The Modern-Day Jōb

An Amazing Fable of Truth

Darwin Shurig

Print ISBN: 979-8-9903367-9-7

Publisher: **Author Writer's Academy**

AWA Literary Agency, United States

Senior Editor: Marjah Simon

www.AWA4Life.com

Cover Design and Illustrations - Author Writer's Academy

Foreword

It is a rare and extraordinary thing to encounter a book that speaks directly to the soul—offering both profound truth and a deeply moving narrative. ***The Modern-Day Jōb: An Amazing Fable of Truth*** is one such work, and it is my honor to introduce it to you.

This remarkable novel tells the story of Darius, a man whose journey through personal anguish—marked by the pain of divorce and spiritual struggles—mirrors the trials of the biblical Jōb. In a reflection of his own spiritual awakening, Darwin takes us on a journey that is at once heart-wrenching and redemptive. Through Darius's story, readers are invited to face their own struggles, confront the demonic forces of despair and doubt, and ultimately rediscover the life-changing power of truth and a healing relationship with God.

I first came to know Darwin at a difficult time in his own life. He reached out to me and opened himself up with such courage and vulnerability that I couldn't help but feel connected. He was not only experiencing challenges in his life but also in the spiritual realm, and as we spoke, I could sense his hunger for healing and deeper truth.

It is humbling to know that those conversations became part of the inspiration for Darius's journey, who, like Darwin, takes a bold step forward to seek help and renewal. That small act of courage, both for Darwin and Darius, was a turning point that God used in a mighty way.

As someone who has spent years in ministry, teaching, and writing about spiritual warfare and the power of prayer, I recognize the importance of a work like this. Darwin's fable does what few books can—it blends storytelling with theology, creating a narrative that is as instructive as it is enlightening. It echoes the themes of my own work, yet Darwin's approach stands out for its artistry and ability to touch the heart in a unique and unforgettable way.

My connection to this book is not just professional—it is deeply personal. In my own life, I have faced moments of uncertainty and struggle, where God's truth was my only anchor. I believe this book will serve as the same beacon of hope for countless others, helping readers to see their own pain through the lens of God's divine purpose.

Darwin has given us more than a story—he has given us a gift. He reminds us that through faith, perseverance, and a willingness to confront our deepest fears, we can overcome the challenges that life places before us. And just as Darius finds healing and truth, so too can we.

As you turn these pages, prepare yourself for a journey of the heart, mind, and spirit. You will find yourself challenged, comforted, and inspired. My prayer is that **The Modern-Day Jōb** will touch your life and give you hope—a light in the darkness.

May this book strengthen your faith, deepen your understanding of God's love, and equip you for your own battles in the spiritual realm.

In His service,

Steve Hemphill

Author, Speaker, and Teacher

Readers who wish to explore Steve's insights further can delve into his numerous titles:

My Search for the Real Heaven, My Search for Prayers Satan Hates, What Are The Stakes?, God's Power For Our Daily Battles, 12 Spiritual Weapons, Dante's Hairy Scary Dreams (children's book)

Dedication

I want to dedicate this book first to **my Lord and Savior, Jesus Christ** –
thank you Lord for never giving up on me
and for your unbelievable Love and Grace.
Secondly, to **my children** –
I love you all so much.

But I also want to dedicate this book to

anyone who needs a guiding light or a helping hand –

no matter who you are or where you are in your life,

I hope this book helps you to move through life more gracefully

and avoid some of those hardships.

I hope that within these pages you find the permission you need

to give yourself grace and begin your journey

to find self-love and truth.

Acknowledgments

I want to thank **Marjah and her remarkable team** for helping me navigate this amazing journey of authorship to bring this work to life. Writing a book is an interesting challenge, and I can't imagine what it was like in the days of the past, sitting around trying to type out words on a typewriter. Wow ... I have so much admiration for those who were pioneers in the early days of book authorship; each one of them has my respect.

My editors, **Emily and Emma**, were indispensable in supporting me not just in word-smithing or configuration but in their kindness, encouragement, and overall support.

I am indebted to **Marjah** for her support and belief in me that this project was worthy, needed to be written, and that it could impact the world in a positive fashion. I am humbled and grateful.

Thank you, **Steve Hemphill**, for your kindness, support, your work, and the incredible mission that Acts of Faith is bringing the world. It is desperately needed, and I am grateful God brought you into my life, my friend.

Thank you, **Dr. Whitman**, for being one of the kindest and most beautiful people that I have ever met, for your book, and for your willingness to meet with me so that I could share the healing aspects of your work in the most transparent possible fashion. God definitely broke the mold when he blessed the world with you!

A huge shout of thanks to my friend, **Jeff Borkowski**, for his amazing mission to help men grow in awareness and give them the tools to be better husbands, fathers, and strengthen the family unit. God's idea of family and marriage has been under attack for some time and your valuable work is greatly needed. Thank you for being so kind to me and encouraging me to write!

Thank you, **G.S. Youngblood**, for your exceptional work on polarity, masculine and feminine energy, and changing my life with your incredible truths and introducing me to the art of embodiment. I believe no young man should graduate high school without reading "The Masculine in Relationship."

Thank you, **Josh Hudson**, for creating the Marriage Reset Program and giving men looking to grow and increase their awareness in a positive, masculine frame the resources, tools, and support in an incredible format.

Thank you to all my BIAs – You are my brothers and I love every one of you. I am always here if you need anything.

Thank you, **David Hawkins**, for bringing the most amazing work to the world and changing my life in so many ways, including self-healing. I can't wait to meet you someday! The conversations will be remarkable if you will so kindly humble me.

Tony Robbins – What is there to say? The world has been amazed, blessed, and has been trying to keep up with your excellence for decades; your impact is hard to measure. Thank you for helping me change my belief system, my personal system for valuation, and too many other items to mention. I am so grateful for the TR Platinum World and the incredible friends I have met because of your unbelievable work. Life changing... I love you all.

Thank you, **Dr. Joe Dispenza**. Your work is supernatural, just like your story and the value you bring to the world. The ability to change the software system of the mind to create the genes we truly want for mental, emotional, and physical health is priceless. Is it odd or is it God?

Thank you, **Kevin Zedai**, for everything you are doing with Warrior Notes Ministry, your teaching of the Word, the Gifts of the Spirit, the Holy Spirit, and coffee talks ... The rabbit holes and books your influence led me to have been life-changing. I can only imagine how God smiles on the work you are doing.

Thank you, **David Platt**, for writing "Radical" and its influence to read the entire Bible in a year. That decision has changed my life more than any other decision I have made. If we seek him, we will truly find him. The Bible isn't meant to be easy to read, and the more we do the work with a humble heart, the more he shows us. The Sword of the Spirit is Absolute Truth.

Thank you, **Jonathan Cahn**. It's hard to even explain how much you have blessed me with your work in understanding the history of the Bible, the truth of prophecy, and understanding one's destiny. I had never heard of a Messianic Jew before and to find out

I was one ... Amazing! I look forward to being in Israel with you in the future.

There are many friends that I could thank for encouraging me to write and believing in me; you know who you are and I appreciate you.

Thank you to the real Larissa – I will forever be indebted to you, my beautiful friend.

> **Thank you, Bubba** – I had never met a Prophet before; you are truly amazing. Thank you for everything, but you already know, I have no doubt.

Thank you to both of the men from my church, Our Father's House, whom I had never met previously, that God encouraged me through to finish this work. At one point, I was stuck at 120 pages, unsure, and had not written in 6 weeks.

> The first man came up to me and said, "God gave me a word for you." He was uncomfortable and said "this might seem strange..." I laughed and told him, "Brother, if you knew what the last two years have been like, you wouldn't be worried. Praise Jesus! Let's hear it." He said, "Well, God gave me a vision of you when I saw you enter the church. You were sitting at a desk and were supposed to be writing. God said you have been going through a very difficult time and are doubting yourself. He said to trust Him and get back to writing because it is going to bless so many people." Then he said, "I don't know if that means anything to you..?" After they picked me back up off the floor, I explained how much it did, and I got back to work.

The second man was months later, nearer the finish line, who told me that God wanted me to press on because this testimony would matter. Thank you.

Lastly, but most importantly, I want to thank my Creator, Elohim, Yaweh, Jehovah, or as I have come to fondly think of him as the song's words have been in my head every day since last year, the great I AM. Thank you for being the ultimate power in the universe, the only one true God, for the redemptive blood of your son Yashua, and the Holy Spirit. Thank you for your angels. Thank you for creating me, forgiving me, never giving up on me, and for your amazing Grace. Thank you for knowing what needed to be removed and for all of the incredible people you have been bringing into my life.

Thank you for giving me Grace as I initially ran from your direction for this assignment. If it wasn't for You, I would never have had the courage to write this book. Thank you for being patient with me and forgiving me each time I thought and said, "This is crazy!" Instead of realizing that "No! This is God, and this is Amazing!"

And finally, thank you for changing my thought process and vocabulary, because everything You do cannot truly be expressed with human words. I praise you and I thank you, Father.

TABLE OF CONTENTS

TABLE OF CONTENTS

TABLE OF CONTENTS

TABLE OF CONTENTS

Jōb 1-12

There once was a man named Jōb who lived in the land of Uz. He was blameless—a man of complete integrity. He feared God and stayed away from evil. He had seven sons and three daughters. He owned 7,000 sheep, 3,000 camels, 500 teams of oxen, and 500 female donkeys. He also had many servants. He was, in fact, the richest person in that entire area.

Jōb's sons would take turns preparing feasts in their homes, and they would also invite their three sisters to celebrate with them. When these celebrations ended—sometimes after several days—Jōb would purify his children. He would get up early in the morning and offer a burnt offering for each of them. For Jōb said to himself, "Perhaps my children have sinned and have cursed God in their hearts." This was Jōb's regular practice.

One day, the members of the heavenly court came to present themselves before the Lord, and the Accuser, Satan, came with them. "Where have you come from?" the Lord asked Satan.

Satan answered the Lord, "I have been patrolling the earth, watching everything that's going on."

Then the Lord asked Satan, "Have you noticed my servant Jōb? He is the finest man in all the earth. He is blameless—a man of complete integrity. He fears God and stays away from evil."

Satan replied to the Lord, "Yes, but Jōb has good reason to fear God. You have always put a wall of protection around him and his home and his property. You have made him prosper in everything he does. Look how rich he is! But reach out and take away everything he has, and he will surely curse you to your face!"

"All right, you may test him," the Lord said to Satan. "Do whatever you want with everything he possesses, but don't harm him physically." So Satan left the Lord's presence.

Preface

    This is a story about change, growth, and awareness—looking in the mirror first to realize that before this man could look outward, he first had to look upward and then inward. In this journey, **Darius** needed to understand that his challenges stemmed mostly from within, not from the world around him. Perhaps "A Modern-Day Jōb" is somewhat misleading because, on the surface, this man was nothing like Jōb.

    Jōb had material wealth beyond imagining. **Darius** had some financial success, but it was nothing compared to Jōb. Yes, **Darius** had positive attributes, wanted to be kind, and was charitable to a point. **Darius** believed in God but had no understanding of evil, what it meant to be God-fearing, why that might matter, and certainly no concept around the Fear of the Lord being the beginning of wisdom. It's hard to fathom that God might be bragging about him to Satan in the heavenly realm. He was so lost in his own lack of self-worth from his own past, his exploding situation, that he had no true sense of anything outside of the material world and was driven to be successful in the hopes of feeling loved and finding meaning, but unfortunately at a lower level of consciousness and thus low awareness.

God knows each person intimately. He writes our potential, future, and purpose in the Book of Life before we are even born, blows us into life in our mother's womb, and even longs to see us grow ... While **Darius** was far from the epitome of greatness or perfection, he, like every human created by God, was born with a purpose if only he would seek God and learn the truth of it.

Darius was a man who was lost in many ways, suffering without need and, unfortunately, had little awareness of his specific issues or how to fix them. But what if the worst thing that ever happened to you was the *BEST* thing that ever happened to you? Free will is an amazing blessing and yet an incredible challenge, is it not? In every situation, as humans, we get to choose where we focus and to what we give our attention and energy. Where focus goes, energy flows, and our energy is not limitless. Will we focus our energy on negatives and give our attention to that which doesn't benefit us while adding to chaos and conflict, or will we choose God's direction of love, kindness, growth, contribution, forgiveness, and behaviors that lead to harmony and peace? For **Darius**, the question remains: would life happen to him or for him?

In our story, **Darius** seeks God for answers and is given a rude awakening of his failings. At that point, he, like all of us in these challenging situations, has the opportunity to choose whether to go through the doorway to seek truth, which can lead to solutions, answers, and blessings for greater awareness and healing, or focus on lower-level emotions, negativity, and the pain. For **Darius**, there was no turning back and it led to a journey of using the pain of past failures and mistakes to find answers. After being blessed with awareness, he chooses to relentlessly move forward for answers and that leads to truths and tools for transformation.

So why should I tell this story, and why should you be eager to read it? What purpose might it serve?

The concept and understanding of God have changed throughout our history but never more so since we entered the technological age. While aspects of faith have diminished in societal structures, the concept of evil remains universally recognized. Why do we readily comprehend evil yet struggle with the concept of God?

It's an interesting question for me.

Just as some understand evil but not God, others believe in God without acknowledging evil. But believing in one without the other is like believing in the light but not the dark. Darkness is the absence of light. What if similarly evil is the absence of God, or more specifically, the absence of seeking and obeying him, thus increasing our interaction and access to evil?

The data shows that for over thirty years, humanity and certainly the United States has been moving more and more away from the Creator; removing Him from schools, institutions, homes, and increasingly watering down what is moral and right in many areas of life. As we look at the chaos in our politics, our schools, the continued degradation and devaluation of the family unit, an increase in violence and suicides, an explosion of medications for mental health and conditions that barely existed 30 years ago, and our ever increasing tolerance of violent and immoral content from Hollywood, it's hard to miss where we seem to be headed. I understand some people are reluctant to acknowledge or believe in a Creator or that God is real, so imagine how much more difficult it is to have a conversation about evil or the demonic or the supporting human activities around the occult!

Many people today struggle with the concept of the demonic, often associating it with fiction rather than acknowledging its potential reality. And for those that would knock religion, yes, I believe I can understand. In many churches, it's more about man's perspective than obedience to the Word as they put God in a box while picking and choosing what to believe in, depending on how it suits them. I hope that **Darius's** journey of God's word, his experiences, and his exploration of levels of consciousness, energy, and the quantum and spiritual realms, including how they interconnect, raises your eyebrows, piques your curiosity, and potentially opens a door to more curiosity.

I have been asked previously if I had ever seen evil before, and the answer was a most definite yes. As a young child, I encountered a horrific scenario that could have cost me my life. I witnessed evil in the emergency room and hospitals, and it seems to be apparent through time through atrocities, and mass exterminations of humanity. How can there not be evil when an elephant tranquilizer is being used to increase addiction and overdoses for profit? When more people are in slavery than ever before and millions of children are being sold as sex slaves right now? When one of the leading countries puts over 1,000 harmful chemicals in its foods, leading to so many chronic diseases and healthcare waste?

The Bible shares many times that Satan is the ruler of this world, which I never understood. It made no sense to me, but the more I journeyed down my own path of personal revelation, the more I have realized the truth behind that statement. I believe his minions and followers are in every institution and unfortunately, deeply embedded in many of our churches and religious institutions, as well. The occult is everywhere and over the past few years is being unashamedly exhibited at the highest levels right in front of us, whether we are aware or not.

In the past, if you asked me, "Do you believe in God?" I would have said, "Absolutely." If you then asked me, "Do you believe in evil?" I'm sure I would have said, "Yes." "Do you believe in Satan?" "Yes." ... But if you asked me if I believed in the demonic? I would have probably looked at you peculiarly and said something like, "Like *The Exorcist?* Yeah, I've seen the movie!" All while gingerly heading for the closest exit from this obviously mentally confused person.

In the book *The Harbinger*, by Jonathan Cahn, the Prophet tells Noriel that he is being given the clues for his own awakening and like the watcher on the wall, it is his responsibility to sound the alarm or blow the trumpet. I don't share this to compare myself to

Cahn's amazing work. In truth, I had no interest in writing this book when God told me he wanted me to write it, and I ran from it for several months before additional direction was given in a remarkable fashion. I couldn't ignore it anymore.

This is a story about truth, deception, and lack. It is a story about force versus power, higher-level emotions versus lower-level emotions, positive and negative influence, and higher levels of consciousness. It will explore God's perfection and Evil's mirroring and perversion of this perfection. Through the eyes of **Darius**, my hope is that you will find aspects of his journey that bring you hope and possibly a tool or two that leads you to positive solutions that bless your life.

You may choose to simply enjoy the story for what it shares on the surface (I certainly hope you find it interesting and entertaining!) or you may dive deeper to read between the lines and discover something more. Regardless, I ask you, dear reader, if something resonates with you, take it into your heart, hold it close, and look for greater understanding. By doing so, you may find tools and insights that set you on an unalterable path and a transformative journey that blesses you. Will it be easy? No, I cannot promise you it will, but I can assure you it will be worth the effort.

Whether you believe in God or find comfort in another form of faith, we all have an innate desire to understand and live the best life we can or at a higher level of consciousness. Universally, we all wish to feel worthy and find success; to be loved and to be good enough. If you have questions about God, what happens after death, or were hurt by inappropriate use of the idea of religion in the past, I hope you find not only tools that might assist you, but perhaps a curiosity that leads to exploring the truth of your Creator in a way, perhaps, you never have before.

Peter was unique among the disciples, the only one to walk on water, and the first to know that Jesus was the Messiah and the Son of God. I believe he was the only one of the disciples with that high a level of consciousness because he was the one most seeking the Lord. As the Scripture shares over and over, if we seek Him, we will find Him. He is absolute Truth and the Word is the sword of truth.

When God reveals something to you, it doesn't matter what the whole world says.

May God Bless you and yours and I pray that anyone who reads this book is touched in the most beautiful fashion.

All the Best and in His Blessings,

Darwin

Chapter 1
Vacation Interrupted

He sat in the chair, tears staining his cheeks and his head throbbing. Within the four walls of his home office, it had just turned three in the morning, and Darius was still watching a marriage sermon, hoping it would give him an answer.

The last week had been painful; to call it a disaster wouldn't do it justice. Two weeks prior, he had celebrated his 17th Wedding Anniversary with Jessica, commemorating almost 20 years together from the start till now. It wasn't perfect—nothing could be truly perfect—but they loved one another, living with more positives than negatives in the life they had built together. Or at least that is what Darius had always wanted to believe.

The last week was indescribable, but the past year and a half was difficult. He still couldn't believe all the details, even though he re-lived them in his mind too often. It was a life that he would have thought reserved for the big screen; a work of utter fiction—complete bullshit. But, unfortunately, it was not only real, but he was in the starring role.

His "performance" began when his parents moved in with him and his family. His father, Norman, had been battling Parkinson's for years—a devastating disease that aged his mother, Sybil, and deprived his father of his manhood. The disease robbed him of everything he once was and it overwhelmed his mother. She was someone who had control issues and also struggled with feelings of guilt and burden, which made asking for help difficult. But it was Darius, with Jessica's support, who encouraged them to move, assisting them in building a house nearby to be closer to their grandchildren and get support.

However, due to post-pandemic supply chain issues, delay upon delay meant the house wasn't ready on time, so his parents stayed with Darius.

With his father's condition worsening and two energetic dogs, the house became a circus. Yet, despite the difficulties, Darius cherished the time they spent together. He believed it was a blessing that allowed the grandchildren to see Norman daily, provided support for Sybil, and allowed them to care for Norman in a way that wouldn't have been possible if they were elsewhere.

Eventually, the house was built, and they moved his parents in. It was to be the start of a new chapter in all their lives, but two weeks after moving into their new home, Norman passed away in the middle of the night. His final weeks were marked by repeated falls and sleepless nights, as Darius often was called to help him back to bed. It was exhausting. The night his mother called to say his father had passed away, Darius had a guilty sense of relief that his father finally had the peace he sought.

Darius drove over and once in the room, he confirmed that his father was gone. He was not a stranger to death, having worked as a respiratory therapist in his past, but this was his father. His mother thought he was still breathing, but it was obvious that his lifeless body had moved on to God. The two of them stood heartbroken, staring at his lifeless body.

It was a painful moment, but nothing compared to what was to come.

The sermon ended and Darius sat thinking about the content, feeling numb.

It had been five days since they had changed their flights and returned home with their youngest son. It was supposed to be their week away, a chance for him to step away from his business and relax with his wife and Ben. It had only lasted three days.

So wrapped up in work, he hadn't noticed how distant Jessica had become, but he was at least aware enough to realize the need for them to get away, to decompress and reconnect. He had no idea evil had infiltrated their family and their businesses.

Before they left, she was gone almost every evening and on the plane, she was silent. It was as if she were avoiding him, refusing to make eye contact or touch him entirely. This person was not like his wife at all; she was quiet and unhappy, her mind wandering elsewhere.

He tried to engage with her a couple of different times, but she wasn't having any of it. At one point, their son left to go work out, and he had a chance to talk to her alone in the condo. Lovingly, playfully, he wrapped his arms around her.

At first, she allowed it and leaned into his chest as she had a million times over the last 20 years.

"We need to talk," he said, trying to keep a smile on his face. "I want to know what's been going on. What's upset you? If it is something I've done, I'm sorry, but—"

Saying "sorry" was like a cannon going off.

Something snapped in Jessica.

Her head flew back and she swiftly moved away from his arms. Her demeanor immediately became dark and ominous, and her voice deepened as she flatly said, "What are you sorry for?"

The hairs on Darius' arms stood up and a chill ran down his spine as he looked at her with confusion. He didn't know what she was upset about. He racked his head, but struggled to find any specific example.

"For my part in our challenges," he said, quickly adding, "And what I have done to upset you."

He wasn't looking at his wife anymore; he wasn't sure who he was looking at. Her voice was different and she was lifeless.

"I can't do this anymore."

Her words added to his confusion. Her words hurt.

"What do you mean?"

"My tank is empty," she declared, voice cold and emotionless. "I just can't do it anymore."

Darius was confused and still didn't understand what was happening.

"Well, let's figure this out. We can fill your tank back up. Let's go to counseling."

"No," she abruptly stated. "I don't want to go to counseling."

"What are you saying?" He asked. "17 years of marriage, 20 years together, the life we have built, and it's over? You're not even willing to have a conversation or work at anything?"

She looked at him with a cold expression. "That's right."

Darius felt like he'd been hit by a truck; he just stared at her, paralyzed, as tears started down his cheeks. Jessica just looked at him, emotionless.

This would be the start of what would be the most painful and challenging journey of his life. A journey that, at the time, Darius had no idea would lead him to blessings of spiritual, emotional, and physical healing for which he would be forever grateful ...

Chapter 2
Did You Get Them All?

T he first he had heard of Larissa was how she helped kids overcome a variety of cognitive and behavioral issues. It was Jessica who told him about Larissa and the work she did. She was an emotional trauma therapist, someone who could help their son. Darius didn't completely understand, but he had no issues with it if Jessica thought it would help.

His youngest son had so many issues with his emotions, struggling with anxiety and anger, which often made communication difficult—especially if it didn't go his way.

After the first appointment, there was an obvious sense of calm about their son. He came home, exhausted, and went to sleep. It was unusual, but the counselor ensured this was normal.

His wife scheduled an appointment for herself and encouraged Darius to do the same. He wasn't sure what it would entail exactly, but he had read about emotional trauma when he worked in the hospital. He understood the body could carry scars from traumatic events for years if they weren't handled properly. He wasn't sure what he would gain from such an appointment, but with a smile, he agreed and booked it.

Darius's initial appointments had been before they left for Mexico. He hadn't known what to expect, but from the moment he entered the room, he felt positive energy from Larissa.

"What *exactly* do you do?" He asked.

Larissa explained her practices, how trauma was kept in the body, and touched on the esoteric more than the logical. He asked her about the children she had helped. Her answer caught his attention and he definitely wanted to ask some follow-up questions later.

She had been hesitant to explain in detail, but Darius had just stared at her and then continued prodding.

"When you talk about night terrors, there is something ominous about the way you say it," he said awkwardly. "Why?"

She had paused to consider his question. "There are a lot of influences in this world—good and bad. I deal with a lot of people, with a lot of children, and when it comes to night terrors, sometimes there is additional work to do."

He had looked at her, holding her gaze. "What type of work?"

After a few seconds, she said, "Evil spirits."

As Darius processed it, he frowned and then found himself laughing. "Are you talking about *real* demons?"

Larissa's expression hadn't changed. "It's not a concept or idea people handle well. Most react just like that. But, yes."

Despite his faith, he was detail-oriented, logical, and analytical. None of this made any sense and was nothing more than fantasy. Wasn't it, he thought to himself?

"How often do you deal with that?"

She looked a little uncomfortable, but she knew he wasn't going to leave the topic until he had some form of clarity.

"Okay," she conceded, "I'll give you an example. There was a family that I have known for a few years who brought their daughter to me. She was a pretty, bright little girl, when all of a sudden, she started having a lot of issues, including night terrors, behavioral issues, school issues, all sorts of issues. This was going on for several months before her mother brought her to me for help.

"As we started into prayer and then the muscle testing, I could tell something wasn't right, and the girl became very uncomfortable. Suddenly, she jumped up and said, 'I don't want to be here. We are leaving.' The mother interjected, trying to explain to her daughter that I was only there to help and that she needed to give me more time. But the girl grabbed her mother by the throat and lifted her up off the floor and—"

"What the fuck!"

Shocked, Larissa looked at him.

"Uh, sorry," he stammered, collecting himself. "What did you do?"

Larissa said the girl had seven demons in her and explained how she had begun praying silently, exorcizing the girl. She spoke of how the girl, still holding her mother in the air, turned her head to look at Larissa and asked her what she was doing. He was relieved to hear that the girl had dropped her mother, leaving her sobbing on the floor and then the child walked across the room to stand directly in front of Larissa.

"She looked me straight in the eye, speaking in a strange voice that wasn't hers and said, 'What are you doing?' I replied, 'Praying for you.' At that point I had rebuked six of the demons, and the little girl cocked her head and asked me, 'Did you get them all?!' I continued praying out loud and the little girl suddenly fell to the floor as the last spirit left her."

At the time, Darius didn't know what to say. He was full of questions, but when he opened his mouth, the father inside him emerged and asked how the girl was. "So how is she? Is she okay?"

Larissa nodded and said, "Hasn't had any issues since and is doing great."

Darius was a man of faith; he knew what it meant to believe without needing to see, but all that seemed far-fetched. "Are you going to cut the head off a chicken?" He asked with a wry smile.

"No, there will be none of that," she laughed and replied, "We will pray together before, during, and after to help some of the issues leave your body. So what is it you want to focus on?"

"I—"

Words seemed to catch in his throat. In truth, he didn't know why he was there.

"Have you had many traumatic experiences in your life?"

Darius frowned. "Some, I suspect."

She gave him all the time he needed as he searched his memory for something that could satisfy.

"My life has been interesting and plenty of challenges, but maybe we could start with an accident I had a long time ago? An accident in high school caused my left hip to ache, and since then, it's always hurt. It's never a matter of *if* it hurts or not, but *how* much it hurts."

She began the process, saying a prayer over him and focusing her questions on the circumstances surrounding his old hip injury. She asked about his life, specifically his childhood, and Darius felt comfortable sharing with her. As she asked questions, her fingers moved in different sequences over his body as she performed muscle testing while looking at charts.

He had only had his driver's license for a few months, and as he messed with the radio while coming up to an old iron bridge, the right tire went off the pavement and into a rut. Shaken, he overcorrected twice as the car skidded across the bridge and then flew off a 50-foot embankment and into a tree.

It wasn't the greatest end to a sophomore track meet. He had to be cut out of the car and taken via helicopter to the capital's trauma unit for care. Amazingly, he had no broken bones or major complications, but the pain in his left hip had hurt him his entire life. After the car accident, he always had pain in his left hip, and his legs seemed asymmetrical.

Again, Larissa asked him about stress, about his own thoughts and feelings. Darius told her that he ran a business and that his and Jessica's busy schedules were stressful. He added that, oftentimes, he felt unworthy and didn't like, let alone love, himself.

To that, Larissa replied, "Could you tell me more?"

He couldn't. It was too hard to explain. But he was able to confess that these thoughts were ones he had carried with him for most of his life.

Larissa shifted in her chair. Her fingers moved in a blur as she continued muscle testing, ready to ask another question, when suddenly a shadow passed across her face.

"Something is blocking me."

Darius looked at her curiously with an inquisitive look on his face. "What do you mean?"

"Well, it can mean a couple different things."

"Like what?"

Larissa didn't say anything.

"What do you mean by blocked?" Darius asked again.

She sat back, placing a hand to her temple. Almost exhausted, she explained what it meant when she was "blocked." It sounded like something from a horror movie; the presence of "an influence" that he could only compare to demons and devils that prowled nightmarish fiction.

"Are you saying I'm possessed?" He laughed, looking at her strangely.

"No," she replied, giving an answer that only added to his confusion.

"Then what do you mean by 'an influence?'"

"There are a lot of things that can influence us. Just as we can feel positive energies, there are also negative energies that can impact us in a similar way. No, I don't think you are possessed, but I do think you have something trying to influence you. When it happens, I get a serious headache."

He could hear the sincerity in her words—the concern as well.

Chapter 3
A Demon Cord

Darius wasn't sure about the work Larissa was doing, but he had to admit he was fascinated. Since their first meeting, he had done more reading on muscle testing and wanted to understand better what she was doing and how it was working. He had no doubt that the body held on to certain emotions and traumas but wasn't really clear on *how* it worked.

Larissa shared some of her methods as well as some pretty interesting stories and perspectives in their first meeting. It was only supposed to last 45 minutes, and yet they had spent well over an hour together. It was hard for Darius to deny; he was curious to meet with her again.

After the initial greetings, when they next met, they spoke about their first meeting, and again Larissa asked what he wanted to focus on. He wasn't sure, and so she decided to return to his injury and what had blocked her, saying there was still more they could extract and through that, they could begin to talk about his childhood.

Darius agreed and the appointment began with Larissa praying. Afterward, she asked him a series of questions and started the muscle test as she consulted several charts. After finishing the testing, she tapped the top of his head before handing him the magnet as she ran several others over his back.

"Repeat after me," she started.

I release the feelings of hopelessness that I inherited from my Father. I don't have to hold on to this feeling anymore. I am worthy, was created special by God, and I don't have to hold on to this emotion. I release it to God.

I release the feelings of low self-esteem. I know that I am valuable and can live out my life according to my gifts and the blessings God has given me, and I don't have to hold on to this feeling any longer. I release it to God.

I release the feelings of not being valued and feeling like I am taken for granted that I inherited from my father. I can live a life of value and being appreciated, and I release this feeling to God.

I release the feelings of fear, despair, hopelessness, and worry that have been in my body since high school and the accident. I can live a life of optimism, joy, blessings, and confidence. I release these feelings and give them to God.

I release the feelings of panic that I felt when I was 16 and understand I don't have to carry this feeling anymore. I can be confident that I am loved, and I release this feeling to God.

As she finished up the process, she pulled out his report and asked him how he felt.

Darius paused. "I feel fine, not really any different."

"Well, you might feel fatigued later and make sure to drink plenty of water."

He nodded but said nothing more.

"How does your hip feel?"

"It hurts less."

It was her turn to nod. "Okay. Good," she said. "I have taken over 20 emotions out of your hip, but I think you might have structural damage that I can't help you with. I am going to refer you to a chiropractor who does holistic work. I think Dr. Whitman could fix the structural damage."

"Where is he?" Darius asked, taking the doctor's details.

"In Brazil, but people come from all over to see him for all kinds of issues."

He looked at her with curiosity and she returned the look with a smile.

"Well, he's not just a chiropractor. He helps people reset their system of metals, chemically, physically, and emotionally using muscle testing, manipulation, supplements, and various treatments, but I suggest considering getting a consultation from him to see if he can help you."

Again, Darius nodded and let Larissa finish with her report. She took him through all of the emotion removed from his hip, before suddenly stopping. A slight frown appeared on her face, her brow furrowing. For a moment, Darius just observed her, but then a familiar shadow crossed her.

"What's wrong?" He finally asked.

"I know what was blocking me last time; you have a demon chord on your left hip."

Startled, he continued to watch her as she started to explain "demon cording." Apparently, it was a means for the demonic to influence a person through a connecting channel, almost like a conduit for electricity.

"What does that mean?"

Larissa stopped him with a gentle gesture before he could batter her with more questions. "Well, your chord has seven channels or doors."

"What are they?" Darius asked with concern.

"I don't know yet, Darius. Something traumatic caused it … probably the car accident. We're out of time to deal with it tonight, but we need to remove it."

Darius was baffled and sat there quietly. He couldn't wrap his head around it, but he was eager to understand it.

"Okay," he said with as much certainty as finality, "Let's schedule another appointment, but we are headed to Mexico with our son in a few days, so it will have to be when we get back."

Chapter 4
Eyes to See & Ears to Hear

The shock remained. Why had Jessica let them fly all the way here only to unload all of this on him and then pack up and leave just like that? Who does that on a vacation!?

Darius couldn't fathom it, but he wanted to understand; he was desperate to. He prayed like he had never prayed in his life. He asked God to give him direction, to bring insight, to give him the words and actions he needed to save his marriage. What had caused this and how could he fix it?

"Please give me the answers I need. Bless our marriage. Help us find a way through this bump. Help me understand my wife, let me connect with her and her with me. Please keep our family safe; keep us together."

He combined his own words with the Lord's Prayer, alternating between them one after another. He looked up different verses, looking for answers.

Where were the words that could show him the way?

He did this until he passed out, and he did it again when he awoke until he would pass out again. The nights were the only times he could remember, sitting on the patio looking out toward the ocean and drinking a beer or two to numb his thoughts before returning to his prayers; the days were a total blur.

It was in the middle of the third night before flying home, as he had lost count of how many times he woke from restless slumber, that Darius experienced something else in his prayers. It was a weight, like a ton of bricks—something he could hardly describe, even if he wanted to.

There wasn't an angel or a bright light, nor the sounds of a marching band or tunes of a choir, but he was hit with a divine awareness that was nothing like anything he had ever experienced. It was like God had heard his prayers and said, "Okay, you really want to know?"

For the first time in his life, he could see himself as he truly was through another's eyes and saw the challenges of his marriage in his wife's eyes.

It horrified him.

He had spent so many years watching the world, watching his world through his own eyes. He couldn't remember a time when he stopped to look at this through her eyes—through Jessica's eyes. They were husband and wife, they were a unit, one flesh just as was written in Genesis, Matthew, Mark, and Ephesians, and yet he realized they were anything but one unit at this point.

God pulled back the curtain and showed him his reality. In grace, God revealed his lack, his neediness, and how little worth, respect, and care Darius gave to himself. In this moment, Darius saw a shell of what should have been a man, a man who had failed to honor himself and protect his wife's heart or hear her voice in the way it was meant to be heard. He saw how he victimized himself in areas and was ... selfish in a way that was now obvious to him.

His heart hurt and his head throbbed. For the first time in his life, he realized he loved her, but he had always truly loved her selfishly. The relationship was built on what he could get out of the relationship versus what he could do for her. He had never given her an agape love—unselfish and not wanting or asking anything in return. How clearly he could see his failings from his mood swings and temper to his habit of distancing himself after an argument, and he was appalled.

How exhausting it would be to be around someone that behaves like that?

The flight home was long, draining, and became the precursor to an incredibly long week where he and Jessica had minimal communication. In fact, he didn't see her much at all, save for one night when she did eventually come home.

The memory of that night in Mexico lingered; a sweet haunt that wouldn't leave him be. So that night, Darius tried to talk to her. His intention was to share with her what God had revealed to him, and through his vulnerability, find a way to connect that might help her open up and share more details. His heart was aflutter, filled with anticipation and anxiety. He wanted to make this work; he wanted to make it right.

"Jessica—"

He interrupted himself. She wasn't interested.

She stood in their bedroom, stoic and unfriendly as she desperately tried to avoid him. There was no emotion in her expression, but her expression was one that ended the conversation before it even began.

"Please," he said, "Can we talk? We need to talk."

"No, I don't want to talk to you," she said, shaking her head. "I am going to a counseling appointment on Tuesday and am not going to talk to you before then."

Darius looked at her. "Are you just going to this appointment to get approval to divorce me?"

"I can't answer that."

"You are making me feel like there is no hope for our marriage."

Jessica's expression shifted. It was cold, like the harshest chill of winter; it made his heart heavy and chills run up his spine.

"I can't give you any hope," she said flatly, ominously.

He stood there quietly for a minute, maybe more. A thousand thoughts and even more questions flooded him. Finally, he found words, unsure if they were the right words but knowing them true. "I don't know who you are anymore," he said. "This isn't you."

Jessica gave no reply; she simply turned and walked out of the room.

***

That week, he had gone to dinner with his mother. It was mostly uncomfortable silence as Darius drove them to the restaurant. He felt a significant amount of stress, and his mother probably didn't know what to say, he thought. After sitting and ordering their food, they began to discuss the situation.

"How are things going?" she asked.

"Not good," he admitted. "She hasn't come home any night this week, so far. She apparently has a counseling appointment, which will determine if she is going to move forward with filing for divorce or not."

"Your father and I always worked out our differences, and hopefully, she will want to work through it. I can't imagine you two not being together," she said.

Darius told his mother about praying in Mexico for two nights straight and God opening his eyes to his worst flaws. "I realize that I didn't look at our challenges through her eyes often enough."

"She gets frustrated with how you speak to her sometimes," his mother said curtly, her head nodding.

Darius just looked at his mother in disbelief. "Why would you say that?" he stammered.

"Sometimes you're just short and don't speak nicely."

"Do you really think I need you to kick me when I am down?" Darius exclaimed. "This is the hardest situation in my life. I love her. I don't want to lose my wife or have my family break up."

"I am not doing that. You are just being sensitive," she stated with a frown on her face.

"Would Jesus treat someone like this, Mom?" he asked.

"He might," she stated matter of factly, holding his gaze.

Unbelievable, Darius thought. He looked at his mother, shaking his head. "In the Chosen, when Mary Magdalene messes up and goes back to her prior bar life, Peter and Matthew go and find her. She is embarrassed and doesn't want to face Jesus. When she meets Jesus, he says, 'Did you never think you were going to make a mistake again?' Then he says, 'You are forgiven.' No, I don't think he would treat me this way."

The tension continued to grow as his mother just sat there glaring at him with eyes tinted with anger. Darius couldn't believe it. Nothing else was said as they finished eating and he drove her home.

He helped her out of the car and into her home as they said a quick good night. As Darius drove home, he couldn't wrap his head around the bizarre conversation. Who needs enemies, he thought.

Chapter 5
A Prayer Battle for Love

He still hadn't seen much of his wife, but on Sunday, they had planned to have the family over after church for Sunday dinner. At church, Jessica was like a zombie, numb and silent, something for him to avoid, whether he wanted to or not. It was a state of being Darius had grown reluctantly accustomed to, but it was still so strange to be so close yet unable to touch her. Then, after church, she disappeared, leaving to run errands and not to return until before it was time to make dinner.

Darius spent the afternoon doing yard work, trapped in his own thoughts. What the hell was going on? Nothing made sense to him anymore. He mowed the grass and tears began to flow down his face.

That is when it hit him.

He slammed the breaks of the mower and called Larissa. It went straight to voicemail. Darius shook his head and composed a text: *please call me if you can, when you can. Something very strange is happening and I need your help.*

It wasn't long before she texted back, apologizing and asking what was wrong. The two proceeded to exchange texts, one after the other.

Have you seen Jessica since her last appointment?

No, why?

What happened at her last appointment? Was she unhappy, distant, struggling?

> *I can't say a whole lot without her permission, but I can say she wasn't unhappy. She told me the two of you had a good marriage, and that she wanted to make it a great marriage.*

Darius read the text again. It didn't make any sense. The next thing he sent was an account of their trip to Mexico, his wife's avoidance and reluctance to speak, and that she had stated their marriage was over.

A few minutes later, his phone rang.

Larissa asked him to recount the events of the past few weeks, and he did so in a voice high with anxiety. On the other side of the phone, he heard Larissa take a deep breath.

"It sounds like you have a serious problem and may have some influence. Do I have your permission to check the house and her car for evil spirits?" she asked.

"Yes."

It was quiet for a minute and then as she came back on, she said, "You are surrounded by influence. There are two in your house right now, and four are with your wife in her car right now."

"What do I do?!" he yelled.

She could do little to calm him from the other side of the phone, but she did try. "Darius," she started, getting his attention, "You can handle this as you are a believer and one of God's children. I'm going to send you prayers and exorcisms, and you need to go into the house and go through each room and bless the rooms and exorcize them from the property and then do the same thing on the outside. After you do that, call me back and we can check the property again."

He waited for Larissa to send him everything he would need. He then went into the house and fervently exorcized each room; then went out and did the prayers again at each corner of the house. As he went, he got more excited and feverish, gaining momentum with each prayer. At the last corner, he jumped for joy and thanked the Lord.

A weight lifted and he was giddy like a child. He called Larissa when he was done and urgently asked what she sensed now. His relief was immense as she told him both of them were gone.

"What do I do about the ones in her car?"

"Wait until she comes home. You can exorcize them one at a time from your office when she makes dinner."

Over and over, he thanked her. He would owe her forever.

They hung up, agreeing to reconnect later that night after Jessica returned home.

It was a restless, anxiety-filled wait for his wife to come home. Evil spirits ... Demons ... Exorcisms ... It was all so unbelievable. He tried to recall everything that had happened this past year; how long had these influences been in his life, in *their* life? He couldn't think straight; the adrenaline was all-consuming and overwhelming.

But Jessica still wasn't home. She was supposed to be home at 5 and it was almost 6.

Darius stared at his phone, frustration building with each unanswered call. He had tried reaching Jessica multiple times, only to be met with silence. Each call diverted to voicemail, each text left without a response. Finally, a message popped up:

> *I'm not cooking dinner. I don't know what I was thinking. I can't do it.*

He was relieved to hear from her.

That's okay. You don't need to cook. When are you coming home?

I'm not coming home. I don't want anyone to see me like this.

Where are you? Are you with Ash?

He looked at the message for a moment.

He was surprised he had asked that, but they had been spending a lot of time together both at work and after work lately.

I am in a parking lot, and I am a mess.

Just come home.

No, I am not coming home. I don't want the kids to see me.

Darius took a breath; how was he to respond—how would anyone respond?

Okay, just tell me where you are. I'll come to you.

No. I don't want to see you.

At that, Darius quickly pulled up the tracking system they had on their iPhones, only to find she had disabled it so he couldn't locate her.

Frustrated, worried, and with little other option, he called Larissa. He told her everything: his wife wasn't coming home and he was desperate for Larissa's advice. She asked if he could get Jessica to go to a friend's to stay the night. He said he could try, but he followed it with a question, asking what he was to do about the exorcism. Larissa didn't know. She had only ever practiced such things up close. But she said it could be possible.

It *could* be possible. The words gave him hope.

When he got off the phone, he texted Jessica, asking if she would not come home, would she go stay with Beth, one of her best friends. He then texted Beth as well, asking if she knew where Jessica was. While he awaited a response, he started to go through the incantations to exorcize them, including adding in new verses: another from John and one from Mark.

Then Beth texted him, reiterating the words of his wife. She told him while Jessica was with her, he was not to come, that Jessica didn't want to see him. The affirmations hurt, but Darius messaged back, ensuring that he wasn't going anywhere. He just wanted to know where she was and that she was safe.

For the next two hours, Darius prayed fervently, reciting passages to remove the demonic presence from his wife. Since God had opened his eyes in Mexico, he had never felt more compassion and empathy for her. The love he felt now, amidst their struggles, was overwhelming. Protecting his family had always been his priority, but this situation took that commitment to a whole new level.

After what felt like an eternity, he texted Larissa. She told him that two of the demons were gone, but one had attached itself to Jessica's dress. Confused, Darius called her.

"I've only seen this a few times," Larissa explained, "But sometimes the spirit doesn't want to leave so badly that it attaches to a clothing article or an object."

"What do we do now?" Darius asked, bewildered.

"The only way I know how to remove it is to remove the object. She has to take the dress off, and then we have to get it away from her."

Darius sighed, realizing the difficulty of this next step. "Maybe I can get Beth to help with that if she stays there," he suggested.

He messaged Beth again, asking if she could give Jessica some pajamas for the evening. Understandably, the response carried an air of confusion, but at Darius's insistence, Beth said she would try.

Finally, relief. It was small, but it was there—though not enough to calm him.

The night wore on, and Darius set in for a long vigil. He was determined to do everything he could to stay awake and keep praying, invoking God's power to exorcize the last two, including the one from Jessica's dress. It was exhausting, but he had done it twice in Mexico without the same passion and energy that drove him now. Protecting his wife and family fueled his prayers.

At 10:00 PM, a text from Beth came in:

> *I tried to get her to take the dress off multiple times, but she won't do it. She's going to sleep in it.*

The words resigned Darius to a sleepless night. It would be long and difficult; it would drain him physically, mentally, and spiritually, but he would press onward. His love for Jessica and his family gave him strength. He dozed off a few times, but each time he woke, just as he did in Mexico, he resumed his prayers.

He barely noticed the sun rise.

Exhausted, he fumbled with his phone, not even registering the time as he opened up his text thread with Larissa and sent a message asking if she was up and if he could call her.

When she finally responded and he called her, her voice was incredulous. "What did you do?"

"What do you mean?" Darius asked, confused.

"I've never seen an evil spirit removed from an article of clothing or an object before—and it's gone."

Darius wanted to jump for joy. "Thank God!" he exclaimed. "I prayed all night, fervently and without cease, intermixing the Scriptures into the exorcism with all my heart."

Larissa was quiet for a few seconds. "That's just beautiful," she finally said. "Keep me posted when she gets home."

"Okay," Darius agreed. Then, in a quiet voice, he asked, "Larissa … will she be my wife again now? Does this mean I'll get her back?"

There was a pause before Larissa responded. "Darius … I know your love for your wife and your family. Your actions and intentions over the last day have been remarkable and beautiful to see. But you have to understand that six demons have been affecting your family. This didn't happen overnight. Just as they had the ability to influence you, these demons have the ability to influence your wife, but they don't replace your actual issues, what she is holding in or what gave them access initially. So I have to caution you; you can't expect that this is over—that she's going to come home and jump into your arms."

Darius nodded to himself. It wasn't what he wanted to hear, but there was a part of him that expected it. Maybe, even if it wouldn't be immediate, this would allow them to reconnect and rebuild their marriage.

An hour later, Darius heard the garage door open and the sound of Jessica's footsteps as she walked slowly down the hallway to their bedroom.

When he saw her, his heart swelled with love, joy, and happiness. The most remarkable feeling washed over him as he looked into her eyes—it was Jessica. It was his wife, truly herself, for the first time since before they left for Mexico. Like Larissa had warned, she was not running into his arms, but at least she didn't seem like a completely different person anymore.

They exchanged a quiet glance before she went into the bathroom and closed the door to shower. The moment he heard the water run, Darius wasted no time gathering up the dress and burying it at the bottom of the dumpster.

Chapter 6

Stakes & Spiritual Surprises

A s time passed, more often than not, Darius felt like he was losing his mind. His life was spiraling out of control.

His marriage, his life, and his business were all struggling ... Everything was crumbling around him, and there was nothing he could do to stop it, no matter how hard he tried.

The guilt he felt after God opened his eyes in Mexico was ... significant. He knew everything wasn't his fault, but being able to see his faults clearly now made it tough to swallow. Sitting, waiting for his appointment with Larissa, he started to think about behaviors, poor decisions, and conflicts from the past and couldn't stop thinking about the demon cord. What did it mean? He was here to find that out.

Larissa's previous client was leaving and smiled at him. Darius just stared at her quietly, too deep in his thoughts to return a smile. Larissa appeared in the doorway afterward and welcomed him in, asking how he was as he passed her.

"I am a bit shell-shocked," he admitted, taking a seat in her office. "I don't understand. I've been trying to, but I can't. I don't know what's going on. Where did they come from? How did they get into our house?"

Again, he began to rattle off questions, one after another, not taking a breath as he tried to extract all of his thoughts in an instant.

"It could be for multiple reasons or from different sources," Larissa said. "You need to read *What Are the Stakes?* and consider Steve's direction—you're under attack and probably have been for some time."

"Who is Steve?" Darius asked.

"Steve Hemphill. He's a Christian author," she explained, pulling out what looked like red garden stakes with Scripture written on them. Larissa told him the stakes were rooted in Old Testament practices, similar to marking homes during Passover. They symbolically bless and dedicate land to God.

She mentioned her house and office were staked, and Darius quietly absorbed this, thinking about his own troubles. His wife's business partner was a lesbian, there were affairs in the office that his wife had told him about, and he'd been having a lot of employee issues at work. One longtime employee had recently started behaving bizarrely. His mind raced, recalling personal struggles over the years, including his oldest child's bipolar disorder and the resulting crises.

Larissa continued, explaining that evil tries to infiltrate her office every week or two. Sometimes, the stakes are mysteriously pulled halfway out of the ground, but she replaces them. She also suggested using frankincense to bless doorways and windows.

"So, how are things going?" she asked, formally starting their appointment.

Darius updated Larissa on his situation, explaining that his wife wanted him to move out, but he hadn't yet. He admitted his heart was broken, and he was uncertain about what to do, hoping that the exorcism might have changed things. Larissa reminded him that while the evil influence had been temporarily removed, the underlying human issues remained. Those problems didn't arise overnight and wouldn't be resolved quickly; both he and his wife had personal challenges to work through. She advised him to keep praying and be patient, while he hoped his wife might still want to work on their marriage.

Darius mentioned that their children were very confused as they hadn't seen the separation coming. He noted that everything seemed to change after their trip to Mexico, which even their son had noticed.

Larissa encouraged him to keep praying and lean on God. They then discussed focusing on the "cord" during the session, with Larissa clarifying that any influence from the cord was more about its impact on Darius directly over the years rather than the house. He quietly nodded and Larissa proceeded with her muscle testing.

"We're going to pray over your hip and cut the cord. We're going to remove it from you. Repeat after me."

Together, they recited prayers, the same prayers they had many times before. Then she stopped and asked, "What happened when you were 36?"

Nothing immediately came to mind, so Darius just shrugged.

Larissa cocked her head. "There was something around that time. There are a lot of negative emotions tied to you from around that time. A sense of failure, perhaps? Think about it."

He tried to do as she asked, casting his mind back almost 20 years. Suddenly, his eyes widened. When he was 36, he would have been in the middle of his ex-wife taking him back to court. They were going through a full-blown custody evaluation, which was just as stressful as it was expensive. Then, in the middle of it, he lost his job. He had to borrow money from his parents to continue paying child support, and even though he found some work as a respiratory therapist, he was only getting a few shifts, nowhere near what his previous job had paid or enough to cover their expenses.

Larissa listened intently as he recounted the whole story. When he got to the end, all she could say was: "That must have been hard."

"I hadn't thought about it like that, but yes, I felt like a failure. After that, I started having panic attacks. I would get short of breath a little and I was definitely anxious so they put me on anti-anxiety medication to help."

She nodded. "That makes sense."

They talked about other moments in his life, going as far back as his late teens. Back then, basketball was his greatest passion; it formed the map for his entire future. But from a tense relationship with the coach to cutting the tendon in his hand in a freak accident at a friend's house the week before the season started, things didn't go exactly as planned.

He had also thought he was in love when he headed to college and that girl had broken up with him the weekend before they left for college.

Larissa continued to take notes, but when he finished speaking, there was a moment of silence between them. Darius was the first to break it.

"So, what about the cord?" he asked.

Larissa put down her pen and looked at him. "Have I mentioned the seven doors to seven emotions?"

Darius shook his head.

"Well, the seven doors for this cord are: Impatience, Unforgiveness, Suppression of Others, Fear, Rejection, Prejudice, and Cynicism. Whenever you felt one of those emotions, it was most likely because of that cord. The evil spirit that placed it there was able to come back through that doorway in a sense and potentially influence your behavior. While you were responsible for your own behaviors, the spirit would use the cord to create an influence to cause pain and disruption to the person and people around you."

It was awful to think about. Even as she continued her explanation, she listed all of the other emotions that could be used to open those doors.

"Do you remember something that happened at the age of 7 that was traumatic?" she asked.

His head was swimming again as he thought about the past, but somehow, the question still caught him off guard.

"I don't know. There are a lot of things I don't remember about my younger years. Does this have anything to do with the sexual trauma you picked up on my first appointment?"

A curious Darius shifted in his chair and caught sight of Larissa's notes. The word "terror" was written by itself, the most recent thing she had etched on the page.

"Terror?"

"Yes," Larissa said, confidently. "You absorbed the emotion from someone around you. It could have been a parent or a friend or something else."

Together, they prayed and released the weight from Darius's past.

As the appointment came to an end, he felt calmer, more relaxed than he could ever remember. He was as light as a feather. Again, Larissa told him that he would probably feel exhausted later.

Darius rose from the chair and began to make his way out of the room, when he stopped. "Can I ask you another question?"

He could hear Larissa laugh.

"Of course."

"How often does this happen? How often do you deal with—" The word still caught in the back of his throat; there was still a part of him that struggled to believe it. " With spirits?"

"Well, about 75% of the time, I am dealing with people and trauma, and oftentimes, the rest involves evil influence. It's not something people think about or even consider, but we need to be cautious and aware of what we allow into our minds and homes as those energies, those spirits, are incredibly powerful. It's interesting because I can say spirits or evil influence and people seem to understand, but if I say the word demon, it gets a completely different reaction even though it means the same thing."

Larissa rose from her chair to see him out. They had already gone over their time, but still Darius had questions.

"One more question, please," he begged as she went to open the office door.

"One more," she repeated with a smile.

"Did you ever talk about any of this, about the demonic, evil influences, or spirits, with Jessica?"

Larissa shook her head. "She knew that I worked with kids and situations where there is evil influence but no details like we have discussed. When she and Ben came for an appointment, we discussed it."

"So how often do you talk about these things?" Darius asked.

"Are you serious?" She laughed, but quieted when she saw that he was, indeed, serious. "Almost never. If I did, people would think I was crazy."

"Why did you tell me, then?"

"You really want to know?"

He nodded and she sighed.

"First, you weren't going to stop asking and prying and secondly, it was obvious the first time you came in here that you were struggling and had issues, but ... " She paused. "But you also had the Holy Spirit in your heart."

They stood there for a minute before Darius broke the silence again.

"I owe you and will always owe you no matter what happens," he said. "What you have done for me and my family and how you are helping me, I will never forget or be able to repay. If I can ever do anything for you, don't hesitate."

She gave him a quick hug, thanked him, and told him she would be praying for the family.

"Until our next appointment," she said.

"Until our next appointment," he smiled.

As soon as he got home, Darius searched Amazon and immediately ordered the book by Steve Hemphill that Larissa had recommended.

Chapter 7
You're Moving Out

So much had rested on Jessica's appointment with the counselor. It was what would apparently determine whether or not they would work on salvaging their years together or if it was all over.

Darius had tried to distract himself from it. He had buried himself in his work but would take 30-minute breaks when he would leave to cry. He didn't want others to see how broken he really was, how sleep-deprived and fractured he had become since their trip to Mexico. He had to be strong, or at least appear to be strong, for his team and his business. But when it came close to the time Jessica was to meet with the counselor, he left, drove to the park, sat in his car, and prayed for an hour.

Finally, he received a text. She was not making any rash decisions, but he needed to move out of the house; they would work on themselves and then see what happens. It was hard to keep his head straight. Darius sat with tears in his eyes, contemplating the text. On the one hand, he was expecting her to tell him she wanted a divorce, so in a sense, it was a victory—a chance they could reconcile. On the other hand, where was he going to go?

It was a question he had no answer to. It took him two days of thinking about the situation before he finally decided to start packing up some clothes in his car. Darius didn't want to move out, but he didn't know what else to do. He had talked about moving into the basement, but she didn't want their other older son being "displaced," as she put it. What did she think was going to happen? But after everything he had seen, after everything that happened, he knew better than to argue.

Later, he would wonder why he hadn't just decided to stay in the house and let her move out if she wanted. But at that moment, he didn't have the capacity to think that way. Darius loved her and wanted to give her space, believing they would go to counseling and work on their marriage.

He had already decided to join the Marriage Reset Program, attend 1-1 counseling and group therapy, and devote himself to his "studies," determined to better his understanding of his faith, himself, and his relationship. He would get all the support he could and knew that he would do his part to work on himself and change, in a positive fashion, from what God had clearly shown him about his issues in Mexico to help them get through this challenging time.

Early on a Thursday morning, he started loading his car. He let Jessica know he would be gone by the following morning. She had been staying at a friend's house nearby and would only come home after she knew he was long gone and at the office. She wouldn't allow him to see her, even in passing.

Where will you be staying?

It was the first time she had reached out to him since all of this began, and he ignored it.

The text had caught him off guard ... It was the first time in some time she had shown any concern about him. But there really wasn't any place for him to go other than the office. He could ask a friend or go to his mother's house, but right now, he didn't want to look at any of those options.

He looked at the text again, not sure why he was unwilling to give her an answer.

Darius left his phone to the side and continued ferrying stuff to the car. One trip, then another, and then, while he was in the bathroom packing a few more things, he heard the front door open.

His mind first thought it was just one of the older kids coming to check on him. He stood in the bathroom, continuing to pack.

A few moments later, Jessica came around the corner and into the bathroom. She stared at him and him at her.

"Are you not going to tell me where you are going?" she asked.

"What difference does it make?" he asked in reply, his voice, accidentally, as cold as hers had become.

Darius took his things from the bathroom and walked past her, twisting his body so as to not bump into her. She grunted as he passed, her frustration evident. He ignored it, continuing on his way. He made his way down the hall and out into the garage.

The door opened shortly behind him.

He turned to see that Jessica had followed him. She didn't say anything, but this was perhaps the last chance he would have to say something to her, at least for a long time to come.

"I don't want this," he started. "I love you. If you need anything, please, let me know."

As he turned to get into the car, he heard her say, "I am sorry."

He stopped and as he turned back, she was walking up to him. When she stopped, she was so close, for the first time since before Mexico. She didn't touch him, but she looked at him and he could see himself reflected in her beautiful eyes. This was the woman he knew ... It was his wife, *his* Jessica, and he loved her.

"I know we can work through this, Jessica. I love you."

She reached out and grabbed him, nestling into him, and they embraced. "I love you," she said.

His heart almost exploded. He hugged her back and told her he loved her again before kissing her forehead.

But the moment ended as quickly as it started.

She let him go and left.

Darius drove to the office, head swimming. That was the first time she had told him she loved him in so long—in too long. It was overwhelming. It was shocking. It was distressing. It was joyous. It ... gave him hope.

Chapter 8
So, There Is Hope?

Darius couldn't get the image of his wife out of his head. He imagined seeing them together: Jessica seemingly being herself; then, through his own eyes, he would walk over to hug her, feeling her warmth against his and smelling the fragrance in her hair. He would hear her laugh and feel himself smile. But then, a chill would fill the room and she would spring from his arms. She would transform, almost levitating in front of him. He would no longer be looking at his wife; he was looking at ... something else, something soulless, void of light and life and full of hate.

It was an image that was there whenever he closed his eyes.

Darius was excited about his first Marriage Reset counseling appointment. The Zoom meeting opened and his potential counselor, Kristen, lit up the screen. She exuded confidence and with the smile on her face beaming, an air of peace and compassion. This was their introductory call to see if they would work together.

"Hello Darius," she said, with a warm, welcoming smile.

He opened his heart to Kristen, explaining he had issues he didn't understand and a sense of unworthiness that had crept in out of nowhere. He explained his current situation, as well as he could, and that, at the end of all of this, he wanted to and was ready to do whatever it would take to fix what was happening.

Then his heart sank listening to Kristen, full of the weight of understanding.

Kristen explained that "this," all of it, was probably not as sudden as it felt; his wife had most likely considered this for the past 2–3 years and only now was she ready to make her decision, which was part of the reason why it felt so dramatic. But Kristen also assured him he wasn't alone in this experience. There were over 700 men in this program, all who were going through similar experiences of shock and grief.

"With some, their wives are having an affair, with others, their wives came home to tell them it simply wasn't working and that they needed something to change, and then the last third, their wives told them it was over and walked out with no interest in working on the marriage."

Darius felt he was among that last third. It didn't bring him much comfort, but, then again, by her expression, Kristen didn't expect it to.

With a soft smile, she read through her notes, commenting on her observations. She noted how she concluded that Darius was an over-achiever, someone who was driven and would always be driven. But she encouraged him to slow down, to take his time, work through the counseling modules, and attend the group counseling weekly. She invited him to return to see her regularly so they could continue their work together. Then, most of all, she told him to give his wife space and time.

The weight grew heavier and heavier, causing him to almost sink into his chair from the pressure. He knew she was right. He was happy, comfortable even, when he was moving a hundred miles a minute; maybe it *was* time he put on the breaks and stopped rushing into things.

He nodded, agreeing to the trajectory she set him on, and thanked her.

She told him that his love for his family was beautiful and that if he did the work, there was hope.

There was hope.

Chapter 9
God Has You, Son

After Darius got the book *What Are The Stakes?*, he couldn't put it down. He was a fairly fast reader, even more so now that the situation added a certain sense of urgency. But it was content that made an impact as well—he had never read anything like it in his life.

The first story in the book grabbed his attention, but he supposed with a topic like this, talking about demons, what did he expect? It wasn't going to be a slow introduction.

Steve started off sharing the harrowing experience of an unexpected and terrifying encounter during what should have been a routine Bible study. He had been meeting regularly with Sam, a man who seemed entirely ordinary until one fateful evening when something profoundly disturbing occurred.

On that night, Steve invited Sam over to his home for another study session, just as they had done several times before. Everything seemed normal at first, but the atmosphere shifted abruptly when Sam, without any warning, started to behave erratically and Steve asked him to leave.

Sam's voice changed, sounding almost otherworldly, as he refused to go. He then lunged at Steve with a strength that defied his size, wrapping him in a vice-like grip. In a moment of desperation, Steve passionately stated, "Jesus is Lord!", commanding whatever force was driving the young man to leave.

Incredibly, Sam immediately released Steve and backed away, as if an invisible force had intervened.

But the ordeal wasn't over. Sam began to hurl objects—pots, pans, and kitchen utensils—at Steve, all while standing just ten feet away. Despite the barrage, not a single item hit him, as if he were being protected by an unseen shield. As the situation had escalated, Steve managed to step outside and call 911. Inside the house, Sam's rampage continued, causing extensive damage. He flipped over a baby grand piano, shattered windows, and destroyed much of the home's interior—all within a matter of minutes.

Darius's eyes were opened after finishing that story and he stopped to think about a quote from C.S. Lewis. **"Are you a missionary or an imposter?"** Darius felt like he had been an imposter more than a missionary for most of his life, though he had started to change that 8 years ago. He had been on 6 mission trips to support a school in the Dominican Republic and planned to go to Africa later this year to support a new clinic. It was his dream to start a charitable foundation in the next few years and the goal was to give $400k to charity, as well. He didn't want to be an imposter, and he wanted to keep growing charitable contributions.

His mind returned to the book as he turned the page and kept reading. What the heck would he do or how would he react if someone started destroying his house like that? He probably wouldn't handle it well, and definitely wouldn't have been aware enough to handle it in a spiritual way by going to God. He shook his head; he couldn't help but admire Steve.

With that thought, he dove into the next story in Steve's book.

It was an unsettling experience of a woman who began suffering from intense demonic nightmares after returning from a mission trip overseas. They were unlike anything she had ever experienced, leaving her terrified and unable to sleep. Each night, she would wake up in a cold sweat, vividly recalling the terrifying visions and sensing the presence of demonic figures in her room, watching her. Desperate for help, she reached out to Steve, and after some reflection, he asked if she had brought anything back from her trip. She mentioned a brochure about a local god and a letter dismissing Jesus in favor of Buddha. He suggested she burn those items and "stake out" her apartment with spiritual warfare stakes, praying for God's protection.

It sounded unbelievable. Yet, to her relief, the nightmares ceased immediately.

Sometime later, the nightmares returned, leaving her in a state of panic. After going back to Steve for help, she revealed that she had been seeing someone who was not a good person. She had unwittingly given evil an open door back into her home. He advised her to sever ties with him and to cleanse her home again. She followed this advice, adding even more spiritual protection, and the demonic attacks stopped once more.

Darius and his family had been blessed to travel a lot over the years, including a trip to Greece, and multiple trips to Europe. And similarly, on the trip to Greece, he had bought himself and his boys' small statues which included one of Hercules, Leonidas, and Achilles, as well as a Gladiator sword. They had always brought back souvenirs, but he had never thought about these items potentially having any significance to idols or lesser gods, which were actually demons. Outside of the times he had read about Jesus exorcising demons, he had never really thought of demons or even evil spirits.

Darius couldn't stop thinking about that last story as he thought about his family's travels, particularly their trip to Africa. During that trip, they had visited an African village and brought back several items that made him wonder if they had opened the door to evil. His wife had been given a female necklace as a gift that went with a mating ritual and had bought some kitchen items. Darius had brought back a Chieftain's club, which was a gift given to him when his wife got the necklace and a spear along with artwork.

His head continued to swim, and he couldn't put the book down.

Steve expressed that the words we speak and the actions we take in the physical realm carry significant weight and have real consequences in the eternal realm. When we bind an evil entity in the name of Jesus, it is bound, and when we command in His name, those commands must be obeyed. Darius was overwhelmed with the idea of what he was reading. It wasn't simply positive thinking; it was a spiritual reality affirmed by Scripture. Steve was saying that the Bible teaches us that what we declare in faith, in alignment with God's Word, manifests in the unseen realm.

It made Darius's head spin contemplating the idea of binding in God's name, in the name of Jesus. He was also starting to think about Scripture in the context of what comes out of our mouths being a blessing or a curse. Proverbs 18:21, he thought, reminds us that our words can bring life or death, and those who speak with wisdom will be rewarded.

Darius couldn't stop thinking about the past. Was he really that blind to reality? To whom God was and the idea or context of evil? If someone had told him about this book in the past or that his family was under attack by evil influence or demons, he would have thought they had lost their mind. He was wondering if was losing his mind over the past few weeks.

He kept reading.

As the strange and supernatural experiences kept occurring for Steve, his skeptical wife insisted he not share them with anyone. People would think he was bonkers, completely mad. However, as the stories kept happening and from credible sources, finally, even his wife softened and got to the point where she was excited to hear about the positive things that God was doing through Steve helping people.

Yeah, welcome to the family, Darius, he thought to himself with a grin.

How would he tell anyone what he was learning? They would think he's crazy.

Hey, what's going on?

Well, my wife doesn't think she loves me anymore and doesn't want to work on the marriage.

That sucks. What happened?

I really had no idea she was this unhappy.

Seriously?

No, seriously. I mean, our marriage isn't perfect, and we have struggled to communicate but we didn't even know she had ADHD until a year ago. Yes, of course, I thought most of the problem was her until God gave me eyes to see and ears to hear down in Mexico.

What?

You know, I stayed up for nearly three nights asking for God to help me and then he finally showed me what an asshole I can sometimes be and that I have a lot of scars from the past that need healing to do. The main point is that I can see through her eyes now and I know what to work on. I know what has destroyed our polarity.

Polarity? Are you a fucking battery, man?

It's about positive and negative masculinity and positive and negative feminine traits. You see these have a major impact on polarity in a relationship.

Blank stare with a chorus of crickets.

Seriously, though, I realize I could have handled things better and I am now realizing I have a lot of work to do on myself, but I am willing to do it.

And she's not?

It doesn't look like it but I think I understand why.

Why?

Well, demons are influencing her. So, she just needs a little old fashioned Catholic exorcism, like in the movies and I think we can work it out.

And with that, they would have him on the next train to looney town as the winner of "Who wants to be in a straitjacket?!"

Darius literally shook his head in disgust and dug back into the book.

The next story was about a married man with kids who looked like he had a good life but who, behind the scenes, was living a different, darker life. He was addicted to pornography, was spending money they didn't have, and eventually, his wife finally got wise to his issues and they were struggling to stay together, sleeping in separate rooms. The man attended a lecture at their church where Steve was doing a sermon around his book called *My Search for Prayers Prayers Satan Hates*. In the lecture, Steve discussed how many Christians were clueless about the demonic, that they were everywhere in the Bible and were territorial.

It was the kind of message you'd expect from Hollywood in some big blockbuster feature film. But after hearing Steve's sermon, the man told him he thought he had a demon issue while explaining his addiction and the surprising fact that he couldn't read the Bible. He shared that every time he tried to read the Bible or pray, his words would be blocked.

After going through a series of prayers with Steve, this man went home and staked his house out and could read the Bible and pray for the first time in years.

Demons work to destroy marriages? The thought troubled Darius. He could see how something that hated God would want to destroy marriage since God created marriage, but were they working to destroy his?

As Darius read on, there were multiple stories on children being affected by the demonic, including how they go after innocent children in their dreams. It made him think about Larissa saying that night terrors with children almost always had to do with demons from her experience. How often were these things preying on children?

He started into the next story. A shy girl recounted a dramatic encounter: the day after the staking, an ominous man approached her, exuding a palpable sense of evil. Despite his efforts, he was unable to cross an invisible barrier at the edge of the staked area, as if restrained by an unseen force. It was sharing the point that God is still in charge if you let Him be, and that while evil wanted to create chaos and nightmares, they were repelled by areas dedicated to God.

Darius thought about the idea of someone trying to step over a property line and not being able to. It made him think of the time he had been canoeing with his dad, uncle, and cousin and had asked to stay behind with the canoes while they drove back to get the other car. It was one of the scariest things he could remember in his life, and it was strange to him that it popped into his mind now.

He was pretty naïve as a kid and maybe even sometimes as an adult about certain things, but he was definitely not a worldly kid growing up. He had never stayed in a nice hotel until he won a sales contest in college. They had grown up in KOAs, or campgrounds of America, in a pop-up trailer as his parents couldn't afford for them to stay in hotels, which was fine. It really made him appreciate everything he had earned and all the things he had been able to do for his children. But even without a lot of awareness, it astonished him he knew exactly what was happening.

A man had driven by and leered at him through the car window. He asked where his parents were, and a young Darius knew that he needed to lie. He told the man that they were down by the water getting another canoe out, and for a moment, that seemed to satisfy the man. He drove on, parked, disappeared into the brush, but then came back about five minutes later, walking straight toward Darius.

He had gone to check and knew that Darius had lied.

He asked Darius to come with him, but there was nothing good about this man. He intended to harm him, badly.

Darius said no multiple times, but no longer satisfied and growing impatient, the man started to walk around the canoe. Darius told him to stay away and started swinging the paddle in an attempt to defend and protect himself. The man had ... literally snarled at him with hate. He was more beast than man.

After what seemed like an eternity, the man took off when another car approached.

Darius had never forgotten that episode or the terror he had felt, the evil in the man, and his entire body trembling with fear ... What would have happened if things had gone just a little bit differently?

***

It was some point around 3 AM when Darius set the book down and fell asleep on the couch in his office. The next morning, he got up, read Scripture, meditated, and worked out, and then did some business items. His mind was all over the place; meditation was a challenge and going through the first few modules of the Marriage Rest Program wasn't a lot of fun. As blind as he had been to what was happening around him, he was intuitive enough to realize there wasn't much coming that was going to be fun.

In the early afternoon, he jumped back into the book and finished it. Like the first half of the book, the remaining chapters were more unbelievable stories of demon-influenced horrors that were stopped miraculously through acknowledging the behaviors that had led to them, repenting, and staking out the area with Steve's stakes. Amazing stories of children being afflicted and then after staking, everything ended. Events that should have killed people on staked out land and they weren't harmed and even cars that were staked out getting in collisions when those in the accident weren't harmed.

Darius sat in the empty office and the wheels of his mind couldn't stop spinning. He was overwhelmed mentally and couldn't stop thinking about past events. His youngest son, Ben, bullied one of his friends this past year, and it was recorded on video. It was horrifying to watch and Darius couldn't believe it at the time. His daughter, Alexandra, had been through so many challenges in high school, including an attempted suicide, which Darius miraculously realized in time to take her to the hospital before it was too late. His other son, Sheehan, had moved to a private school for his junior year because they felt he needed a more academically challenging environment. He was also a talented basketball player and could have played in college after being the only junior named to the Marion All-County Honors. But his senior year had been ruined by a prank during an overnight team building session, leading to Sheehan being suspended for the first half of the season. Similar to what had happened to Darius.

So many other negative events came to his mind.

He thought about some of his family's bizarre behavior and past events of conflict, shame, guilt, and his grandparents. After passing away, both grandparents had left a will and designated one of their children to be the executor of their estate. But in both situations, his parent's siblings had started taking items from the home without consent, essentially stealing from the estates. It had caused major conflict, and those relationships never recovered.

Darius's mind came back to the demon chord, which still disturbed him greatly. He thought of his past poor behaviors, including the times he had gotten drunk, times he hadn't been kind or gracious to others, or hadn't given his wife grace. He thought about his deep dislike for himself in particular and how he didn't speak nicely to himself and would get stuck in negative thought patterns. It was sobering, to say the least, and Darius sensed that regardless of what his wife did, he was never going to be the same.

He sat back, feeling a weight on his shoulders. Then, as he set the book aside, he decided that he had to meet Steve. Darius made a living "cold calling" people and didn't have to think about it twice; he found his information and sent him a message through Facebook Messenger on Saturday afternoon.

Sunday, he followed his new routine with meditation, went to church, and then was doing some prep work for the week when he received a message back.

How did you find me?

I have been dealing with some crazy things, my wife doesn't want to be married anymore, and a lady told me to get your book, which I just read.

Okay, can you talk this evening?

Yes!

Late Sunday evening, Darius was sitting at his office desk working when the message came in from Steve asking if he was available to call and talk. A minute later, they were on FaceTime video.

"Nice to meet you, Darius," Steve said.

"You as well, Steve. I really appreciate your time and your book has … It's blown my mind." Darius said, his face taught with concern.

"Tell me what's going on," Steve said.

Darius gave Steve a short synopsis of the challenges of the last year, filling in all the gaps with the discoveries he was making—one after another.

"Oh boy, you are definitely dealing with some challenges for sure," Steve responded, nodding his head with a sympathetic expression on his face.

"I don't know what to do!" Darius exclaimed.

"Have you ordered stakes? Steve asked.

Darius nodded. "Yes, yesterday, after I finished the book. I plan to stake out my house, my office building, my mom's house, and my daughter's apartment to start with."

"Okay, Darius, that's a great start. Just keep praying, stay in your Bible, and keep doing the work you're doing with this new men's marriage program. Control what you can control and leave the rest to God."

Steve led Darius in a prayer, asking for calmness, peace, and blessings on Darius's family. He prayed that God would show His power and glory while protecting the covenant of the marriage and being an example to the children. He prayed that God would lead Darius closer to Him, give him direction, and soften Jessica's heart.

At the end of the prayer, Darius thanked Steve and then started to cry softly, his speech as rapid as it was muffled. "I don't want to lose my wife or have my family broken, I love them so very much and—"

"Son, son … " Steve kindly interrupted. "Stop."

Darius stopped in mid-sentence, his face calming as he looked at Steve.

"God has you, son," he stated. "He is in total control, and He has you. You need to understand how much God loves you. God loves you so much. He hears all prayers, and He uses everything for His good. Your family is going to be fine. God is in charge."

Darius smiled and slowly nodded. "Thank you, Steve."

"Stay in touch and I'll be praying for you," Steve said before hanging up.

Darius sat in the office thinking about the idea of not understanding how much God loved him and that he was in charge, hearing all prayers. God had most certainly been listening in Mexico as Darius prayed incessantly. There was no other answer that made any sense to Darius, particularly when he had been given an understanding and truth that he didn't like. No, he hadn't heard a voice, witnessed a vision, flash of light or fireworks, but the thoughts had been formed clearly in his head and they weren't his thoughts. God had revealed to Darius the truth of where he was lacking in the fruits of the spirit and his mistakes.

Darius thought about Steve, his kindness, and how genuine he was. Steve seemed to give off an aura of kindness and love. Oddly, he suddenly thought if there was a real Santa Claus, he would behave like Steve in their call. Shaking his head, he opened up his phone and order two more of Steve's books, *Prayers Satan Hates and My Search for the Real Heaven*

Chapter 10
A Marriage Reset

T wo weeks later, Darius was excited to talk to Kristen again after having some work under his belt.

"Alright, Darius, let's dive in. There are four key legs to this program. I'll briefly cover them, and, by the end of this call, my goal is for you to walk away with actionable steps, steps that leave you confident in your ability to succeed here."

Kristen shifted her gaze, looking directly into her camera and waiting for his acknowledgment.

Darius nodded. "Sounds good."

Kristen smiled. "Great. First, the course. Were you able to log in and complete Level 0?"

"I believe so," Darius replied, tapping his notebook. "I've got six and a half pages of notes, watched all the videos, and did that painful exercise on how badly I've been messing up. Not fun, but I should be prepared."

Kristen laughed lightly. "That's good progress. The course is designed to be done one module a day, to really let you lean into it.

But from what you've told me, it sounds like you enjoy seeing the bigger picture first, right?"

Darius gave a small shrug. "Yeah, that's just how my brain works."

"And that's okay, too. Some men go through the program multiple times, and every time, they gain new insights. So, keep that in mind as you continue. Now, the second leg of the program: the Facebook group. Honestly, this is my favorite part of the program. The community is incredible. The men in this group are powerful, kind, and deeply masculine. It's a safe space for vulnerability and growth. I really encourage you to dig in there, to lean on your brothers-in-arms. Men who engage with the group find the most success."

Darius shifted in his chair. "I guess my hesitation with Facebook is ... Well, people put up these fake fronts, you know? But for this purpose, I can see the value."

Kristen nodded, understanding. "That's a valid concern, but let me assure you, this group isn't about pretending. Only men who've invested in themselves and this journey are there. It's a sanctuary for real, raw support. It sounds like you're ready to engage with that."

Darius considered her words, nodding slightly.

"So you'll also be assigned a Customer Success Manager, or CSM, who will check in with you. They'll help you with day-to-day questions, like strategizing communication with your wife, for example. It's a great resource."

Darius leaned forward, taking a few notes as she spoke. "Is that the person who gives feedback on things like text threads with your wife? That's a big reason I'm doing this. I've made a lot of progress, but I need this to become part of who I am, not just something I do occasionally."

Kristen smiled. "Exactly. You'll see men in the group posting their communication challenges and wins all the time. It's a powerful tool for growth. Now, the third leg is the group calls. These happen four times a week. What time zone are you in?"

"Eastern," Darius replied. "I'm in Indiana."

Kristen chuckled. "I grew up in Michigan but live in Florida now. Anyway, the calls are held Tuesday, Wednesday, Thursday, and Sunday. Each coach has their own style, some structured, some free-flowing. They're about 75 minutes and focus on coaching, collaboration, and even one-on-one moments. They're high-value sessions, and you can attend as many as you'd like."

"I'm looking forward to joining the call tomorrow," Darius added.

"Perfect. I'll see you there. Now, the final leg is the War Room calls. These are strategic one-on-one sessions. I'll be your coach unless you prefer to work with a man."

"No, I want you," Darius said without hesitation.

Kristen grinned. "I'm honored. I'll send you my scheduling link after this call. These sessions are 30 minutes, focused, and tailored to your needs. Before each session, I'll ask you a few questions to ensure we're prepared to tackle what's most pressing."

Darius leaned back, rubbing his chin. "That sounds like what I need. I've done a lot of the work, watched the videos, taken notes, but when my wife said she was leaving me, I panicked. I did everything wrong, pursued her, pushed too hard. I made it worse. Now, I'm trying to approach things differently. She's noticed, too, which is encouraging, but I need to be strategic."

Kristen tilted her head. "Darius, give yourself some grace. Your logical, strategic mind is one of your greatest strengths, but it can also make things harder when emotions are involved. The key here is balancing that logic with presence and compassion. Let's take a moment to celebrate how far you've come already."

Darius exhaled, a small smile tugging at the corners of his mouth.

"Your wife wants to feel seen and safe. Those are the two fundamental needs for a woman. When she doesn't feel seen, when you disengage or bury yourself in work, it hurts her deeply. And when she doesn't feel safe, whether that's emotional or otherwise, it creates a barrier."

"And that's the thing," Darius began, his voice measured, almost hesitant. "I didn't get it before, but I do now. I'm ... so logical. Like, my brain processes things really, really fast. Everything gets filtered through this lens of analysis."

"That's a core difference in communication between men and women," she said. "Men tend to approach things with logic and structure. Women ... We're like a song. Full of high pitches and low notes, indirect and flowing. Even though a lot of our communication, the nonverbals especially, might overlap, the way we arrive at connection is different."

Darius shifted in his chair. He had thought about this distinction before, but hearing it framed this way brought a fresh clarity.

Kristen continued, her tone soft yet deliberate. "You know, in the Marriage Reset Program, Josh talks about the fundamental human needs, and for women, two stand out to me as absolutely vital: the need to feel seen and the need to feel safe. If I don't feel seen, through verbal and nonverbal communication, or if I don't feel safe, well, it's impossible to thrive in that space."

Darius nodded, his brow furrowing slightly. "Yeah. That makes sense. And when I went through his list of reasons why women leave their marriages, I could pinpoint four or five that I've failed at. That realization hit me like a ton of bricks."

"What stood out the most?" she prompted.

He exhaled deeply, his fingers tracing the edge of the notebook on his lap. "The one about emotional connection. How a husband doesn't try to understand his wife. I stopped trying, years ago. I disengaged. She doesn't feel good about herself because of me, because I make her feel worse about herself. That's something I never wanted to do, but I did it anyway."

He paused, running a hand over his face. "And I've been distant. Burying myself in work, especially over the last ten months. I mean, it's been hell in the business. We're growing, but we've made no money for months, and I had to borrow just to keep things afloat. But we've also learned so much, about our weaknesses, about what needs fixing in the business. And we're fixing it. It's this strange paradox. I've spent so much energy on saving the business, thinking it would secure our future, but I didn't realize I was sacrificing our present."

She gave him a sympathetic smile, her expression one of both understanding and challenge. "So, now you have clarity. You've identified the problem. That's powerful. What's your plan?"

He straightened, determination flickering in his eyes. "I've got the right lens now. I see what the issue is. If she gives me a chance, I can fix this. I *will* fix this."

"Good," she said. "But fixing it starts with showing up, consistently. With communication. Women crave meaning behind words, meaning that aligns with action. You said it yourself: she needs to feel seen and safe. How are you addressing that, day by day?"

He hesitated. "I mean, I'm logical to a fault, right? She's not. She's ... free-flowing, unpredictable. That's the polarity that drew us to each other in the first place. I used to love that about her. But I let it turn into frustration instead of strength."

"Exactly," she said. "That opposite energy is what creates balance. When you're fully grounded, open, and present, you help her thrive in her flow. That's when connection grows."

Darius nodded slowly, the weight of her words resonating deeply. "You're right. It's like ... She's amazing. Everyone loves her. And I've let my impatience and my need for structure erode that admiration. But I see it now. I see how I've failed to be present for her. I've been thinking about everything through the lens of what she's not doing for me. But now ... " He swallowed hard. "Now I see it's about what I'm not doing for her."

"Presence is everything. It's not about fixing her; it's about showing up fully, authentically, without judgment. She needs to feel your compassion and your focus, not just in words but in energy. Like when you're here, talking to me, your intensity, your focus ... It's powerful. Channel that, but in a way that's soft and inviting."

He chuckled. "You're spot on. People always think I'm intense, a hardass, even. But inside, I'm a pushover. A total softie."

"I can see that," she laughed. "And that softness is a strength too. Lean into it. She'll respond to your openness, your ability to hold space for her. It's not about solving her scattered energy or her quirks. It's about being with her, present and grounded, no matter what. Do you meditate?"

"I pray a lot," he replied, "But, well, no, I mean, for me, meditation is when I go hiking or scuba diving, those times when I get to decompress."

"You know, I like to look at prayer as talking to God and meditation as listening to God. So I would like for you to be more intentional about it. Try to dedicate 10 minutes every morning to intentionally have that time to listen, whatever that looks like for you, but the point is you're doing it with intention. You're just being present and listening."

Darius exhaled deeply, the tension in his shoulders easing ever so slightly. "I can do that," he said finally. "I always say: Seek truth, determine your values, be intentional—"

"And then practicing it," Kristen added.

He laughed. "Correct."

Chapter 11
Get the Straight Jacket

I t was a Sunday afternoon and Darius was at the office waiting to take a video call with one of his remote employees, Stygall, who was due to work onsite for the coming week. They had worked together some years ago and had become fast friends, staying in touch long after departing corporate America until Stygall finally joined his company earlier that year.

Like most people in his life, Stygall was aware of the general turmoil that plagued Darius's life but none of the details. So it must have been quite the shock when he joined the call, said, "How are you doing, brother?" and Darius confided some of the details. He had stayed at his house before and didn't see this coming.

"I'm doing the best I can, man," he said, getting choked up. "I love her. I love her ... I don't want any of this."

"It's going to be alright. Just give her time and God will get you through this," Stygall said, offering as much comfort as he could through the screen. "We all go through challenges; Sharon and I have certainly had ours. Don't worry, brother, it's going to be alright."

"I know … I know. I just have to keep praying, be faithful, and work on myself."

"Are you going to counseling?"

Darius nodded and told him about Marriage Reset—and about how he found it at 3 AM when this all started. "It's about controlling your emotions and behaviors. It's centered around the idea that life is happening for you, not to you, and I'm starting to learn about polarity. There are a lot of modules, and I've just started. I had my first appointment with my one-on-one counselor, and she seems pretty awesome. I was—" Darius paused, almost chuckling to himself, thinking about his first meeting with Kristen. "I was basically a disaster in the first session."

"What do you mean?" Stygall asked.

"I was talking a mile a minute, she had to keep slowing me down, I would, but then I would speed up again, and eventually, I just lost it. Cried like a little bitch."

Stygall laughed out loud; his musical belly laugh that made anyone around him want to smile and laugh too. "Ah, man. It's going to be alright."

"Thank you, Stygall," Darius said, laughing at himself for the first time in a while.

"You are welcome; we are praying for you and I am here if you need anything."

The rest of the meeting went as Darius had originally expected it to go. They discussed the coming week, the training they were going to do, and the plan for the next 90 days. It was focused, productive, and Darius would dare even say "normal."

"Is there anything else?"

The question brought that sense of normality to an end, and Darius paused, contemplating whether or not he would tell his friend anymore.

"What's up, man?"

It was as if, in that moment at that very second, Darius was split in two. There was a part of him that wanted to nod and smile and say, "Yeah, sure, see you next week!" But then, there was the other side of him. The side that feared sounding crazy but that wanted more than anything to share the truth.

"I want to share some other things with you, not about work, but you're going to think I'm fucking crazy."

Stygall laughed again. "Well, try me."

"You might regret—"

"Try me," he repeated.

After a few seconds, Darius found the courage. "Well, I'm probably nuts for telling you but I need to share this with someone."

He wasn't sure Stygall was fully prepared for the barrage that was about to come his way. Up until this point, Darius had only shared that Jessica had pulled the rug out from under him in Mexico and was looking at the possibility of a divorce. Anything supernatural, anything demonic, was kept off the table. But now he brought it all to bear.

He didn't know if he resembled a mad man on the other side of the screen as he told Stygall about his meetings with Larissa as well as everything that came after, but while the "more reasonable" part of him was likely screaming for him to shut up, this part of him was itching to confide in a friend. Whether it was the need to either validate he wasn't losing his mind or maybe for someone to tell him he *was* bonkers and go right ahead with the straight jacket, he wasn't going to stop until everything was out and in the open.

Stygall didn't say a word; he never interrupted, not even once. He sat there, listening intently with a stone-like expression on his face. Even when Darius was done, ready to call it a day from the exhaustion of it all, Stygall still said nothing.

After a moment of silence, Darius asked, with as much of a jesting tone as he could muster, "So how quickly can I expect your resignation because your boss has completely and utterly gone nuts?"

"I would never quit on you," Stygall said. "Dude, I love you, and this ... this just makes me want to be there for you even more. I'm not going anywhere; in fact, I'm going to get Steve's book and read it myself."

Chapter 12
Therapy or a Bullet

After his second week attending the Marriage Reset group sessions, Darius had started keeping in touch with some of the other men through Facebook. There, he would post daily about the work he was doing and interact with the others who were doing much the same.

It felt strange to be a part of a community again, but it was interesting for him to see how right Kristen was—to see just how many people there were who were having similar issues. They might have been completely different on the surface, but underneath, Darius could see the similarities, and he could see parts of himself reflected in many of them.

One of the first exercises in the initial module required each man to create a video discussing how they planned to win back their wife. The goal was to envision the relationship six months down the line, using positive, masculine language to describe the changes. Darius recorded several takes on his phone before he finally felt comfortable enough to post it on the MRP Facebook page. Kristen had emphasized the importance of fully immersing himself in the program to achieve meaningful results. This meant diligently working through the modules, attending at least 2–3 of the weekly group meetings, participating in individual counseling sessions, and posting daily about his progress.

Darius was more than ready to commit. As a lifelong overachiever, he recognized the need to change and was determined to do whatever it took to save his marriage. He loved his wife, and his children, and believed he was starting to understand her perspective on his failings. Although she hadn't shared her feelings with him directly, Darius had begun to gain insights from the program and was eager to continue learning.

The community offered a wealth of resources, and Darius planned to make the most of them. It quickly became clear who was genuinely committed to the work, who was struggling, and who had been in the program long enough to appear more grounded. Most of the men seemed to have good intentions and were genuinely trying to improve their lives. While a few came off as narcissistic or abrasive, the majority were decent, well-meaning men who were simply lost and trying to find their way.

Occasionally, senior members would harshly critique newcomers, and after Darius posted his first video, a seasoned member commented:

"Hmmm, there's a lot to unpack here, but I'll start by saying you don't come across as confident or masculine in this video. If you want to get your wife back or even be worthy of her, you need to take care of your body first. A masculine man prioritizes his physical health, watches what he eats, and maintains good physical condition. If you neglect your body, you'll likely neglect other important things, like your wife. Show some self-respect. Hit the gym."

Darius was taken aback. He hadn't seen himself as out of shape and felt defensive. He re-watched the video, looking for "evidence" to refute the comment. Sure, maybe it wasn't the best angle, but he was in decent shape—actually better than decent. He'd lost 12 pounds through fasting even before the marital issues began, and after Mexico, he'd shed another 10 pounds. For the first time in ages, he was close to his college weight.

With fingers on the keyboard and the first few words already ready to go, he stopped.

"Darius, take a breath and stop to think," he heard Kristen say in his head.

He deleted the start of his comment almost instantly. This was a behavior he was trying to break; he wouldn't let himself fall back into old habits and react defensively.

He decided to leave it be and later that evening, the sudden irony of his situation did not go unnoticed. The group call focused on how to maintain a masculine frame when responding to criticism; responding with calmness, confidence, and emotional stability, rather than reacting impulsively or defensively. It was about not letting criticism undermine your sense of self-worth and to distinguish between constructive criticisms and subjective criticisms. Then, respond versus react, and sometimes, the response might be not responding at all.

It was a great call, one that gave Darius the confidence to say he was moving in the right direction. Then another opportunity presented itself when one of the men, Todd, messaged him asking if he'd be up for getting in touch outside of MRP. Keen to connect with other men who were going through experiences similar to his own, Darius said yes and eagerly awaited the time of their call.

Todd was both everything he expected and nothing like he expected. He was measured and collected; he was a nice guy who had a couple of kids who he loved dearly. Then, he began to talk about his own situation. Unlike Darius, he had been going through whatever "this" was for over three years and Marriage Reset wasn't the first program he had attended to try and help his marriage and improve himself.

Three years ... He couldn't even begin to imagine what that was like.

It was something Darius truly admired, but he certainly hoped that he wasn't still in "this" three years from now. Though, in the 30 minutes in which they spoke, Todd showed Darius something. He showed him there was still a bright side to all of this: there was still a chance.

**

His first appointment with his wife's counselor, Sharon, had been delayed a few weeks because she was on vacation, which wasn't ideal in the middle of this crisis. Darius was conflicted to say the least seeing her, but he had little choice as Jessica wouldn't go to anyone else. They had a challenging history with Sharon—at least from Darius's perspective.

It was frustrating because he felt that Sharon had told them certain things separately and then changed her narrative once they were together. Darius was by no means perfect and, since Mexico, had a whole new awareness of his deficiencies, but he wasn't a narcissist.

The second time they had gone to her, his wife had accused him of being a narcissist and that Sharon thought he had aspects of it. After he had gotten that accusation, he had researched the traits, including taking an assessment, and it wasn't an appropriate or fair label. The assessment showed he had 3 out 12 traits. However, it was a perspective that Jessica seemed to take to, one Sharon encouraged and one that soured Darius's perspective of Sharon. That situation had hurt him greatly, and it took him a long time to get over it; in fact, maybe he really never had.

But this would be the third time they would be counseling with Sharon—unless his wife had already been going to her on her own without his knowledge, which he had to assume was a possibility.

Two weeks after coming home from Mexico, Darius was still a wreck. He was getting little to no sleep; he was exhausted and heartbroken at the same time. As he got on the video call with Sharon, his anxiety rose a little in anticipation of talking to her. He liked her but didn't trust her.

She was kind to him and compassionate while asking how he was doing. Darius talked fast as he told her he was scared, exhausted, and didn't understand what was happening. After he gave her his perspective of the synopsis, Sharon told him the first step was making sure he was mentally well and getting sleep.

"Are you open to taking something for sleep?" she asked. "I'd like to encourage you to go on Trazodone, which acts as a sedative. It's a tried and true old-school medication that works really well. I have asked family physicians to prescribe it on a few occasions for this very thing."

He wasted no time agreeing. "I need sleep and I know I need sleep," he said, "So yes, I'll take it."

She nodded. "I will call your family doctor today to ask him to prescribe it."

"Okay," he said.

Sharon took a breath before continuing. "Now, here is what I want you to hear. You need to go very, very slowly. Slow down, that's number one. Number two ... get comfortable being uncomfortable," she said. "Jessica needs space and has a lack of trust in you to hold a boundary."

Darius looked at her dazed and confused, but nodded his head slowly. "I believe I understand that I have bulldozed her with logic, though I didn't understand that previously."

"You have to understand that Jessica takes a lot of things in and then buries them down deeply inside. So that means that something has hit her deeply, flipped a switch, and she has a lot to work through right now."

He just looked at her, nodding his head, and said, "Okay."

Sharon held his gaze. "So let me repeat: 1. Go slow. 2. Get comfortable with being uncomfortable. 3. There are no immediate solutions to this. 4. Your mental wellness has to be a priority, so please pull back on your solution energy to this situation and bring it back to Darius. 5. You *need* to sleep and need to eat."

She took a moment and smiled at him.

"I want you to be at peace with yourself," she said. "I want you to work at believing Jessica when she says she needs space. You have to help her know that you will hold your side of the boundaries she is setting. If you do, that might help her soften her heart."

Darius just nodded. "Okay, I understand. I love her and I will do whatever I need to support her and work through this."

He paused, a thousand thoughts suddenly coming to the front of his mind.

"Do you think she is having an affair?" he asked.

She shook her head slowly. "I didn't see any signs to make me think that, but she is very confused, and I truthfully don't know what is going on. I want to help, though. Take care of yourself, give her space and I'll get with both of you again in the next few weeks. Hopefully, in time, we can get you both in the room or on a video call together."

"Okay," he said again as the video call clicked off.

***

That evening, Darius was in a deep state of contemplation driving to the office from the gym. He had worked out, gotten cleaned up, and was headed back to get situated for the night. Darius tried not to think about it but living out of the office sucked. It didn't really matter that he couldn't cook anything because he had very little appetite, but living and working out of the same place just wasn't ideal. Everyone needs a change of scenery, and right now, his scenery was changing very little.

As he pulled up to the office and parked, he felt the most uneasy and ominous feeling. It was odd.

Suddenly, he heard in his mind, "You should put the pistol in your mouth and blow your brains out."

Darius froze and looked down to his right at the 9 MM Sig Sauer P320 sitting between the driver's seat and the console. He suddenly pictured the gun in his mouth and his brains splattering over the windshield as he pulled the trigger.

"You should put the pistol in your mouth and blow your brains out," the words urged again.

Darius suddenly snapped out of his frozen state and bolted from the car.

He ran to the front door, praying as he went. Panicked, he unlocked the door and went inside. He felt like the voice was following him. He went to the conference table, sat down, and started praying. Ephesians 6:10-13, reciting the words of exorcism over himself and the building, and finishing with 2 Timothy 1:7.

He sat there in an agitated state and realized sweat stuck to his brow. The ominous feeling faded. The voice gone.

What in the world is happening to me?

It wouldn't be the last time that thought would cross his mind. It would be a restless night on the office couch nestled in his sleeping bag once again wondering if he was losing his mind.

Chapter 13
Anything Strange Ever Happen?

Dude, we need to talk. This book is incredible.

Yeah, I know. How far along are you?

I bought it on audio right after we got off our call and can't stop listening. I am about half way through. I just finished staking my house out.

Darius stopped and read the text again. It had been a week since Darius had ordered stakes of his own and they hadn't arrived yet, but Stygall, who had *just* started reading the book, had already finished staking his house? Quickly and more than a little curious, Darius texted back asking how.

I went to Wal-Mart, bought the stakes and a magic marker, and wrote the Scripture on the stakes myself.

What a go-getter was all Darius could think, but when he probed Stygall further, curious to know why he was so quick to stake his house, he was met with:

I'll tell you tomorrow. You aren't going to believe it!

"Yeah," Darius said to himself, looking at the text and shaking his head. He couldn't help but crack a smile. "*I'm* not going to believe *you.*"

It was a joke that tickled him for the rest of the day, but the curiosity lasted much longer. What in the world would make Stygall do that? The question was an itch he couldn't scratch, and he couldn't wait to find out why.

The next morning, he woke and followed his new routine, which helped distract him, but his curiosity was building. He stood in the airport, which wasn't at all busy, and waited for Stygall to show up.

When Stygall did eventually show up, bag to his side, the two men embraced and walked to Darius's car. It was slow and quiet with the conversation short.

"How was the flight?" Darius asked.

"All good. No issues," Stygall responded.

Darius popped the trunk of his car and loaded the bag into it as Stygall climbed into the passenger's seat.

He pulled away from the terminal and all was quiet; Darius could hardly handle it. He wanted to know what was going on, but the conversation that did fill the air was consumed by "small talk." They talked about Stygall's family for a few miles, discussed some business items for the next few, resumed the silence for half a mile or so … and then finally Darius couldn't handle it any longer.

"Brother, you got to tell me what the deal is with the stakes!"

Stygall was quiet for a minute and then, after consideration, he said, "I know, man. I will. Let's get someplace where we can sit down, grab a bite to eat … someplace quiet. Then I'll tell you."

"Okay."

Firehouse wasn't usually busy, and the food was more than acceptable. It was somewhere Darius would occasionally stop, so he knew it was the kind of place that would fit Stygall's cryptic requirement. He parked the car and then they went in to place their order. For Darius, the usual, and for Stygall, one more, with drinks for two. Then they went and sat in the back corner, sitting in silence until the food arrived.

As they began eating, finally, Stygall spoke up.

"Okay, here's the deal. I'm going to share several things with you, and you'll need to shelve them until I finish going through the timeline. Don't worry, it'll all make sense by the end."

"Okay," Darius nodded. "I understand."

Stygall took a deep breath, gathering his thoughts before continuing. "So, we basically raised our boys in the house we're living in now. We moved in when Zach was four, before Ian was born. Everything was great at first. We loved the house and were excited about it.

"But about six months after we moved in, Zach started having night terrors. And I'm not talking about the occasional bad dream. These were awful, ongoing for a few years, and nothing we tried helped. We went to doctors and counselors, but nothing worked. It was beyond words—you had to experience it to understand. But after about three years, they finally stopped."

Darius's eyes widened, but he simply nodded, allowing Stygall to continue.

"One summer, while we were having a cookout with some new neighbors, one guy asked if anything strange had ever happened in the house. I gave him a peculiar look and asked why. He just shrugged me off. 'No reason,' he said. As I thought about it, I remembered the door lock on one of the upstairs bedrooms. I shared now that I think about it, there was something strange when we moved in. One of the upstairs bedrooms had a lock on the outside of the door, in the hallway, which was really strange.

"All the guy said was 'That makes sense.'"

"I was like, 'What?'"

"He went on to explain that the previous occupants had a young boy who had severe issues and frequent outbursts of anger. As he grew older, they couldn't control him and ended up locking him in his room. Tragically, he committed suicide in that house."

"That's awful," Darius said, shocked.

Stygall nodded. "Yeah. We never would have bought the house if we'd known."

He took another breath and sip of his drink, wetting his palette and clearing his throat. "Then, you told me about your situation, and I was thinking, what in the world? I know you and I love you, man. I know you're not crazy, and I believe in both God and the reality of evil. I've made my own mistakes—things you don't know about that were really bad."

Darius tilted his head and said, "Look, brother, we've all made mistakes and done things we regret."

"Yes, but—" Stygall stopped, clearly not wanting to delve any further into that part of the story. "Let's just say, your story made me reconsider some of my past and I will share more with you later."

Darius nodded. "I completely understand. I'm doing the same thing."

"So, the night I got the book, I listened to the first six chapters and I went to bed thinking about it. I listened to more the next day, and then it talked about night terrors."

A chill ran up Darius's spine, but he held his tongue and let Stygall continue.

"I first thought about Zach when we first moved in, but about four months ago, Ian started having night terrors. It was like the past was repeating itself."

"Holy shit!" Darius exclaimed without thinking.

"Yeah," Stygall said. "I went straight to the store, bought the stakes, put the verses on them, and staked out our house Monday night."

They sat in silence for a moment until Darius asked, "So, has he had any since?"

"No, not last night at least."

"I'll send you the Scriptures and prayers of exorcism that Larissa gave me. They should help; they helped me."

"Yeah, do that," Stygall replied with a grim expression. "Do that."

The next few days were busy as they worked in the office, developing a strategy for growth and figuring out how Stygall would expand the business in North Carolina. The week came and went, and soon came Thursday night, when Darius dropped Stygall off at the airport.

Stygall embraced him, thanked him for the training and support, and promised to continue praying for his marriage and family. "Stay faithful, stay positive, and remember that God has a plan and is in charge," he said.

Darius nodded, returning the embrace. "Let me know if you need anything," he replied.

There was no further discussion about the stakes, the demonic, or the situation for either of them until later that night. Darius found himself shaking his head when he received a text from Stygall. After staking the house, their youngest child hadn't had a nightmare for the fourth consecutive night—something that hadn't happened in months.

"You couldn't make this stuff up if you tried," Darius muttered aloud.

Since everything happened, since this other world was slowly starting to reveal itself to him, Darius was struggling to make sense of the world. How could Christians believe in a God and His son, Jesus, and not talk about the truth of evil and the demonic? They were everywhere in the Bible! Steve Hemphill's books were opening his eyes to truths that led to a lot more questions and he realized this journey was just starting.

Through it all, through his reading, new and old, he felt he had opened himself to a different kind of realization. Not only would he never be the same, his realization of the truth of the enemy enhanced his faith in his Creator and the idea of destiny. He was just starting to understand prophecy and had had no understanding of it previously. The truth of it was almost unbelievable! Remarkable. God wrote about each person in the Book of Life/Lamb before they were born. Wouldn't that mean each person has their own personal prophecy on their life?

It continued to make him realize that he couldn't stop moving to learn and grow, to change aspects of his life, and reconsider what it meant to have true faith. The Book of Jōb kept coming back to him and Hemphill's words in *Prayers Satan Hates*

Chapter 14
Reasons for an Exodus

I t had been a few days, but he finally had some time to log in and continue working on the modules for the Marriage Reset Program. His determination and drive were still as strong as ever; he wanted to be one of the fifteen-percenters who came into the program and was able to come out the other side, however long that might take, with his family and marriage still intact. But above all else, he was determined to stay committed, stay focused on improving himself, and showing his wife those positive changes so that they could keep their family together.

From Darius' perspective, there had been a lot more positives than negatives. Since his eyes had been opened, he certainly saw the areas that he needed to work on and grow, but he loved his wife and knew that they could work through this.

So, on that note, Darious decided to dive right into the module titled: The Vicious Cycle and the Infinity Loop.

It didn't cause his determination to waver, but there was something about the title of this module that dropped a rock in his stomach.

It talked about how people tend to push each other away out of fear, often creating negative interactions instead of positive ones. It emphasized the need to see each other through the lens of our inner child, asking us to consider how we were showing up in our relationships. Were we showing up as a spouse, a parent, or maybe as a wounded 7-year-old child? Or as a teenager carrying scars from the past?

The exercise focused on understanding the pains and wounds that shape our reactions. In different situations, we often react defensively rather than seeing what the other person needs and where they're coming from at that moment.

He sat there, shaking his head, looking at his notes, thinking about his relationship with Jessica. It hit him—they both had the same unmet attachment need. They had both played each role in the past. But it was clear now: he was a "pursuer," and she was a "withdrawer." While he had never fully understood it before, this cycle had been playing out in their marriage for years, on and off.

What made the realization worse was what came next.

In his first counseling session, Kristen had mentioned that most women she counseled had been considering divorce for up to three years before they brought it forward to their husbands. It was a thought that made Darius numb, and that feeling was once again present as he stared at the title.

This sucks, he thought.

As he pulled up the next document and module titled: "The 10 Main Reasons Why Wives Divorce Their Husbands," it once again emphasized the importance of safety, respect, and empathy. It mentioned how many women didn't feel appreciated or understood, and that if they did, they would feel closer to their husbands. Over time, this loss of connection leads to a loss of trust.

He scanned the list. The number one reason for this disconnection was a lack of emotional connection. Husbands often didn't understand their wives—or worse, didn't even try to.

Guilty, he thought, readying himself for the next bitter pill.

Number two was financial struggles, with husbands not doing enough about it. Well, that wasn't him. He had always provided. He'd given his family financial security, and there had never been a shortage of trips or comforts.

Number three hit closer to home: a distant husband who doesn't give enough attention, often burying himself in work. He underlined that one. When things weren't going well, he would pull back, becoming quiet, aloof, and distant—throwing himself into work as if that would solve the problem. It was his default move. Provide more. But clearly, it hadn't solved anything.

Number four was poor communication—spouses who couldn't resolve conflicts. That one stung, too. In recent years, they'd just stopped trying.

Number five was about controlling or aggressive husbands. That wasn't him. But wives feeling unappreciated and resentful? He suspected that might be true. He didn't quite understand why, but from everything he was learning and reading, it was clear—he hadn't made her feel heard or appreciated. She must have felt incredibly frustrated.

Number seven dealt with poor sex lives and a lack of intimacy. That one confused him. They'd been married for 17 years and had been together for 20, and even up until the week before she told him she no longer wanted to be married, they were still intimate two to three times a week. She often seemed satisfied, too—but, maybe he was clueless. He'd never thought of her as someone who could fake that. But clearly, there was so much he didn't understand. So maybe his assumptions no longer held any weight. To do things the way she was doing them, she clearly hadn't been transparent.

Number eight was about changing values, growing apart instead of together. Number nine was infidelity. That wasn't the case, at least not on his part. Number ten covered addiction—substances, alcohol, porn, and the like. He had never been interested in porn; he saw it as poison. But alcohol? They had definitely been drinking more since the pandemic. Still, he didn't consider himself an alcoholic. He wasn't the type to get drunk or dependent on it, though he had used it as a crutch more than once. That's why he'd cut down on drinking after everything happened—he realized that when he was upset or stressed, or when others were drinking, he tended to join in. He made a promise to himself that moving forward, he wouldn't drink because he was upset or just because others were doing it.

As he looked over the list, three or maybe four of these reasons seemed to explain their problems. At least there wasn't any abuse, drugs, or infidelity—or so he hoped.

The modules were eye-opening, forcing him to think about responsibility, about how we are each responsible for our own happiness. Life was happening *for* him, not *to* him. More than once, it had been said in the program that every man there was receiving a blessing, even if their marriage couldn't be saved. He knew the prior, and hoped the latter wouldn't come to fruition.

But he did have to admit that this whole experience and his wife, as the program always stated, had done him a huge favor. He had the opportunity to open his eyes to where things had gone wrong, and how, moving forward, he might be able to fix it. Worst case, he could change for a better life moving forward.

Chapter 15
Thanks, Mom

I t was difficult, to say the least, and at most, he didn't have the words to describe it. The silence was deafening. He was doing better—he knew that much. But he also knew he wasn't quite where he wanted to be, not yet. The first few counseling sessions had made a difference. He was sleeping more, working out regularly, and leaning into positive behaviors. He wasn't drinking, wasn't losing his temper. Still, living out of his office felt far from ideal.

He had found some comfort in the books by Steve Hemphill, and his emotional trauma therapy sessions were helping too. Meditation and breathing exercises had been recent additions, and he embraced these new habits as ways to manage his blood pressure. The holistic doctor he'd heard about gave him some hope. But in truth, it sucked. He felt alone and detached, as if he were standing outside his life, watching it unfold without him. Each day felt like an empty cycle he couldn't escape.

It would be a few weeks before he'd have his next counseling session with the therapist his wife had chosen, though he'd already had two with Kristen, his counselor from the Marriage Reset Program, and those helped. A lot. He had dug into the program's modules, realizing just how much work lay ahead, but he was ready for it.

In the meantime, he had ordered the stakes, inspired by Steve's words and warnings, and when they arrived, he took them out to four corners of his office property, placed each stake, and said prayers over the land, dedicating it to God. The truth of the biblical practice and the amazing stories Steve shared brought him some peace. Then, he faced a challenge: how to perform the same blessing ritual at home.

He wasn't living there anymore, but the timing worked out unexpectedly. Jessica had texted to say she'd be out of town visiting her father and asked if he'd like to spend Father's Day weekend at the house with the kids. Eagerly, he agreed.

Walking into the house was surreal. It felt both familiar and foreign, almost like a dream. He was thrilled to be in his own bed, but it no longer felt truly his. The memories hit hard—of a life that now seemed to exist only in fragments. It was torture. But then he thought of the program's advice: he was choosing to suffer. He tried to reframe the experience, telling himself to focus on the chance to be with his kids instead.

That night, with his son out at the gym, he got to work. He placed stakes around the perimeter of the property and the house, praying over each corner and blessing the land. The book talked about one man who did it, calling it a double moat! It was serious to him—this was his family, his home. He'd do whatever it took to bring peace and protection. He added stakes to the bedroom, closet, and bathroom, believing it would bring harmony and safeguard the space. He even wanted to add stakes to Jessica's car, just as he had done in his own car.

One of the stories in the book talked about a horrible car accident that happened in which the family involved all should have died. Remarkably, while most of the car was destroyed, not one person in the car was hurt. The family had staked their car. It seemed unbelievable, but with everything he had seen, he wanted that kind of protection for his wife. It was an impossible task, but he thought maybe one of his kids could help him do it.

The weekend was peaceful. They spent time outside, watched movies together, and he worked hard to stay present. This was his greatest struggle—the realization of how often he'd been physically there but mentally absent and how many moments he'd missed. The awareness was both painful and motivating. His Marriage Reset sessions echoed in his mind: "In this experience, your wife has given you the greatest gift she could have ever given you." It didn't feel like a gift right now, but he understood the meaning. If this hadn't happened, he might not have gotten the awareness to face these issues.

Reflecting on why he'd never liked himself, why he'd struggled to be present, he began to see a path forward. He didn't have many answers yet, and he knew he had a long road ahead. But he wouldn't stop attending therapy or counseling, wouldn't stop reading, and wouldn't stop doing the hard work of self-examination. The program connected him with other men who had turned things around. He was determined to be one of them.

The situation with his mother was getting more uncomfortable. The same day he staked his house and office, he had driven over with a set to bless her house. The response he had received wasn't what he expected. She was worried it would cause a problem with the lawnmower when the hired workers took care of the lawn.

Darius couldn't help himself as he laughed. "So, you think these plastic tent stakes are going to hurt the blades on a lawnmower? They will be flush with the ground so the lawnmower won't touch the stakes. They wouldn't affect the mower blades anyway. The blades would just destroy the tent stake."

"You know it's okay for you to answer my questions, Darius. Sometimes people need more information."

As he placed them at each corner of her property, she stood outside watching him with a peculiar look on her face. She thinks I am crazy, he thought.

The next day, he and his son, Sheehan, had gone to breakfast with his mother. It didn't go much better than the dinner he had with her before he moved out of the house. In the middle of the conversation, she looked over at Sheehan and said, "You know, your Dad put stakes around my property."

Sheehan smiled and said, "Oh … "

"I am wondering if he's losing his mind."

She said it like Darius wasn't even present, and he and his son just sat there in surprised silence as she continued to talk as if she never even said it, moving on to share a story about her neighbors.

He and Sheehan shared a look.

At one point, Darius shared that he was going shopping that weekend because of the weight he had lost. After losing 10 lbs from the intermittent fasting, the stress of the separation had led him to lose another 10 lbs and none of his pants fit. He needed a new wardrobe and had finally set aside the time to go out and get it.

"Don't get rid of any of your clothes," his mother said, curtly.

Sheehan laughed as Darius cooley smiled back. "That's nice of you to say, Mother."

As she just looked at him, Darius decided he was going to have to start limiting the time he spent around her. Healthy boundaries as the Marriage Reset module explained.

Chapter 16
An Organic Odyssey

D r. Whitman's clinic was a little out of the way—a 45-minute drive that seemed so much longer as Darius drove to his first appointment with Andrea, a close friend and member of his staff, in the passenger seat. If it had been anyone else who recommended such a thing, he might have refused, but coming from Larissa, he thought it worth a try. He was already fascinated by her methods and had downloaded an app to learn about tapping and how it was used to relax the body's system and help create coherence. This was just the next step in that journey.

The clinic was tucked behind a gas station and a fast-food joint. It certainly didn't look like a place people would drive for hours from all across the states to visit. Getting out of the car, they made their way into the clinic. The inside was just as simple as the outside, with a small waiting area and reception desk tucked in the corner. Behind it sat a petite Asian woman with her hair tied back and a smile on her face.

"Hello," she said, her accent noticeable but her voice gentle.

"Hello," Darius and Andrea said in unison.

"You have an appointment?"

"Yes," Andrea confirmed, "Darius and Andrea for our first appointment."

For a moment, she looked away from them and toward her computer screen, eyes flickering as she scrolled down the screen, likely searching for their names. Her smile widened. "Have a seat. I will let you know when the rooms are ready."

Darius chuckled quietly to himself—she was a sweet lady.

They only sat for a few minutes before another woman came into the waiting room. She was short, stocky, with brown hair that came down just past her shoulders. Like the receptionist, she wore a smile on her face and had a demeanor that made the room want to smile with her.

"Hello, I'm Cheryl. Which one of you would like to go first?"

Darius and Andrea shared a curious glance and Cheryl laughed.

"Don't worry, it's just for some preliminary tests so that we can get a base on you. I'll take one of you first and then when another room opens up, we'll take the other through for their tests. After this, you will meet with either Dr. Whitman or our other doctor."

They nodded and when she asked again, who wanted to go first, Darius nodded toward Andrea. "We can let the real boss go first," he said.

Andrea laughed, shaking her head as she got up from the seat and followed Cheryl out of the waiting area and down a hallway.

It was the receptionist who eventually came to collect Darius, and together, they walked down the same hallway but into another room. She asked him to take off his shoes and sit up on a patient table while she prepared the equipment. She attached several things around his waist and a small oximeter with a probe to his finger.

"We will measure you for cardiac, brain rhythm, oxygen, and measure your balance as well."

"Balance?" he asked.

She nodded, reassuring him that this was all standard procedure. She then left the room, came back, took some measurements, asked him to stand up and then to balance on an object. It was something so simple, but the instant he did it, he could feel something wasn't right. The object was unbalanced; it wobbled underfoot, and he struggled to keep his balance.

As he stood, balancing awkwardly, she asked him to take a deep breath while she manipulated aspects of the device and wrote down numbers on her pad. After several manipulations, she told him to take a seat while she finished up, and as he did, he tried to look at the sheet.

She smiled and let him look.

Instinctively he made quizzical noises reading through the numbers, he could make sense of quite a few of them, but then he spied the notations: Fall Risk. She thought he was a "fall risk"? He knew his balance was average at best, but he always thought himself to be in great shape. He was 51 and worked out, but if that wasn't enough to be in good shape, let alone great shape, what would he look like in another 10 years?

She led him from one room and into the next, introducing him to Dr. Adrienne as Dr. Whitman was with Andrea. Darius sat down on the chair across from her, she peered at his charts and paperwork with a serious expression. They walked through his health history and his current routine and diet.

He admitted he drank regularly before June, but had cut liquor out of his life and was drinking very little now. He didn't eat a lot of bread, nor did he buy fast food—and when he did, it was from establishments that were supposed to have good meat without antibiotics or hormones. He didn't eat organic foods, just whatever was available at the store, but he never thought it would cause an issue. She then explained rather curtly that he would need to start changing what he ate and becoming more aware of what he was putting into his body.

"You're going to have to start looking at labels, and it's going to shock you," she said. "If you can't pronounce it, it's probably made in a lab and isn't good for you. You'll want to eliminate those types of products from your life. Find a store that sells organic food, and even then, you'll need to carefully check the labels before you buy."

"Okay," he replied. "So, no eating out?"

She shook her head. "Not for a while. Your body is out of homeostasis, and you need to reset it first. We'll test you for chemicals, pesticides, yeasts, parasites, and more—both physical and emotional—to identify where the issues are. Whatever the biggest issue is, that will be our first focus. As that gets fixed, other areas may then become the key focus. We'll adjust as needed."

"Parasites?" He said aloud, somewhat surprised.

"Yes, parasites," she confirmed. "Most people have been out of harmony with their bodies for so long due to chemicals in what they consume. When issues start, they go to the doctor, who prescribes more chemicals made in a lab. These are just Band-Aids that then lead to more issues for the body. The body remains in constant stress and can't heal or repair itself. We'll help you identify the problems, clean them out of your system, and get your body into a position where it can heal. So, the first stage is getting the body out of danger, then into a state where it can repair, and finally into a state where it is healing."

During that time, she emphasized, it would be vital for Darius to eat organic foods, drink clean water, and take necessary supplements based on his deficiencies to help detoxify his body.

"So, no eating out?" Darius asked again, trying to grasp the full extent of the changes.

"No," she reiterated. "Not for a while, if you can help it. Most places you eat will have chemicals in the sauces and antibiotics and hormones along with chemicals in the meat. After you reset your body and allow it to heal, you'll be able to cheat occasionally, as your body won't be in a traumatic state anymore. But you'll still need to eat healthily and avoid the things that caused your issues in the first place."

"Okay," he said, reflecting on the challenge ahead. He didn't think it would be a problem for him. He was determined to get off the medications, especially after his recent heart scare.

Darius decided months ago, before everything fell apart, that they were—no, *that he was* drinking too much. Alcohol had always been a part of their marriage, and he had been drinking since college. It was ingrained in his career, especially in sales and working with hospital administrators and doctors, where dinners often involved wine, scotch, or other alcohol. He mirrored them, thinking that was what a good salesperson did, and over time, he developed a taste for it all—whiskey, scotch, wine, beer.

After turning 50 at the beginning of the year, he had started to think seriously about his relationship with alcohol. Something felt off. They were always on the go, always busy, always on their phones, and usually, alcohol was involved. It was then that he decided to take a break from drinking, to reset and reconsider his relationship with alcohol.

Becoming consistently sober, he started to confront his growing dislike for himself in a more serious way, trying to understand his sense of unworthiness and why he didn't like himself. He realized he often drank either because others were drinking and it was expected, or because he was stressed or unhappy, using it as a crutch. Then there were times when he tried, in a way, to hurt himself. It was strange to say, but he knew it was true. When things were really stressful and he was already tipsy, he would do shots— until he passed out. It didn't happen regularly but it was like a form of self-punishment. The next morning, he would wake up perplexed, questioning his behavior: "What the hell is wrong with you? You're an idiot! Why would you do that?"

But it was just another aspect of the deterioration of his relationship with Jessica, a disconnection he didn't understand. When he decided to take a break from alcohol and told her, he got very little response. In fact, she seemed upset, which he found odd.

It was around the same time that he had his heart scan, and the results were alarming. They found calcium deposits in his arteries and told him he needed to start cholesterol and high blood pressure medications immediately and undergo a cardiac stress test ASAP because he was at risk of a "widowmaker" heart attack. The news shocked Darius; it was a wake-up call. He had always thought of himself as being in good shape—his weight was fine, and he was fairly muscular. But the reality was different, and as the year progressed, it became harder to ignore.

Now, he couldn't ignore it, even if he wanted to.

Dr. Adrienne asked if he had any more questions, and Darius thought for a second.

"Well," he started, "I've started to get a rash in my armpits. It's uncomfortable, and no matter what I try, I can't seem to get rid of it."

"That's probably because of the antiperspirant you're using," she explained. "Different aluminum compounds are used in different antiperspirants, most of which can be irritants to the skin."

"Aluminum?"

"Yes, there are just as many chemicals in consumer products as there are in the foods we eat. It's crazy."

"What deodorant do you use?" he asked, curiously.

"I don't wear deodorant," she replied.

"Huh? How—How do you not stink?"

She laughed, thankfully not taking offense to his question.

"Because I don't put crap in my body," she answered with a clever smirk.

He laughed, shaking his head slowly from side to side. "Well, I'll have to test that theory after I change my diet. But I'll stink to high heaven with the way I work out if I don't wear deodorant."

"You can Google it, but there are different products out there, particularly those with a charcoal base for deodorant. Just make sure you check the ingredients because some products market themselves as all-natural but still aren't 100% clean."

"Okay," he nodded. "What about shampoo, toothpaste, and other things like that?"

She gave him a couple of brands to consider. "As you start to explore, you'll figure out what works for you and what your options are."

"So, what happens next? How much does it cost to enter the program?"

"That depends," she explained. "It's different for everyone based on their challenges and what's in their body. When you come back, we'll go through your report in detail, and then we'll do diagnostics with muscle testing to determine what supplements you'll need to help flush out your body. If you commit to the program by eating healthy and taking the supplements, you'll heal your body."

"How long does it take?"

"That depends too," she smiled. "It depends on what needs fixing to get your body back into homeostasis and how well you follow the program. If you don't have the discipline to make the necessary changes to eat healthily or clean out your system with the supplements, then it's not worth your time or money because you won't get better."

"Will I have to take the supplements indefinitely?"

"Some people continue to take certain ones, like amino acids, because the food we eat just isn't as nutritious as it used to be. But most supplements are only needed temporarily to flush out the chemicals or pesticides in your body so it can heal. After you heal, you can indulge occasionally in less healthy foods, but you'll want to eat healthy and choose organic options without chemicals, hormones, antibiotics, and pesticides 70–80% of the time. Otherwise, you'll just end up with the same issues again."

He listened intently. How did he not know this? Why had no one told him before?

"We'll give you Dr. Whitman's book, with reading assignments, so you understand what's going on with your body," she continued. "You'll also get educational pamphlets throughout the program on eating and taking care of your health. At first, you'll come in once a week for the first six to eight weeks, then every other week, and eventually, once a month if you're progressing well. As you go through the program, we'll retest you at each level to see if you're still compromised, in healing, or in repair."

"I understand," he said, slowly nodding his head. "I'm disciplined enough to do this, and I want to get off the medications I'm on."

"Just remember," she said, her expression becoming more serious, "We can't recommend that you stop your medications. We can tell you where you stand and how you're doing, but you need to see the physician who prescribed them and get retested with them."

Liability, baby, liability, he thought to himself. "I understand," he said, knowing he didn't plan on needing nor getting his family doctor's permission. If people came from all over to see this doctor and heal, then he was determined to make sure this program worked for him too.

Chapter 17
Celebrate Yourself!

I t hadn't been long since he and Kristen met, but even in such a short period of time, so much had changed, and he was excited to share the work he had done and the progress he had made. The Zoom call connected, and Kristen greeted him with a warm smile. She went through the pleasantries, they caught up on the events of the day, and soon the topic turned to Darius.

"So," Darius began, his voice hesitant as he tried to organize the swirl of thoughts in his mind. "First, I haven't really had any direct interaction with her, but I'm practicing the idea of it, being more conscious, with my staff, my kids, anyone I interact with personally."

Kristen was beaming on the screen. "I love that. You're applying this in all your relationships. What specifically are you doing?"

"I consciously, like, at work, right? I'm working to be intentional. I think everything through before I say it. And if I had been doing that at home, the way I do at work, I don't think we'd even be here. I mean, I could be wrong, but I think … I think if I'd just taken time to listen, to really verify what she's saying before I responded, we wouldn't have hit this wall. It's just—" He paused, catching his breath for a moment, though his mind clearly raced ahead. "I realize I bulldozed her sometimes. My logical brain just kicks in, and I run her over. I don't mean to. But I do. And now I'm trying, trying so hard, to get the cadence right. The thought process. So that, when we have a chance to reconnect, she feels heard. Seen. Validated."

The words poured out like a torrent, his voice rising and falling, nearly breathless as he moved to the next point without pause.

"And then you said to celebrate wins, right? Write down one thing. I mean, I haven't written anything yet, but I remember everything. My memory's … it's too good sometimes, honestly. It's almost a problem." He let out a nervous laugh, quickly shifting back to seriousness. "But this last Wednesday, God, it was brutal. The silence between us is deafening. Like, just sitting there, not hearing from her. It's torture. I miss her. I miss being home. I miss … the normalcy, you know? So I keep myself busy. But then the clock hits six or seven, and I can't go home. Usually, by then, we'd be texting, figuring out dinner or whatever. And now? Nothing. It's just this … void." His voice cracked, but he pushed forward, not allowing himself the space to falter.

"And since all this started, I haven't been sleeping, like, at all. Two hours here, four hours there. It's been hell. But I'm getting better, I think. I finally had my first counseling session with Sharon. You know, the one who knows both of us? She knows me, us, and that was … I mean, it was huge for me. It's been a month since all of this blindsided me, and, like, I'm still reeling. I can't wrap my head around it. Her mom, her best friends, our kids, my mom, they're all confused. None of it makes sense. None of them saw this coming."

His voice quickened, as if the speed could somehow untangle the chaos in his mind. "It's like we went from fine, everything seemed fine, to this. 'I don't want to be married anymore.' Just like that. And then she goes to one counseling session, comes back, and tells me to leave. Just leave. Get out. And I've been trying so hard to piece it together, but it's like this puzzle with half the pieces missing. Talking to Sharon helped some, though. It was the first real insight I've gotten. I've been praying nonstop ... And then there's the meditation, two straight weeks now. Between five and ten minutes each morning, before prayer and Scripture. And it's crazy, but I already feel a difference. Like, something is ... quieter. Calmer."

He laughed again, a short, humorless sound. "It's not just me, either. Two friends, one guy, one girl, they've noticed it. Without me even saying anything. The guy was like, 'Man, you're really present, intentional.' And her best friend, well, she said something similar. She told me to just keep doing what I'm doing. She could tell I'm working hard. That meant something, you know? It's like, like proof that I'm not just spinning my wheels here. But Wednesday was rough. I lost it, completely, at the end of the day. My logical mind ... It's like a curse sometimes. I couldn't stop thinking, running through scenarios. Was she having an affair? Could that even be possible? I mean, none of this adds up. And when you're exhausted, when you're not sleeping, it's like the worst thoughts creep in. Evil thoughts, even. And I just ... I had to stop myself. I went to the park, and I prayed. I prayed hard. And then I called her friend, not to put her in the middle, but I needed ... something. Anything. And she said ... She said it's not what I think. That whatever this is, it's deeper than any of us realized. But she also told me to keep going. To stay the course. She could hear the difference. That mattered. I'm doing the work. I'm showing up. And for the first time in a long time, I feel like—"

"Darius, Darius," Kristen said, finally interrupting him. "Can we, can we slow down for a minute?"

He took a breath, a proper breath for the first time in a while. "Yeah, yeah, I'm sorry."

Kristen laughed. "No, I'm sorry, this is our first proper call and I didn't set any expectations. So I love your wrap up of all these things, but what I would like to do is to bring more intention into it. So let's pause and talk about these things a little bit more."

Darius nodded.

"So, awareness is a powerful first step forward, but what I want to know is, has there been a moment this week where you noticed a difference?"

Darius's face softened as a memory surfaced. "Yeah," he said. "Last night, I spent three hours with my 14-year-old. He brought up a couple of things, stuff that, honestly, didn't seem very interesting at first. Normally, I might not have really been paying attention. But I caught myself. I leaned in, got more engaged. We ended up going for a walk and talking for much longer than usual. It felt ... good. Like we connected on a deeper level."

Kristen's eyes lit up. "That's an amazing example. And it's something I can relate to as a parent."

Darius chuckled softly. "Yeah, and we laughed a lot. It was nice. My middle son, the 21-year-old, the pilot, and I are wired similarly, so we've always had that natural bond. But my 14-year-old? He shares some of his Mom's traits even though he has some of my good and bad traits, as well ... There's always been this dynamic where he'd go to her for everything because he knew he'd get a yes. I was always the bad guy." He paused, his smile fading slightly.

"That sounds tough," Kristen said gently.

"It was. But a few months ago, before this started with my wife, I decided to approach things differently—less conflict, more collaboration. And it's working. Last night, he told me, 'Every time I see you, every time I think about you, I just get happy.' That hit me hard. It was ... incredible."

Kristen smiled. "That kind of feedback is priceless. It sounds like it's validating the work you're doing."

"It is," Darius said. "It gives me hope. I keep thinking, maybe my wife can't say yes to us right now because she doesn't know if I'll really be different. But when we're finally around each other again, she'll see it. I know she will."

Kristen let the moment linger before gently steering the conversation. "Let's talk about celebrating yourself. You said you've been more consciously aware of it. How have you celebrated yourself this week?"

Darius's brow furrowed. "Honestly? It's been hard to celebrate myself in this situation."

Kristen tilted her head, her voice soft but firm. "It's not about celebrating yourself because of the situation. It's about looking within, reminding yourself that you're worthy, and celebrating that."

Darius sat back, considering her words. "Okay," he said finally. "That makes sense. I have been focusing on the ways I'm able to be a blessing to others. For example, the charities I support. One of them is a healthcare clinic in Africa. I'm visiting for the first time in August. They sent me a picture recently of a baby whose life was saved because of equipment we provided."

"That's incredible, Darius," Kristen said.

He nodded. "It is. There are other things too. My business has been growing, and I've been building a stronger professional presence. I was just accepted onto the advisory board of a medical device company. My first compensated board position! A post I made about it went viral, and it's brought so much attention to what we're doing. It feels good to see the fruit of those efforts."

"That's so worth celebrating, Darius. You're seeing the impact of your goodness and generosity."

"Yeah," he said quietly. "And I'm proud of that. I've been thinking a lot about who I am now versus who I was five or ten years ago. Back then, if something like this had happened, I'd have been a mess. Probably drinking too much, angry at the world. But now? I've leaned completely into God. I know this is just the beginning of what I need to change, but I'm staying focused. I'm working to take the high road and I'm praying for her and our family four or five times a day. I'm proud of that."

Kristen's eyes glistened as she spoke. "I'm proud of you, too. What you've described, your intentionality, your faith, your growth, it's amazing. I want to encourage you to keep celebrating yourself. From your heart."

Chapter 18
Brothers in Arms

S itting at the desk in the corner of his office, Darius pulled up his laptop and readied himself for the Marriage Reset group call. After three weeks, it was his ninth call, and he had already learned a lot from his Brothers in Arms and was looking forward to the Monday night discussion. Mondays were focused on the different things that the men wanted to learn or the challenges they were having, whether that be with themselves or with their spouse. It was led by Kristen, which gave everyone a unique perspective as she had nearly 20 years of experience working with both men and women going through the rollercoaster of divorce.

The men joined one by one, and quickly, the online room had 110 men joining the call. Kristen welcomed them all and expressed her excitement at seeing so many new and returning faces. Darius only recognized five of the men on the call, but in comparison to some of his other Brothers in Arms, he was still one of the "rookies," so he wasn't surprised there weren't more familiar faces.

Kristen began the session and asked if anybody had anything to share. Online hands went up, and she brought to the "stage" one of the younger men in the group. Darius hadn't seen him before, and from the gestures shared among some of the other men on the call, they didn't recognize him either, but they seemed to know something Darius didn't.

He introduced himself as Robbie, and immediately started to talk about his challenges: the things his wife was doing. They were currently separated, but he seemed almost obsessed with what she was doing on her social media. He believed the things she was posting were not okay and he voiced how often he called her out on it.

Suddenly, the reactions of the other men made sense; they were welcoming a newcomer. You could almost always tell when somebody had been doing the work and growing in their level of consciousness versus one that wasn't or that was new to the tools and materials. Darius dove headfirst into everything he could from the moment he joined because he wanted to learn as much as he could. It was clear Robbie was just starting this process. You could tell by his sharp tone, condescending language, and rising frustration.

"And then—"

"I'm going to stop you there," Kristen said. "What exactly are you trying to accomplish by getting on her for her social media posts?"

Suddenly, the tension could be cut with a knife. Kristen had struck a nerve.

"Well, I mean, we're still married," Robbie started, trying to swallow his frustration. "Just because we're separated doesn't mean she can be putting that on social media."

"Do you think maybe she's doing that to get a reaction out of you?"

"I don't know, but it's just not really appropriate, you know? She should be thinking about this instead of—"

Kristen stopped him again. "Okay, first you need to get out of her head."

As Darius looked between the different cameras on the call he saw the wave of agreement from the other members.

"You control you," Kristen continued, "You control what your behaviors and actions are, whether you're doing the work or not. You don't know what she's thinking, and you're not in great communication with her right now so you need to get out of her head and stop projecting your thoughts, opinions, and judgments onto her. That's not helpful to you."

While the rest of the online room seemed to get it, Robbie didn't. He had nothing more to say, but you could see, and feel, his frustration.

"Well, okay," he said, biting back again, "But she has to be responsible for what she's doing."

Kristen would say one thing and then he would bite back with something else, always coming back to "But she has to ... "

"Okay, let's park this," he heard Kristen say, pulling him back to the present and away from his thoughts. Then she recommended he connect offline with two Brothers in Arms that had made comments in the chat to try to help give him some perspective.

As Darius watched, he wondered if this had ever been his reflection—had there been a time when he thought, acted, and reacted just like this? God, he hoped not. He had a lot to learn and work to do, but he was glad he wasn't completely unaware of his failings as some new members were.

"Let's get to the next person."

Jorge was pulled to the stage next—a big guy from New York who had spoken on one of Darius's first group calls. It had been quite the introduction to the group. He'd taken to the stage, gone off on a tangent, started calling his wife names, and then got muted by Kristen. It was only one experience, but it was enough for Darius to think, "Oh, here we go again," the moment Kristen unmuted him.

"All right, Jorge, what's going on?" She asked, giving him her full focus.

With that, it was like releasing horses from the starting gates or a bullet from a gun—he was off! He spoke so fast Darius could only catch snippets:

"My daughter started ... "

" ... her friend too was ... "

" ... and then she got involved."

"It was all a big mess but she just ... "

" ... and I was pulling my hair out."

"You know, sometimes she's a right crazy bi—"

Kristen muted him immediately. "We're not going to talk like that. Not about our wives, our ex-wives, or anybody, understand? We're going to respect each other and keep it positive and going in the right direction."

She waited a moment before unmuting him.

"I'm sorry."

Jorge calmed down and started to talk slower but then got caught up in starting another negative story about his wife. That was the last clear thing Darius heard before Jorge unleashed another tirade. Darius heard him mention something about "five years ago," and then Kristen's voice cut through:

"Jorge, take a breath. Where are you going with all of this?"

Darius laughed, seeing a crowd of smiling men on his screen— they knew the answer before Jorge even said it.

"I don't know ... Uh, sorry."

Kristen nodded. "Then let's shelve this for now until you do."

There were a few more men pulled onto the stage, Brothers in Arms, who were willing to share and looking for advice. For now, Darius was content listening to their stories and perspectives and taking a few notes here and there about things he wanted to reflect on at a later date. But then Bryce, a member from Australia, was brought to the stage.

"Welcome from Down Under," Kristen said with a smile on her face. "It's really great to see you again, Bryce. You have been doing so much work and you have really come a long way in the five months that you've been a part of this program, and I saw some of your posts this past week on the group section and I thought they were beautiful. So I just wanted to honor you."

"I really appreciate it, and I really appreciate you," he replied. "When I first started in the program, I was very much focused on myself. My behaviors were somewhat selfish, and I was not in a positive masculine frame. Like many of us, I was showing up with so many negative masculine traits and because of that, I wasn't really listening to my wife. I wasn't validating her and was allowing myself to be a victim of my frustrations around her behaviors. I didn't have boundaries of what was acceptable or not acceptable and I responded to things over-emotionally."

The beginning of Bryce's journey was almost a perfect reflection of Darius's. He shuffled in his chair and gave the screen his full, undivided attention, searching for an answer in this strange reflection.

"We've been separated for about 6 months now, but because of the work I've been doing, we're now communicating in a very healthy fashion." Bryce let out a hopeful laugh. "There is even talk of the possibility of her not filing for divorce, something I would not have thought possible when I first joined this program."

There was a moment of silence, filled with grace, before Kristen smiled and said, "That's because you're showing up in a completely different way now."

"Yes, yes, you're right. Before, I was always trying to solve the problem, whatever it was, and now I listen. I listen to understand and validate what she's thinking, and then I ask her questions. The entire conversation is just different, and over the last few months, our conversations have lasted longer. And then this last week, we actually met for dinner to discuss a couple of things. It was incredible, you know, because it wasn't only productive, but we actually laughed a few times as well."

That was the ideal. It was what the outcome Darius hoped he would achieve with all of his own hard work.

"I just want to take a moment to honor you and the work you're doing, as well as this community of men," Kristen said. "Everything you are doing is not only supporting yourself, but also your fellow Brothers in Arms, and you should all be proud of that."

Bryce nodded, as well as a few of the other men on the screen. "Absolutely. Two of my brothers, I told them about this dinner about a week before it happened, and they both were right behind me. They helped me get into a positive mental frame and made sure I showed up in the right way. And that wasn't even the coolest thing about it."

"What was it?"

"At the end of the dinner, my wife hugged me and told me that she really enjoyed the dinner and that she saw the effort I was putting out."

Kristen applauded him, and the men, silent in their little boxes, also clapped and cheered. Even Darius couldn't help but be fueled by the ovation, evermore determined to ensure that this could be his future. This was exactly why he had signed up for the Marriage Reset Program in the first place, to have the tools to build better and healthier relationships, to have more positive interactions, to show up in a different, more genuine and positive way, and to reconnect with Jessica. He was in a difficult situation, but now he could see the possible light at the end of the tunnel, and in the last hour of the call, more of the seasoned Brothers in Arms shared their wins.

As Darius got off the call, he smiled and thought about how energized he felt and how suddenly grateful he was to be a part of this program and community. It made him optimistic that there could be hope for their future together; he just had to work hard.

	Statement	Grade
1	**Disfigured men are givers** - They think about making others happy first.	① ② ③ ④ ⑤
2	**Disfigured men often try to fix others** - Instead of allowing others to express their emotions, they try to make others feel good to take	① ② ③ ④ ⑤
3	**Disfigured men seek approval from others** - Particularly wanting approval from those they are close to, like their spouse.	① ② ③ ④ ⑤
4	**Disfigured men avoid conflict** - They try to keep others happy and avoid conflict in unhealthy ways.	① ② ③ ④ ⑤
5	**Disfigured men believe they must hide their perceived flaws and mistakes** - They strive for perfection because they don't like themselves.	① ② ③ ④ ⑤
6	**Disfigured men seek the "right" way to do things** - They become obsessed with doing things perfectly, which leads to judgmental tendencies.	① ② ③ ④ ⑤
7	**Disfigured men repress their feelings** - They avoid feelings, sometimes to the point of constant unhappiness.	① ② ③ ④ ⑤
8	**Disfigured men try to be different from their fathers** - They attempt to surpass their fathers or avoid becoming like them.	① ② ③ ④ ⑤
9	**Disfigured men are more comfortable relating to women than to men** - They may feel more at ease bonding with women.	① ② ③ ④ ⑤
10	**Disfigured men have difficulty making their needs a priority** - They struggle to put their own needs first and often put others' needs ahead.	① ② ③ ④ ⑤
11	**Disfigured men struggle to ask for help** - They are willing to help others but find it difficult to ask for help themselves.	① ② ③ ④ ⑤
12	**Disfigured men make their partner their emotional center** - They unfairly place emotional responsibility on their partner.	① ② ③ ④ ⑤

	Statement	**Grade**
13	**Disfigured men are dishonest** - Not sharing true feelings or needs can be a form of dishonesty.	① ② ③ ④ ⑤
14	**Disfigured men are compartmentalized** - They may separate parts of their lives or emotions, thinking it's better for others.	① ② ③ ④ ⑤
15	**Disfigured men are manipulative** - They manipulate situations or others, even if unintentionally, especially when blaming others for their unhappiness.	① ② ③ ④ ⑤
16	**Disfigured men are controlling** - Making someone feel guilty is considered a form of control.	① ② ③ ④ ⑤
17	**Disfigured men give to get** - They engage in covert contracts, doing things with hidden expectations.	① ② ③ ④ ⑤
18	**Disfigured men are passive-aggressive** - They may act out in childish ways when not getting what they want.	① ② ③ ④ ⑤
19	**Disfigured men are full of rage** - They may have a long fuse but explode when it runs out, though much of the anger is often directed inward.	① ② ③ ④ ⑤
20	**Disfigured men are addictive** - They may have addictive personalities or behaviors, such as reliance on alcohol or other vices.	① ② ③ ④ ⑤
21	**Disfigured men have difficulty setting boundaries** - They often don't understand boundaries or struggle to maintain them.	① ② ③ ④ ⑤
22	**Disfigured men are frequently isolated** - They may prefer isolation or believe others wouldn't like them if they were truly known.	① ② ③ ④ ⑤
23	**Disfigured men are attracted to people or situations that need fixing** - They prefer helping others as a way to avoid facing their own problems.	① ② ③ ④ ⑤

Chapter 19
The Disfigured Man

He had heard other men in the group sessions talk about "The Disfigured Man" but never really knew what it meant. He had assumed it was another module in the program, and he was right. However, with the video pulled up on the computer, waiting for him to click play, he wasn't so sure he wanted to know what it meant.

Letting his curiosity drive him, rather than his fear, he moved the cursor across the screen and started the video.

With a series of shifting infographics, the video delved into the concept of manhood: the defeat of childhood narcissism. It explained that men who are "too nice" often exhibit a form of selfishness. The video also mentioned the egocentric mindset, where individuals believe that everything, good or bad, happens because of them. Men who fit into this category were labeled as "the disfigured man." These men often experience something called toxic shame—the belief that they are inherently bad and unworthy of love. They don't want, or don't know how, to receive love, which leads to repressed sexuality. As a result, they tend to treat themselves poorly, whether through alcohol abuse, mental or physical neglect, or other self-destructive behaviors and can make poor sexual choices.

As Darius watched, the video continued to explain that this usually stems from an unhealthy relationship with one's parents: a distant, emotionally unavailable father and an overbearing, critical mother. Darius paused the video. The realization hit hard. It struck close to home. He took a deep breath and hit play again.

It went on to describe how these dynamics shape a boy's identity, forcing him to seek it from his mother, and in turn, the mother, wanting to mold her son into something more like herself, feminizing him. This causes the boy to become passive, not embodying the healthy masculine traits needed to fulfill a woman or thrive in the world. Without these traits, the boy—now a man—struggles to survive. In trying to gain his mother's approval, he grows into a distorted model of masculinity, one that becomes problematic when he tries to connect with others. Women, who naturally want to bond with a masculine man, are put off by his neediness and weakness. Instead of connecting in a masculine way, he connects in a fragile, dependent way, which breeds resentment and anger.

Darius found himself reflecting on his own childhood. His father and his grandfather sometimes dealt with depression, and he always found it hard to talk about anything of real substance with his dad. Sure, he'd talk about sports, the weather, or nature, but never about things that truly mattered. Darius loved his dad. He had always been around, but sometimes in a distant, detached way. In hindsight, Darius thought his father had been somewhat selfish. He winced, thinking that way about his deceased father, particularly in consideration of his own selfishness, but this was about positive change through transparent discovery.

His mother, on the other hand, had always had the ability to be … overbearing. Growing up, and over the years, no matter what Darius did, it never seemed enough to make her happy. She tended to be critical. He remembered once thinking that even if he cured cancer, his mother would ask, "Why did you do it that way?"

Sitting staring at the now-black screen, he needed a minute to process it all. Darius realized how deeply this "disfigured man" resonated with his own upbringing; it felt as though his childhood had just been explained to him in a way he had never seen before.

Thoughts, feelings, and time passed before he pulled up the next section of the module: a list of 23 statements that he had to answer to determine where he fell on the spectrum of the disfigured man. It was simple: read the statement and give yourself a grade, 1–5, as to how much that sounded like you, one being not at all and five being almost definitely.

"This is going to suck," he said, bracing himself.

Number one, disfigured men are givers. He sat back in the chair and looked at the ceiling. He could be a giver, but he could also be rather selfish. He wanted people to be happy, but he didn't think that he was someone who was always trying to make them happy. It was the first question and he was contemplatively stalled. He took a breath, put a ? next to it, and moved on; he could come back to it later.

The next one: Disfigured men often try to fix others. He reflected on that, though not for long. He was always trying to fix something when it was wrong and could only presume that would extend to other people, too. And taking credit for things? Unfortunately, that was probably true as well. It also fed into number three: A disfigured man seeks approval from others. Totally, particularly him trying to get approval from his wife. He definitely wanted other people's approval, of course, but more than anything, he wanted hers.

Number four, "Disfigured men avoid conflict." More likely, I create conflict by trying to avoid it, he thought. Like any husband, he didn't want his wife to be unhappy, but wasn't a little bit of conflict normal? And he certainly had a tendency to avoid conflict in an unhealthy way. Again, it rolled perfectly into the next one: Disfigured men believe they must hide their perceived flaws and mistakes. This, he realized, was a major issue. He had to be perfect, he couldn't make mistakes, but then what he really realized was how exhausting that must be to be around. Not only did he hold himself to a standard he couldn't achieve, but he also then projected that standard onto everyone around him. No, it wasn't all the time, but it wasn't fair. It created conflict. And it showed him how insecure he really was.

Almost halfway, he thought, hoping it would act as a pep talk to push him onward.

Number seven: Disfigured men repress their feelings. *Come on*, he thought, feeling all of the pep disappear and a tear come to his eye. He was too often moody, dower, and down. Now, for the first time, he thought about the fact that maybe, in the past, he had just been looking for reasons to be unhappy. What a horrible way to live, and what fun for someone else to be around someone like that …

Darius wiped his eyes and shook himself. "Next one," he rather curtly said aloud.

Number eight: Disfigured men often try to be different from their fathers. He thought back to his childhood again. Never did he ever think that he'd be like his dad, but he did know that he wanted to be more than him. His dad was … afraid of being successful, at least in Darius's opinion, as he pondered the question. He was one of the smartest men Darius knew, but he had no ambition to be something greater than a teacher. Or was that the perception and Dad had ambition inside but was afraid to try? There was nothing wrong with the life his dad had made for himself, and there was certainly nothing wrong with being a teacher—in fact, Darius was always proud of his dad's profession—but if he had tried, could his dad have done so much more?

He found himself smirking. I guess I am trying to be different from my dad, he thought.

The next three were somewhat easy to answer, even though the answers to the latter two differed from the first. He had never felt comfortable around women; in fact, he actually felt uncomfortable around most adults, regardless of their gender, preferring the company of himself or his children. Then, with regards to putting his own needs first, he quickly realized that was probably a problem for him. Then he thought about the next one: Disfigured men have difficulty asking for help. Another hit to the head of the nail. He always had a horrible time asking for help, even when he was more than willing to help others.

Number twelve: Disfigured men often make their partner their emotional center. For the first time, he realized he had completely put that on his wife unfairly, and in doing so, had probably made her withdraw even more.

Darius took a moment away from the computer, getting a glass of water and taking a moment to clear his head. It was the first time he was actually aware of how sore it was.

"Nearly there," he said, rubbing his temple as he made his way back to his desk.

Disfigured men are dishonest.

Disfigured men are compartmentalized.

Disfigured men are manipulative.

Disfigured men are controlling.

Disfigured men give to get.

It was like a barrage—one that did nothing to help his headache.

He was dishonest, in a sense. He'd always thought of himself as being an extremely honest person, but then, not sharing openly, that's just as bad as lying, right? Then maybe he was compartmentalized. Their communication was ... not good. He came back to examining himself: he too often overshared and that made it worse as, more often than not, he wasn't making the person feel heard and validated.

Manipulative? Controlling? Surely not. But then he shook his head. Surely indeed. He put all of the responsibility for their unhappiness on Jessica; intentional or not, that was manipulative. From that manipulation, she likely felt extremely guilty about a lot of things and was that not a form of control?

At least he could say with some confidence that he never did anything with the expectation of getting anything back. He never partook in "covert contracts," but did that really count for anything if he was unconsciously being dishonest and manipulating the woman he loved?

Wait, no, he thought. That wasn't truthful! He did things or agreed to things too often he didn't want to do and then expected sex? Sounded like a covert contract!

The realization washed over him. He never really set any healthy boundaries.

Darius felt almost sick.

Number eighteen and nineteen were somewhat similar, but something that only added to the weight pressing down on him. Maybe he was a little passive aggressive? He did have a habit of acting like a child and doing back to her anything she did to him that he didn't like. He had always felt that was the only way to get through to her because she wouldn't change her behavior even if he shared his feelings. Was that accurate? He might have had a bit of a short fuse, but it had gotten longer over the years and most of his anger was directed toward himself.

The next one made him smile. Number twenty: Disfigured men are addictive. Well, he'd always thought if he were a criminal, he'd probably be a pretty good criminal, or if he was doing drugs, it wouldn't be good, so this was probably true.

Final three, he thought, with an ounce of renewed vigor.

Number twenty-one: Disfigured men have difficulty setting boundaries. Darius wasn't sure about that one, but given the track record of so many of the other statements, there was probably some truth in it. It was likely a much bigger problem than he realized.

Then came number twenty-two, and he stopped. On the worksheet, it stated that men with Toxic Shame tend to end up with women that have bipolar disorder, ADHD, or similar challenges, because it allows them not to have to look at themselves. Lord, Darius thought. Two marriages with his first wife being bipolar and his second having ADHD.

This exercise fucking sucks, he thought.

Darius sat back, took a drink, and looked at his results. For fourteen out of twenty-three, he scored himself 4/5, five of the twenty-three were smack in the middle ... It didn't really matter about the rest because that was nineteen, nineteen out of twenty-three when comparing himself to the "ideal" description of the disfigured man.

He thought about the emotional trauma therapy sessions he'd been having with Larissa and how eye-opening they had been. The baggage he'd carried since early childhood was staggering. His parents must have fought a lot when he was young. He reflected on his childhood, on what an angry environment it had been: the conflict, shouting, the locked doors. The discipline. A lot of it he had blocked out, but the truth was he had never felt like anything he did was good enough. Those memories had been repressed, but after the last session, it was as clear as if it had just happened.

As he sat there, tears started to roll down his face. He realized why he had always pushed himself so hard—he was driven by fear of failure, more than any desire for success. It was always the stick over the carrot. His feelings of worthlessness, fear of rejection, hopelessness, and self-loathing suddenly made sense. He had never truly understood them before, but now, for the first time, they were coming into focus. And it was horrifying.

The idea of divorce felt devastating to him. But what also became painfully clear was how, over the course of this bleak year, as each new situation arose and the pressure mounted, his behavior had only worsened.

Chapter 20
F'ing Toxic Shame

Darius sat there, staring blankly at the computer screen, unsure of how long he'd been in that daze. At some point, he blinked, but still didn't fully grasp what he was thinking. The situation he was in felt unbearable, and it seemed even worse after everything he'd just processed. Why? Because the truth had hit him hard.

Feelings of worthlessness, fear of rejection, hopelessness, and self-loathing flooded his mind. For the first time, he could actually identify and name these emotions and behaviors. And that realization was terrifying. The pain of his marriage falling apart, of knowing his wife no longer seemed to love him or care enough to fight for their relationship, was bad enough. But now, as he worked through this exercise, the truth about himself became impossible to ignore.

He was forced to confront the patterns of his behavior over the past 20 years—habits and actions that, in many ways, had sabotaged their happiness. It was glaringly obvious now, and the weight of it felt crushing.

But as shameful as it was, as much as he didn't want their marriage to end, he realized he had to continue to embrace this. As the program always said, "This was happening for you, not to you." He had to stop and thank God for the opportunity that he now had to transform into who he was meant to be, because surely God hadn't meant for him to be this. Then he thought of the demonic … No, God definitely didn't mean for him to be this way.

Darius looked at the next aspect of the exercise, the "Exploring Toxic Shame" part, almost feeling too discouraged to move forward. But, like he always had, he sucked it up and moved forward with the next set of questions.

He started by writing:

I feel hope, I feel worthy, and for the first time, at the age of 51, I'm starting to understand my purpose in life. Now, I've got to just figure out how to keep moving forward and learn to forgive myself for how I've hurt her and for my part in putting us in this situation.

He looked at the first question, and really just steeped in it for a second. Why would it seem rational for a person to try to hide certain things about themselves or to become something different? What would be the reason for that? He thought about it, and the sad realization was that he really didn't have a strong understanding or awareness of what he was doing or why he was doing it.

Even though it seemed so obvious now, Darius couldn't help but reflect on how different he felt. Going through the emotional trauma therapy sessions had helped release so much of his anxiety, leaving him with a completely different outlook, even in the middle of this difficult situation.

When he thought about the question at hand, the answer came to him immediately: they wouldn't do that at all. Why would someone hide who they really are unless they were dealing with feelings of worthlessness, fear of rejection, or some other irrational reasons? It made no sense. Worse still, it set the stage for relationships—any relationship—to be built on dishonesty and a lack of transparency. He thought about Matthew 7:24-27. How could a relationship endure or grow if it was built on a false foundation?

As Darius considered the second question, "Why do people change who they really are?" the answer seemed clear yet unsettling. They want something. And, irrationally, they believe that changing aspects of who they are is the way to get it. But is that healthy? A lot of it came down to fear—fear that people wouldn't like the person they truly were.

A wave of sadness washed over him as he thought about his own experiences. Even at a young age, he never really felt adequate around people. Sure, he got attention in sports and always made good grades, but he still didn't feel like he fit in, especially in college. Despite his accomplishments, there was always a lingering sense of discomfort, particularly in different social groups. Why? Because deep down, he just never felt worthy. There was always something to prove.

Reflecting on this, Darius realized that in many relationships—especially with his wife—it must have been exhausting sometimes to be around someone constantly trying to prove himself. Whether it was through knowing more, being more successful, chasing something outside of the family or always having something to say, it made him wonder: had he been trying to "one-up" people all along?

He shook his head, putting the thought to the side for now as he moved onto the next question.

Darius began reflecting on the perspective he'd had growing up and the reality of his family's dysfunction. He'd always tried to convince himself that his childhood had been great, but deep down, he knew that was a facade he had wanted. The truth was, it had been chaotic and often filled with anger. Conflict was a constant presence. The anger that surrounded him and his sister growing up seemed to explain their deep-rooted insecurities.

He remembered the physical punishments—being hit with fly swatters, belts, tree branches they called "switches," smacked in the face, and even once being severely whipped with a hanger. As he thought about it, he didn't feel anger toward his parents. He believed they did the best they could, even though they had clearly carried their own burdens—anger, guilt, and shame passed down from their own childhoods. While Darius believed in discipline and had no qualms about smacking his children on the hand or bottom when necessary, he began to question the extreme physical discipline he had endured. It made him pause, especially when he reflected on the constant feeling of disappointment from his mother. He realized that he had never felt like it was okay to be himself; his thoughts, feelings, and even his identity had seemed to be met with disapproval and that had left him feeling sad and unworthy.

As he looked back at his parents' dynamic and his need to please his mother, he realized how much the exercise he'd been working through made sense. The concept of "toxic shame" hit him hard. The shame he carried wasn't just about feeling like a failure. It was a deeper, more profound belief that he wasn't worthy of love or approval. That realization was both eye-opening and painful.

Still, Darius didn't want to blame anyone, not his parents or anyone else. What he wanted was understanding and healing. More than anything, he wanted to change. He thought about his wife; she hadn't intentionally made him feel unworthy. In reflecting on her lack of presence and the ADHD diagnosis, maybe he had taken her consistent lack of presence as meaning that he wasn't worthy? No, it wasn't all his fault, and he knew that.

He also thought about his sister. His perception was she had always felt so inferior to everyone around her, which could make her overbearing, constantly acting like she knew everything and was right about every topic. It exhausted people, and now Darius could see how her own insecurities had shaped her behavior. She and his mother could have a tendency to talk at people versus with them.

He then thought about himself—how he'd always told himself that he didn't care what people thought of him. But now he realized that wasn't entirely true. His indifference had mostly come from a place of insecurity. He cared deeply about many things—his family, how he presented himself to the world, his work, and the charities he was involved in. It was all confusing, but the more he thought about it, the more he understood that this was only the beginning. He had opened up a can of worms, and while it wasn't pleasant, he knew he had to eat the whole can and keep moving forward. Now that he had awareness, he was determined to grow, learn, and change.

As Darius reflected on the next question, it hit him: what would life be like if he didn't care what others thought? If he stopped seeking the approval of women, how would that change his relationships? The question made him pause, and as the truth sank in, his stomach dropped. He started to recognize the pattern of dysfunction that had marked so many of his relationships with women. There was no escaping the truth—it all traced back to his relationship with his mother. It had shaped him, not only in how he related to her but in the type of women he was drawn to. Conflict seemed to follow him, even with his sister. His relationship with her had never been healthy either.

What if things had been different? What if he could respond to life with positive masculine traits, the kind he'd been reading about in his new books, particularly *The Masculine in Relationship* by G.S. Youngblood? Too often, he realized, he reacted rather than responded, whether it was with his wife, mother, or sister. His instinct was to immediately react to a situation instead of pausing to consider it from a rational place. He thought about how powerful it could be to stay in a positive masculine frame. Instead of allowing another's actions or his emotions to control him, what if he could pause, listen, and validate what the other person was saying—

whether or not it was rational, accurate, or made sense? It wasn't about agreeing; it was about acknowledging their emotional state, hearing them, and then responding in a more appropriate fashion.

He realized now that responding immediately wasn't always necessary. Sometimes, the best response was no response at all. He needed to understand how to control his emotions, to give himself those three to four seconds to pause before responding, especially in emotional situations. It had been one of the reasons he started watching Josh Hudson's video every day. It was only five minutes long, but it gave him a vital reminder: pause, validate, and understand. Connect with the other person's emotion, thank them for sharing, and then determine whether to apologize or ask what they needed, depending on the situation. That small shift in consciousness could have prevented many of the conflicts in his life, especially in the last 20 years. He was certain of it.

The bottom line was, if he had developed a healthier perspective on this question earlier, he would have been more secure in himself. He would have stopped looking to his wife for validation, stopped expecting her to make him feel like he was a worthy man. He realized how much happier she might have been if she didn't feel responsible for his happiness or the happiness of their marriage. His neediness, particularly when it came to their relationship, and even their intimacy, disgusted him now. He felt ashamed. He had put too much pressure on her, expecting her to be responsible for his contentment, even at times in the bedroom.

If he could have let go of that neediness, things might have been different. He wouldn't have worried so much about their time together, in group settings or in private moments. Why couldn't he just be grateful for their time together, to simply enjoy being around each other? If he had taken that approach, wouldn't she have been more relaxed? He realized he was putting too much blame on himself, but it didn't matter.

Darius dropped his head in his hands. None of this stuff was fun. None of it. He had stared into the world countless times over the years, on hikes, at the ocean, on the deck, trying to understand the emptiness in himself. He had never seen himself in such clarity. All the scars, all the mistakes ... Maybe ignorance is bliss, he thought.

He swallowed the lump building in the back of his throat and sat back, returning his gaze to the screen. *Maybe ignorance is bliss, but in ignorance, how am I ever going to change, how am I ever going to fix this? No, I'll never turn back now I know the truth.*

He glanced over the list, reflecting on the question: what examples could he write down of situations where he had tried to hide or distract attention from his perceived flaws? How effective had he been in keeping those flaws hidden from the people he loved? A wave of frustration washed over him. He rubbed his hands over his face and closed his eyes for a few seconds, massaging his scalp as he contemplated his past.

The truth was, his insecurities had manifested in harmful and unhealthy ways. As he thought back, he realized he had developed more than one coping mechanism that simply wasn't healthy. He could clearly see healthier options from the support material he was reading. "Hey, babe, I'd love to do something together, just the two of us, but let's go out with them first. Then we can have thirty minutes of alone time later." Why couldn't he just express what he wanted from a positive masculine perspective? The literature he had been studying made it clear: it didn't matter whether he got what he wanted; he was still in control of his emotions. A positive masculine man could ask for what he wanted, and if he didn't receive it, that was perfectly okay.

Then the realization hit him. "Well, guess what, genius? You're here for a reason because you didn't know how to do these things." He hadn't even been aware of the tools available to him. Why hadn't anyone shared these insights or books with him twenty or thirty years ago? Most of the behaviors he had adopted were just not effective at all. It would have been better to understand from the start the importance of honesty and transparency in a healthy way.

If he found himself with someone who didn't want that, it probably wasn't the right relationship for him.

As he reflected on this, he thought about his own children. He realized how important it would be to teach them these lessons, to make them aware of these concepts. He wished someone had done the same for him when he was younger. There needs to be a program for young boys in high school or college to learn this.

As he looked at the last question:

Do you believe that people can see your human imperfections and still love you? How would you be different if you knew that people who care about you would never leave you or stop loving you, no matter what?

That question made him ponder. Unconditional love. Agape love. God's love. How amazing would that be to have someone who loved you unconditionally?

Pretty amazing, he thought, coming face to face with the reality of his own situation.

If he were more transparent, easygoing, and less judgmental, he would be more enjoyable to be around. People would likely appreciate the company of someone secure in themselves and their masculinity. The more he could be present in the moment and appreciate others, the more he would realize it was okay to have imperfections, to not be perfect, and to not know everything. Instead of judging others, he would let go of projecting his own insecurities onto them.

He recognized that placing such high standards on himself—standards he could rarely meet—only set him up for failure. It was exhausting to think about how he had turned those unrealistic expectations onto others. How could they ever measure up when he himself couldn't?

The thought weighed heavily on him as he longed to be like the other men he observed in the program. He admired the positive masculine traits they embodied, traits he aspired to adopt himself. At least six or seven areas in his life needed to change, as he found himself exhibiting negative masculine traits. Yet, through this journey, he understood that the more he worked on personal growth and could lift others up, the more enjoyable he would be to be around.

He pondered the concept of living in the moment, letting go of negative thoughts and traits that had developed from his past. What would it be like to simply be present, to appreciate whatever was happening right now? He had always been the type to hurry from one thing to the next, never pausing to truly appreciate the many positive experiences life offered in the moment. For the first time, he thought he might finally understand why.

Fucking toxic shame.

Chapter 21
That Voodoo You Do

From the start, Darius sensed this meeting with Sharon would be different. She wasn't like Larissa or Kristen, but she was Jessica's preferred counselor. He went for Jessica, not for himself. But this wasn't like the first session, where he'd felt a hint of hope from simply opening up and knowing there was work to be done. When he got on the video call, right away, she got straight to the point.

"You haven't been following through, Darius. You're supposed to be giving her space and going slow."

Darius resisted the urge to defend himself but took the chance to calmly explain an inaccuracy in what she was claiming. "I haven't reached out to her in eight days," he replied.

"Yes, but you reached out multiple times before that," she said.

He nodded slowly. "It's been difficult, especially with how sudden it was and the lack of communication. It's hard to sit with that, knowing her ring was at the jeweler for months and she never picked it up."

Sharon nodded too, seemingly understanding his frustrations.

As they continued, she asked him about his routines and sleep. He explained that he was getting more rest than before, though the sleep aid she recommended had been a disaster. He also mentioned that he'd taken on some new habits: breathing exercises, starting counseling through the Marriage Reset Program, and even meditating.

"How long do you meditate?" she asked.

"I'm up to ten minutes now," he said.

She acknowledged that as progress, but then her tone shifted. "Darius," she said, "There are some concerns about your behavior."

He raised an eyebrow, confused. "My behavior?"

"Yes. Some things you've done are, well … concerning."

"Like what?"

"The way you reached out to her despite her request for space. And … what you did to the house."

He paused, wondering if she somehow knew about the stakes he'd placed around his property as part of the blessing ritual. "You mean blessing my house?" He asked.

She sidestepped his comment. "It's … Well, it's more about everything in combination. There's concern you may be manic."

Darius took a breath. "Manic? I haven't been sleeping well, I'll give you that, but I'm clear-headed. I'm functioning. Go look at the regular videos we record for social media or the podcasts, I am around my employees every day and any of them would tell you I am not manic."

She let out a small sigh. "I'm not so sure, Darius, but it's tough that I always have to be the one in your life to tell you the difficult things."

The difficult things?

Darius grimaced, though externally his expression remained unphased. He knew exactly what she meant by that. Nearly a decade ago, he and Jessica had both attended Sharon's counseling sessions, and in that session, Sharon implied to Jessica that Darius was narcissistic. This was completely different, but the tone, the sigh, and the words—all of it reminded him of that conversation with Sharon. At that point, he could start to see where this seemed to be headed.

And then, the request came.

"Would you be open to a psychological evaluation?"

Darius stared. "A what?"

"A psychological evaluation," she repeated.

"You want me to have a psych eval?"

"Yes," she replied. "It's just to be sure, for your sake—and for the kids."

"Because I blessed my house?" he asked, barely containing his disbelief.

"It's not that any one thing is bad, Darius. It's the overall picture."

He took a breath. "Sharon, aren't you a Christian counselor?"

"Yes, I am."

"Well, my wife told me you advised her to kick me out. I just don't see how that fits with Christian principles, especially when there's no abuse or addiction involved."

"That's not true," Sharon replied quickly. "I told her that space might help, but I didn't say she should kick you out."

"Well, that's not what she told me," Darius replied, frustrated. He typed a note in his file: Jessica thinks I'm losing it and wants me to see a shrink. Somebody is being dishonest with the separation.

He stared at the screen as she continued her appeal for the evaluation. "Would you?" she asked.

Despite the bubbling that seemed to rise in his chest, like a kettle ready to boil over, Darius kept himself calm. "I'll think about it," he said, as honestly as he could, adding, "But if I do, then it's only fair that we, Jessica and I, both agree to do one."

Sharon said nothing, and he felt himself withdrawing. But as the call was about to end, Sharon said, "But really Darius ... *Voodoo?*"

The call ended.

Voodoo? Darius thought. What the hell is she talking about?

Sitting back, he exhaled, mentally sorting through the meeting. "This is insane; they think I am doing voodoo and want me to have a psychological evaluation? Maybe they need an evaluation!"

It didn't bode well; this didn't feel like the actions of someone who was willing to work things out.

Not at all.

Chapter 22
The Detour Begins

J essica had taken her ring to be cleaned and repaired months ago. She told him about it at the time, but recently, she had mentioned that it still wasn't ready. That week, however, he received a call from the jeweler. They informed him that they had reached out to Jessica multiple times, but she hadn't picked up the ring. Confused and hurt, he sent her a text about it. Her reply was "angry"—she said she had been too busy to make the trip to get it. Frustrated, she added that if he wanted her to wear the ring so badly, he could go pick it up and bring it to her himself.

The next day, he drove to the jeweler, collected the ring, and placed it by her bed. The whole situation was becoming more and more clear to him—Jessica had already made up her mind about their relationship. He didn't want to accept it, but the signs were becoming harder to ignore because she was so hostile.

If he was honest with himself, and he was certainly trying to be, he'd really shot himself in the foot. She'd told him to give her space, but didn't really explain what that meant so he pursued her to find an answer—something he was learning through the Marriage Reset Program was the opposite of what he should have done. While still at home the first week, he'd bought the book *The Love Dare* by Alex Kendrick and Stephen Kendrick, and on the fifth day, she had adamantly told him to stop reading the book! After moving out, he'd texted her more than once, each time hoping for something different. Then came a wake-up call from one of her friends.

> *You're not doing what she asked. Don't reach out to her unless it's about the kids or business.*
>
> *Okay.*

He couldn't find any other words to say.

The next mistake came when he tried reaching out to a coworker of hers, hoping to find out if she was having an affair. But Jessica was right there with her when he'd sent the message, and within ten minutes, his phone buzzed.

> *If you want to know something, ask me, not my friends.*
>
> *Wouldn't that be novel? It would sure make things easier. But you're not willing to communicate about anything.*
>
> *I need space.*
>
> *I'm not right in the head. I can't think straight, and you're not right either.*
>
> *You act like you hate me. You won't talk. I'm in the dark and living out of my office.*

His message was left unread for a while, before eventually his phone buzzed again:

We need space. Respect it and stop reaching out. Don't text my friends.

What the hell? he thought. They're my friends, too.

It was almost impossible to fathom.

Being surrounded by the life they had built together, but having no access to it anymore; it was an unbearable form of misery. The restaurants they used to go to, their home, the friends they used to visit—all of it was right there, yet he couldn't be a part of any of it. Occasionally, he would see a black vehicle drive by that looked like hers—or maybe it even was hers—and he would find himself looking, hoping, wondering. But what was he going to do? Chase after it like a dog chasing a car?

He needed to get out of the area. He needed to escape and clear his mind. One of his oldest and closest friends was in North Carolina. It was the second charity his business had started supporting—a therapeutic horse ranch. He and Brett had been friends for nearly 30 years. They first met working in hospitals and hit it off instantly. Over the years, he also became close friends with Brett's wife, Hannah, and their children. Darius and Jessica had visited North Carolina with their own kids many times, staying with the family.

When Brett and Hannah had moved to North Carolina, they set up the charity because their daughter faced challenges. Her growth plates hadn't developed properly, which affected almost every aspect of her daily life. But she was a beautiful young girl, with a lighthearted spirit and an infectious laugh. Darius had always admired both Brett and Hannah deeply. They were remarkable parents, raising such an incredible child despite the difficulties. While Darius had had some struggles with his kids—both had their challenges, bipolar and ADHD—he was amazed at Brett and Hannah's patience and grace. To Darius, they were the epitome of resilience and strength and Christian parenting. Their daughter and boys were wonderful to be around.

Brett had also been the one who, almost 10 years ago, gave him the book: *You Can't Out Give God* by Dr. Hickey. That book had been the catalyst for Darius's shift in perspective on charitable giving. It opened his heart to the importance of giving and was a significant reason why, when he started his own business, he committed to donating 10% of every placement he made, a percentage of his business revenue, to charity. That seed of generosity God had planted was watered by Brett, and it had grown into something fundamental to Darius's life and values.

The Ahearns knew what was going on, and they were praying for him. They told him that if he needed to get away, he was welcome to come stay with them. So, he decided to pack up the car, go to North Carolina, stay with his friends, and help out by volunteering at the therapeutic ranch. It seemed like the best option. His heart was broken, and he knew he was in a state of shock. Helping others, especially the kids at the ranch, would take his mind off his pain while also giving him a much-needed change of scenery.

The day before he left, Darius watched a sermon called "The Detour," sent to him by Larissa just a few days earlier. It was as if the whole thing had been written specifically for him. The minister spoke about the plans we make versus what God sometimes has in store for us, and how, when things aren't going well, we need to realize who's truly in charge. We have to let go and allow God to lead us through the detours in our lives. This message struck Darius powerfully—he felt like he had no control over anything at this point.

The past year for Darius had been incredibly tough: his father had passed away, the business faced major setbacks, and three key employees betrayed his trust—one setting up a competing company, another becoming increasingly difficult and had to be let go, and the third pursuing law school behind his back while still expecting to be paid full-time. It felt like everything was falling apart.

For weeks, he had felt like he was in freefall, grappling with a personal and professional crisis. Jōb was a character he hadn't felt connected to before, but as he reread the story for the first time in years after hearing that sermon, he couldn't help but relate to the trials and challenges Jōb had faced. Yes, Darius's trials and suffering were nothing compared to Jōb he knew but his situation felt overwhelming for him. He felt like he was living through his own "Jōb-like" year of suffering and hardship and this could be exactly what he needed to begin to heal.

It would be a nearly ten-hour drive to get to the ranch—a long drive with way too much time to think. He decided to buy a couple of audiobooks for the drive, one of which was *The Case for Christ* by Lee Strobel. Darius had read the book several times in the past, but it had been four or five years, and he felt that with everything going on, it was something he needed to revisit. Listening to it seemed like the perfect opportunity during the drive. The journey itself was beautiful and went by smoothly, offering him time for reflection and prayer.

In the car, as he listened, Darius realized how much of the book he had forgotten. It was remarkable how many aspects of Jesus' life and works were historically validated through evidence. This book had been instrumental in solidifying his belief in God the first time he read it. Strobel, a former atheist and Pulitzer Prize-winning journalist, had set out to disprove the resurrection of Jesus after his wife converted to Christianity. As an atheist, Strobel couldn't believe in Christ's resurrection, so he approached the subject as a case reporter—meticulously interviewing experts and gathering research. Through this process, Strobel found overwhelming evidence of Christ's resurrection and ultimately gave his life to Christ.

For Darius, this book had always reinforced why his faith was important and why he needed to live according to the principles he believed in. As he listened, the message struck him even harder now, particularly in light of the personal challenges he was facing. His eyes had been opened to his flaws, his mistakes, and areas he needed to improve, both as a man and as a husband. It made him think deeply about the decisions he was making in life and reaffirmed his desire to live with more intention and purpose. It was a reminder that he needed to keep working on himself, growing spiritually, and striving to live out his faith, especially during such a difficult time.

Coming to his first stop, he hit pause and pulled into a gas station in Virginia. With a smile on his face, he saw the Bojangles sign across the way and decided to grab lunch. It brought back a flood of memories. Bojangles was always a fun inside joke with his family. Whenever they would go to Florida or Georgia, or any place where there was a Bojangles, it would always be a go-to destination. And every time, without fail, they would sit down with their food, and he would say in a funny southern drawl, "Bojangles, chicken and biscuits." And every time, without fail, the kids would laugh and it put a big smile on his face.

The memory brought a smile to his face, a small moment of joy amidst the chaos that seemed to fill his life. He was excited to see his friends and felt a sense of relief with the change of scenery.

On the highway, his mind started to reflect. Darius had been devouring anything he could find from the Marriage Reset Program. He found himself diving into the modules three to four evenings a week, determined to better understand his wife's needs, address his own misunderstandings, and begin reprogramming his unhelpful mental patterns. But it was only after his third emotional trauma therapy session with Larissa, that he felt he experienced remarkable progress.

The first two sessions had left him feeling unchanged. But then, during the third session, something incredible happened. It felt as if a 200-pound weight had been lifted off his back, like a blind man suddenly given the ability to see.

If someone had asked him in the past if he suffered from anxiety, he would have laughed and said, "Are you serious?" In fact, he almost did when Larissa first asked it. Yet, the reality was it was pouring out of his eyeballs. he had been living with incredible anxiety—and he hadn't even realized it.

Throughout his life, there were moments when he knew he was hurting, that he was somehow damaged. He often rationalized it by thinking he had scars on his heart, but he never fully understood the why, the how, or the extent of the damage. But now, he realized, a significant part of his heartache stemmed from the constant challenges he faced with the women in his life.

His relationship with his mother had always been difficult. Then marrying his first wife had been a foolish decision, one he later realized was a continuation of his lifelong search for love. It was a disaster from the start.

All he had to do was tell the story of the wedding day and subsequent honeymoon. The church he grew up in and they were supposed to get married in had a boiler explode and was badly damaged, so they had gone to the Baptist Church asking if that would be an option. They were reluctant but it was a small town and everyone knew his family so they had relented. It was a hot July day and the air conditioning didn't work; they were told not to turn on any ceiling fans because with the candles it would be a fire hazard. When they had gone outside to take pictures, someone had turned on a fan and the unity candle had set the altar ablaze. Darius had come in with the altar engulfed and had sprinted to the kitchen to grab the fire extinguisher. As he came running back to put it out, there was the photographer trying to use his tuxedo jacket to put it out! Needless to say, the church leadership was less than happy and the damages to the altar and his suit weren't slight.

As the honeymoon in the Bahamas started to sour with arguing, it was cut short by a hurricane with 100-mile-per-hour winds. They boarded a ship back to Florida with high swells and his new bride threw up regularly on the trip back. It was a highlight that described most of the marriage.

While he hadn't fully grasped his own issues at the time, he could vividly recall her struggles and pains. During their eight years together, conflict dominated their lives, and happiness was a rarity for either of them. Later, he would learn she was bi-polar and potentially had something called Borderline Personality Disorder, and after reading, *I Hate You, Please Don't Leave Me* by Jerold J. Kreisman and Hal Straus and *Walking on Eggshells* by Paul T. Mason and Randi Kreger, he was amazed at how relevant it was to their situation. The books described so many things he had experienced.

His relationship with his sister was also fraught with strife and conflict. Then there were his daughter's struggles, which began to seriously impact their family as she became a teenager. This included two trips to the stress center, a suicide attempt, and a lot of conflict

And now ... Now, there was Jessica.

One of the things that Darius couldn't move past was how sudden all of this seemed. She hadn't spoken or asked about going to counseling. She hadn't complained to him about anything new or particularly specific. True, he had maybe not been around as much as he would have liked, but he had been dealing with so much in the business that just kind of became his priority. But even if it was, was it enough to dismantle everything they had built together over the last 20 years? Yes, there were certainly times that he found her frustrating, and, like most couples, they had issues, but it didn't change the fact that he loved her and he was committed to her and their family

As he considered his past and the spiritual awakening in Mexico, the ominous truth being reinforced was that he had to take ownership of his part of all aspects of the past. He had to keep looking at himself for answers wherever the truth led and to clean out his faults.

The audiobook had become a dull drone in the background, mixed with the monotonous sound of the car's engine. He had about 4 or 5 hours left in the drive.

His mind drifted through eras of his past when times seemed better ...

Anytime the topic of marriage arose, he would suggest destination weddings. On the rare occasions they had those conversations, his view was that traditional weddings wasted an immense amount of money, often spent on everyone except the bride and groom. From his perspective, all that money went toward extravagant receptions, with people drinking at open bars while the newlyweds were left feeling stressed and unable to enjoy their own celebration.

His perspective was spending the money on the rings and making memories, and when Jessica said, "Yes," that's exactly what they did. A destination wedding over three days with close friends and family that was incredible, beautiful, and full of fun and relaxation for everyone—including the bride and groom.

After that, they honeymooned in Italy. Eleven days traveling from Milan to Lake Maggiore to Verona, to Venice to Ramini to San. Gimignano to Siena, Florence, Rome, Naples, Pompeii ... It was even more magical. Amazing. The best thing he had ever done at that point in his life and a big reason for that was because it was done with her, with her smile and in her company.

It was a dream made real, and their honeymoon was only one of many memories they shared over the years.

For the longest time, they had enjoyed trips to her family's lake house, spending summers with friends and family there every year. But then, for reasons he didn't fully grasp, they stopped going. In the last three to four years, things had changed—especially after moving into their current house, leaving behind the home where they had raised their kids for the first fifteen years of their relationship. It hadn't dawned on him until their current issues, while they had family photos hanging everywhere in their first house where they lived 14 years, Jessica had no family photos hanging in their house now. Why had he missed that?

Yet, Darius felt that the good memories outweighed the bad. He had always viewed his wife as a happy and generous person, not fake by any means, which made it all the more confusing when his counselor mentioned that she had likely been contemplating divorce for the last two to three years without ever saying a word. Had he been really that naive, that clueless about the state of their relationship?

In his mind, there had been countless special moments. As he reflected on the trauma of their situation and engaged in self-evaluation, he realized that while he excelled at the big occasions—planning trips and providing financially—he struggled with the smaller, more meaningful gestures, like celebrating birthdays or simply doing thoughtful things for her during the week. He had to admit that he wasn't present enough, and the Marriage Reset program made it painfully clear that he hadn't been taking charge at home the last few years. Though he didn't fully understand everything, it was obvious he fell into the same category as many other men in the program.

He felt that the crux of the issue lay in his failure to validate her feelings and make her feel heard. Their communication challenges often led to shutdowns, with him becoming angry and silent during disputes instead of working on a positive resolution. He had reached a point where, when problems arose, his instinct was to work harder and provide more because he didn't know how else to cope.

Still, he cherished many experiences they had shared—like their trips to Paris, Ireland, river cruises, and traveling the states. But now, he found himself questioning many aspects of what he thought he knew. One memory haunted him more than others: the trip to Africa the previous year. It had always been a dream trip for him, and he thought it was for her as well. Achieving a significant business goal was the reason they had gone, and she had insisted on joining him, adamant that he wasn't going without her.

The trip had been nothing short of magical. They got along beautifully, with no arguments or disputes that he could recall. It felt like a movie—witnessing the great migration, seeing hippos, and experiencing the Big Five: lions, elephants, and more. There were smiles, joy, and incredible memories captured in photos and videos. The intimacy they shared during the trip reminded him of their honeymoon in Italy. How could it all change so drastically? How could he go from that blissful experience to six to eight months later, facing her assertion that it was over, that she wouldn't work on it or seek counseling?

He realized that he was running this scenario through his mind while taking all the responsibility and no account of his wife's issues or failures in the marriage, but he could only focus on his challenges. Now, this new version of her acted as if she couldn't stand him, avoiding him at every turn, as if she utterly despised him.

Chapter 23
Healing With Horses

When he finally arrived at the Ahearns' horse ranch, a smile spread across his face. The place was filled with cherished memories. They had acquired it through an auction—about 40 or 50 acres featuring a stunning 7,000-square-foot home. With twelve horses, the ranch served anywhere from 30 to 40 children and adults with disabilities at any given time. They didn't make a profit from the venture and relied heavily on donations and volunteers to keep it running. To Darius, it was a noble cause and just one more thing he admired about his friends.

As he entered the gate using the code, it swung open, and he drove up to park in his usual spot to the right of the garage. He got out and started to walk toward the front when he spotted his buddy standing on the porch, two beers in hand.

He came up the steps and Brett gave him a huge hug. He could feel the cold glass bottle wet his back, but he didn't care; Darius embraced him back.

"I love you, man," Brett said.

"I love you too," Darius replied.

Brett pulled away and handed over the beer. "I know this is hard, but you'll get through it."

Darius's smile weakened, the memories brought forth by the long car ride still forefront and raw. "I know," he said, certainty absent from his voice.

They went around the deck and sat down to talk. Before he arrived, Darius had told Brett about the book *What Are the Stakes?* and shared some details over the phone. Brett mentioned that he had read the book and found it remarkable. However, he also shared some troubling news: things had not been going well for the charity.

"What do you mean?" Darius asked, surprised.

Brett sighed. "We've just had all kinds of problems. Not enough volunteers. One volunteer was even stealing from us—just a lot of strange things."

"Really?" Darius replied, still in disbelief.

"Yeah," Brett continued. "We've been trying to decide if maybe what it's telling us is that we need to shut the charity down or combine with somebody else. We're just not sure we can keep it going."

As they discussed the challenges surrounding the charity, Hannah came in and sat down, giving Darius a big hug and a kiss on his cheek. "I just don't understand," she said. "Last year, we were all together for your birthday. She's your soulmate. You guys were in love."

Darius looked at her, feeling a mix of sadness and confusion. "It's just ... she's not the same now. I can't explain it, but everything is different. She doesn't want anything to do with me."

Hannah responded, "Well, it's going to change. She's going to change her mind. You'll see."

Then the book came up again, and Hannah said, "I just don't even understand."

Brett chimed in, "Well, evil's real just like God's real. Nobody wants to talk about these kinds of things, but there are many examples of it throughout the Bible and life."

Darius nodded. "Yeah, that was the thing I had no idea about. It's been eye opening and how come it's not talked about more in church? Among a lot of things I didn't understand, I didn't realize how some of my behavior and my lack of worthiness must have been very difficult to deal with—just being so needy. I had no idea that I had so many of those traits. I realize now that I really didn't like myself a whole lot, and I've never felt worthy or spoken nicely to myself either. But I just had no awareness of how it affected her or how I wasn't being a leader."

"Come on, man," Brett said. "You've always been a great dad. You've always loved her. You've always provided. You've done the best you could."

"I know that's true, but it doesn't change the fact that I have a lot of work to do on myself and changes that need to be made," Darius replied.

There was silence as they both took a drink, and then it quickly disappeared, as conversation resumed—this time with Hannah's much-welcomed input. Darius had forgotten what it was like to just chat; even if they were talking about everything that had happened since they last got together, it was broken up by drinks and laughter. It was as if things were normal for the first time in a while.

Then the topic turned back to the challenges the charity was facing. Darius wanted to know more, but when Brett started listing everything, it seemed near-endless.

As Darius sat there in stunned silence, Brett finally shared a realization. "I don't know why we ever stopped the weekly Bible study we had going on here."

"What do you mean?" Darius asked. "When was that?"

"It stopped a few years ago," Brett said. "But it is interesting that when that was going on, everything was at its best. We had the most volunteers, the most kids. Right now, we have people on a waiting list. We can't even take them on because we don't have enough volunteers."

"Well, I would say that evil probably doesn't like the good that you're doing," Darius said. "While I would have never said this in the past, based on what I'm experiencing in my own situation, you're probably under attack. They didn't like me giving more money each year and leaning into God more and more, even with all my challenges. They certainly don't like what you're doing. You need to stake your place out."

Brett smiled. "The stakes were ordered yesterday, man, so we'll get it all done this week after the riding show. I've got enough to go to each corner of the property, the entire 50 acres."

"Awesome," Darius replied. "We'll bless the entire property and give it to Him."

They clinked their beer glasses together; Darius taking a sip of his while Brett finished off his.

"Sounds like a plan," Hannah said, giving Darius another big hug. "You know, this is your home. So make yourself at home. Whatever you need, whatever you want. I'll be cooking dinner on certain nights when we're here. In a few days, we have to go to Georgia for a competition, so you'll be here alone, but there's a freezer stocked with meat. You can cook whatever you want."

Darius's smile grew again. "It's so good to see you guys. I love you, and I appreciate your prayers. I appreciate you giving me a place to come and get away to reset my mind. It will be nice to be able to work out here, jump in the pool every now and then, ride the horses, and help out with the charity."

"We're glad to have you," Hannah replied.

Chapter 24
Hey, It's Jeff

He had been stuck in limbo with little to no communication from his wife. Even in North Carolina, time seemed to drag on, and the more effort he poured into the Marriage Reset Program, the more he began to understand the situation—and himself—but the more he understood, the more the outlook didn't seem positive. Still, he knew he had to give her space.

One of the books he was reading during this time was *The Way of the Superior Man* by David Deida. It was fascinating so far, though certain parts made him uncomfortable—especially sections about sexual relationships, which seemed to promote promiscuity in ways that didn't align with who he was or what he wanted.

When he was younger, he had taken sex far too lightly. The work he'd been doing in the program, particularly through The Disfigured Man, forced him to confront those past decisions. Before he was married, he'd been with many women, a fact he was now ashamed of. Looking back, he realized that most of those encounters hadn't brought him happiness. Instead, they had been rooted in toxic shame and a constant need to seek love and validation, stemming from his belief that he was never good enough.

That realization had hit him hard. It wasn't just about physical intimacy; it was about the emotional void he'd been trying to fill. As the program taught, a healthy person gives love freely rather than seeking it. He now understood how unhealthy and flawed his approach had been in the past. As he continued to dive into the Bible, the truth of the demonic, and considering the chord, as well, he was wondering how generational curses might play into his life. Just like the demonic, prophecy, and spiritual realms, the idea of curses or blessings was becoming evident. He had so much to learn.

Despite its challenging content, the author spoke about carrying yourself with confidence, yet not egotistically, embracing your masculine frame. This involved listening, validating, and connecting to a woman's emotions, all while maintaining control over your own feelings. One example stood out: the comparison to a lighthouse standing firm on the shore. No matter how fierce the storm became, no matter how overwhelming or irrational her emotions were, the lighthouse remained unmoved. It didn't matter if she was upset over something that didn't make sense, if her memory was faulty, or if her anger seemed unwarranted. As a masculine man, the key was to stand strong, like the lighthouse against the crashing waves.

In the same way, the exercise he'd been practicing taught him to pause for three to four seconds before responding. It was important to validate what was being said, reflect it, and connect with the emotion underneath. That was not an easy task. From Darius's perspective, it took time to identify the right emotion to connect with, but he was starting to understand how to practice it. He was learning examples to thank a woman for her vulnerability and then ask for what she needed or apologize if that was required.

That aligned with the principles taught in the Marriage Reset Program, as well as those in *The Way of the Superior Man*. A truly positive masculine man, the book explained, knew who he was, what he wanted, and had no hesitation in asking for it. Whether or not he received what he asked for didn't matter. If he didn't get it, his emotional state wouldn't change. And if he did get it, that was fine, but regardless of the situation or challenge, he would handle it based on his core values, not on his emotions or negative masculine traits.

Darius appreciated this book's insights and had begun reading others as well, like *Better Man, Better Marriage* by Jeff Borkoski. That book, however, was a tough pill to swallow. As he read, he couldn't help but feel he was failing in many areas. About 60% of the book felt like a checklist of mistakes he had made. Still, he found the material invaluable, and Borkoski's humor made the hard truths easier to digest.

One evening, after the Ahearns had left for Atlanta, Darius decided to visit one of his favorite joints in Durham called Bull City Burger and Brewery. He ordered the burger of the month, sampled a few beers before settling on an IPA, and sat in the corner with his laptop. After enjoying his meal, he decided to finish the last chapters of *Better Man, Better Marriage*.

As he closed the book, he felt a mix of frustration and gratitude. *Why had nobody taught me any of this before?* he wondered. At 51 years old, it was a hard realization, but he was thankful to finally be learning.

The book ended with a note from the author that included an email address and phone number. On a whim, Darius decided to send a text.

"Hi Jeff, My name is Darius. I just finished reading your book Better Man, Better Marriage. I've been going through a very difficult time. My wife isn't sure she wants to stay married after 17 years and 20 years together. It's been incredibly tough, but your book has opened my eyes to so many things I didn't understand

before. I just wanted to thank you. I can't imagine how many men you've helped. This is a must-read for anyone married, or planning to marry. Thank you."

About 40 minutes later, as Darius worked on his laptop, his phone rang. He looked down and couldn't believe it—the number was the same one he'd texted earlier. He answered cautiously.

"Hello, this is Darius."

"Hey, it's Jeff Borkoski."

Darius was stunned. A huge smile spread across his face and his thoughts escaped him. "Wow."

Jeff laughed. "I just had to call and say your text was awesome. This is why I wrote the book, and it means the world to me to hear that it helped you."

They talked for about thirty minutes about the book and what Darius was going through. As he shared his situation, Jeff grew a little quiet, listening intently. After a pause, he said, "Oh man, look, I get it, but here's the thing, you have to give yourself grace. You have awareness now. Yes, you're only a couple of months in, but you're doing the work. You joined the program, and from what I can tell, it sounds like a great program. You're going to be in such a better place. And really ... just like my ex ... and I know she's not your ex, you're still married. So there's a possibility, man, that God could work through this and the situation could be reversed. Your marriage could still be saved." He paused before continuing, "But no matter what, she's done you a great favor. You're being awakened now. And just look at the work you're doing, it's incredible."

Darius felt a wave of gratitude wash over him, and then Jeff added, "If you want, I'd love to send you some of the material I share with the men I coach. It could really help."

Darius didn't hesitate. "Are you kidding? Absolutely! I'd love to see it."

Jeff smiled. "One of the things I'm going to send you is a video by Ryan Holiday. It's something I recommend to all my clients. You know, the guy who writes those books on Stoicism?"

Darius nodded. "Yeah, I know him and have several of his books."

"Exactly," Jeff said. "The video is something you watch every single day when you wake up. It's all about making a choice, choosing who you want to be, what you want to stand for, and deciding whether or not you'll let things affect you. It's all about taking control of your future."

Darius felt a spark of excitement. "That sounds amazing. I'd love to have that."

Jeff agreed, "I'll send it over as soon as we get off the phone."

Darius then mentioned, "There are a lot of guys in the Marriage Reset Program who are reading your book, and it's been a great help to many of them. I'm going to order the other one you have, *The Wife Magnet*, too."

"I really appreciate that," Jeff said. "Stay in touch and let me know if there's anything I can do for you. It was great talking to you."

After the call, Darius sat back with a smile. He felt renewed hope, not just for his marriage, but for himself. Jeff's journey from failure to growth inspired him. If Jeff could transform his pain into something that helped others, maybe Darius could do the same. He had a sense they were going to become good friends.

***

Darius left Bull Brewery, shaking his head with a grin as he slid into his car, heading back to the house. Meeting Jeff Borkoski—amazing. The encounter left him buzzing with a renewed sense of energy, though his thoughts quickly returned to his growing to-do list and tasks for the week. Tomorrow, he'd planned to saddle up one of the horses for a long ride through the woods. It was time he allowed himself a moment of solitude.

His phone buzzed—a text from his mother. He'd been meaning to call her back, so he hit FaceTime, the call connecting after a few rings. The small talk started in the usual way, with his mom's familiar, nervous energy in every syllable. Since his father passed, she had only grown more anxious as it had been very tough on her.

She asked him about his recent days, so he told her about meeting the author of *Better Man, Better Marriage*. Her reaction was a quiet "Oh," before quickly changing the topic. She asked how he was doing, prompting him to say honestly, "It's difficult. I'm hopeful we can work things out, but it's not going great."

He hesitated, thinking about things that had weighed on him since he left for North Carolina. For a while, he didn't say anything, just considering how much had changed—and how much was still to change.

"What are you planning to do for Ben?" She asked, cutting into his thoughts. "You need to be around for him, you know."

He took a deep breath. "Mom, I'm doing the best I can. She has him constantly on the run. He's out of state with her right now anyway."

"I don't understand why you left. How are you going to go to counseling?" She said.

Darius's jaw tensed, but he measured himself and made himself respond without emotion or sarcasm. "You understand that you can do counseling without being in person? There is video."

A quiet pause followed. Then, she asked, "Well, you can answer my questions, Darius. Have you tried to communicate with her?"

"No," he replied, keeping his tone steady. "We still aren't communicating. She's not willing to right now and doesn't want to hear from me."

"Well, she's just mad at you because you don't talk very nicely sometimes, Darius," she said, her voice sharp.

Darius felt his jaw tighten. This was the pattern—criticism cloaked as concern, pushing at his patience. In the past, he would've reacted, but lately, he'd been working on setting boundaries, saying "No" instead of allowing himself to be pulled down by her remarks. "Mom, I've told you nicely, several times, I'm not going to be spoken to like that," he said.

"Oh, you're just being insecure," she replied, brushing off his words.

"No, this has happened repeatedly. I'm dealing with a lot right now, and I don't need you kicking me while I'm down," he said, keeping his tone controlled.

"You're being ridiculous and too sensitive," she replied, dismissing him in the same way he was becoming so accustomed to—as if he were the one at fault for even bringing it up.

Frustrated, he took a breath, steadying himself. "If you keep treating me like I'm the problem for standing up for myself, I'm hanging up," he said firmly. As his mother continued, he sighed, said okay then, goodnight and hung up the call as she was in mid-sentence.

As he sat in the quiet, he wondered how his own mother could treat him so unkindly.

Then, his thoughts turned to another hurt he'd been carrying. Since moving out, his wife had begun hosting gatherings at the house—events where his mother and friends they'd shared for years came by, like nothing had changed. Initially, Darius had tried to brush it off, telling himself it didn't matter. But the more he thought about it, the more it stung. These were people he'd celebrated Christmas and Thanksgiving with, people he'd believed were friends. The old him would have swept it under the rug, but he stopped and admitted it pissed him off and sat in the feeling.

He thought about how strange it felt that they hadn't once checked on him, never reached out to see how he was holding up. He'd lived out of his office while they enjoyed the pool and house he'd worked hard to pay for. If the tables were turned, he couldn't imagine going to a friend's home to party while they were struggling, separated, and living out of an office.

Frustrated, he let the anger simmer, and then slowly released it, a skill he was learning through the program. He was reading about emotional release in *The Untethered Soul* and was excited to get into the works of David Hawkins to better learn how to process emotions instead of letting them overtake you.

As he walked into the Ahearn's house, he thought about how little support he felt from his mother. Every interaction seemed to sap his energy, leaving him feeling unmoored. It was as if she was on his wife's side, more loyal to her than to him, her own son.

Chapter 25
Darius—You Have Mail

T he thing that was really difficult for Darius to deal with was the realization of how blind he had been to the challenges going on between him and Jessica. There were so many signs that he was oblivious to that now seemed so obvious, and now he realized how the mounting stress and pressure had forced him to wear blinders that narrowed his vision more and more with each new problem.

He was so focused on saving the business, on providing for his family, on ensuring that they had financial security that he missed everything else happening around him.

With all the work he had been doing through the program— through counseling, emotional trauma therapy, and adding embodiment, breathing exercises, and meditation—he had started to do cold plunges as well. He was working so hard to grow, to look in the mirror, to change, and to recognize his faults. One of the biggest challenges had been truly forgiving himself for his mistakes, his idiosyncrasies, and the things he had done that caused friction in their marriage.

But now those blinders were off, and with this awareness and clarity came another realization: it certainly was not all his fault.

There were so many signs that he had just missed because of the anxiety and the pressure he was dealing with. Looking back, he could clearly remember situations, comments, and unkind facial expressions that he had failed to acknowledge at the time. Now, they were all too clear. Things she had said, like if he hadn't been trying to grow the business, they could have been doing so much more with the money. She was spending so much more time around her business partner and their employees, which wasn't positive because the group wasn't a positive influence and tended to create chaos.

Over the last few years, they had really continued to grow apart. They used to be involved in each other's social activities, but two years ago, he had kind of gotten uninvited from her real estate events because her business partner didn't like him. It was a strange situation. He didn't have an issue with lesbians in general, but historically, they had never really tended to like him, and he never quite understood why. Her business partner, with whom he had initially gotten along fine, had started becoming very unfriendly toward him. After that, Jessica would go to her events with her partner instead of him.

There were just so many examples of them continuing to become more distant, and communication had always been a struggle for them.

With her ADHD diagnosis, which had just happened a year and a half prior, it brought a lot of answers but also a lot of challenges. It gave them an explanation as to why she was not always present or listening, why she could be so flighty or skittish, and why sometimes she appeared as if she was all over the place. But, in hindsight, he could see now how he had never been particularly patient with her—something he was ashamed of and wanted to change.

But at this point, even though it had been eight weeks since the "breakup," there had been no communication—no specifics on her feelings or what she thought. While he had a strong sense of clarity from all the work he was doing, including the books he was reading, he still felt in the dark. The counseling sessions and group discussions were helpful; he was learning about communication challenges between men and women, as well as the dynamics of polarity.

He was also seeing examples of other men's successes and failures, which made him realize so many reasons why she could be frustrated. He understood the main reasons why a woman might file for divorce, especially when a man is completely unaware it's coming. But the more work he did, and the longer it went on, the more he realized all those little things he missed.

He missed the things that frustrated him about her, the things that were not loving or respectful, the things that, when he looked with this new perspective, made him realize that there were many things about the last few years that he wasn't necessarily happy about either. All "the little things."

It was obvious that as he had grown his business, and after she'd gone into business for herself, they had been steadily growing apart. If he were honest with himself, the idea of how many of the situations that had occurred over the last three to four months, before she told him it was over, had gone unnoticed by him was embarrassing, painful, and a little mind-boggling all at the same time. Yet, through this entire process, he still believed that things could get better. He was 100% convinced in his heart that change was possible. He remembered a few years earlier, grappling with some of her behaviors and frustrations, wondering if he even wanted to stay in the marriage any longer.

Sometimes, he had felt incredibly lonely because she was often not present, and there were many aspects of his background—clinically, in business, and other areas—that he couldn't discuss with her. It was hard to explain, but it added to his feelings of disconnect and loneliness. However, the truth was that he was very loyal, and he probably would never leave her. Did that mean that if things continued to get worse, he wouldn't want change, demand change, or put his foot down? No. He certainly realized he had been asleep at the wheel regarding her needs and hadn't been seeing things through her eyes.

However, now he had eyes to see and ears to hear. Now he could see his failings and challenges with his unworthiness, anxiety, needy behaviors, and lack of emotional control during conflicts, and was absorbing everything Marriage Reset was teaching. He was learning about polarity and the differences between positive and negative masculine and feminine traits. If they had had these tools—if he had just had the understanding—he believed with all his heart that their relationship would have been completely different. Now, he was learning how to help a woman connect with her feminine energy.

The program constantly emphasized that feelings, emotions, and love could be retriggered and transformed. While it took time to reach their current state of disconnect, he learned that with two people willing to work on it—armed with the right tools and support—the situation could improve much faster than it had taken to break everything down. For Darius, his belief in God and the covenant of their marriage drove him. He wanted to protect his family and children from the pain of a broken marriage and the consequences that would inevitably follow. He would do anything to avoid that brokenness, to grow, and to restore the relationship.

At the same time, he had to stop beating himself up because it wasn't all his fault. There were plenty of things she could have done differently, and she could have communicated her feelings better. Clearly, she had been holding a lot inside for it to reach this breaking point.

***

That Wednesday, following the best night's sleep he had had to date, Darius pulled himself from bed feeling good. While in Indiana, while everything was going downhill, he hadn't slept more than two to four hours at a time; he had been in bad shape, physically, mentally, emotionally ... Through the Marriage Reset Program and taking control of his own life and health, he had made progress in a few of these areas. At least in North Carolina, it seemed he was starting to make significant progress.

In his routines, he was consistently meditating, working out, continuing with his modules, and reconnecting with Scripture; seeing the horses and the solitude of the change of scenery was good for his mental processes and he was in a much better place. Going through his routine, he then spent part of the morning out with the horses. They were always so amazing, so loving, and just put him in a sense of peace.

After seeing the horses, Darius would clean up and get to work in the office Brett had set him up in. After a busy day, he was going to relax and cook some dinner. That's when the email came in.

It was from Jessica.

His heart skipped a beat as he pulled it up on his phone. It was long, so long the thumb of the scrollbar was almost impossible to see. He started reading and was barely a sentence in when he felt the pit open in his stomach. It wasn't at all what he hoped for.

It was a laundry list of grievances.

You're a horrible husband.

You're a horrible father.

You have no friends.

You have no redeemable qualities.

You made me feel ugly.

You made me feel dumb.

I was embarrassed by you ... by the way you spoke, the way you behaved, the way you drank.

Her list, her reasons, everything she shared across the near-three pages of the email ... It was horrible. It was so unfair. She brought up things from the past, including one item she was angry about from 14 years ago. Almost three pages of nastiness. Had she been holding all of this in for the 20 years they had been together? Did she have any happy memories from their time together?

It was as if someone opened a spigot; tears flowing endlessly as he came to the end of the email.

Please wait at least 48 hours before responding.

Jessica.

Wait 48 hours? What exactly was there to say to this?

He certainly couldn't tell her what he truly thought—that a lot of what she said wasn't entirely fair, and some of it wasn't even true. Of course, some of it was true, especially over the last three or four years, but it was hard to reconcile how their relationship had deteriorated so much. How had things gotten this bad? It was a question that weighed heavily on his mind as he sat there, replaying their conversations in his head.

He reflected on some of the things she had said, accusations that cut him deeply. She told him that he had made her feel like she wasn't smart enough, like she wasn't pretty enough, like her body wasn't good enough. He couldn't even understand where some of those feelings had come from. He'd never intended to make her feel that way. The idea that she had carried these emotions, possibly for years, was overwhelming to him. How had they drifted so far apart, to the point where she felt so diminished and unseen?

It all felt surreal. As he sat with those thoughts, a heavy sadness settled over him. Could their marriage even be saved? How could they ever come back from this? The possibility of divorce loomed larger in his mind, and it terrified him. He didn't want to give up on their life together, but at the same time, he couldn't see a clear path forward. The gap between them seemed too wide and her laundry list of accusations too long.

Darius couldn't eat—his appetite had completely vanished. Before he knew it, he found himself at the Ahearns' wine cabinet, opening a bottle of Pinot Noir. He walked out onto the deck, looking out over the trees, his heart heavy with the weight of it all. Sitting there, he began crying, praying, and drinking. It wasn't the best combination, and he knew that, but at that moment, it felt like all he could manage.

He had cut down on alcohol significantly since everything began falling apart. He'd made a decision to avoid hard liquor altogether—maybe the occasional beer or glass of wine, but he had mostly stayed away from it. Yet tonight was different. The emotional toll was too much to bear, and the bottle of wine offered a temporary escape from the overwhelming sadness and helplessness that had been suffocating him. He knew this wasn't the healthiest way to cope, but in that moment, it was all he had left to cling to. The tears, the prayers, and the wine swirled together as he sat there, trying to make sense of it all.

Storm clouds rolled in, and suddenly, it was a deluge. Lightning flashed in the distance and the loud sounds of thunder shook the countryside. Wind whipped through the trees, spooking the horses in the barn. Darius sat there watching the storm, trying to lose himself in the majesty of it. When that didn't work, he tried to watch a movie on his phone. The screen was blurry through the intermittent tears and the sounds were garbled, mixed with the storm and the torrent of thoughts that wouldn't seem to settle no matter how much wine he drank.

***

Darius woke up sometime after dawn, still outside on the lawn chair with an empty bottle of wine lying beside him. He tried to pull the weariness and fatigue from his mind, wondering if the whole thing was a cruel figment of his imagination.

If only.

The email was there at the top of his inbox.

How in the world was he supposed to respond to that? He had around 48 hours to figure it out. With that weight on his shoulders, he decided it was definitely time to schedule another appointment with Kristen.

Chapter 26
Healing Over Anger

" So, how can I help?"

Darius sighed, still trying to find the words. "Well, I don't know. My response keeps shifting, I've rewritten it at least ten times, and every time I pray about it, I want to make sure I don't react. I want to get this right, you know? I want her to feel validated. I'm trying to account for everything she's saying, and I'm hopeful because I hope she'll see that I get it, you know, that it's alright, and she'll open up—" He could see Kristen shaking her head on the other camera. "No, it won't?"

"No, not that it won't. It's more that you have an expectation already."

"I don't have any expectations," he said quickly. "I just want ... Well, I guess what I'm saying is, I'm prepared for her to react negatively or even neutrally. But I'm hoping for something better."

"But that's still an expectation."

Darius let out a long breath, feeling his old self trying to claw out and snap back. "Okay, I see that. But ... I feel like something has to happen. Right? I can't just not send it."

"Hold on. Slow down for a second."

"I just want to make sure I'm doing this right. I want to respond in the best way I can, that's all."

"And what does 'the right way' mean to you?" she asked, tilting her head ever so slightly.

Darius thought for a moment before speaking slowly. "Well, the 'right way' to me is about not reacting like I would've in the past. I want to use the tools we've been talking about so she feels validated. I can't just jump in with my own emotions. I have to show her I understand her first. I don't want to bypass her feelings and start problem-solving."

Kristen gave a small nod. "That sounds good. But what's the challenge?"

"The challenge is I don't want her to feel like I'm ignoring her. She pointed out those things, and I don't want her to think I'm brushing them off. So, I feel like I need to address every point she made, but I also don't want to be defensive. Should I validate her first and then go into each specific point, or just skip over it and focus on the bigger picture?"

"Well, you're looking at it from a very different lens now. You have to remember, Darius, her memories may not even be entirely accurate. But they are her feelings, and feelings don't always follow logic. Think of her accusations like sticky notes she's pulling off herself and giving to you. 'Here, take this. I don't want it anymore.' That's why your response matters. Not to defend yourself or correct her memories, but to help her begin to heal."

Darius's shoulders relaxed a little, as if the weight of her words clicked into place. "Yeah, I think that makes sense ... It's like she's sharing her whole life with me, everything she's been holding on to."

Kristen nodded. "Exactly. And that's where the challenge comes in. You've got to absorb those emotions before you respond. Don't just react to the things that upset you; recognize that she's been carrying these feelings for years, and that's why she 'snapped.'"

"I had no idea. I look back now, and I can see how much I hurt her. I didn't even understand the fear of rejection, the hopelessness she must have been feeling. And I can see where I sabotaged things with my own issues."

"You've been doing the work, Darius. We've talked about your self-worth, about recognizing that you are enough. You've come a long way in seeing where your own insecurities have played into this."

He nodded slowly, feeling the weight of his words. "Yeah, I used to feel broken, but now I don't. I know I have value. I have purpose now, and I can be the best version of myself. It's like ... I'm more present now. I'm not rushing through life anymore."

Kristen smiled. "That's powerful. It's not just about doing things for yourself, but for the people around you. Your kids, your wife, your friends, they'll feel the difference now that you're showing up, confident and humble."

"I want them to feel uplifted when they're around me," Darius added quietly. "I want to be able to give them the good stuff, the fruits of the spirit, rather than anger or sarcasm."

Kristen nodded, almost prideful in the smile she gave him. "And you're doing it. So, about this draft you're working on, do you want some feedback?"

He simply nodded.

"This is a shift in behavior, right? The first draft you sent me was ... chaotic. You were reacting. But now, you've slowed down. You're thinking it through. You've given yourself a huge gift by taking a step back. You're not rushing, and that's where growth happens. Just remember, this isn't about fixing things for her."

"So, I shouldn't try to fix it. I'm not supposed to explain everything away or question her feelings. I just need to validate her, and then share what I'm doing on my end."

Kristen smiled. "Exactly. It's not your job to fix her. You're validating her feelings, acknowledging what she's been carrying, and then moving forward with what you're doing to better yourself and your relationship."

Darius paused, processing her words. "That makes sense. I think I was worried that if I didn't address everything, I'd be ignoring her. But it's about validating her first, then showing her the changes I'm making."

"Right. You're leading by example, not by pointing out her faults. Show her the changes in you, without pressuring her to do the same."

"I think I get it now. I don't have to go through every point in her letter; I can just focus on the bigger picture and how I'm growing."

Kristen's smile was warm. "Exactly. You're learning to be present, and that's the key."

Darius chuckled. "I've been practicing patience, too. I used to be so impatient, but now I'm starting to see the value in waiting. I asked God to help me with patience, and He's been giving me what I asked for!"

"Patience is part of the process. Every challenge is an opportunity for growth. And look at how far you've come. Remember when we first met, Darius?"

He smiled almost sheepishly thinking back to their first meeting.

"All of these challenges, all of these tests, they're opportunities for you to rise above mediocrity. It's not going to be easy. It's not for the faint of heart. But you can look at it in your own way. And when

I heard your story, I was like, 'Wow, what a gift. Jessica is sharing her heart with you.' And you reacted and responded in all kinds of ways, which is completely understandable. You're human too. You're allowed to feel all of this. But now you're giving yourself the space to experience it fully, whether it's anger, sadness, resentment ... You know, you've probably gone through 30 or 40 different emotions in the last few days. And that's okay."

They took a moment to really appreciate the journey. She was right; there was still a long way to go, but he had come so far. "Yeah, it's been tough," he admitted, with a smile. "But I feel like I'm learning how to be patient with myself and others. I still have a long way to go, but I'm trying."

"And that's what matters. Remember, you don't have to have everything figured out right now. You're doing the work. You're growing. On that note, I want to recommend a book for you as a business owner that I think you would appreciate. It's called *The 15 Commitments of Conscious Leadership*."

"Thanks, Kristen. I'll definitely check it out and make a few more edits and then send you the next draft."

"Sounds good," she replied with a nod. "Keep working through it. I'm proud of you."

***

Darius sat for a moment, staring at the screen. The call with Kristen had brought him a lot of clarity, but there was still more he wanted to explore. Shifting in his chair and leaning over the desk, he opened up the Marriage Reset Program and began flipping through the modules focused on resentment and anger.

Overall, he felt he was doing well in this area. He firmly believed that resentment and anger only hurt the person holding them, not the one they were directed toward. He also felt the book *The Bait of*

Satan explained it perfectly from a spiritual standpoint. Evil used anger and resentment to add to chaos.

You can't live in the past.

If you stay stuck in the past, it will end the future.

The key was to move forward. If you were still angry or resentful, it meant you weren't fully committed, you weren't all in. When you could forgive yourself—and your partner—it was a sign of complete acceptance. It meant the things that once bothered you wouldn't even cross your mind anymore.

He thought about David Hawkins and his work on levels of consciousness. The book *Letting Go: The Pathway of Surrender* had come highly recommended by the men in the program, and Darius was eager to dive in. He had always struggled with negative flow loops—ruminating on the same negative thoughts without being able to shake them off. From everything he'd heard about Hawkins's work, he believed it could help him manage that. And it was clear from this module that he was right.

Darius listened to Josh Hudson, the program instructor, discuss in one module about how resentment and anger tend to attract more resentment and anger. Birds of a feather, right? When you focus on anger, you become angrier. It wasn't just about anger, either. Josh spoke of drug addicts he'd worked with—people living in shame and guilt, trapped in a level of consciousness so low it was practically nothingness. The rock bottom. The kind of place where people felt so lost they ended up overdosing. On the other end of the spectrum, though, were higher emotions—joy, peace, love, goodness—the fruits of the spirit, Darius thought.

The module encouraged him to continue progressing in his healing. One part of the program included a Hawaiian meditation for self-love and radical forgiveness, called Ho'oponopono. The name was a mouthful, and Darius chuckled to himself as he tried to pronounce it and failed more than once. He'd first tried it before coming to North Carolina, a 20-minute session that left him lying on the floor of his office, tears streaming down his face. It had been unlike anything he'd ever experienced.

The module continued, talking about the need to choose to forgive and let go. Josh reminded them that by the time a woman reached this point in a marriage, she'd often been contemplating divorce for two or three years. Darius now understood the dynamics. As he listened, he realized he had to stop blaming himself for the confusion in their relationship. He couldn't allow resentment, emotional withdrawal, or fear to take root. Those were the things that had brought them here. He believed he understood his failings, particularly over the last 3–4 years.

He had to change. He had to learn how to communicate differently, how to pause, validate, and connect with her feelings. He was getting better at it, using the techniques with his staff and others. But with Jessica? He was frustrated because he wasn't getting up to bat.

As he listened to other men in the program share their wins and losses, he often felt a twinge of jealousy. How could he be sure of his progress when he wasn't even able to have a conversation with his wife? Now she had shared so much, things from years ago—resentments he hadn't even realized were there. The email from Hell ... The psych eval ... Things didn't look even slightly promising as she seemed intent on only blaming Darius for their challenges. But he knew he had to focus on what he could control.

The video suggested an exercise to help reframe thoughts. Darius wrote down his frustration: *Jessica gives more emotion and energy to everyone else but me.* As he followed the steps of the exercise, he began to see things differently. Was this thought true? No, not really. Was he certain of it? Probably not. He realized how many times he hadn't acknowledged her struggles—her ADHD, her people-pleasing tendencies, and how she feared letting others down. At that moment, he was hit with a painful realization. She wasn't neglecting him because she didn't care; maybe she was simply overwhelmed.

He thought about the way he had reacted in the past—making unhelpful comments, getting frustrated. That had only pushed them further apart. But what would he have done without that thought? He realized that if he could stop the negative loop, things might change. With more reflection, Darius saw where he had failed: I should have been more empathetic, more loving, more focused on her needs instead of my own.

Tears welled up in his eyes. *I am such a pussy*, he thought. The exercise had hit him hard, but it was powerful. He was starting to understand things he had missed for years. As he returned to the video, Josh spoke about the prefrontal cortex, explaining how monks, with their deep meditations, had brainwave patterns of coherence and clarity. Just one week of doing the exercises in the program could help Darius achieve the same level of focus.

Josh emphasized that true forgiveness meant removing all resentment and negative energy. It was about self-love and radical forgiveness. This was the key to moving forward. The video suggested incorporating these exercises into a daily practice, something some men had done regularly for an entire year.

The message was clear: if you wanted to reach your potential, you couldn't remain the person you had been. What had gotten you here—those patterns of behavior—wouldn't get you to where you needed to be. You couldn't be like a buoy in the ocean, bobbing up and down in the swell. You had to get yourself grounded. Only then could you become a safe haven for the love you wanted to offer.

Darius reflected on the last part of the video: "You must look at everything that has happened like it's a gift." His past weakness had brought him to this moment of awakening and as painful as it had been, it was a gift. Jessica had shared her truth, which may or may not be accurate, but at least now he knew what was real for her. And it was up to him to be honest with himself about how he had failed in their relationship.

It wasn't about saving his marriage anymore—it was about changing himself. He thought about the hateful-sounding email he'd received. A lot of it wasn't fair, but surprisingly, he wasn't angry with her. For the first time in his life, he realized he could love her unconditionally, or at least move toward that.

He started the Hawaiian healing prayer, Ho'oponopono, taking deep breaths as the soothing music filled the room. "I love you. I'm sorry. Please forgive me. Thank you." The words felt powerful as he repeated them. Each time he did this exercise, he continued to release the pain and negative thoughts that had bound him. Looking back on everything that had led him to this point and realized that this journey, painful as it was, *was* changing him.

As the meditation ended, Darius lay there, tears streaming down his face, again. He felt lighter, as though something deep inside him had shifted. This is working, he thought. He wasn't the same man who had started this journey. No matter what happened, he knew he would be grateful for this experience. Because he would never go back to being blind to his own behaviors or feeling unworthy. He would never again fail to show up for the people he loved.

Chapter 27
How Many Demons Are There?

T he Ahearns were gone for eight days while Darius was there, including over the 4th of July weekend. It still amazed Darius that he had to go to D.C. to the embassy to get a Visa for his trip to Liberia—what were the odds he would end up supporting a clinic in one of two countries in Africa that you had to get a visa to visit? Crazy. He would have flown to D.C., but because of the decision to come to North Carolina, he was only about a 5-hour drive away, so he decided to spend that weekend in D.C., getting his Visa and enjoying the festivities since he had never visited the capital for the 4th.

Halfway through the drive, thoughts of the past returned to his mind. The night before, he had made a list of regrets during their marriage and he had been planning on sending it to Jessica, but his counselor had told him that was a bad idea. He ultimately agreed and didn't send it, but it did cause old memories and thoughts to resurface. The Bible said that if we acknowledged our sins and repented, we would be forgiven. That morning's Scripture reading was on repentance and forgiveness, including Acts 3:19: *"Therefore repent and turn back, so that your sins may be blotted out,"* out and 1 John 1:9: *"If we confess our sins, he is faithful and just, so that he will forgive us our sins and will cleanse us from all unrighteousness."* He also read in Matthew 5:28 that if a man looks at a woman with lustful intent, he has already committed adultery in his heart. It also stated clearly that if we didn't forgive others, God wouldn't forgive us. It was like it was guiding him in a direction to seek forgiveness for his past, and for those in his past.

As he drove, he was suddenly overcome with emotion and pulled over into a rest area.

While he had never physically committed adultery and had been faithful in his marriage, he had certainly looked lustfully at other women. It was the strangest thing to Darius, but, in that rest area, he felt an incredible and overwhelming urge to pray. For thirty minutes, Darius sat there in tears and repented for any past scenario he could think of where he had looked at a woman inappropriately or thought about them physically. He prayed God would show him any other sins he was unaware of and needed to repent for. Then he thought about any grievance he had or anyone who had ever wronged him or been unkind to him. Darius forgave them out loud and prayed a prayer of blessing for each person.

As he finished, he was amazed by the most incredible sense of peace that he felt. He smiled, shaking his head as he got back onto the interstate.

D.C. was packed as he got into the city with locals and tons of tourists here for the independence celebration. Darius made his way to the embassy, found a place to park, and went inside. It was smaller than he had imagined, and he didn't have to wait very long before being helped.

"Do you have your passport and vaccination documents?" The woman asked.

"Yes," Darius smiled, handing them over.

After examining the documents, she asked for his Visa application, which he happily handed over. She went in back for a few minutes and then came back out. After taking his cashier's check for the fee, she told him to come back in a few hours to pick up his Visa.

Darius made his way to an outdoor café for lunch and to catch up on some work. Then when the hour was up, he returned to the embassy and picked up his Visa. After that, he headed downtown to the Marriott he had booked, checked in, and walked to the National Mall. It was getting dark, but there were still people everywhere.

It was a beautiful night as he walked between the monuments and found a place on the grass near the Washington Monument. The fireworks display started an hour later and it was magnificent. Darius thought about the freedoms they had and how grateful he was to those who defended their freedoms.

As it ended, he got up and walked back toward his hotel, thinking he might find a place to grab a beer. But as he came to the first hotel on a corner, there was a commotion going on.

A crowd of people stood around watching two paramedics try to get a very large woman onto an ambulance stretcher. She was in great distress and appeared to be having severe seizures; her face contorting in agony.

Darius stood just 10 feet away and watched as they tried to secure her flailing arms and help her on the stretcher, when he suddenly had the most ominous feeling. It was the feeling he had when he had staked out his home, when the suicidal thoughts had entered his mind before, and one late night in his office ... The hairs stood up on his arms and he felt a dark presence! Evil ... The demonic! He put his hand on the rosary under his shirt and started to pray Ephesians and the words he had memorized to exorcise an unclean spirit directing them at the patient.

Finally, they got her strapped on the stretcher and started moving toward the back of the ambulance. Darius continued to pray and watch as they put her into the ambulance with the two paramedics struggling against the woman's arms as her body continued contorting in different directions. As he finished the prayers, the ambulance doors shut.

He stood there looking at the ambulance; the menacing feeling was suddenly gone. Then, no more than a minute later, the most peculiar thing happened.

Suddenly, the woman's head popped up into view from the back window of the ambulance. She was slowly taking off her oxygen mask and was no longer thrashing about. Darius could barely see both paramedics who had been struggling with her stop what they were doing. The lady was talking with them seemingly disoriented but no longer in distress. After a few minutes the back doors opened back up with the patient sitting calmly talking to the paramedic.

Darius slowly shook his head. His first thought was he was losing his mind and then he told himself to stop. It was incredible. He turned his back and headed back to his hotel and grabbed a small bottle of wine from the hotel store.

Sitting in his room with a glass of wine, he thought about the demonic. It was the fifth time since coming back from Mexico that he had prayed for deliverance or believed he was exorcising an evil spirit. All five times, he had felt a cold, dark, and evil presence, and all five times after praying—through the prayers that Larissa had given him—the feeling and fear he felt had immediately left.

Darius had been starting to collect Scripture on his phone since this seemingly insane journey started after talking to Larissa. He opened the note on his phone and pulled up Scripture.

Psalms 106:35-38: *"but they mingled with the nations and learned their works, and served their idols, which became a snare to them. They even sacrificed their sons and daughters to the demons, and they poured out innocent blood, the blood of their sons and daughters, whom they sacrificed to the idols of Canaan, and so the land was defiled with the blood."*

Colossians 1:16: *"because all things in the heavens and on the earth were created by him, things visible and things invisible, whether thrones or dominions or rulers or powers, all things were created through him and for him."*

He finished his second glass of wine and thought about those verses and again about Ephesians. Principalities, cosmic forces in this current darkness, spirits of evil in the heavenly realms. What in the world, Darius thought. All of those things ... They were demons? Unclean spirits, evil spirits, demons were all the same thing, but ... How many demons did Satan have? Were there as many demons as there were angels?

The Bible only talked about three angels by name that Darius could think of: Michael, Gabriel, and Satan. However, there were many references in the Bible to angelic, to the armies of God, to His angels, and to the messengers. It talked about a lot of angels, but were there really that many demons for them to combat? It was mind-blowing.

Darius looked at the wine bottle and decided he was done.

His decision earlier in the year to stop drinking had been a smart one and he had physically felt a lot better. After Jessica's decision, he had continued to stay away from liquor but would have a beer or a glass of wine here and there. But tonight, the more he went down this rabbit hole, the more he realized being intoxicated was a really bad idea. He scrolled back to the top of the note in his phone where he was keeping his newest verses, the ones he wanted to memorize and understand. There he had copied a paragraph from the last two pages of Steve's book, *Prayers Satan Hates*

"I hear stories from others (and had other experiences myself" that make me realize how active Satan is in his efforts to lead us away from God, and focus on people at strategic moments in their lives to thwart the good they will do. By that I don't mean Satan knows the future, because only God knows every detail of our future. I do think Satan and his forces work diligently to stop the plans of God in people's life as their direction begins to unfold, making it more and more obvious that the light of the Kingdom of God is shining through those individuals. When the light gets brighter, Satan works to put it out. Quickly and thoroughly. How about you? Is your light shining brighter for God? If so, Satan is noticing you, so you will become more and more of a target. But don't worry, he that is in us (God's Holy Spirit) is greater than he that is in the world (Satan)."

Reading that had hit Darius deeply—it was why he had copied it into his phone.

He rubbed his hands over his face, then stared out the window at the D.C. skyline and his stomach dropped. For the first time, he was starting to understand. I shouldn't be removing demons from anyone who doesn't want them removed, he suddenly thought. Dear Lord ... What in the world is going on? I am nobody. My family history is a mess. What in the world is going on?

Darius thought about how he had lived his life before, giving so little to God and worried about so many things that didn't matter. He had been moving toward God more and more the last eight years but it had been accelerating the past four. Now he felt sad thinking about what God must have been thinking all those years, waiting on Darius to wake up. What had God wanted from him ... for him all this time? Darius knew it was so much more than he had been doing.

Was giving the amount of money he had been giving, what he wanted to give in the future, and starting a charity enough to become a target for the Father of Lies? How could that be?

It was nothing in the grand scheme of things; a speck of sand on the beach. Darius got in bed, prayed, and tried to go to sleep. He was going to get up early for the drive back to North Carolina.

Chapter 28
Breathing With Ben

D arius called Sully, a dear friend and one of the most faithful men he had ever met, and after sharing the details of the email, Sully only grunted.

"Well, it doesn't sound like she left much to the imagination. But like Hemphill's work showed you, Satan doesn't like where you have been headed and he always goes after the weakest links to get at us."

"What do you mean?" Darius asked.

"Jessica, of course," He said rather bluntly. "Satan is going after her. It's easier to go after her through the secular world and in the chaos of her office versus coming directly at you. The charitable contributions are growing and your desire to start a charity ... The Evil One definitely wants to extinguish that, bro."

Darius sat reflecting. "Yeah, I guess that makes sense."

"Look man, we have to understand that everything in the spiritual world is way ahead of the physical. Most people don't understand that and the demonic is attacking us in advance in the spiritual realm."

"I don't think I had any understanding of that any more than I realized what was real about evil or the truth of the demonic all throughout the Bible. I read Hemphill's book, *In Search Of The Real Heaven*. It talks about the seven spiritual realms and prophecy. I had no idea that 40–50% of the gospels are prophecies. I had forgotten about how remarkable the prophecy of the Bible is and how unlikely from an odds standpoint."

Sully nodded. "Yeah, man, I mean if you understand prophecy alone, it takes 100 times more faith to be a non-believer!"

They laughed together.

"Yeah, Darius, when you understand the spiritual realms, you have to understand the demonic has been working on your house and family for some time. It didn't just happen overnight, just like that trauma therapist lady told you."

Darius told him about the rumors of the affair along with the psych eval request and Sully moaned out loud. "Oh Lord, Satan would certainly love to have that as a prize! But, dude, you should totally do the psych evaluation ASAP."

Darius was surprised. "Are you serious? That's ridiculous, man!"

"Of course it is!" Sully laughed. "She is the one that could use one based on her behavior, but that's how this stuff works. The one doing something inappropriate accuses the other. They project what they are doing, man, so if she is having an affair, which sounds likely, she is already positioning against you legally. But who cares?! You would pass that evaluation with flying colors. Plus, God would be smiling as you explained the factual Scripture around using stakes with Scripture to bless the house."

Darius was silent for a moment. "I hadn't thought of it that way, but you are right. I told them I'd be happy to do it if she was. I will just keep praying the affair isn't true. What a mess ... Man, I have just made so many mistakes in the business, in my marriage. I hired so badly—"

"Wow, man," Sully interrupted him. "Every time I talk to you, you are beating yourself up. Stop it. the people you hired, you know what ... maybe you hired badly and maybe you hired them so God could allow you plant seeds in them while teaching you something? Your marriage. It takes two and it's not easy but you are loyal, a provider, a hard worker, and while it's admirable you are admitting your mistakes let's not forget who is fighting and who's running. I don't want to hear you beating yourself up anymore. All right?"

Darius smiled and nodded. "Okay, man. Yes, I just want to own my part, lean into God and change and grow where I need to. Thank you for the direction and your prayers."

"Well brother, you know you're the first on the list here with the prayer warriors. The Fathers are always asking about you and wanting me to send you goodies and more rosaries."

"I appreciate it and you. If you get a chance, check out this book I just finished called *The Language of God*. The author, this guy Francis Collins, was an atheist who was the head of the Human Genome Project, a PhD that became a Christian. It's remarkable!"

"I am swamped as always but I'll try to check it out. Stay strong and keep working," Sully said.

After finishing the call with Sully and getting in the car, Darius was filled with excitement as he drove to pick up his youngest son from the airport. It had been a tough year, but the prospect of spending a week together in North Carolina, away from the distractions of everyday life, was something both of them needed. His son had asked to visit the Ahearns' horse ranch after finding out his dad had headed there.

When Darius saw his son walk out of the airport terminal, he felt a surge of happiness. They shared a warm hug, and as they made their way back to the ranch, they chatted about everything and nothing.

"How's everything been going?" His son asked.

"It's good. Just business," Darius replied with a smile. "I'm enjoying the horses and the peace and quiet. And I'm still working on myself."

His son glanced over, curious. "What do you mean?"

"Well," Darius explained, "I'm in this new marriage program. I've been doing counseling—group therapy three times a week with other men, one-on-one sessions, reading, studying, really diving deep into some stuff."

"Like what?"

"How to communicate better, listen more effectively, process old trauma, and deal with some unhealthy habits. I thought maybe I could share some of what I've learned with you while you're here."

"Oh?" His son raised an eyebrow, intrigued.

Darius smiled. "Look, I love you, but you've got some of my, well ... let's say, 'less ideal traits.' Like you tend to bottle things up and get angry quickly when things don't go your way."

His son laughed a little, nodding. "Fair enough."

"So, here's what I'm thinking," Darius continued. "While you're here, I'd love for us to wake up early together, spend some time in Scripture and meditation, and I can show you a few of these breathing exercises and communication techniques I've been working on. Sound good?"

"Yeah, sounds good."

***

That evening, after a delicious meal prepared by Hannah, they gathered around the table with everyone, laughter and playful banter filling the room. The stakes had arrived and Brett and Darius made the plans to bless the property later in the week. After dinner, they went outside to see the horses, eventually winding down for the night. And after that, Darius and his son went up to get ready for bed.

"Okay. Let me walk you through these," Darius said as they entered one of the spare rooms. He cleared a space on the floor and set up his phone so they could follow along with the different tutorials. "This first one is called Ujjayi Breathing. You breathe with your mouth closed, pressing your lips together."

"So you just breathe through your nose?"

Darius laughed. "Not quite. You breathe against your closed lips. I'll try to show you."

He did his best to mimic the video and his son tried his best to mimic him, bursting out laughing after only a few moments.

"I don't think I'm doing it right, Dad."

"Yeah, it took me a bit, too," Darius chuckled, setting up the video for the next technique. "Let's keep going. This next one is a lung expander. Take a deep breath, then take a few quick sips of air to really fill up your lungs and hold for seven seconds."

After ten repetitions, they moved onto another technique called the Breath of Fire, panting with closed mouths, and another called Ego Eradicator, which involved holding their arms straight up and breathing rapidly. The video was demonstrated by Russell Brand who shared the name and laughed when he commented, "And who needs it more than me!"

Darius and his son laughed out loud.

The final exercise was the Wim Hof breathing technique.

"This one is my favorite," Darius said, switching the video over. "It's a powerful method created by this guy from Poland, the 'Iceman.'"

His son laughed, "Why do they call him that?"

"He's famous for his ability to withstand extreme cold. But for now, we'll stick to the breathing."

They lay down, taking 30 deep breaths in a circular fashion without pause, then holding their breath for a minute and a half and repeating the cycle twice. By the end, they were both relaxed, basking in a sense of calm.

"Wow," his son whispered. "That was ... awesome."

Darius smiled. "Glad you enjoyed it. This is my favorite, too, and you know, the more you do these types of embodiment exercises, you're strengthening your constitution. You're strengthening your emotional fortitude so that when things happen, you remain in your positive masculine frame, instead of moving into negative emotions and negative masculine traits."

"I don't really understand that bit."

"Yeah, well, that comes with the practice, too," Darius chuckled.

***

The next morning, they rose early to study Scripture, do breathing exercises, meditate, and work out together. Then, after a hearty breakfast, they spent some time with the horses. Later, Darius turned to his son and said, "I want to show you something I've been learning, a communication technique. Watch this video with me."

They watched a clip of Josh Hudson that explained a process of communication: pausing, validating the other person's feelings, acknowledging emotions, and responding with empathy. Darius looked over at his son. "Do you see how this could help with Mom, or even with friends or coaches?"

His son, Ben, stared at him, a little confused.

"Alright," Darius continued, "Mom asks you to do something. What do you usually do?"

Ben smiled, but didn't answer.

"You typically react," Darius said, "and start running your mouth. Then what happens?"

"She gets mad," Ben muttered. "Yells at me ... says stuff."

"Yeah, and you make everything worse. It's not really respectful, is it?"

Ben shrugged.

"Let's say your coach tells you to do something, or your girlfriend. By working on this skill set, you could really improve your communication, and earn people's respect."

Ben nodded but remained silent.

"Let's do a roleplay," Darius said. "I'll be you."

Ben raised an eyebrow. "Okay," he said, a smile tugging at the corner of his mouth.

"Say to me, 'I told you that you couldn't go unless you cleaned your room!'"

Ben grinned, then exaggerated his voice to sound like a high-pitched woman. "I told you that you couldn't go anywhere unless you cleaned your room!"

Darius laughed. "Nice voice." He waited a beat before continuing. "Pause. So you're frustrated because I didn't clean my room like I was supposed to?"

Ben hesitated but nodded. "Yeah."

"You feel that I don't respect you because I didn't do what I was supposed to do?"

Ben looked at him, eyes wide. "What am I supposed to do or say?"

They both laughed.

"Just say, 'That's right,'" Darius coached.

"That's right," Ben repeated, still laughing.

"I'm sorry," Darius said. "Thank you for explaining that to me. I'm sorry I didn't do it, and I'll do better. What do you need me to do?"

Ben blinked, a little thrown off. He didn't answer immediately.

"You get the idea?" Darius asked.

Ben paused, then nodded slowly. "Yeah, I think so."

"Okay," Darius said, shifting gears. "Let's do another one. Let's pretend it's your girlfriend." He smiled at his son. "I'll ask you."

"Alright," Ben said, trying to stifle his amusement.

Darius cleared his throat and adopted a serious tone. "You know, it really ticks me off when you tell me you're going to be here at 5:00 and then you're late."

Ben just stared at him.

"You're mad at me because I'm late," Darius prompted.

Ben squinted. "Yeah."

"And you feel...?" Darius trailed off, pushing his son to dig deeper.

"I don't know, Dad," Ben said, shrugging.

"I know, son," Darius said softly. "This part is the hardest, really understanding and connecting with the feeling. But I'm telling you, if you work at it, you'll get better and better. I know I'm starting to get more comfortable with it."

He paused, considering. "Alright, here's how I would handle it. Ask me again."

Ben nodded, taking a deep breath. "It really upsets me that you're late."

Darius paused, mirroring the situation. "So, you're upset because I wasn't here at 5 like I said I would be?"

"Yes," Ben said, more emphatically this time, with a smile.

"You feel like I don't really care about you because I didn't follow through when I said I'd be here?"

Ben blinked, surprised.

Darius smiled, reaching out to place a hand on his son's shoulder. "Thank you for being vulnerable and sharing that with me. I do care about you. And I'm sorry I didn't manage my time better. What do you need from me?"

Ben smacked Darius lightly on the shoulder. "Nothing."

Darius chuckled. "You can use these tools in just about any situation. But I'm telling you, if I had had this skill set when your Mom and I were in conflict, I bet 70 to 80% of the issues could've been avoided."

Ben, still grinning, nodded thoughtfully. "I talked to her last night."

"Oh yeah?" Darius raised an eyebrow. "What did she say?"

"I told her what you have been teaching me," Ben grinned. "She was surprised."

"There you go," Darius said, chuckling.

"She thought it was positive," Ben added, a little proud.

"Well, there you go," Darius said. "Alright, I need to get ready for some business meetings, so hang out, do whatever. Tonight, we'll head into town for dinner, okay?"

They hugged, and Darius pulled back. "I love you, son."

"I love you, Dad," Ben replied.

Chapter 29
Blessing the Land

J essica's letter had pushed him into a brief tailspin. He found solace—or at least distraction—in their wine fridge, drinking through a bottle and a half on the first night and finishing another bottle the next. He wasn't proud of it, but he reminded himself he was human. The horses wouldn't tattle.

Still, he wasn't going to let this setback derail him. Darius was learning that it wasn't about being right; it was about being kind to her, and to himself.

With each step he took, Darius felt a growing sense of doubt. He questioned whether he had gotten it all wrong—Jessica's actions and the things she said in her letter left him grappling with disbelief. It was hard to shake the feeling that there might have been someone else involved or, more troubling, that it just didn't matter what he did because, in her mind, she had already decided that it was over. She was just now getting around to telling him.

But as blind as he had been to everything, his time in North Carolina had reaped great reward. The time he had spent with his son was incredible, and the bond they were forming was beautiful to witness. They had spent a day helping with the horses and children who came to ride them. The arena was filled with smiles and laughter, and Darius felt immense pride watching his son interact so kindly with the participants. He snapped a few photos and sent them to his wife—his only communication with her since she had sent the letter outlining his deficiencies. He thought it might be a kind gesture, and she thanked him for it.

One weekend, the two of them visited friends in Raleigh and spent the day with paintball guns, running through the woods and laughing as they fired shots at each other. After they finished, he went to the car to get some things and change clothes before dinner. It was then that he received a text from Jessica about the bills and their financial situation.

The business hadn't made money in six months, and the large tax bill was looming over them. He responded, acknowledging that he wasn't sure about the specifics of one bill, but that their financial situation was indeed tight. He had explained to her multiple times that it wasn't good and why they couldn't afford for him to get an apartment. They had a huge tax bill the previous year but Darius had been able to put money aside to cover it. With this year's difficulties, that wasn't the case for this tax burden.

Her response came quickly, a reminder that he needed to focus on work. Maybe he was spending too much time on social media, doing podcasts and activities that didn't generate income. He was good at recruiting and making money and that was what he should be focused on.

Darius read the message, shaking his head. *What a b—*, he thought. *It's like she's living in an alternate universe.* The irony wasn't lost on him. He thought about how he could respond, then he smiled thinking about responding versus reacting.

"Baby, I love you and am grateful for your recognition of my talents and your kind direction and insights. I can assure you, even now, I am more loyal and motivated to provide for you financially than ever before!"

He said it out loud in a sincere, kind, and loving voice.

He couldn't help but laugh out loud, appreciating the humor in the moment. It had been so absurd that he almost sent it just for the reaction it would get.

But, instead, he chose not to respond at all. Sometimes, silence spoke louder than words. It was a small victory that he was laughing. Smiling at the ridiculous thought, he put his phone away and rejoined his son, getting changed for the cinema and for dinner.

As the movie finished and the night wound down, they sat having pizza at a local brewery, and over a beer, Darius couldn't help but think that his wife would have liked this place, a spot that would have felt like home if they were all together. His son was certainly enjoying it, and it was nice to once again spend that time with him.

Their final day before heading back to Indiana was just as eventful as the previous, and that night, Hannah made a delicious meal, complete with dessert, and they sat outside, visiting and savoring the moment. The day before, they had gone to church and then walked the entire acreage of the ranch. The stakes from Hemphill's company Active Faith had come in and as they walked, they placed 16 stakes in all to bless the land with the kids joining them. At each stake, they took turns praying and blessing them individually. At the last stake, Darius blessed the entire property and all stakes together.

"Father, we give this land to you," Darius prayed. "Make it a safe haven for your Word, your people and your work. Protect it from anything that isn't from you and remove any evil that may be hidden here. Cover this property with the blood of Jesus and bless it as we dedicate it to you. We give you our talents, our assets, and our home. Lead us and guide us according to your will."

Brett and Hannah looked at each other, moved. "That was really beautiful," Hannah said, looking out over the property with a peaceful expression. Brett added, "It's so interesting, thinking back to when we had that Bible study here. The charity was thriving then." He paused. "We never should have stopped it. This past year has been strange."

"I think it's fair to say that evil doesn't want you to succeed, especially with the good work you're doing. Start it back up!" Darius said. "God can change things just as quickly and I pray that he does that for you and for the charity. You're doing amazing work."

They embraced, shared a final moment of gratitude, and Darius reflected on the time spent in North Carolina. It had been well needed, and he felt truly grateful for these friends of nearly 30 years. Time didn't matter; each time they met, it felt like no time had passed at all. Brett had even told Jacob, his youngest son, no matter how long it had been, it was as if they'd seen each other just yesterday. Those were rare friendships, and Darius felt blessed the same as Brett.

As they packed up the car, Darius and his son said their goodbyes, wishing their friends well. The drive back to Indiana would be long, but Darius was curious about what would come next. In a few weeks, he'd be heading to Africa—another chapter of his story that, despite the uncertainty, he was excited to see unfold.

Chapter 30
Letting Go & Dark Memories

Darius walked into Larissa's office, his mind a whirlwind of emotions. Tumultuous was the word that popped into his head to really describe it all. *There's one for Scrabble*, he thought with a faint smile.

Larissa greeted him with a warm smile. "How are you?"

He laughed. "The Twilight Zone, Larissa. The Twilight Zone."

She gave him a knowing look, shaking her head as he sank onto the couch, visibly stressed. "How are you, *really*?" She pressed.

"Well, pretty good for a guy who apparently needs a psych evaluation," he quipped with a weak smile.

She shook her head again, her expression serious. "Darius, I don't know what to tell you. After talking to her, my perspective is ... she's just looking for a reason to get divorced."

Darius sat silently, processing her words, then let out a long breath. "Yeah, well, as soon as her favorite counselor brought up a psych evaluation, I knew there probably wasn't going to be a happy ending to this."

"Darius, listen," Lindsay said earnestly, "You've done an amazing job. I've never seen anyone fight for their marriage like you have. But there's something else going on here."

He leaned forward. "What happened when you talked to her?"

"She wasn't interested in hearing anything I had to say. It was almost like she was trying to get me to agree that you needed this evaluation. I tried to explain to her that everything you've done was out of love, that you read the book, followed its guidance, and acted to protect your family. But ... she wasn't open to it. She was just trying to talk me into agreeing with her."

Darius clenched his jaw. "Yeah, I get it," he said softly.

"Just keep moving forward, Darius. You're doing the best you can. Keep praying. But you have to accept that some things might be out of your control."

He nodded. "I understand. So much is happening that I can't control."

They talked briefly about his business. Darius explained his vision to grow it for the sake of charity, only for Larissa to ask a piercing question: "What if the business goes away? What if everything about it disappears?"

Darius froze, then looked at her, puzzled. "Well, it's His business. Every time I've tried to take control, it hasn't gone well," he admitted. "I thought I was making progress spiritually, but now, after everything that has happened and what I am learning, it feels like I was a drunken sloth crawling forward instead of on a spiritual walk." Darius held up his fingers and made a dramatic motion with them as he emphasized spiritual walk.

Larissa laughed, and he joined in.

"I mean, if it all goes away, it all goes away. None of it matters. I just want to use the gifts God's given me to help people. But looking back, I see how much I focused on building assets and planning for retirement without asking God what He wanted. I was doing it from a secular perspective of wealth."

Larissa nodded. "And what if it does all go away?"

"Maybe that's okay," Darius said after a pause. "Jōb lost everything and look what happened there. I pray that prayer every day for myself, and all the men's marriages in the MRP, and for our marriage. What also amazes me, even as unkind as she is about ... well everything, and even if she is having an affair, I am willing to forgive her and work through it.

Darius paused.

"I knew right away when I got on the counseling call with Sharon, it didn't feel right. After she told me Jessica wanted me to take a psych evaluation, as we were getting off the call, she said I was doing voodoo."

"Voodoo?" Larissa echoed.

"Yeah, apparently, because of the stakes, they think I'm performing some kind of voodoo on the house," Darius said, shaking his head in disbelief. "I mean, that's crazy. It's like she thinks I'm cutting up chickens and splattering blood on the walls."

Larissa smirked but gave him a reassuring look. "Darius, you're not going to let this bother you, are you?"

"I mean, it *is* pretty crazy," he replied.

"Let me remind you of something," Larissa began. "They accused Jesus of casting out demons by the power of the devil, called him Beelzebub. They said he was crazy, practicing witchcraft. And he was the Son of God."

"Yes," Darius nodded slowly. "That's true."

"Well then," she continued, "What does that say about your situation?"

He shrugged.

"It means you're blessing your land, acting out of love for your family, and staying grounded in Scripture. If anything, this just means you're on the right track. I'd take it as a 'red badge of courage.'"

Darius sighed, then smiled. "Yeah, I see what you mean. Thanks for saying that."

Larissa patted his shoulder. "Alright. Let's focus on you. What do you want to work on today?"

Darius leaned back thoughtfully. "Honestly, there's so much," he admitted. "My counselor, Kristen, has been helping me realize just how unhealthy some of my relationships have been ... to my mom, and an unhealthy attachment to Jessica. I've started reading David Hawkins's *Letting Go*, and some of the guys in the marriage group recommended *The Masculine in Relationship*. I feel like I'm learning for the first time what it means to understand polarity and healthy relationships. It's overwhelming, but I'm grateful for the chance to grow."

"That's fantastic, Darius," Larissa said. "What else has been going on?"

He hesitated. "Well, obviously there's the whole psych evaluation thing, and then there's the hate mail ... I just ... I don't think this is going to end well. I've been praying, but I'm pretty sure she's in a relationship with another woman that she works with."

"What makes you think that?"

"There's a lot of talk around town," he said, sighing. "It's come from multiple places about her and her coworker and my intuition keeps nagging at me. Plus, so many things I missed because of the stress of the business issues, anxiety ... As I am working on myself through MRP and with you, cleaning out my issues, I see many things clearly that I missed before."

"Like what?" Larissa asked.

"Things she said, how she acted, certain behaviors," Darius started. "A month before this all started, she was telling me she needed to get away from her business partner and the people in that office. It was not healthy, they were a bad influence, and there were several affairs going on. Then she told me about one of the employees, Ash, who was having an affair with a married woman. We discussed options for her to leave. I was happy about it because I had told her three years previously that it was a mistake to go into business with her partner."

Larissa nodded slowly. "I know your wife and her partner are going through a dissolution of their business but I am not sure I understand."

Darius stared at Larissa. "That entire conversation with Jessica ... She was very quiet and withdrawn. Also, I know that she was spending a lot of time around Ash after hours. Multiple people told me." He paused. "What I completely missed about Jessica's behavior and the way she was talking ... It was shame, Larissa. The affair she was describing was her own. I am almost certain now, though I am still praying that I am wrong."

I've been praying, and I'll keep praying, but ... I don't think this is something I can fix. Unless God softens her heart, it feels like this is the end of the road."

Larissa nodded sympathetically. "You're doing everything you can. Just keep praying."

"I am," Darius said. "And I've been working on setting boundaries, especially with my mom. I don't want to be the person I used to be. When she started saying unkind things about me the other day, I told her I wouldn't accept that and got off the phone. Of course, she called me sensitive. But I stayed calm, said goodbye, and hung up."

"Good for you, Darius," Larissa said. "You're honoring yourself, and that's a big step."

"Yeah, I just keep thinking about what the Bible says," Darius said. "'If you have faith, you can tell a mountain to move into the water, and it will be done. But when you pray, fix your grudges with others so your Father will hear your prayers.' I don't want to hold any grudges against my Mom or Jessica, even if they've been ... Let's just say unkind."

Larissa chuckled. "I get what you mean."

"I've been thinking about it a lot," Darius continued. "I'm grateful for the growth I've experienced, even though it's been painful. I wish things could be different, but I'm starting to accept that I can't control their choices. All I can do is keep showing up as the best version of myself."

Larissa nodded. "That's all you can do. Let's start the process. I think we should focus on your heart walls again, especially your relationships with your Mom and Jessica."

Darius smiled wryly. "Alright, hit me."

They both laughed, and Larissa began. As she worked, memories and emotions surfaced, each tied to specific points in Darius's life: lack of control and low self-esteem at age 5; blaming, dread, fear, and anger at age 5; shock, unworthiness, and worthlessness at age 8; betrayal and love unreceived at age 2; frustration and being taken for granted at age 12; absorbed horror from his mother at age 5.

"Wow," Darius said, shaking his head. "That's a lot."

"It really is," Larissa said. "There was obviously so much going on when you were younger."

She guided him through some affirmations:

I am free to be at peace with my mom. I am free to show myself grace and forgiveness. I can accept grace. I am free to set Godly boundaries and not accept certain behaviors. I am free to feel secure, wanted, and loved. I am free to be hopeful for a loving relationship in the future.

Darius repeated each statement, nodding slowly as the words sank in.

Larissa continued:

I am free to have unconditional love and to feel worthy of love. I am free to have healthy relationships with my mom, Jessica, or someone God has planned for me in the future. I am free to be loved and to give love. And I am free to move forward when the time is right.

Darius let out a deep sigh, his shoulders relaxing. "Wow. I feel good. I just want to do what's right, but the situation with my Mom is still so confusing."

Larissa frowned thoughtfully, tilting her head as she often did. "Darius, sometimes walking away is the healthiest choice. The Bible shows us that setting boundaries is okay. You're honoring your relationships by wanting healthy relationships, but you're also allowed to protect yourself from harm."

Darius nodded slowly. "I don't want to have grudges or anger, but I'm not going to let myself be treated like that anymore. I don't want to react in unhealthy ways. I've done that before, and it doesn't help anyone."

"You're making progress," Larissa said. "There's a lot of trauma you're working through, and that's okay. You're allowed to choose relationships that bring healing and growth."

Darius gave her a small smile. "Thanks, Larissa. I just want to handle this the right way."

"And you are," she said gently. "Keep trusting God and giving yourself grace. You're on the right path."

***

The next morning after their meeting, Darius awoke to the sound of his alarm—something that rarely happened anymore. But it didn't come as a complete surprise as he always felt drained after his sessions with Larissa.

Getting ready and heading out, he sat on the deck and read his Scripture and then began his meditation. In the silence, in the peace of the moment, he suddenly started to feel awful. It came in flash memories that were buried deep and were now resurfacing in his mind.

He was 8. He was with his babysitter and she had molested him multiple times. Together in his room. Together in his bed. He was confused. Scared. Frustrated. Touched.

Oh my God, Darius thought, a rush of emotions overcoming him as if the memories had occurred only yesterday. His heart stopped for a moment as another wave hit him, bringing back something he had long buried.

And then he realized it wasn't the first time something like this had happened. As he tried to recall the shadows of his early childhood, a fog settled over him. He could barely remember much from those early years, but there was a sense of something dark—a shadowy figure of a man. He didn't know who it was but he sensed he was around four years old.

This memory was different. Fainter, murkier, yet it left him violated. shamed. It was painful, confusing, and deeply unsettling. The memory wasn't clear, just the impression of it. Tears began streaming down his face as the realization sank in.

God help me.

He sat there, trying to think, trying to breathe. But the weight of the memory, of everything it implied, was suffocating. And yet, as he wrestled with it, something strange began to happen. Pieces of his past, parts of himself that had never quite made sense, began to fall into place. His behaviors, his struggles with shame, his cycles of self-doubt—they all seemed tied to this pain.

Maybe, he thought, I can give myself a little more grace now.

But grace wasn't his strength. His heart ached with guilt and shame, emotions that had shadowed him his entire life. He thought about his parents—the regular conflict between them growing up, the disfigured man exercise he had done in counseling, and how it all seemed connected. Growing up, he had always carried the weight of guilt, as if all the dysfunction was his fault.

Then his mind shifted to his own mistakes. His decisions in college and after, seeking love through promiscuity rather than giving it authentically. A pattern of victimhood, of acting out, of craving validation yet never feeling worthy of it. It was almost too much to comprehend.

"How?" he whispered. "How could I have forgotten this? Why now?"

He took a deep, shuddering breath, his thoughts spiraling.

I'm intelligent. I've done good things. I love my family. I loved my wife. I love my children. All I ever wanted was to provide for them, to be worthy of them. And yet, here I am, sitting in the rubble of my choices, my unawareness. How did I end up here? How did I hurt them? I never meant to.

The weight of it all pressed on him, but somewhere in the storm of his mind, a small, steady voice emerged.

"This isn't all my fault," it said.

He closed his eyes and listened.

"I didn't ask for this. I didn't choose to be shaped by these shadows, this evil. And I didn't remember, not until now. I didn't have the tools to understand or to stop the cycles that came out of this pain."

He exhaled slowly, the tension in his body easing slightly. It's time, he thought. Time for some grace. Time to give myself a break.

He repeated the words in his mind, letting them sink in.

"Thank God," he murmured. "Thank God for eyes to see and ears to hear, even if it's painful. Thank God for the chance to change. To move in the right direction. for the opportunity for spiritual, emotional, and physical healing."

The memories hadn't stopped hurting. The shame and regret hadn't disappeared. But there was a flicker of hope now, a sense of purpose in the pain. He didn't have to be perfect; he just had to keep growing.

Darius straightened in his seat, took another deep breath, and whispered, "I'm working my ass off. That has to count for something."

Chapter 31
Business for Dummies

After ending the conversation with a potential client, Darius leaned back in his chair and stared at the ceiling, slowly shaking his head. It was a business deal he had hoped would materialize, but he'd just been informed that the positions were going to be put on hold. More of the same disappointing news. He rubbed his eyes and temples, feeling the weight of a very difficult year bearing down on him. Not only had he faced numerous challenges in his personal life, but the state of the business and the economy felt like a punch in the gut.

Darius had never owned a business before. He had pursued an MBA, which he often joked meant he knew how to run a business just like someone who had stayed in many hotels knew how to operate a hotel. The truth was, unless you had actually run or started a business, you probably had no idea what you were doing, regardless of your qualifications. He thought it was similar to how no one could fully understand the struggles of cancer unless they or a loved one had experienced it firsthand. Having worked on the oncology ward at University Hospital in the past, he knew just how emotional and challenging that environment could be, even as a clinician trying to help patients.

When he started his business, he had no experience in the industry and had never been a business owner before. It was both eye-opening and stressful. For the first eight or nine months, he worked clinically to generate income for his family's needs and bills until the company began to turn a profit. It took him six and a half months to start making money, and just thinking about it made him feel a little queasy. It was one of the hardest things he had ever done, regularly working a 12-hour night shift at the hospital, getting home to sleep two hours before getting up and drinking a Mountain Dew Kickstart before working 8–10 hours trying to build the business. It was tortuous, but he made it work because it was all for his family.

At the time, the financial boat was starting to leak, and they were almost out of money. The fact that the company finally started making money couldn't have come at a better time; had it taken much longer, things could have turned ugly very quickly. He wouldn't want to have to do it again.

It certainly didn't help that Darius had started the company in the midst of the last recession and economic downturn. He had often read that launching a business during tough times was supposed to be one of the best times to do it. The theory was simple: if you could survive and succeed when the economy was struggling, then you could make it through anything.

It seemed like there was a lot of truth to the idea that starting a business during tough times could test resilience. While it had certainly made things more emotionally challenging, Darius couldn't ignore the fact that his company had grown from earning a quarter of a million dollars to over $600,000 in the span of just a few years. Encouraged by that growth, he'd decided to start hiring and scaling, and the year before, his business had grossed over $2 million. But in hindsight, it all felt like a bit of a house of cards.

Darius realized he had been blind to so many things, not just in his personal life but also in the business world. Some of the issues he'd been facing head-on in the past few months had affected both realms. Yes, his resilience and hard work had helped him get to where he was, but he also recognized that much of his motivation came from a place of fear—fear of losing what he had built. It had driven him to succeed, but perhaps also contributed to his blind spots.

He had read about the statistics: roughly 40% of businesses don't make it through their first two years. Darius had started his company as part of a franchise, and five other businesses had launched at the same time as his. Three of those didn't make it past the two-year mark. He had always been grateful to be one of the fortunate ones, fully aware of the challenges that most businesses face. Of those that survive the first two years, only about half make it to five years, and 80% don't last a decade.

Despite the odds, his company had thrived. He was grateful for the success and the lifestyle it had provided his family. He had no debt for the last three to four years, owned the company outright, and had paid back the retirement savings he had used to start the business. He had been able to invest in buildings, stocks, and bless his family with trips, enjoying the ability to travel and dine out whenever they wanted.

But now, Darius could see how some of the very traits that fueled his success—his grit, his drive—had also blinded him. Those same qualities that had helped him push through challenges had kept him from seeing the cracks in his business model and personal life. It was a bitter realization.

Despite doing many things well, the past year had been marked by significant mistakes—especially in hiring. He had brought on several employees that, in hindsight, he had no business hiring, but at the time, he was blind to it. The upside, however, was that these mistakes forced him to take a closer look at the hiring process, leading him to develop better tools for his company to have a better cultural fit with new employees. If he hadn't made those errors, he might never have delved so deeply into understanding how crucial cultural alignment is for a successful team.

One of the books that had been particularly eye-opening for him was *Hiring for Attitude* by Mark Murphy, which presented data on hiring across various industries and company sizes. The statistics revealed something surprising: only 11% of misfires—hires that didn't work out—were due to a lack of the required skills. The remaining 89% failed because of issues related to emotional intelligence, poor temperament, difficulty working with others, and low motivation. It emphasized how important it was to hire people who not only had the right skills but also fit into the company's culture.

Darius realized how important it was to hire individuals whose personal "why" aligned with the company's mission and vision. This alignment led to higher employee engagement and fewer wasted resources. Unfortunately, he had hired several people based on gut feelings, previous friendships or a quick assessment, thinking they would be positive additions, but they simply hadn't worked out.

What made the situation even worse was that Darius had brought in four other hires to boost profitability, and none of them had delivered. His personal efforts had been generating plenty of revenue, but instead of using the profits to make his life easier, he invested in bad hires and buildings.

What baffled Darius most was not just that he had kept these people for so long, but that none of them, except for Antonio, seemed interested in following the successful systems he had already put in place. Antonio had worked hard and had great numbers but he just struggled to get results. Despite the proof of his methods, they resisted, unwilling to embrace the very strategies that could have led to their own success.

On top of that, he had spent money attending conferences he thought would be beneficial and poured resources into trying to land government contracts—potentially lucrative opportunities that ultimately went nowhere. Then, earlier in the year, the economy froze. Of the nine clients who had brought in significant business in the previous two quarters, only one remained active. The loss in revenue was staggering, and the betrayal from the former employee only deepened the blow. It was like being hit from all sides at once.

Financially, it was a disaster—the possible divorce only made it worse as now the majority of his assets were frozen. Darius was running out of money, and none of them could make sense of why they couldn't get new business. He was working as hard and efficiently as ever and it was one no after another. The employees left were wondering if they had been blacklisted in the industry. They had a unique value proposition in the marketplace, utilizing video technology, and their results were impressive, especially when it came to efficiency. And yet, the jobs weren't coming in anymore.

The company's fixed costs hadn't been an issue back when they were pulling in the kind of revenue they had over the past three years. But now, things were different. The weight of the business collapsing alongside his personal struggles was taking an emotional toll.

Guilt gnawed at him. He couldn't stop thinking about the ways he had contributed to this mess—his mindset of lack, his feelings of unworthiness, and how they had driven him to act like a victim too often. Shaking his head, he forced himself not to fall back into those thoughts. He'd worked so hard to change, to let go of the past, take accountability, and move forward. He was learning to stay in a more positive, masculine frame—controlling his emotions, focusing on what mattered, and truly believing that life was happening for him, not to him.

He was grateful for the chance to make these changes, but still ... did everything have to happen all at once? The Bible said God wouldn't give you more than you could handle, but holy cow, did He really have to have this much confidence in him?

He felt like he was getting closer and closer to the edge of a cliff, but in the back of his mind, he held onto the thought that things would get better.

Chapter 32
Listening to God

D arius sat on the blanket, meditating as soft singing floated around him. Nearly eleven weeks had passed since he and his wife had separated. So much had shifted in his life—so much he'd learned about himself—and yet, so much still remained unclear.

On one hand, it was remarkable to see how much he'd grown in this short period. He was immersed in the Marriage Reset Program, diving into three group sessions a week, individual counseling, modules, reading materials, and connecting regularly with his Brothers in Arms, all of whom were on a similar journey. He felt he was finally seeing his own flaws clearly, recognizing the conflicts he'd contributed to over the years. While he knew he wasn't the only one responsible, he felt an overwhelming need to hold himself accountable.

For the first time, he understood the impact of his moodiness, selfishness, and aloofness; he could see how he wasn't present sometimes, both for himself and for his marriage—for Jessica. He had completed the exercises, which were painful in their own way, but had opened his eyes to patterns that had long been buried. He realized how much of his past behavior had been driven by a lack of self-worth. He'd been hurtful to himself, defensive, and driven by negative self-talk.

Now what he wanted to do more than anything was to continue to lean into God, continue to look in the mirror, to be accountable, and to grow. Things were improving and meditation was helping. Initially, he could barely manage five minutes of just sitting and clearing his mind; now, he was up to fifteen or even twenty minutes a day, letting go of his thoughts and trying to embrace a quiet, centered stillness.

Kristen once told him, "Prayer is speaking to God, and meditation is listening." This had become his new rhythm: beginning each session with a prayer, asking God to guide him, then sitting in silence, open to whatever message might come. A book he'd recently read, *The Art of Embodiment*, likened meditation to a movie screen: as thoughts arise, imagine them appearing and gently push them off the screen to return to a clear state. This technique resonated with him and was helping him enter a deeper meditative state.

As he worked through his journey, he was astonished at how his focus and mental clarity were improving. Once burdened with relentless anxiety, he now found himself reading faster and more deeply, finishing books like *The Five Love Languages* by Gary Chapman in only a few days. It was an eye-opener, giving him insight into how he might have failed in understanding Jessica's love language. He recognized that her primary language might have been words of affirmation and acts of service—areas where he now realized he'd likely been lacking.

And as he read further, he found himself confused about even his own needs—he had no clue what his own love languages were.

His needs were more aligned with quality time and physical touch, though not merely for sex, but for intimacy through connection and presence. Yet, reflecting on his past, he acknowledged he had struggled with showing empathy and being present. He thought about the countless times he had withdrawn out of frustration, creating a barrier between them. And though he knew both of them had their shortcomings, he felt that if they'd been able to communicate better, things might have been different.

He'd often questioned why they hadn't communicated these things better. Perhaps she'd tried to reach out in her own ways, but he'd been too wrapped up in his own issues to see it. He realized now how much he had wanted a meaningful connection—mental, emotional, and physical.

The Marriage Reset Program had also opened his eyes to something deeper: how their relationship had become a cycle of self-fulfilling behaviors. He now believed that they both wanted the same things—a safe, fulfilling connection—but their individual traumas and past wounds had shaped their approach. This dynamic led them to work against each other rather than with each other, despite a mutual desire for intimacy and understanding.

At the end of *The Five Love Languages*, he'd read a story about a woman whose marriage had seemed beyond hope. The counselor had asked her if she'd be willing to try one last approach. She agreed and asked her husband weekly what she could do to be a better wife. This small act eventually softened their relationship. Darius found himself deeply moved by this example.

Each day, he became more committed to this journey, seeing it not as a means to repair his lost marriage, but to truly transform himself. He was learning to shed his fears and open himself to the possibilities of change, carrying forward the wisdom he was gaining with every step. For now, his focus was on keeping his heart and mind open, regardless of what lay ahead.

Darius took a deep breath, centering himself as he considered the journey he was on. He was still working on the fundamental challenges of self-awareness, growing as a person and as a man, and letting go of his reactive tendencies. It wasn't easy. Each new layer of understanding seemed to reveal even more areas that needed attention. But as he could look up to the sky and see the clouds change shape, he could look back on where he was and see how far he had come. In a way, each small step felt like a triumph, a sign of progress, even if the bigger picture sometimes felt overwhelming.

The story of the woman who'd been advised to pour love and kindness into her marriage, only to find herself loving her husband again, lingered in Darius's mind. It was a story of ironic healing, and Darius wondered if such an approach could work in his life too. While it didn't seem likely, Darius was willing to play that role for Jessica if she had a change of heart.

He had already noticed the undercurrent of growth in his heart—a new ability to love his wife unselfishly. His old way of loving her had been rooted in what he got from her love, her affection, and her attention. But now, he felt a pull toward giving, nurturing, and supporting her, not to fulfill his own needs, but because he genuinely wanted her to feel loved and cherished.

Darius's thoughts turned to prayer. He reminded himself of the fruits of the spirit—love, joy, peace, patience, kindness, goodness/generosity, faithfulness, gentleness, and self-control. These qualities had become his guideposts, the virtues he wanted to embody not just in his marriage but in every part of his life. In the quiet of his mind, he called upon them for guidance on how to continue down this path even when it felt steep and uncertain. He prayed for his wife, that she might also find healing and growth. And he prayed for their marriage, that it might someday be restored on the foundation of two people touched by God, with increased awareness, healed through an unselfish love, and a potential example for others struggling. At this point, that seemed the only possibility for their marital salvation.

Chapter 33
Flying With Doubt

D arius was on his way to Africa. He woke up to the flight attendant bringing a chicken meal that tasted like the plastic wrap with a cold pasta side and a roll so dry that it could kill someone if he had decided to throw it hard enough. It was airplane food; what else did he expect? After eating half of it, he decided he wasn't hungry enough to eat the rest. He got up, stretched in the aisle, hit the bathroom, and then sat back down in his seat thinking about watching a movie.

After perusing the movies, he watched 15 minutes of a drama, felt dumber for the effort, and decided he just couldn't do it and turned it off. Ever since the rug was pulled out from under him, he'd had a really hard time watching TV. He had such a sense of urgency to keep learning and trying to understand. If it didn't activate his mind, he wasn't interested because he didn't want to be numb or unconscious. Maybe he didn't feel he had the time to waste.

He grabbed Dr. Whitman's book (*You Don't Have to Live with Chronic Pain – No Matter What Your Doctor or Aunt Betty Says*) and decided to jump into the next chapter: "Diet and Nutrition That

Heals, Functional-Neural-Bioenergetic Testing (FNBT), Primary Physiological Priority (PPP), and Functional Bioenergetic/Central Nervous System (FBE/CNS) Synergy (Syn) ... ”

Was he getting paid for acronyms? he thought, laughing.

> **"By examining the fields, channels, and bodies of subtle anatomy you can potentially diagnose problems before they occur or diagnose them accurately and holistically if symptoms are already present."**

Once again, this chapter started off with a testimonial and it rocked his world just trying to wrap his head around it.

The patient was a woman who was almost bedridden with enough issues for a whole hospital wing, forget about one person: fibromyalgia, high blood pressure, depression, migraines, and pre-diabetic among other issues who was in adult diapers, had a catheter in and was sleeping most of the day. She had zero quality of life, and her husband was raising their kids alone.

Without much hope, some friends told them about Whitman and she made the two and a half hour trip to see him with little to no expectations. According to the testimonial, after just two visits, she had less pain and more energy, though still with a hefty dose of skepticism, but she continued to make the drive to see him.

After a month, the woman was pain free, diaper free, had gotten rid of nine medications, and she and her husband are hiking!

In less than six months, this woman received the miracle she had been praying for and her medical doctors couldn't explain it.

Darius couldn't explain it either, but he found it fascinating. Was this what Larissa was talking about when she said that everything is made of energy, when she tried to explain muscle testing and tapping to him?

As he continued into the chapter, he really got intrigued because it started to talk about muscle testing, describing one of the techniques called O-ring testing. It used an example of an atheist going weak during a muscle test and a believer having a muscle to stay strong at the mention of the word God, regardless of whether it was conscious acknowledgement or not. The book stated that muscle testing was bioenergetics testing—a "fail proof human lie detector test."

What in the world?

Apparently, through muscle testing, Dr. Whitman could identify functional issues before the patient even had symptoms, in theory, and, as the book showed, in practice, one could fix issues or eliminate a pathology before it physically showed up. Darius was fascinated and confused. The testimonials in this book were like miracles and yet this guy had been doing this work for 40 years. Why in the heck weren't there more holistic doctors like this?

As he read on, Dr. Whitman explained how using neural-bio genetic frequencies of colors along with O-ring testing could determine certain health issues and risk hazards, including heart attack, stroke, diabetes, and issues implicated in causing Alzheimer's Disease, which had a strong connection with too much aluminum in the brain. Why in the world would a people or a country of people start putting all these chemicals in food and consumer goods that can hurt you? It made no sense to him. Inflammation was essentially the cause of most issues, but the book was not easy reading.

Then he hit the topic of GERD, or Gastroesophageal Reflux Disease, which he had been fighting for fourteen years. He was the only immediate member of his family, including his late father, mother, and sister, who hadn't had an ulcer. Once he started getting bad indigestion, his family doctor at the time told him there was no sense fighting his genetics anymore and it was time to go on medication. The first one being Ranitidine, which he had taken for nine years, twice a day, without fail. If he took it, there would be no reflux and if he didn't, he could feel it within an hour after he should have taken it. Then, after putting Ranitidine in his body twice a day for nine years, they took it off the shelf because it was causing cancer. They switched him to another medication called Famotidine.

Whitman described that he was able to use KST testing, diet modification to organic healthier options, and natural supplements to completely eliminate GERD and reflux. He then described how these medications override the autonomic nervous system to achieve temporary relief while never fixing the underlying cause and creating other symptoms.

Yeah, like mother fucking cancer, he thought.

Sorry God, he then thought sheepishly. His language had always fluctuated and never had an issue using foul language for humor, though he had toned it down significantly in recent years as God had become a more central figure in his life. However, after the current situation and his aggressive diving into the Bible, he was working hard to consciously change what came out of his mouth.

As Darius dug into the next eighty-three pages, he was continuously mesmerized and blown away by what the book was sharing as Dr. Whitman went into the primary energy points and acupuncture points while describing the diagnosis, underlying cause, and treatment of a myriad of issues. Too many medications in the world of Big Pharma were treating symptoms and not causes while creating more issues leading to more medications.

It reminded Darius of another book that had impacted him greatly over 10 years ago: *The Healing of America*. The author personally experienced several different countries' healthcare systems, including the UK, France, Taiwan, and others while comparing the efficiency and expense to the U.S. systems. The data was astonishing and while the U.S. was the number one spender on healthcare per capita, it was nowhere near the best in outcomes or efficiency. It was a rather remarkable read for him at the time as he realized the U.S. was the only industrialized country that didn't truly consider healthcare as a citizen's right, allowing insurance companies to profit so greatly.

Darius shook his head. Unbelievable. Just unbelievable. There was no way he was going to continue taking some of his medications and not going on Whitman's program. What a blessing this like . Where had he been all this time and why did it have to come to this for him to hear about him?

A foreword between chapter four and five caught his attention. The author. The name. David Hawkins. There he was again, Darius thought.

He started to make notations with his pen because he kept noticing ADHD, mood swings, allergies, and other items that made him think of his family and he wanted to make sure he could go back and find that information. His main focus was his own challenges but if he could help his wife or children, obviously he wanted to, assuming his wife would ever speak to him again but he knew he couldn't think like that.

***

During his flights, Darius had finished the book *Radical* by David Platt and was amazed by it.

One of his favorite parts of the book was about a student in Indonesia on a mission trip to share the gospel in a predominantly muslim area. The guy was a badass, a black belt in Karate, Ju-Jitsu, and Taekwondo. While in a house sharing the gospel in a smaller village, a witch doctor had come to the front of the home and started yelling at him. He was cursing him and wanting him to come out and fight him. The missionary's first thought was, I am going to go out there and kick his ass. Then he calmed and said, "No, I let the Lord do my fighting for me."

He walked out as the witch doctor continued to shout at him, and finally, after another threat of violence, he said again, "I let the Lord do my fighting for me now." The witch doctor went to open his mouth, started choking, and fell over dead. The missionary and the people watching looked on in amazement.

In the Lord's name, most of the village was baptized that day!

Darius was blown away. The book challenged the reader to go on mission trips, pray consistently and even pray for people in other countries regularly, and to read the entire Bible in one year. Darius thought about that and nodded slowly to himself. Yes, starting now, starting with this trip, I will do that, he decided.

After praying for his family, he took a nap.

The next stop he didn't have to get off and waited patiently on the plane until they took off to his final destination of Monrovia, Liberia. Halfway through the flight, Darius couldn't help but think about his circumstances. *What am I doing?* he wondered. *My wife is going to leave me, my business isn't doing well, and I am running out of money. In the middle of it, I am flying around the world to a country I would never go to so I can help people I don't know ...* Weren't there people in Indiana or a million other places closer that he could do something good? The plane ticket alone had cost him almost $2,500, and he had given the clinic $1,000 last month. I hope you know what you're doing, Darius, he thought once again.

He felt confused, unsure, foolish, and suddenly defeated. He closed his eyes and tried not to think about his circumstances as a tear rolled down his cheek. It wasn't long until the vibration from the plane and the darkness led him off into a restless sleep.

Darius awoke from the flight attendant shaking his shoulder as they had landed in Liberia. After waiting to get off the plane, he collected his bag and walked out to arrivals, where he saw Chea waiting.

They embraced as Chea asked. "How was the travel? It is so good to see you, my friend."

"It was long, Chea, but I am here." Darius shared an exhausted smile, trying to hide his discouragement as he still had no idea what he was doing here.

Chea smacked him on the back. "I know it's a long trip. Let's get you to your hotel so you can rest up for tomorrow."

The car came around and Darius loaded in the back. It was a long, bumpy, and dark ride to the hotel. The roads were not good as there were constant stops with a lot of potholes creating an uncomfortable ride. Darius was mostly quiet as he leaned against the side window trying not to think negatively.

"I hope you know what you're doing," that inner voice echoed.

Chapter 34

A Clinic in Need

After a long, weary ride, Darius finally reached his hotel and settled into his modest room. It was small, furnished with a refrigerator, a narrow closet, and a separate bathroom, but it was enough. Exhausted, he quickly drifted to sleep. He and Chea had arranged to meet the next morning, around 8:30 or 9:00, though Darius had encouraged him to come early for breakfast if he wanted.

When Darius woke, he checked his phone; no new messages. He paused, thinking again about where he was. Monrovia, Liberia. The strangeness of being here, in this corner of Africa he'd never imagined visiting, struck him anew. Shaking off the feeling, he opened his phone and began reading Scripture. Every day, he marveled at how the verses seemed to speak directly to his circumstances.

After his Scripture reading, he went through his breathing exercises, the embodiment routine that kept him centered, then made his way to breakfast on the third floor. Hotel breakfasts outside the U.S. always fascinated him; the buffet included some usual items but also some surprises like baked beans. Baked beans for breakfast.

When in Rome, he thought, as he added a spoonful to his plate.

Just as he was settling in with his coffee and food, a message arrived from Chea: *transportation would be there shortly*. He had explained that timing here could be unpredictable—traffic, police stops, equipment issues, all potential delays. Darius finished his breakfast and headed to the lobby to wait. The lobby itself was decorated with African masks, shields, and art, grounding him in his new surroundings. Soon, a small van pulled up outside, and Chea climbed out to greet him with a big smile. At around six-foot-one with a lean build, Chea's eyes and broad smile made an impression. They embraced warmly, and Chea introduced him to the driver before the two of them climbed into the van.

"How was your sleep?" Chea asked as they got settled. Darius told him about his morning routine, mentioning the breathing exercises.

"Embodiment?" Chea asked, curious.

Darius explained, and Chea nodded with interest. "You're welcome to join me anytime," he offered. "We can do the exercises, then dive into Scripture and prayer together."

Chea's eyes lit up. "I'll come by earlier tomorrow, then! With traffic and transport, it's always hard to tell what time things will happen, but I'll make it work."

"So, what's the plan for today?" Darius asked.

Chea began outlining their day as the van navigated the crowded streets of Monrovia. "First, we'll head to the clinic so you can meet the staff and get a feel for our operations. We'll work with patients today, then tonight, I'll bring you back to the hotel. Tomorrow, we'll go to the construction site for apartments and I'll show you the land we could buy for a new clinic site. And if all goes well, we can help with construction."

Darius nodded, taking it all in. They'd been discussing the clinic's future, a vision to move away from their current rental. Land in Liberia was surprisingly affordable—$6,000 for over an acre and a half. With another $60,000, they could build a permanent clinic, an unimaginable cost savings compared to U.S. healthcare construction.

When the van eventually pulled up to the clinic, Darius examined the modest structure. The building was rough—concrete blocks with a metal roof and open windows. As he got out of the van and went inside, Chea explained that power outages were frequent and often lasted a day or more. Darius met the nurses and staff, and Chea showed him a small room where he could leave his things.

"Today, I'll show you around the clinic, then you can work in the lab with Owen," Chea explained.

"Sounds good!" Darius replied. As they walked toward the back of the clinic, he met Monique, who would be cooking for him during his stay.

"Is there anything special you like?" Monique asked.

Darius smiled. "I'll try anything. African food sounds perfect," he replied enthusiastically.

They moved back inside, where Chea showed him a few more rooms before introducing him to Owen in the lab. Patients were beginning to arrive, and they were a weary-looking group. Darius took in their sad expressions; some appeared visibly uncomfortable, struggling with various ailments. He put on gloves and scanned the equipment around him. It was shockingly outdated—really, really old.

Soon, a young woman, likely in her early twenties, arrived as the first patient of the day. She didn't speak English, so Owen communicated with her as he drew her blood. Darius assisted, placing the sample into the centrifuge and disposing of other items. Afterward, Owen asked her for a urine sample.

When she returned, Owen handed the sample to Darius, who labeled it and set it for processing. As she left, Darius glanced over and saw Owen preparing to recap the needle.

"Whoa," Darius cautioned, alarmed.

Owen hesitated, looking at him.

Darius was astonished. He started working in the hospital in the early 1990s and he hadn't seen equipment or procedures like this since then. With the advances in equipment, it was unheard of to be actively recapping a needle. One wrong move and they'd prick themselves. Updated equipment had been available for decades now, improving safety and preventing accidents that would expose practitioners to bloodborne illnesses like HIV, hepatitis, and antibiotic-resistant bacteria. Recapping needles was reckless.

"What are you doing?" Darius asked, incredulous.

"We have no choice," Owen replied. "We only have so many supplies and this is what we have."

Darius bit his tongue, doing his best to remain calm. He didn't want to alarm the staff.

"What's her diagnosis?" he asked after a moment.

"Malaria, yellow fever, and gonorrhea."

Darius's stomach tightened. He worked to keep his face neutral, but the emotions were overwhelming. As Owen stepped out to call in the next patient, Darius turned toward the wall, feeling tears arise. It was unbelievable. He was in a clinic on the other side of the world, using outdated tools and limited resources to treat a young woman with multiple serious infections. They were following all the protocols he'd expect: keeping the space as clean as they could despite it being in the open air, disposing of materials safely, taking care of their patients with utmost dedication, but if they simply had access to modern equipment ... The thought struck him as deeply unfair—almost unacceptable.

"Get it together," he told himself.

These people couldn't see him break down; they couldn't see him cry. He steadied himself, taking a deep breath and drawing from the breathing exercises he'd practiced. Within seconds, the torrent of emotion calmed; his mind and body overcoming the feelings. That embodiment work was worth money, he thought, turning back around and returning to work.

Chapter 35
African Baptism

At the end of the day, as the clinic emptied out, a few staff members spoke to Darius before they left—a couple even thanked him for being there. As they gathered in the back of the clinic, Monique was preparing Monrovian ribs with rice and a special sauce. The smell was enough to make Darius realize how hungry he actually was, and when he sat down, it was quickly satiated by an incredible plate of food.

"Wow," Darius said, looking at Monique. "This is fantastic."

She smiled, nodding.

As Darius finished, he realized no one else was eating. After he got up, Chea asked if he had gotten his fill. After responding, he realized Chea was letting everyone else know they could eat what was left. Darius felt numb. If he had understood that, he would have eaten less.

Lesson learned, he thought, understanding how valuable a meal was here.

After the others finished eating, they headed outside to prepare for the ride back to the hotel. On the way, they discussed the day's work and the equipment they needed. Tomorrow, they would visit the construction site to see the land where a new clinic would eventually be built. Afterward, they'd join some staff members for dinner to review the clinic's finances and discuss future plans. When they reached his hotel, they clasped hands and hugged in a friendly farewell.

"I'll see you tomorrow," Chea said. "I'll come early so we can go over breathing exercises and pray together."

***

The next morning, Darius woke to a message from Chea, saying he'd be an hour late due to an issue with the van.

Things like this always come up.

No worries. I'll be here.

When Chea finally arrived, Darius went down to greet him and bring him up to his room. He showed Chea videos demonstrating two exercises: the Breath of Life and the lung expander. Chea nodded. "I think I got it." They went through the exercises, ending with Wim Hof's exercises. Afterward, they lay back in relaxation—Chea sprawled comically across the small hotel couch. His expression was one of wonder. "Wow, that's amazing."

"Isn't it?" Darius laughed. "Every time I do it, I feel so peaceful."

They took out Scripture, and Darius led them in prayer, then they took turns reading. Darius was particularly fond of the Magnificat, a Catholic devotional he'd been reading daily for years. Though not Catholic himself, he loved its mix of Old and New

Testament passages and insights from saints and martyrs. That day's reading touched on faith in adversity. When they finished, both laughed, realizing how much it applied to their situations.

After breakfast, they headed out in the new vehicle, a Pathfinder. As they drove, Chea asked, "What do you notice about the traffic?"

Darius looked around and finally noticed something unusual. "A lot of these vehicles don't have license plates."

Chea smiled. "Yes. The corruption here is so bad that many people don't register their cars. The police often pull people over just to collect bribes, so locals just skip the plates and use that money for bribes instead."

Soon after, almost in irony, they encountered a police checkpoint. Chea told the driver, "Just keep going," but he hesitated and pulled over. Chea, usually quiet and reserved, stepped out with a commanding presence, speaking firmly to the officers. After some back and forth, he borrowed the driver's phone to make a call, and 20 minutes later, they were allowed to leave.

"What happened?" Darius asked.

"Just like I said, they wanted a bribe," Chea replied.

Darius raised an eyebrow. "And?"

"I threatened to call one of the senior managers over at the police station," Chea said with a grin. "They let me go right away."

Darius shook his head. "So, what would have happened if you actually called them?"

Chea smiled. "Well, I try not to make that call unless I absolutely have to. Most of the time, I refuse to pay the bribes. But if things get really out of hand, I'll call in a favor, and they'll handle it."

"So, just like that?"

"Yeah. But you don't want to rely on those favors unless it's really necessary," Chea said with a shrug.

Arriving at the worksite, Monique was already preparing an outdoor fire, explaining that she'd be cooking fish, chicken, and another local dish Darius could barely pronounce. He laughed. "It sounds amazing!" Monique assured him that anything he left would be safe, and then they walked down the dirt road to the construction area.

Chea introduced Darius to the workers, explaining that he was one of the missionaries supporting their efforts. Darius was handed work gloves and began helping to place bricks on the wall under construction. The foreman, Samuel, scolded him a few times for wasting materials, and Darius tried hard to improve while maintaining his balance on the wall. His legs and arms burned with the unfamiliar exertion, but the workers' singing and laughter kept him motivated.

Finally, it was time for lunch. Darius walked back up the hill with the others. They prayed over the food, and as they ate, Darius noticed children and other people arriving. Chea explained that they'd soon have a baptism ceremony. Darius had only baptized his two older children, but today he'd have the chance to baptize people here in Africa. He could barely contain his excitement.

During lunch, Darius made sure to leave enough for the others after the experience at the clinic. When he finished, Monique gathered the uneaten food, mixing it with other leftovers and dividing it among several of the men, who shared utensils and ate around a single container. Darius felt a lump in his throat, thinking of the abundance in the U.S. that many took for granted. He said a silent prayer, grateful for his blessings and for these people.

The afternoon flew by as they continued work, and when it was time for the baptisms, Darius's heart raced with excitement. About 30 people, including children, gathered around. Chea introduced Darius, explaining the meaning of baptism. Darius led a prayer, asking for the Holy Spirit to touch each of them. When he invited questions, one man raised his hand.

"Sometimes," the man began, "I drink too much and make bad choices. Can I still be saved?"

"Absolutely. God loves you. He made you special," Darius said, looking around at the people gathered, each watching him intently. "He made each and every one of you special. He wrote about you in the Book of Life, the Lamb's Book, before you were even born. He breathed life into you in your mother's womb. And He forgives sins. We all sin; we all make mistakes."

Darius looked at the man in front of him and smiled. "Yes, you absolutely can be baptized. You can be saved. And guess what? Even after that, you're going to make mistakes—I make mistakes all the time and have drunk too much also. But you can always come back to Him. The enemy wants you to believe you're not good enough, that you're not worthy, and that there's no way God could love you."

Darius's voice softened. "But I'm here to tell you, He absolutely loves you. You could never make a mistake or commit a sin so great that He wouldn't forgive you, wouldn't take you back. Just keep moving toward him and try to remove those sins."

The man nodded, and smiles broke out across the faces of those gathered around. The baptism that followed was one of the most incredible experiences Darius had ever witnessed. They stood on a dirt hill, surrounded by dust and sparse vegetation, in a humble area of a country halfway around the world. Yet, here he was, praying with these people.

At the construction site, in a rubber tub on a mound of dirt, he baptized eight people that day, including three children. With each person, he prayed over them, guiding them to profess, "Jesus is the Christ, the Son of the living God. I give Him my life and accept Him as my Lord and Savior." After each prayer, he submerged them in water and, as he lifted them back up, cheers and applause erupted. He embraced each one with joy.

When it was done, the entire group prayed together, and shouts of celebration filled the air, carried by a chorus of voices. Darius's heart felt full. As he and Chea embraced, Darius took a deep breath, savoring the moment.

"All right," Chea said, smiling. "Let's head back to the hotel so you can get cleaned up, and then we'll go to dinner."

As they made their way back, Darius smiled to himself. What a remarkable day, he thought, reflecting on the journey that had brought him here. Just days ago, he had been on the plane, wondering what he was doing, questioning if he should even come to a place he'd never imagined visiting. Yet now, he felt certain that God had led him here for a purpose. Now, he knew without a doubt that he was exactly where he was meant to be.

Chapter 36
A Dance Move or Two

T he drive back to the hotel was uneventful, but the past two days had been nothing short of remarkable, and he felt overjoyed and at peace, even amidst all the chaos around him. He also thought about the fear related to his marriage and family situation, but those thoughts seemed distant now.

He loved what he did from a business standpoint, but his long-term goal was to start a charitable foundation. Within the next ten years, he hoped to spend half of his time doing charitable work like this. It was what he truly wanted to do.

He took the time to freshen up and then left the hotel to make his way to the nearby restaurant where they were getting together for dinner. It was a little over half a mile away, and as he entered, he saw Chea, Monique, a couple of client employees, and the driver sitting at a table outside. He walked over, greeted everyone with hugs, and sat down. Then the waitress came over to take their order.

"What would you like?" she asked.

As Darius scanned the menu, he looked up. "What type of beer do you have? I'd love to try a local African beer."

Monique recommended one, ordering one for herself too, and the waitress headed off to fetch it while they scanned their options for dinner.

"So what do you think?" Chea asked.

"Well, you know me, I like almost everything," Darius reflected. "All the food Monique has made has been fantastic so far. These ribs look pretty good, but if you guys want to order for the table, I'm fine with that too."

"Ah, we've done enough picking your food for you," Monique laughed. "We're going to let you pick something this time."

Darius nodded, deciding on the ribs and a local rice side dish to go with it. The night was beautiful with a cool breeze, and music played in the background.

"Is this a place that you come often?" Darius asked.

"Well, not often," Chea said, "But they have music sometimes. People here love to dance and sing, so places like this tend to have bands or spaces where people can come and dance."

"What do they like to dance to?" Darius asked.

Chea laughed. "Actually, they do a lot of disco-type music here."

Darius shook his head, chuckling, trying to picture it. He looked across the courtyard into the indoor area and saw a couple of people dancing and the waitress returning with their beers.

Darius took a sip.

Chea smiled. "What do you think?"

"It's not bad at all," Darius replied. "I'm more of an IPA or imperial stout type of guy, but I always like to try whatever the local beer is when I'm somewhere new."

The waitress took their orders and disappeared again, leaving a moment of silence at the table before Chea started a new conversation.

"Today was interesting."

"How so?" Darius asked.

"You're quite genuine," Chea said matter-of-factly.

Darius cocked his head and raised an eyebrow with a half-grin. "I hope so. But what do you mean by that?"

"Well, I knew you cared about charity, doing the things you've done," Chea said. "When your company bought our first ultrasound, that was a big deal. You coming here is obviously a big commitment. The money you've spent is significant. But sometimes people do things because they feel like they have to or because it's expected. I don't think that's the case with you."

Darius looked at him seriously. "I certainly don't feel like I have to do this. I never in a million years thought I'd be coming to Liberia or supporting a clinic here. I didn't even expect to be supporting one in a country where you actually have to go to the embassy to get a Visa."

Chea paused, took a drink of his beer, and looked back up at Darius. "Yes, I understand. But after watching you over the last two days, in the clinic, helping with construction, praying, baptizing those people today, you were completely in your element. You were happy. None of it was forced. It was all real. And I just think it's a beautiful thing. I'm grateful."

Darius looked at him, paused for a couple of seconds, and said, "Thank you. I receive what you're saying, and I appreciate it. Something I've never been good at, and I'm working on, is receiving and accepting even a compliment."

He looked back down at his beer, took a sip, then looked back at Chea. "You know, none of this is by accident. Us meeting, me being here, I have to tell you, on the plane, I had some difficult moments.

It's a long flight. I was thinking about how hard my personal situation is with my wife and how the business is struggling. Spending money to come here, it cost me over $2,000 for the flight, which is incredible. I probably shouldn't have spent that money. I started doubting myself on the plane. But in the last two days, what a blessing. I know exactly what I'm doing because this is where I'm supposed to be, and I know that I'll be back."

Chea smiled. "Your story is amazing, and I'm grateful not only to know you but to have the opportunity to support your dream. Tomorrow, we're going to visit the clinic, stake out a couple of homes, and the construction site. We're going to give the land back to God, a place that has been filled with corruption and evil. In a country that has known so much civil war and atrocities, we're going to bless this land."

"Amen," Darius said with a smile. "That is amazing. What if it snowballs? What if the clinic becomes self-sustaining? What if we're back with more people, helping more people, and we start to bless more land, more lives?"

Chea nodded. "Yes, what a beautiful thing."

The waitress returned with their food, and over the meal, things shifted again as Darius brought up the topic of business.

"I want to talk about the next clinic site," he said. "What's the rent for the facility?"

"That was covered by charitable funds? $4,000 for two years," Chea replied.

"$4,000 for two years?" Darius echoed. "That's remarkable."

"Yeah," Chea nodded.

"Okay," Darius continued, "How much is the land going to cost?"

"It'll be about $6,000," Chea answered.

"$6,000?" Darius asked, surprised. "How big is the land?"

"A little less than an acre and a half," Chea explained.

Darius shook his head in disbelief. "In the United States, commercial property for a clinic would be in the hundreds of thousands. $600,000 to over $1 million or more, even in the Midwest. It's incredible."

Chea nodded. "Yes, it's a great opportunity here."

Darius asked, "How much will it cost to build the clinic?"

"About $60,000," Chea replied.

"$60,000 for a whole clinic?" Darius repeated. "That's crazy!"

They continued discussing the clinic's needs, and Darius was amazed at how efficiently the operation was run. They even talked about labor costs—nurses and clinicians worked for only $380 per month. Darius was stunned.

"You're kidding," he said. "$380 a month?"

"No, I'm not kidding," Chea replied.

"Okay, well, what's the total cost for running the clinic for the year?"

"It's $46,000," Chea said.

Darius absorbed the numbers. The clinic was operating at a fraction of the cost compared to similar operations in the U.S. If the clinic could become self-sustaining, they wouldn't need as many contributions. And if they didn't need as many contributions, then they wouldn't need to worry about what kind of people were sending them the contributions in the first place. The clinic could reach more people, treat more people, and in doing so, it could also fund itself.

"What does the clinic need to start getting patients who can actually pay for themselves?" Darius asked.

Chea thought for a moment. "Well, better equipment would be a good start. And honestly, a more professional space for the patients wouldn't hurt, either."

"What about the location? Is it good enough, or should you look somewhere else?" he asked.

"The location's fine," Chea replied, nodding. "The land we're looking at isn't any harder to reach than any other options around here. It's more about what we can offer when they get there."

"Got it. And do you have a rough idea on the cost for the major items? Like an X-ray machine or lab equipment to handle CBCs and other diagnostic tests?"

"Brand new equipment is pricey, but I'd have to go back and check the specifics," Chea answered.

"Alright. If we were able to acquire those things, maybe we could look for options for equipment that are still valuable but might be phased out of the market soon. Some tech from, say, the last five to eight years that could still serve the clinic well. Companies might even be willing to donate it and get the tax write-off rather than resell it at a lower cost."

"That's a good idea." Chea raised his eyebrows, intrigued. "Is this something you've done before?"

"No, not really," Darius admitted, shrugging. "Just thinking out loud. It's been a while since my MBA accounting classes, but I'm just trying to look at it from a P&L standpoint. Thinking outside the box."

"Well, I appreciate it," Chea assured him.

Darius continued, "The other thing I've thought about is that once you have the right equipment and can attract patients who can pay, the clinic could generate more income. You shared with me what the reimbursement rates might be per patient if we had the equipment to do in-house lab work and X-rays."

He flipped open his notebook, it's showing him his calculations. "If you brought in even seven to nine new patients a month, and maybe did three to four of these specific tests a week, the clinic would actually turn a profit. Instead of losing $35,000 a year, it could make around $10,000."

Chea's face lit up with a smile. "That would be amazing."

"And you could market that," Darius added. "You know, it's still hard for me to wrap my head around, coming from the U.S., I don't worry about malaria, yellow fever, or typhoid. I'm vaccinated against two of them and take pills for the other while I'm here. Yet the majority of people here, who face these threats daily, aren't vaccinated at all."

Chea nodded, a hint of sadness in his eyes. "Over 90% aren't vaccinated. It's terrible, isn't it?"

"More than that," Darius replied, his tone hardening. "It's obscene."

A look was shared around the table. They didn't quite understand what he meant.

Darius took a sip of his beer, cleared his throat, and apologized, "Sorry, it's horrible, a travesty, it shouldn't be that way. But what if we could create an initiative? What if we could incentivize people to come to the clinic? What if, for every procedure they pay for, we could vaccinate one or two people in the community?"

Chea's eyes widened. "Yes! What if, in 5 to 8 years, 50 or 60% of the population is vaccinated?"

"That would be incredible," Darius said.

As they finished their meal, they put away thoughts of business and "clocked out" for the evening. They talked about the usual things—family, local customs, the simple pleasures of relaxing together. At one point, the door swung open as a group left the dance floor, and a burst of loud music filled the air. Darius jumped up, surprising everyone, and broke into a series of dance moves. Laughter erupted around him as Chea shook his head, grinning.

Monique leapt to her feet, joining Darius, and together they fell into a fun, easy rhythm. People leaving the restaurant stopped to stare, some laughing and clapping. One of the patrons shouted, "A white Michael Jackson!" which set off another round of laughter. When the song ended, Monique and Darius exchanged a quick, cheerful hug before they sat back down, still chuckling.

"My brother," Chea said, shaking his head, "I didn't know you had those kinds of moves."

Darius laughed, shrugging. "What can I say? I love to dance. I might have a move or two up my sleeve."

When the evening wound down, they dropped him off at his hotel. Darius hugged Chea, expressing his thanks for all their help with planning the clinic.

"I'll pick you up in the morning," Chea said. "We'll do our breathing exercises, read a bit of Scripture, have breakfast, and then head to the clinic to get everything ready for patients."

Darius nodded, smiling. "And tomorrow night, dinner. Then Sunday, church. And after that, I head home. It's amazing how quickly it's gone by."

"Have a great night," Chea said, waving.

Darius waved back. "You too."

Chapter 37
The Spirit on Fire

As Chea arrived at the hotel to pick him up, Darius reflected on the previous day at the clinic. It felt similar to their first day: the clinic was crowded, mostly with people unable to pay for the services offered. The atmosphere was heavy, and Darius couldn't help but feel the weight of it all. He had helped with stocking supplies, distributing medications, and doing many of the same tasks as before. A media crew had arrived, something Darius hadn't known was part of the plan. They asked some interesting questions, and though he was caught off guard, Darius answered as best as he could.

Later that evening, their focus shifted to the clinic, the house where Chea's son lived, and the construction site. Several employees joined them as they planted stakes in the ground, praying and blessing the land before handing it over to God. It was a powerful moment for Darius, marking his final day in Africa before heading home.

They drove toward the church. Chea and Darius chatted about the week's events, making small talk until they reached an intersection and were suddenly pulled over. Chea told the driver to keep going, but that wasn't an option. The police asked the driver to step out, and the situation quickly escalated. Darius watched the commotion, the back-and-forth dialogue growing more tense. It felt like an eternity, and when he finally checked his watch, nearly 20 minutes had passed.

Eventually, Chea and the driver returned to the vehicle, and they continued on their way.

Darius, curious, asked, "What happened?"

Chea shook his head in frustration. "I had to give them a bribe," he said. "The paperwork and everything were fine, but they weren't making it easy. I knew it would take too long, and we wouldn't make it to church if we went through official channels, so I decided to handle it this way. I didn't want to call in a favor from the station."

"Well, at least it's over," Darius said, relieved.

As they pulled into the church parking lot, Darius could feel the energy in the air change. And as they walked in, he realized he stuck out like a sore thumb as the church was packed, buzzing with excitement. It was a decent-sized building, two stories with beautiful décor, and Darius couldn't help but feel a bit overwhelmed by the crowd.

People were already singing and dancing in the pre-service festivities, creating an atmosphere that felt more like a Super Bowl event than a typical church service. An ensemble of musicians played instruments on one side of the stage, while the congregation clapped and danced to the music.

As Chea led Darius to his seat, he noticed there wasn't an empty spot to be found, not even standing room. People filled every inch of the space, spilling outside the building. He couldn't help but think, the only reason they got a seat was because Chea knew someone. As the music continued, Darius found himself raising his hands in the air, singing along with all his heart. He felt a power, a warmth, that was unlike anything he had ever experienced before.

This must be what the Holy Spirit feels like, he thought.

During the pre-service, he exchanged high-fives and backslaps with the people around him, all of them smiling kindly at him. It was a far cry from the churches back home in the States, where the energy didn't come close to matching what Darius was experiencing now. As the minister was introduced, Darius had no idea what to expect next.

When the sermon began, Darius's jaw nearly hit the floor. The minister's focus was on spiritual warfare and the demonic, of all things. He looked up at the ceiling, as if he were looking toward God, Himself. *Are you kidding me?* Darius thought. He had traveled halfway around the world to support a clinic in a country he had never visited, spent days navigating an experience that had made little sense at times, and now, in this church filled with energy and life, the sermon was on covering the topic that infiltrated his home and taken him completely unaware.

As the minister passionately spoke, Darius quickly pulled out a notebook and began to write furiously. The words were powerful. The minister explained how even those who are saved, who know God, can still be vulnerable to demonic influence if they aren't living in the right way, staying vigilant, and protecting themselves spiritually. Darius couldn't write fast enough as Scripture after Scripture supported what the minister was saying.

It was a remarkable experience, one that Darius couldn't shake as the sermon came to a close. He sat there, processing everything, feeling as though he had just received a massive revelation. Afterward, he spoke with some of the people around him, who welcomed him warmly and asked if he'd return. "I definitely will," Darius replied with a laugh. "But I live in the States, so it might be a while. Maybe next year." The congregation smiled, saying, "Whenever you come back, you'll be welcome here."

Chea, who hadn't been able to sit with Darius during the service, came to get him and asked, "What did you think of that?"

Darius grinned. "Are you kidding me? The Holy Spirit was everywhere in here. I've never felt anything like it in my life."

"It's a remarkable church," Chea said with a smile.

They left the church and returned to the hotel, where the staff was waiting. They ordered food, sat outside, and discussed their next steps for the clinic. The weather was beautiful, and the conversation was filled with optimism for the future. It was a peaceful afternoon.

Later, as Darius prepared to leave, he said his goodbyes. Chea promised he would be there at 6 AM to take him to the airport. After a restful night's sleep and catching up on some work, Darius followed his usual morning routine—reading Scripture, meditating, and praying. Chea and Darius talked about various things as they drove to the airport. When they arrived, they hugged and took a picture, capturing the moment that held so much significance for both of them.

Darius entered the line to board the plane, his mind racing.

Chapter 38
Praying With Strangers

As Darius settled into his seat for the first leg of his journey, he couldn't help but reflect on how remarkable this trip had been. Before he had arrived, he had wrestled with anxiety, questioning what he was doing and whether he was even meant to be there. But now, heading home, he felt a deep sense of peace. He was certain that this trip had unfolded exactly as it was supposed to, that God had orchestrated every moment, and that he was exactly where he needed to be.

He thought back to "the Detour" sermon he had listened to all that time ago before going to North Carolina. Darius realized that he was still early in his own detour, but was truly amazed at all the lessons he'd learned over the past few weeks, especially the insights he had gained into prophecy. His understanding of prophecy had been almost non-existent before reading *My Search for the Real Heaven* by Steve Hemphill. It was eye-opening to learn that 40–50% of the Gospels were prophecies, and how much of the Bible, especially the Old Testament, was tied to prophecy. He was particularly struck by the comparison Lee Strobel made in *The Case for Christ* to the odds of just 10 prophecies coming true—if you took a blind man, placed him in the middle of Texas, and asked him to find one specific silver dollar among a 2.5-foot pile that covered the entire state, those would be the odds. To think that 40 prophecies had come true, it left Darius in awe.

Though he still didn't fully grasp the depth of prophecy, he was beginning to understand it in a new way. Heading back to the U.S., Darius felt a greater sense of clarity. He had decided to take on the challenge of reading the entire Bible in a year, starting with the book of Acts.

The flight to Amsterdam was quiet compared to his flight to Africa. Darius immersed himself in the book of Acts, reading it cover to cover. Every miracle, every situation, was almost too much to absorb. It felt like reading it for the first time. He came to understand Pentecost in a way he never had before. The disciples, emboldened after the resurrection, were performing miracle after miracle, and an overwhelming number of people were coming to the Lord. Darius found himself praying, crossing himself, and reflecting on the Father, Son, and Holy Spirit. He had a clear sense of who the Father and the Son were, but for the first time, he began questioning whether he truly understood the Holy Spirit. The book of Acts opened his eyes to a whole new world—a world he didn't fully understand yet.

Three years ago, he couldn't name all of the fruits of the Spirit. Since then, he had not only evaluated himself relevant to those fruits but wanted to earnestly work to develop them in his life. He thought about the gifts of the Spirit and what they meant. What did it mean to have the Holy Spirit within you? He hadn't learned much about prophecy, the Holy Spirit, or spiritual gifts in his church upbringing, but as he read Acts, he felt the weight of it all, moving him deeply.

Tears often welled in his eyes as he read, filled with wonder and awe at what he was learning. By the time the flight landed in Amsterdam, Darius was in a different headspace entirely.

Throughout his travels, Darius had always struggled with the excessiveness of gift-giving, especially around Christmas and birthdays. His family had so much, and yet the gifts often seemed to lose their significance. As his kids grew older, toys and gifts would be opened, used briefly, then abandoned or sold in garage sales. It bothered him deeply. When he first began traveling for work, he would bring back gifts for his children, but over time, he realized that this cycle was futile. He'd traveled extensively during his twelve years in corporate America, but buying presents every time seemed unnecessary. What kind of expectations was he setting? What was he teaching them about materialism? It didn't feel right.

He thought back to how he had avoided getting involved in birthday and Christmas planning, leaving it all to his wife. He cringed at that realization. Part of that was because he felt she consistently overdid it. But as he thought about it, he realized he could be kind to himself. I did the best I could at the time, he reminded himself. He wasn't the man he wanted to be yet, but he was putting in the work and he could give himself grace for how far he had come on this journey.

Darius took a deep breath, releasing the guilt. The next thought that came to him was: what could he do for his family now, now that he was changing in positive ways? He knew he was becoming a better version of himself. His growth was evident.

He spent the next hour wandering the mini shops in the Amsterdam airport, carefully considering what he might buy for each of his kids and his wife. For the first time in a long while, he found joy in the process. The experience wasn't about buying things for the sake of it—it was about showing them that he was thinking of them in a way he hadn't before.

It took some time, but after picking out a few gifts for his family, there was still time before his flight. Darius made himself comfortable in the lounge and got a drink while he waited. The lounge was bustling, but his attention was drawn to a couple seated a few tables away. He had met them earlier as the man had loved the shirt Darius was wearing that had "Defund Politicians" across the front. Their argument was escalating rapidly, voices rising and faces tense. He watched as the man grew defensive, cutting off the woman mid-sentence, his frustration evident. She, in turn, threw her hands up, clearly exasperated.

Darius shook his head. He doesn't even realize what he's doing wrong, he thought. The scene felt eerily familiar, a mirror of his past behavior. He began silently praying for the couple. After several minutes in conflict, they sat there quietly looking in different directions until the man finally got up and left.

When he returned, he walked over to Darius to let him know the gate had been assigned for their flight to NYC. Darius hesitated for a moment, then stood, walking over to their table. "Excuse me," he began, addressing them both. "I don't mean to intrude, and if you'd prefer I leave, just let me know. But I overheard part of your argument."

The woman looked startled, while the man glanced up, guarded. "You heard us?" she asked.

Darius nodded. "Yes, ma'am. It was … kind of loud. I don't mean to intrude but I have been going through a challenging time and have been working on some things that I wanted to share."

The couple exchanged a glance. Then, cautiously, the man said, "Go on."

Darius shared his own struggles on communication with his wife and in general, then shared the process of pause, validate, connect with the emotion, thank the person for sharing and ask what they need. "If I'd known how to approach those moments differently, I might have avoided so much unnecessary conflict," he said. "There's a video I watched every day for months that helped me shift my mindset. Can I show it to you?"

The couple nodded, and Darius pulled out his phone, showing them the video. He explained its core message—how to pause, validate emotions, and avoid defensiveness. As he spoke, the man listened intently as the wife had a blank expression.

Darius looked at the wife and asked if she had any thoughts. She looked pointedly at her husband and said, "It's spot on!"

The man then looked over at Darius. "This stuff really works?"

"It changed my perspective," Darius replied. He recommended Jeff Borkoski's book, explaining how it had helped him recognize and start addressing his shortcomings. The man asked if he would send him the information and they exchanged contact information, and the couple thanked him for stepping in.

Before leaving, Darius asked, "Would you mind if I prayed for you both?"

The couple hesitated, then stood. The three of them were quite the image—two tall, towering African Americans and Darius, a 5'10" Caucasian man—all holding hands in the middle of the crowded lounge. Darius prayed for them as many in the pub looked on at the interesting and unusual sight. When they finished, a few onlookers were smiling and nodding in approval. While Darius gathered his things, the attractive waitress made eye contact with him, smiled and said, "That was beautiful." He smiled back at her.

As Darius walked to his gate, he shook his head in amazement. "Who would've thought?" He muttered to himself, a grin spreading across his face. Two strangers, almost a foot taller than him, holding hands and praying together in the middle of an airport.

***

Settling into his seat on the plane, Darius stowed the gifts he'd bought for his family, retrieved one of his books, and prepared to continue with his new commitment to read the Bible, deciding he would next read Matthew.

His thoughts were interrupted by a woman asking him to move so she could get to her seat. She was sharp and curt, her tone leaving little room for kindness. Darius forced a smile and obliged, stepping aside to let her through.

As they settled in, it quickly became clear she was not an easy seatmate. One of her bags pressed against his leg, and another sprawled across the armrest, encroaching into his space. "Can I help you with that?" Darius offered, still maintaining a pleasant tone.

She glared at him.

"I don't need your help," she snapped.

Inside, he felt his patience waver. But outwardly, he remained calm. "Alright, I understand," he said quietly, adjusting his position to make room.

For the next nine hours, the woman remained distant and unfriendly. Darius sighed inwardly but reminded himself of the lessons he'd been learning. Give her grace, he thought with a small, amused smile. He opened his book, focusing on the words before him and resolving not to let her sour mood affect his own.

The hum of the plane engines was soothing as most passengers had drifted into sleep. The cabin lights were dimmed, casting soft shadows on the interior. Darius had just finished reading Matthew and was diving into Ephesians when he decided to take a break. He scrolled through the in-flight movie selection. On the way to Africa, he'd tried watching two films but couldn't stomach either, abandoning both within 15 minutes. This time, a title caught his eye: Kandahar. He wasn't familiar with it, but it looked promising.

What the heck, he thought, selecting the film.

Surprisingly, 20 minutes in, he found himself engaged, and by the time the credits rolled, he had thoroughly enjoyed it. Feeling a little more relaxed, he decided to take a quick nap.

Soon after, the flight attendants came by with food. Darius stirred as the trolley reached his row. He had resolved to maintain some flexibility with his diet while traveling—organic preferences aside, he'd eat the plane food ... if it was tolerable.

The meal was ... something. But it did meet his standards of "tolerable." Rice, some sort of meat, a roll on the side, and a passable chocolate dessert. He ate half, skipped the roll, and drank water. As he handed his tray back, a crackle over the intercom seized his attention:

"Ladies and gentlemen, if anyone on board has a clinical background, or if there is a physician among us, we have a medical situation. Please press your call button and identify yourself."

Darius hesitated, as he always did in moments like this. He wasn't a doctor, but his clinical experience in ventilators, ICU, and ER settings was significant. Yet he rarely stepped forward in such situations. What if I get it wrong? Or maybe it was a combination of fear and selfishness? Surely someone more qualified will step up. But he was changing and something nudged him this time and he pressed the call button.

A flight attendant appeared quickly. "Excuse me, sir. Are you a doctor?"

"No, ma'am. I'm not a doctor, but I have a clinical background with critical care experience. I'm happy to help if I can."

"Please come with me."

Darius followed her toward the rear of the plane, past the bathrooms, and across to the other aisle before heading forward. "What's going on?" he asked.

"A gentleman is experiencing shortness of breath, and his blood pressure is dropping. We're not exactly sure what's happening."

As they reached the passenger in distress, Darius saw a tall African-American man seated, visibly uncomfortable. Another woman—a nurse—was already there.

"Are you a physician?" The nurse asked Darius.

"No, I'm a respiratory therapist with ICU and ER experience."

They nodded at each other and turned to the man.

"What's going on?" Darius asked.

"I don't know," the man replied, "I just feel really short of breath and uncomfortable."

They quickly hooked him up to the emergency kit to check his vitals. His oxygen saturation was 94%, heart rate 76, and respiratory rate 20. While waiting for his blood pressure reading, Darius asked, "Do you take any medications?"

"No," the man, Ezekiel, replied.

"Any known conditions? Diabetes? Heart issues?"

"No, nothing like that."

The blood pressure cuff displayed 105/78—not alarming but on the lower side.

"Have you experienced this before?"

"No, not really. Maybe for the past hour or so, I've just felt off."

Darius ran through more questions: any recent head trauma, scuba diving, unusual activity? All responses were negative. As the nurse and Darius assessed the situation, they concluded there were no immediate signs of anything critical—no pulmonary embolism, no hemorrhage, nothing life-threatening.

"Well," Darius said finally, "Your vitals are stable, and there's no obvious indication of a serious issue. You should get checked out once you land, and make sure they do full blood work. But for now, I don't know what else we would do. Just some diagnostics done when you land and let someone know if you feel different as the flight continues."

Ezekiel nodded. "Thank you."

Before leaving, Darius paused. "Ezekiel, would it be okay if I prayed for you?"

Ezekiel blinked in surprise but then nodded. "I'd appreciate that."

Darius placed a hand on Ezekiel's shoulder, bowed his head, and prayed. He invoked God's healing and blessings, asking for Ezekiel's health and peace during the flight and beyond. As he finished, Ezekiel looked at him, eyes glistening. "Man, that was amazing. Thank you."

Hours later, the announcement of their impending arrival at LaGuardia stirred Darius from his thoughts. His neighbor—still unfriendly—had barely spoken the entire flight, but after asking for him to let her out so that she could go to the bathroom, Darius took the opportunity to break their silence and hopefully find some common ground to relieve the tension—something the old Darius wouldn't have even cared to try.

"Are you heading to the States for work or vacation?" he asked with a smile.

"I live there," she said curtly, re-affixing her seatbelt.

"Oh, okay. New York or New Jersey?"

"New Jersey. Near Newark."

He persisted. "What do you do for work?"

"I'm a nursing assistant."

Darius's interest was piqued. "That's awesome! I have a clinical background too, worked in critical care for years. So What were you doing in Africa? Do you have family there?"

Her expression softened slightly. "Yes, I was visiting family in Sierra Leone. I'm from there originally."

He nodded. "Must have been nice?"

"It was." She nodded back. "What about you?"

"I support a clinic in Liberia; it's a charity I'm involved with. I was there helping out."

"That's interesting," she said, but then grimaced.

"Are you Okay?" Darius asked, concerned. She looked at him.

"I'm ... I'm fine," she stated.

"Okay," Darius replied. "But I don't mean to pry, but your facial expression ... It looked like you were in pain."

She met his gaze and sighed. "Yeah, yeah, I'm in pain."

"What are you in pain from?" Darius asked gently.

Her name was Susanna, and she looked down at the floor before looking back up at him. "I was in a bad accident a few years ago, and it's been extremely difficult. My back has been hurt. It's been a lot of challenges. I've been through a lot of rehab, a lot of physical therapy, and nothing's really helped. So I'm in pain ... a lot."

Darius looked at her, his expression softening. "I'm so sorry," he said. "I understand what it's like to be in pain."

She looked at him, and he continued, "There's probably no comparison. I'm not in pain now, but my left hip has been in pain for a lot of my life. And I understand how chronic pain can be very difficult. It sounds like you've had a lot to deal with."

"Yes," Susanna replied quietly. "It was very difficult for several years. And sometimes it's hard to work, so it's been difficult financially too."

"How did it happen?" Darius asked.

Susanna started to explain, telling him how someone had run a red light and hit her car. She pulled out her phone and began showing him pictures of the accident, as well as photos of herself in the hospital and undergoing physical therapy.

"Oh my," Darius said, his heart heavy with sympathy.

Susanna nodded as she put her phone away, and Darius paused before saying, "Susanna." She gave him a full look, and the way he said her name made her pause, too. "I would really love to pray for you. I'd like to pray for healing for you, if that's okay."

Her eyes widened, and she seemed somewhat startled. "Pray for me?"

"Yes," he replied. "If that's all right, I'd like to pray for healing for you."

She looked at him for a long moment. "I would be very grateful," she said softly. "Please."

"Will you give me your hands?" Darius asked, and she placed both of her hands in his. Leaning forward, their heads touched, and Darius began to pray for her.

"God, Father, You are our Creator, the infinite power. I pray to You, Father, through the redemptive blood of Your Son, Jesus. I pray, Father, that You would bring blessings down upon Susanna. I pray, Father, that You would bring the healing power of the Holy Spirit all throughout her body. Father, throughout the Bible, You heal, You perform miracles. Jesus raised the dead, He healed the sick, He cast out demons, and He did miracle after miracle. No sickness comes from You, and You have the ability to cure or do anything You want, Father. I pray, Father, that You would bless Susanna, that You would fill her with the Holy Spirit, and that You would grant her healing, healing so remarkable that she would give You all the glory for it. I pray that You would bless her in the days to come in ways that would be phenomenal. Father, we ask all this in Your name, in the name of the Father, the Son, and the Holy Spirit. Amen."

As Darius finished the prayer and moved his head back, he opened his eyes to find Susanna staring at him, tears beginning to trickle down her right cheek. He felt a bit of wetness in his own eyes as he looked at her.

Her face, which had been tense and angry for most of the flight, now appeared softer, more fragile. Darius couldn't place the exact word for it. Optimistic? Vulnerable? She seemed to be all of those things at once.

"Thank you," she whispered, her voice breaking slightly.

He squeezed her hand gently. "You're welcome," he said, his heart full.

She smiled at him, and they both sat back in their seats. As the intercom announced the descent into New York, Darius felt an overwhelming sense of peace in his heart. What a journey, he thought, heart full. Thank God for change, for transformation, for hope. One more flight to go, then I'm home.

Chapter 39
Terrified but Prepared

D arius was nervous. Terrified, if he were to be truly honest. He hadn't seen his wife in over nine weeks. Communication had been sparse, and what little he had received since it all began was unsettling, then he received the "hate-mail" in North Carolina to go along with the request for a psych evaluation because he was the manic, "Dr. Voodoo." And according to Jessica, he should do it for his kids!

His employees varied between disbelief and anger after he shared with them what was going on. Darius and Andrea had staked out and blessed her house, both of them had read *What Are The Stakes?* and knew the office had been blessed. Andrea, in particular, had a very keen perspective.

"It's nice that she was so worried about us," she said bluntly. "We are with you every day, over 40 hours a week, and not once has she reached out to see if we are okay since you are so unstable." Darius and Jake, another member of his staff, had gotten quite the laugh of that, though Andrea hadn't even cracked a smile showing her displeasure. "You are the last person who needs a psych evaluation. It's ridiculous at best."

Then, almost out of the blue, Jessica reached out, asking to meet. He wasn't naive enough to think that this was a chance for reconciliation. It felt all too clear to him that she was about to tell him it was over. But why? He didn't have answers, only the unsettling feeling that she was already in another relationship.

He tried to push the thought from his mind. Over the past two and a half months, he had grown in ways he hadn't expected, but the more he grew, the more he realized there was still so much work to do. This journey had no end point, no finish line. It was about leveling up—continuing to evolve until he reached what he could only think of as heaven. Tomorrow, he was meeting Jessica in the park, and he was going to be the case study for everyone else tonight in the Marriage Reset group counseling session. While he was afraid of meeting his wife, he was looking forward to the help of his counselors and Brothers in Arms.

***

"You've really helped me out, Sebastian. I can't thank you enough for all the time you've given me this past week," Darius said, his voice crackling over the call.

Sebastian laughed. "Hey, no need to thank me, brother. We're in this together. I know you're going through hell, and I've been there. You're not alone."

Sebastian was based in Europe; he was a fellow Brother in Arms, and his story had become a source of inspiration. Sebastian had been through hell. His wife had had an affair and even lived with the man for a while. Despite everything, they had worked through it and were now together again. It was an amazing turnaround though they seemed to happen regularly.

Darius wanted that too—the miracle of things turning around, the chance to rebuild, to come out of this stronger.

"But sometimes," he admitted, "It feels like no matter how much I work on myself, it won't make a difference. She has no idea who I am now. She doesn't know the changes or appears to care to find out."

Sebastian's voice softened. "Man, you know, we all felt that at one point. But listen, change takes time. It's about duality. You can't let their actions or words define what's truly happening. Just because she acts one way one day and another the next doesn't mean it's what she wants. And remember, none of the affairs last because they are trying to fix their own issues through someone else. Yes, you made mistakes and need to change, but the person that is on the other side of the affair will show their true colors."

"I don't get it on the first part," Darius said, scratching his head.

"You just have to be patient, even when it feels hopeless. Remember, look at her like a five-year-old girl, hurt and scared, talking to her father."

"What?"

"From the call last week?"

Sebastian jogged his memory. It was something one of the other guys said that really caught Darius off-guard. To see yourself as her father? Well, that could be taken from quite a few perspectives, and still it didn't sit right in his mind, no matter which perspective he tried to take.

"Oh, yeah," Darius shifted in his seat. "Honestly, it kind of threw me off at first. I mean, I don't want to see myself as her ... 'daddy.' You know?"

Sebastian laughed. "No, no. That's not what it means. You're not actually her dad or take on the role of her dad, Darius. Think of it more like understanding her wounds and her pain. You know how little kids can be—they lash out, they throw tantrums because they're hurt, not because they actually hate you. You can't take it personally."

"Got it." Darius nodded, thinking it through. "So when she's angry or hurt, just … don't react?"

"Exactly. Stay calm, stay strong. Be the lighthouse on the shore. Let her waves come crashing in, but don't budge. If she's upset, you're there for her. You validate her, hear her, but you don't take it to heart. That's part of being in what we call a 'positive masculine frame,' my friend."

"Yeah, I think I'm finally starting to get that. I've been reading everything, doing all the work, but the hardest part has been not getting a chance to actually show her the changes."

Sebastian nodded. "And that's what's actually working to your advantage. Think about it, Darius—she hasn't seen you in over nine weeks. She has no idea what to expect now. When she sees you calm, stable, not reacting, she won't know what hit her."

Darius paused, taking it in. "I'd never thought of it like that. You think the contrast alone might make a difference?"

"Exactly. She'll see the new you—calm, unshaken. It might take time, maybe a few months, but trust me, even if she says it's over, you don't back down. Stay the course. It's a marathon, not a sprint."

"Sebastian, I'm just scared. What if it's too late?"

"Listen, brother." Sebastian's tone was steady, reassuring. "You've done the work. You're more ready than you think. Most men never make it here—they give up, blame everyone but themselves. But look at you. You've owned your part, admitted where you fell short, found a support system, did the work. That's rare. That's why they call it the one percent."

Darius exhaled, feeling a surge of hope. "Thank you, Sebastian. Really, I don't think I'd be here without you. If I can ever do anything for you, just say the word."

Sebastian's voice softened. "You're going to be fine, Darius. Keep doing what you're doing. Remember—stay steady, be the lighthouse, and let her come to see the man you've become. I'm here for you every step of the way."

***

That night, Darius sat anxiously waiting, facing his laptop waiting for the Marriage Reset counseling session to begin as he would be center stage. Kristen, his counselor, was leading tonight's call and another amazing counselor, Liz, was on that evening as well. There were well over 100 men on the call tonight, Darius noticed including several of his Brothers in Arms among the virtual crowd.

Kristen started welcoming everyone to the call. "I just have to start out by honoring all of you!" she exclaimed. "Here we are on a Wednesday night and we have over 100 men on this call all working to be better. I know I have said this many times but the reason I am a part of this organization is because I am honored to be working for and supporting a community where men are working to grow, to improve on their communication and how they show up, and are responsible for their lives." She paused with a huge smile. "And creating healthier lives and better marriages and families. I am honored to be here and honor you!"

Heads were nodding and many men were showing thumbs up, shaking fists, and showing hands in the air in prayer in response. Positive comments and affirmations were popping up in the group chat, as well. Darius smiled a nervous smile, nodding and took a slow deep breath.

Liz nodded her head and with a big smile said, "Amen."

She then introduced herself. "Look, most of you know my story and if you don't you can go back to that recorded group session. But your main concern is yourself, if you are doing the work and how you show up. You can't decide or determine or have any impact on what is in your wife or girlfriend's head or what they are going to do. What you can do is focus on how you are growing, working on your communication skills, and your emotional intelligence. It's how *you* show up," she stressed.

Heads were nodding all around.

"Remember," Liz continued with a grin on her face, "I got divorced and took my wedding dress and burned it on social media! I despised my ex-husband."

On the Zoom screens, many men, while on mute, were obviously laughing with heads nodding while some newer members were perplexed. Liz was a dynamo and a beautiful person, just like Kristen. Darius had heard her story previously and it was amazing as she and her husband didn't see each other for a year after their divorce, but two years later, after both of them had decided to work on themselves and heal from deep wounds, they got back together and remarried.

Darius was hopeful he could be in the category of men whose wives didn't file, or the 15% who filed and changed their mind. Liz's story was the most unlikely for any man in the program. Only 1% that get divorced remarry.

"We are all here to support your Brother in Arms, Darius," Liz introduced him and the men on the screen waved fists in the air, thumbs up, and a variety of expressions to show their support. "Darius, can you please unmute yourself?"

Darius unmuted himself.

"Darius, Kristen and I, as well as your brothers, are here to support you, but I have Kristen's permission to lead you tonight if that's okay with you."

Darius smiled. "Absolutely, Liz. I appreciate it and want all the help I can get. I also want to thank my brothers and give a shout out to Sebastian, who has been on video calls twice this week to help me prepare and get my mind right."

"Awesome!" Liz said. "Okay, tell us what is going on. What's the update and how can we help?

Darius paused. "Many of you know my story through my regular updates, but I just got back from Africa. When I was in NC before that, I got emails from my wife, which were ... not good. Ugly and incredibly negative. I was hoping when I got back from Africa, we would have a chance to communicate more. I completely stopped with closed loop letters to Jessica after North Carolina. Based on where she is at, it seemed to make no sense. When I got back last week, she sent me a message wanting to meet at the park. I fully expect she is going to tell me it's over."

Liz nodded slowly, eyes fixed on Darius. "Well, how do you feel about that?"

Darius looked down and then back at the screen, hesitated and then said, "I am ... I'm terrified."

"Okay, why are you terrified?"

He looked at her and then glanced at Kristen in the other square as all the men stared at him. "I ... I think it's over."

"Well, what makes you so sure of that?" Liz responded.

"I mean, it's been over nine weeks. As I look back at things ever since she got me to move out of the house, it feels like it was all planned. I don't think she had any intention to work on anything for our marriage. There is no counseling together and the messages she sent were incredibly unkind. I think she is going to file and that's that," Darius replied.

Liz paused and then responded. "Okay. So is your perspective that all you have seen, all the work that you have done, the success stories ... Look, Darius, have you grown?"

Darius held Liz's gaze and slowly nodded his head. "Yes, I know that I have grown and have already changed quite a bit. However, I know I have more work to do and need to keep growing."

"So there is hope." Liz smiled.

Darius smiled. "Okay... yes, there is hope."

"So then why are you terrified?" Liz asked.

He fidgeted in his seat, mind blank feeling stuck. Tears formed in his eyes."Because ... I ... She ... we ... It's almost like she hates me. It seems like there is someone else ... and ... and ..." Darius was fumbling, spitting the words out.

"Darius," Liz interjected, "Take a deep breath."

He paused and took a deep breath. Suddenly, his head cocked sideways and his face and demeanor calmed. "But ... it doesn't matter, does it?" he said calmly. "I don't need to be terrified."

Liz smiled. "What makes you say that? Why not?"

"Because it doesn't matter what she says." He wiped a tear from his eyes, becoming more confident and sitting up straight. "It only matters how I show up. How I treat her and listen. How do I keep moving forward."

Liz had a huge smile on her face and put her hands together in front of her face as if in prayer. Darius could see Kristen shaking her head, smiling in the side square.

Darius continued. "Like Sebastian said, it doesn't matter if she projects on me, what she says, or even if she files. What matters is that I know what I am going to do. I'm going to listen, hear, and validate her, and I'll control my emotions no matter what happens. If I do that, I have nothing to be terrified about. I am moving toward becoming a positive, masculine Godly man."

Several men were nodding and supporting him on muted screens. Darius's confidence continued to grow.

"I have been working my tail off. Working hard to understand the problems and how I added to the issues in our marriage. Even though we have had no communication, I have been doing the work to heal. Attending the group sessions, individual counseling, meeting with his Brothers in Arms, reading ... I've been doing the work to heal. As long as I show up in a positive way, I have nothing to be terrified about because regardless of what she does, I am going to keep moving forward. If we get divorced, it won't matter because I am going to be in such a better place because of the work I have done."

Darius finished, his head slowly nodding and feeling empowered.

As heads nodded on screens, Kristen unmuted herself as Liz, shaking her head, said, "That was beautiful, Darius!"

"Men, I want you all to take a pause and think about what just happened. And I want everyone to take a moment and honor Darius. Because of the work he has been doing, did you just see how he circled back around and worked through the situation on his own?" Kristen said with her beautiful smile, eyes glinting with kindness.

Positive messages started exploding in the group chat as heads bobbed with smiles all around.

"Way to go, brother!"

"Proud of you, man!"

"I just got into this program and have a lot of work to do, but thank you!"

"That was awesome!"

"I am so grateful I get to be your counselor," Kristen began, "And I will never forget our first session, how you were, and how much you have changed in four months. You have done the work and you are going to knock this out of the park."

Darius took a moment, taking it in, and looked at the screen. "Thank you all for your support and help. I will get up tomorrow, keep my routine, and be ready when I get to the park."

As Darius muted his microphone, he leaned back in his chair, sighed and thought how lucky he was that God led him to this program at 3 AM all that time ago.

Chapter 40
Hidden Treasure

By the time he left for the park, a beautiful Saturday morning greeted him, the sun casting golden hues on the world. He felt prepared, having put in the mental and emotional work overall and having stuck to his routine that morning. When he arrived at the designated area—an open space with a small gazebo and a grill—he spotted her car already parked.

She was early.

"You've got this," he murmured to himself. "You've prepared for this moment."

He parked, and quickly said a prayer before stepping out of the car. As he approached the gazebo, Jessica was indeed waiting for him. She stood up, and to his surprise, walked straight toward him and wrapped her arms around him in a hug. He returned it, feeling the tension between them.

"Hello," she said, her voice soft, almost hesitant.

"Hello," Darius replied, his tone steady.

They walked toward the picnic table beneath the gazebo and sat down, two feet apart but facing one another. An anxious Jessica crossed her legs, her gaze drifting anywhere but to him. Darius, on the other hand, felt calm, surprisingly so. His back straight, his posture relaxed but strong, he settled into the conversation.

"It's great to see you," he calmly said. "How are you?"

"I am okay. How are you?" she asked, her voice barely above a whisper.

"I am doing really well overall," he said.

She nodded. "Good. How was Africa?"

"Amazing," Darius smiled.

"That's great," she said, her voice warming a little.

She seemed to look everywhere except at him, and never directly into his eyes. She fidgeted with her fingers. Darius didn't look away. He stayed steady, his gaze soft but unwavering. When there was a brief pause, he asked, "How are things going with your business partner, Michelle? I have heard that it's pretty ugly."

Jessica didn't hesitate. Her voice shifted into something sharp and rapid. "It's been awful. Every interaction with her has been hateful. We're dealing with lawyers, trying to figure out who gets what. She's been bullying me about what's fair, what's mine … I'm not putting up with it anymore. The equity line, the employees, it's all been a mess."

Darius listened, nodding, mirroring her frustration with small gestures of understanding. "I can imagine how difficult that must be. A challenging breakup like that while at the same time being involved in this separation, must be exhausting."

Jessica's gaze finally met his, a flicker of intensity in her eyes. "Yes, it's been one of the worst years of my life. I am not meant to be in business with anyone. I am an empath." She looked away as her voice trailed off.

He sensed she wasn't just talking about business relationships. Empath? he thought. He knew what an Empath was but was surprised as it didn't make a lot of sense to him relevant to Jessica based on his understanding. Darius nodded slowly, acknowledging her pain. "It's been a tough year, I can see that. You've been through a lot. But I'm curious, what if you learned something from all this? If you had the opportunity to work with someone else in business down the road, could you see it working with the right person?"

Jessica immediately shook her head, her expression hardening. "No. I can't. I'll never do that again. People are too difficult. I'm done with it."

"Never again?" Darius asked. "But what if the right opportunity came up? Would you at least be open to it?"

He studied her face as she avoided his gaze again. Listening to her, listening between the lines, he knew deep down what she was trying to say.

"It's not just about business, is it?"

Jessica didn't respond, but she didn't have to. Everything had clearly taken its toll on her—everything with Michelle had been draining. It was obvious that she had never intended to work on them when she asked him to move out. She was removing everything at the same time and had just given herself time to work up to it.

Darius nodded with understanding, but then, gently, he asked, "I understand this is hard for you, and you don't feel like you are meant to be in certain relationships anymore. But I have one favor to ask."

"Anything," she said.

"Please, wait three to six months before filing."

Her eyes widened in disbelief. "What? Six months? I can't wait that long. It's not fair to us, to the kids."

Darius maintained his composure, his voice calm but firm. "Why the rush? You've had this time apart. We've had no time together, and I've been working on myself. I've been going to counseling, learning about my part in our struggles—"

"I just can't," Jessica interrupted, shaking her head. "I took this time to see what I needed and I need to move on."

"Why?" Darius asked gently. "Is there someone else?"

"No," she replied quickly, not looking at him.

"Then why not take a little more time? If there's no one else, what's the rush? Can't we give this a few more months to really consider what's best for our family? For us?"

"Will you be mad at me if I—if I file?"

He met her gaze and his voice remained steady and kind. "Do I look like I'd be mad?" He smiled gently. "I love you. No matter what you do, I won't be angry. My worth, who I am, isn't defined by what anyone else does. I don't get my value from you."

She gave him an odd look, tilting her head, as if trying to decipher something unexpected.

He continued, "I believe we can work through this. I've thought that all along, honestly." He took a breath. "God can fix this."

She blinked, a slight frown creasing her brow, her expression turning almost quizzical, like he was speaking a foreign language.

"I mean it. I know that God can heal us, if we let Him. This time apart, it's a chance to really look at ourselves, our challenges, maybe even fix things in ways we never could before. If we lean into God, we can come back stronger and have the best relationship we have ever had. I even believe that, even if you do file, we will still end up back together."

Now she was staring at him, less quizzical and more like he'd lost his mind. Perhaps this was the first time she was seeing him as a stranger, realizing that maybe she really did know who he was.

"Even if we go through with a divorce, I believe we could still end up together," he said, resolute. "I think the future could be the best time of our lives together."

Her expression didn't soften. In fact, if anything, she seemed even further away from him.

Finally, she replied, "I don't think I can wait."

He hesitated, trying to choose his words carefully. "But what's the hurry? Couldn't we give it a few more months? What's waiting a little longer to be sure? What if you change your mind?"

Jessica didn't respond. She stared at the ground, a distance in her eyes. Darius leaned forward, his voice soft but sincere. "I know you haven't loved me for a few years. And that's okay."

Her eyes snapped up, her demeanor quickly changing as she stated sharply, "That's right."

"But here's the thing," Darius continued. "For almost 20 years, you did."

"Yes," she said quietly as her face softened.

Darius continued. "We've shared a lot of great times, built a family, and shared a lot of love. I believe the good times outweigh the bad. If you loved me for all that time, then you can again. It means, with the right support and focus, we can fall back in love again. Her gaze dropped again, and she rubbed her knee, clearly lost in thought. Darius pressed on. "What if you look back and regret not trying? What if you are like someone who sells a property that you owned for twenty years, thinking it's not worth anything, and then years later, finds out it was full of gold underneath the ground?"

She didn't look at him, her expression unreadable.

"I've been doing the work," Darius said earnestly, "and I'll keep doing it. I'm not giving up on us. We can make this work."

There was a long silence before Jessica stood up, and he followed suit. They exchanged one last hug. As they embraced, Darius whispered, "Just remember, you're not attracted to me anymore so don't grab my ass."

She laughed softly, shaking her head, as they moved out of the embrace but said nothing more. They walked toward their cars, the air between them still thick with unspoken words.

Suddenly, the conversation shifted as Darius brought up the stakes.

Jessica stopped and gave him a steely gaze.

Darius was calm as he explained: "I did it based on Biblical principles. To bring peace to the house during a chaotic time. To bless it, especially during a difficult time for my wife and my family. Maybe someday you will be able to look back and understand it was done out of love."

Jessica's eyes narrowed. "It doesn't matter now," she said curtly, turning toward her car.

Darius stood for a moment, watching her walk away. He sighed deeply, sitting in his car afterward, reflecting on the encounter. It had gone as he expected. She was set on ending things. But he knew he'd handled it well. He'd kept his composure, listened, validated her feelings, and remained calm—even when she seemed confused or surprised by his demeanor. He was proud of himself and grateful for the Marriage Reset Program.

Would it make her reconsider filing? Darius doubted it.

Chapter 41
You're So Special

B efore going to Africa, his operations manager told him that when he came home, he could stay with her and her husband for as long as he needed. They insisted they had more than enough space, letting him know it was more of a command rather than a suggestion—they didn't want him living out of the office anymore.

He thanked them for their kindness and generosity, and said he would be sure not to overstay his welcome. They told him not to be silly, that their home would be his home, and it would be a place where he could rest, heal, and get through this, regardless of what happens.

***

Regardless of what happens ...

Darius lay back on the lounge furniture of the Manns' home thinking about Jessica, about how he missed her, but sincerely wondering what about her he actually missed. Unhealthy attachments...

A beautiful evening was unfolding all around him. The sky was a brilliant purple that faded into a bright cherry; a perfect night that was smudged with a few clouds that kept the dusk air cool. He could hear the birds chirp and sing to one another, and then below their music was the sound of insects chittering. It was peaceful, and he had cozied up to finish *The Masculine in Relationship: A Blueprint for Inspiring the Trust, Lust, and Devotion of a Strong Woman*, by GS Youngblood.

Similar to Jeff Borkowski's *Better Man, Better Marriage*, it struck Darius how much he had been doing "wrong." *The Masculine in Relationship* went into more specific details around polarity and positive versus negative male/female traits.

Suddenly, the sliding glass door opened, and Andrea walked out. "What's wrong?" she asked.

The Manns were special to him and even more so as he was starting to transform and heal. They had allowed him to move out of the office and into their paradise—and he'd forever be grateful for that.

But he hesitated for a few seconds, not even realizing until he became present in the moment that his face was stained with tears. "60% of the content of these books," he started, unsure of where he was going, "I had no idea! I am 51 years old and didn't understand any of this, Andrea. I had no idea when she asked me what I wanted to do for dinner or the weekend and I said, "whatever you want" ... that it was an issue! That I was putting so much on her and not leading. I have been such an asshole, missing in action at home, a completely different man at home the last few years versus the office. I failed her."

It wasn't his first self-abasing tirade. When he had finished, he could hear Kristen's voice telling him to take a breath and stop to think.

Andrea stared at him, letting her own thoughts marinate until she finally said, "Oh my, Darius. You are so special. I am amazed at how broken you are."

Darius, taking a breath, stared back with a look of confusion on his face, not really knowing how to respond.

In the silence, Andrea couldn't help herself and let out a laugh. "Are you serious? Do you know how many people have these issues? So many marriages deal with this and we are all at fault because we are being told we need to be one thing when deep down we know we should be and are meant to be something else.

"It is all out of balance, Darius, but I have never seen a man fight for his marriage more or work so hard to become a better man in the face of adversity than you. I could only hope that if I did this to Rob that he would fight for me and love me as much as you are fighting for Jessica, even if she doesn't understand it."

She was saying what he had come to realize, just in more eloquent words than he could find. He smiled as he knew she was correct.

"Okay, fine," he resigned, laughing with her. "I know what you're doing and, yes, it's working. I hear you, I do, I get it. But ... but if I had understood any of this sooner then maybe it could have been different."

"Yes," she said, flatly, "Maybe it could have been, but she has a part to play as well. The way she has handled this has been horrible, not fair at all. She has made everything worse by not communicating and, right now, she is choosing to be a victim. A very selfish one. Divorce isn't fun and there are two ways it can go. She is lucky you are being so nice because you could be the opposite."

Chapter 42
The Hoosier Healer

D arius sat in the sterile yet oddly inviting office, the faint hum of an air purifier the only background noise as Dr. Whitman leaned forward, his hands folded and his expression softer than he had imagined. He had already talked him through the process in the scientific terms, and vthe tests that he had undergone were nothing if not extensive.

Food sensitivities and allergies, traces of toxic metals, exposure to unnatural or artificial chemicals, immune challenges, and negative responses ... They really left no stone unturned.

"Inflammation," Dr. Whitman explained, "Is the body's alarm system, responding to the chaos we introduce into it. Food sensitivities, heavy metals, chemicals, these are the intruders, and everyone's system reacts differently depending on their environment and what they've been exposed to. We eliminate what the primary culprit is and then reinforce the immune system, because it has the sophistication and ability to remove that sensitivity."

"100% of the time?" Darius asked.

Dr. Whitman shook his head. "No. There are a percentage of patients who have those allergies for the rest of their lives, and those allergies can be dangerous. But in comparison to the average population, this is a very small percentage of people."

"Like Sickle Cell Anemia or Type I Diabetes, for example, while many other issues are created or self-inflicted?" Darius questioned.

Dr. Whitman smiled, faint but knowing. "That's exactly right. For most people, these aren't lifelong sentences; they're learned responses. Even genetic predispositions don't have to be activated, and if we can catch it early, before it expresses itself, we can often reverse it entirely."

"So ... we don't have to be victims of the genes we carry," Darius said. "We can deactivate them, or never activate them in the first place."

"Precisely." Dr. Whitman agreed. "It's not just theory; it's science. And it's happening in real-time, here and now. But it requires work. The right supplements, the right detox protocols, and most importantly, a system strong enough to handle the process."

Dr. Whitman's words flowed on, detailing how amino acids from plant-based sources could rebuild the body's detox pathways, how decades of accumulated toxins could be flushed out, restoring not just health but vitality. It was a rebuilding process—not just a cleansing, but a transformation.

"I'll try to explain it another way," Dr. Whitman continued. "Pain is the body yelling at you. It's not just discomfort; it's a signal, a cry for help. Inflammation, chronic aches, fatigue ... these are all the body's way of saying, 'Something isn't right. Fix me.' But most people? They silence the cry. They take a pill, slap a band-aid on the problem, and move on. They're not fixing it; they're suppressing it."

Darius nodded. He'd lived that truth. Years of masking symptoms with quick fixes, chasing relief without ever asking the deeper question: what's causing this?

"But when you go in and work with the structural problems, you stop suppressing it and start fixing it," he added.

Dr. Whitman nodded. "The body is an intricate system, beautiful, complex, and compassionate. God designed it that way. It's built to heal itself if you give it the tools and remove the barriers. But when you ignore the structural issues and pair that with toxins, food sensitivities, and immune challenges, you're overloading it. It can't keep up. And that's when chronic pain and illness set in. So you've got to address it all."

Shifting the computer screen around so that Darius could see too, Dr. Whitman started to go through his results.

SUBJECTIVE :
Chief Complaint : hip pain
Status : remained unchanged
Discomfort/Pain Intensity / Severity : 5
Timing / Frequency : Constant
Problem side : Left

Notes: The patient updated the changes in their chief complaint(s) as noted above. Sleep issues. Left hip pain.

Pre-existing conditions :
High Blood pressure , High cholesterol , Joint/back pain

OBJECTIVE FINDINGS :
A pre-manipulation P.A.R.T. assessment was performed in the area(s) of chief complaint. Further biomechanical evaluation revealed the presence of additional misaligned segments that are contributing postural imbalance and affecting the chief complaint. The findings are listed in the above P.A.R.T. exam. It was necessary to manipulate the subluxated segments as they are complicating factors. • The patient has had pain for more than eight days: according to the Mercy Guidelines, recovery may take 1.5 times longer. • This case is classified as chronic; lasting more than 16 weeks. According to the Mercy Guidelines, patients with chronic disorders may require more treatment/care to resolve symptomatic episodes.

Patient has right pelvic pattern.
Patient has anatomical short leg.
Patient has 1- inch of right pelvic/leg deficiency.
Patient has facet irritation at L4/5 with counter rotation.

Nutrition:
Color: B/G
PEP -
PPP - Sm. intestines 6
Foods: 8
Immuno: 3
Metals: 7
Chemicals: (2)

There was a lot he understood. There was a note for his "chief complaint" as well as his pre-existing conditions, but then things started to get a little bit muddled—even with his medical background.

Dr. Whitman smiled, clearly seeing his confusion. "Don't worry," he assured, "I'll take you through it all."

"I think I get it," Darius said. "But what I don't quite understand is the numbers?"

"We use it as a guideline," Dr. Whitman began. "When someone comes in, especially someone with complicated issues, I'll often give them a number. A baseline. Let's say they're at a seven, which is bad. That gives us a way to measure progress as we work through the layers."

Darius nodded, eyes narrowing in thought.

"For example," Whitman continued, "I've got a lady right now, a rheumatoid arthritis patient. She was diagnosed just last year. Active inflammation, pain, digestive involvement. It was bad. When she first came in, her inflammation index was sky-high, but we've been working at it. Diet changes, supplements, addressing blockages. I got a call from the office this week, she's down to a two or three now. That's huge."

"Two or three?" Darius repeated, his voice tinged with excitement. "That means her body is healing?"

"Exactly. The inflammatory reaction is calming down. The body wants to repair itself; it's designed to do that. But there are blockages, stressors, toxins, infections, that prevent it from doing the work. Medicine, traditionally, overrides those blockages, but often with a cascade of side effects. What we're doing is removing the barriers altogether so the body can heal naturally."

Darius exhaled slowly. "That's what I want to aim for."

"That's exactly what you want to aim for," Dr. Whitman echoed. "The inflammatory pathways are key. There are five major ones in the body: oxidation, the oxidase pathway, free radicals, nuclear factor kappa-beta, methylation, and nitric oxide. Each of them can play a role in chronic inflammation. That's why, after your initial workup, I ensured we were addressing all of those pathways right from the start."

Darius scribbled the words in his notebook, pausing to underline oxidation and methylation. "So you've refined this process over time, through trial and error, by learning from patient outcomes?"

Dr. Whitman smiled, a faint flicker of deserved pride breaking through his professional demeanor. "Exactly. Early on, we didn't address all these pathways upfront. It took longer to see results, and sometimes, we'd miss the root cause entirely. But through experience, collaboration, and a lot of learning, we've built a more holistic approach. It's faster now, and more effective."

Darius looked up, a question hanging on the edge of his lips. He set his pen down. "And for me?"

Dr. Whitman didn't miss a beat. "Your priority? The biggest issue in your workup wasn't the hip pain, though that's what brought you here. It wasn't even the sleeplessness. For you, the foundational issue is a leaky gut."

Darius blinked. "Leaky gut?"

"The small intestine," Dr. Whitman explained. "When it's compromised, it allows inflammatory factors to leak into your bloodstream, triggering systemic issues. Every single day, it's fueling the very problems you're trying to escape. That's where we start for you."

The room fell silent for a moment as the words sank in. Darius felt a mix of frustration and relief.

"I didn't even realize ... "

"You're not alone," Dr. Whitman said gently. "Most people don't. But once you address the gut, you're not just treating symptoms; you're tackling the root cause. Everything else will start to fall into place. 70% of diseases come from the gut."

Dr. Whitman tapped his pen lightly against the edge of his desk, the rhythmic sound filling the pause between his words.

"What's interesting about your case, Darius," he began, leaning forward, "Is that when you were lying on your stomach, we took that leg differential test. It's a way to measure muscle and mechanical imbalances. Normally, when I turn a patient onto their back, it takes the muscle play out and things balance out. But you? Yours got worse."

Darius frowned, unsure of what to make of the observation.

Whitman continued, his tone shifting, as though pulling back a curtain to reveal a more profound layer. "That tells me there's more going on here than just structural or mechanical issues. The hip, the neck pain, all of it ... it's not just about muscles. There are other factors at play."

Darius tilted his head. "Other factors?"

Dr. Whitman nodded. "Something we don't discuss nearly enough is emotional stress, and, more importantly, the spiritual stress tied to it. These aren't just abstract ideas; they're highly inflammatory. People who've turned away from the spiritual aspects of life, who ignore that essential part of existence? They carry it in their bodies. It becomes part of them, feeding their inflammation."

Darius thought about all of the emotions Larissa had taken out of his body, how it had removed most of his previous anxiety. Spiritual stress ... He thought about the demonic chord and the shock of demonic influence.

"So what is the plan?' Darius asked.

Dr. Whitman smiled. "We will start the plan today if you are ready. Once a week for six weeks, during that time, we run tests, refine the protocols, and assess your progress. Then after six weeks, we do a full rescan and we look at what's improved, what hasn't.

You will move to twice a week for a month or so and then once a week. The body will lead us but everyone is different."

Darius looked up at the ceiling, rubbed his face and looked back at Dr. Whitman. "I can't imagine being out of pain ... Sleeping. I am getting off these medications."

"Darius, everything you are dealing with, we can fix. The body is always ready to heal, Darius. Always," Dr. Whitman said, breaking through his thoughts, "The trick is getting out of its way."

Darius smiled with a determined look on his face. "Let's roll!"

Chapter 43
Anything?

D arius drove through downtown, mind wandering as he headed to dinner with Barry at St Elmo's, one of Indianapolis's famed steak houses where everyone would rave about the shrimp cocktail and the spicy horseradish cocktail sauce that set all senses on fire! The historical venue gave great service, ambience, and food. He hadn't been to such a nice place in a while—business had been tough lately, and with the looming reality of his divorce, finances were a concern.

He had asked her to wait six months; she barely waited two weeks before filing. Since they'd last spoken, her actions seemed to confirm that she'd already detached from their marriage long ago. It was almost as if she'd already considered herself single. The data he'd encountered in the marriage program had mentioned something about this—how, sometimes, one partner quits internally long before the end. But that didn't make it any easier to accept.

He'd always believed she was someone who couldn't pretend— but then he was learning that he had a lot of work to do on his own awareness. Someone who was bringing up grievances from 14 years ago was hardly transparent.

The idea felt impossible. How could someone fake love in this situation? How could she have looked at him, held him, shared life with him, all while supposedly harboring no genuine affection? It didn't make sense to him, and his heart resisted it, clinging to the hope that what they'd had was real.

Yet, as painful as it was, Darius was learning from the experience. He was uncovering layers within himself—layers of emotion, resilience, and understanding that he hadn't tapped into before. He was starting to realize that, while he couldn't control her feelings or actions, he could use this time to examine his own growth and healing, to face the difficult truths about their marriage, and to prepare for whatever lay ahead.

But despite that weight on his shoulders, he was excited to see Barry, a friend who he respected and admired.

Barry was an old colleague, originally from Indiana but now settled in Florida, and they'd gotten to know each other more closely in recent years. He was a sharp, charismatic businessman with a successful career and, seemingly, a happy marriage, something Darius had once imagined he had himself. The two hadn't spoken much since Darius's world had turned upside down, though Barry had reached out repeatedly. Recently, Darius had finally opened up to him about everything—his failing marriage, the business struggles—and Barry, sympathetic, had insisted on taking him out for dinner.

Darius parked, made his way into the restaurant, and found Barry already seated, waiting with a warm smile and ready to give Darius a hearty hug. Barry's familiar presence was grounding, and Darius felt immediately more grounded. They ordered drinks and settled into conversation. Barry didn't sugarcoat things, though; he looked at Darius with concern.

"You've looked better," he said, his eyes sharp but kind.

Darius chuckled. "Yeah, well, it's been pretty difficult. Let's just put it that way."

They spoke openly, Darius sharing the complicated twists of the last year. He couldn't quite believe that his wife no longer wanted to be with him; it still felt surreal. The painful reality that she'd filed for divorce hit him in waves as he recounted the details. Meeting her weeks ago in the park, hoping they might salvage things with counseling, only to realize she was done. Darius opened up, speaking about the heartache and confusion, the hope that maybe, just maybe, she might change her mind.

Barry listened closely. Then, leaning in, he asked, "If you could, would you really do anything to save the marriage?"

Darius paused, taken aback by the question. "Well, yeah, I mean ... I would have done anything," he said, hesitant.

"Anything?" Barry's voice became firmer, his gaze penetrating. "Think about that, man. Really think."

Darius sat back, letting the question hang in the air. "You're right. I wouldn't do anything. Not like that. Not to keep the old marriage."

Barry smiled, satisfied. "Good. The truth is, sometimes life brings us to these crossroads for a reason. It might hurt like hell, but you'll come out stronger for it." He leaned back, eyeing Darius with pride. "You're going to come out of this better than you were before it happened."

Darius explained how he'd been changing, healing—how he'd joined a support group, started meditation, therapy, and even revamped his diet and lifestyle. He spoke about the inner work, cleaning out old emotional wounds, his journey to becoming the best version of himself. He wasn't just transforming physically but mentally and emotionally too.

"I mean, you're not exactly the bubbly, confident Darius I know," Barry said, looking at him with concern. "But I'll tell you this, whatever you're doing, you look great physically."

Darius managed a small smile. "Well, I've been on this new organic diet," he replied. "I started this program after doing a lot of research on the chemicals and pesticides in our food. It's insane, poisons, basically."

Barry's eyebrows shot up. "Huh. Really?"

"Yeah. Had a heart scare a while back, and they had me on multiple medications. I'm now completely off of them, just came off the meds a week or two ago."

"Really?" Barry leaned in as Darius filled him in on the health scare and explained his experience with Dr. Whitman, the holistic doctor he'd been seeing. He talked about the detox program, breathing exercises, and meditation routine that had all become part of his daily life.

"Wow. That's impressive, brother. And it's something to be proud of," Barry nodded. "And as for your marriage ... I'm glad you're holding onto that hope. But sometimes these things happen for a reason, man. You have a beautiful future ahead of you. You're brilliant, you're good-looking, and trust me, you'll be just fine if you end up single."

Darius looked down, his voice soft but resolute. "I know that's what people think, but I'm not interested in that. He paused and asked Barry. "You believe in God, right?

"Yes, of course," Barry nodded.

"The thing is, I never understood the truth about evil, about the demonic," Darius said matter-of-factly.

Barry looked at Darius with no expression. Then, he clapped a hand on Darius's shoulder. "Look, I respect that you aren't ready to date, Darius, and I applaud you for taking the high road. You're a better man for it. But I've been through my own share of heartache, and I'm telling you, getting divorced was painful, but it led me to Laura. She's the kind of woman who can support a business owner, who gets what that life is about. She understands the hard work and

The Modern-Day Job ◆ Chapter 43

sacrifices it takes. Sure, there are challenges, but having someone who truly gets it, who values you and what you're building, that makes all the difference."

Darius nodded, digesting Barry's words as they ordered steaks and sides. The conversation drifted to kids, business, and the pressures of the economy. When their food arrived, they settled into an easy rhythm, swapping stories and sharing laughter over dinner.

When their plates were cleared, Barry leaned back, grinning. "You want dessert?"

Darius chuckled. "I haven't had dessert in a while. I'm on this organic program, remember? Been cooking all my meals for the last two months."

"Okay, then we'll split a dessert. My treat," Barry laughed.

"All right, you twisted my arm," Darius relented, laughing, too.

After dessert, as the evening drew to a close and they readied to part ways, Barry wrapped Darius in a big hug. "Look, man, I'm here for you. I know how rough this is. I've been through it, and it's no joke. I tried reaching out before so you'd know you've got support. I love you, man, and I'm here for whatever you need, anytime."

"Thank you, Barry," Darius replied, deeply moved. "I can't tell you how much that means."

Driving home that night, he thought about Barry's question. He didn't want his old marriage back or this version of his wife. He definitely didn't want his old self back. Yes, he still loved her and cherished his family, but now he understood he wouldn't compromise the growth he'd achieved or settle.

"If you could, would you really do anything to save the marriage?"

For the first time, he could say for certain his answer was no.

Chapter 44
Chemical Candy

He was thrilled to spend some time with his youngest son. Despite the disasters in his marriage and business, their relationship had been steadily improving over the past year. It had always been strained, especially compared to his bond with his other two children, making it harder to connect with his youngest. Parenting differences between him and his wife had often led to arguments over what his son should be allowed to get away with, and Darius had often felt like the "bad guy."

Three months before everything fell apart, Darius had made a decision to approach things differently. He would try to be more accepting, less focused on tough love, and simply love while working on finding more ways to connect. The decision had paid off. Despite the complications of the separation, including not being able to see his son as often, the week they spent together in North Carolina was invaluable. That time had allowed them to grow closer, and it had been a blessing.

Now that Darius was staying at the Manns, it was harder to see his son. His wife had him on the go with friends constantly, and there never seemed to be enough time for just the two of them. The separation had created a lack of structure, much different from a typical divorce. So when they were able to set something in stone rather than just "pencil it in," Darius was more than a little excited to see his son again.

He drove over to pick him up, and as they headed back to the house, they caught up on everything—sports, friends, and life in general. It was a short ten-minute drive, but they had a good conversation.

When they walked in through the front door, his son immediately asked, "What are you going to cook, Dad?"

Darius smiled. "I know you love salmon, so I thought I'd make salmon and broccoli."

"Hey, that works for me," his son responded. "Sounds good."

As they chatted, his son set a bag of Skittles on the kitchen table. Darius grimaced but didn't say anything. Ever since starting the organic program, he had been more conscious of the chemicals in the food they ate. He had re-read sections of Dr. Whitman's book on the subject, and this time, it was to understand how the chemicals affected his wife and son. The first time he'd read it, it had been for his own health, trying to figure out how to get off the medications he was on. But now, he was noticing things like ADHD, allergies, mood swings, and skin challenges, which affected both his son and his wife.

Darius had even compiled a list of the book's key takeaways, specifically focusing on how the chemicals in their food were harming his family. After committing to the program, he had gone to speak with Dr. Whitman about it, and he started making notes, printing out sections, and highlighting the points that applied to Ben. He hoped that by showing his wife the connection between these chemicals and their son's struggles, she might start to see the issue more clearly, even though she wasn't ready to listen to him on the matter yet.

His thoughts went back to his appointment last week with Dr. Whitman. He had excitedly asked Dr. Whitman about ADHD.

Dr. Whitman said. "Darius, it's just a label. It's an accumulation of metals and chemicals that cause little micro-inflammations in the brain, which is why the person has an issue remembering or paying attention."

"So you have gotten kids or adults off of medications for ADHD? Can you help get my son off these meds?" Darius asked.

Dr. Whitman looked intently at Darius, somewhat perplexed by the question. "Yes ... Yes, Darius. We have helped many kids in this situation."

Darius had pointed out another section of the book around allergies and the real causes. "Both my wife and son have horrible allergies and this program could help both of them!" Darius exclaimed.

Dr. Whitman had smiled broadly, shaking his head. Finally, he had patted Darius on the back as he put his arm around him in a loving embrace. "Yes, Darius," he stated affectionately. "I know. I wrote the book."

Darius laughed remembering the conversation.

Dinner put the thought from his mind for now. Instead, they talked about business and other casual topics as he cooked, and after they sat down to eat, his son looked up and said, "Wow, this is great, Dad. Thanks."

"You're welcome. I love you," Darius said.

"I love you, too."

After they finished, Darius cleaned up the dishes and then said, "Hey, I want to share something with you."

"Okay."

"You know I've been on this new diet, right?" Darius began. "I've been doing the organic thing for a few months now, but I'm also going to a holistic doctor about 40 minutes away, and he's been helping me reset my body."

"What do you mean, Dad?"

"Well, a lot of the food we eat has chemicals and pesticides in it, stuff that's made in laboratories, not by God. God made everything naturally, right?"

"Well, yeah, I guess. Food comes from the ground."

"Exactly. Back in the Bible, people lived for hundreds of years. Even after the time of Noah, people still lived over 100 years, but life expectancy has dropped significantly, including going down each of the last three years in the USA. It's the chemicals in our food that are making us sick. They process food and add chemicals to make it last longer, also feeding animals grain instead of grass and using antibiotics and steroids with the animals, but it's not natural. It's not how we were meant to eat."

Darius paused for a moment, allowing his son to take in what he was saying. "I read this book for myself, to figure out how to get off medications—"

"Oh, and how has that helped you, Dad?" His son asked, a hint of sarcasm buried beneath his curiosity.

"Well, as of a few weeks ago, I'm off all the medicines. I don't need any of them anymore. My blood pressure is normal. I feel great. I'm sleeping better. It's made an incredible difference." The two of them smiled at one another, and Darius continued. "But coming to my original point, as I kept reading, I started noticing things about ADHD, irritability, mood swings, allergies ... things that you and Mom deal with."

His son raised an eyebrow. "Wow."

"I'm sending this all to your mom," Darius said. "But if you ever want to try the program I'm doing, I'd love to help you do it. I spoke to Dr. Whitman last week and he has gotten many kids off of ADHD medications."

His son nodded, though a bit uncertain. "Okay."

"Let's do a little experiment," Darius said. "Bring me that candy bag, the Skittles you're eating."

His son brought the bag over, and Darius started reading off the ingredients. "Okay, corn syrup. It's not natural. It's processed and linked to obesity, diabetes, liver disease, and heart problems."

His son frowned. "That's not good."

"Citric acid causes skin irritation, allergies, swelling, and joint stiffness. Tapioca dextrin? Stomach pain, bloating, diarrhea, upset stomach, and, surprise surprise, more allergies."

His son frowned, but Darius wasn't done. "Modified cornstarch? Diarrhea, Crohn's disease, and cancer."

His son's eyes widened. "Crohn's disease?"

"It's an intestinal disorder. It's not good."

They went through the rest of the ingredients. Red 40 damages DNA, causes ADHD, and can lead to cancer. Yellow causes hyperactivity and allergies. Blue causes developmental issues and brain cancer. The list went on, and by the time they were finished, his son looked shocked.

Darius explained further. "These foods are full of chemicals, dyes, and things that our bodies weren't made to handle. They're causing problems that lead to more doctors, more medication, and more Band-Aids. But they don't fix the problem."

"So, you're saying ... I could change what I eat and reset my body?" His son asked, a little skeptical.

"Exactly. The opportunity is there," Darius said. "And you wouldn't need all these medications. You can feel better, just by changing what you eat."

"Huh," his son replied. "Something to think about."

They spent the rest of the evening on the back deck, talking, enjoying the weather, and playing with the dogs. As the night wore on, Darius asked, "Would you like to go do something else later?"

"I can't. Mom has plans for us," his son said.

Darius nodded, masking his frustration. *She's with him all the time and when I get some time with him, she interferes,* he thought. He drove his son back to the house, where they talked more about the upcoming school year and basketball. As they pulled into the driveway, his son leaned over, thanked him for dinner, and gave him a hug.

"I love you, Dad."

"I love you, too."

His son got out of the car and headed inside. Darius watched him go, feeling a mix of emotions. He loved his children more than anything, and the idea that his son might avoid some of the same struggles he'd faced gave him hope. As he drove off, Darius couldn't help but feel grateful for the time they'd spent together, and maybe, just maybe, he had planted some seeds.

Chapter 45
Rise and Shine!

Darius sat on the back deck, looking out over the water. It was beautiful, truly. The Manns had a little slice of paradise here—a gorgeous home. From the upper deck, he could see trees framing the water, while down on the lower level was a cozy fire pit and a dock, stretching out over what he'd call a large pond; it was shallower than a lake. Birds filled the sky, and occasionally, eagles swooped by. He felt peaceful here, grateful for the serenity it offered.

But it wasn't without its bumps.

Early one morning, after his workout and meditation, Darius decided to cook. It was six in the morning, everybody else was still in bed, and he was not yet accustomed to the sensitivity of their gas stove. He cranked up the burner too high and got distracted while rummaging through the fridge. Smoke filled the kitchen, and the smoke alarm erupted. Rob and Andrea came stumbling down the hall, bleary-eyed.

"Oh boy," Rob gruffly stated, while Andrea's expression was tight. As they aired out the room, Darius could only mutter apologies, cheeks burning. Rob shrugged, saying with a grin, "Maybe not cook so early if you're going to burn the house down."

Later, Darius laughed about it, relieved that they took it in stride. Living with the Manns had gone smoother than he'd imagined, despite the occasional missteps. Their spare bed was a single, pushed against the wall, just big enough for him. If he rolled the wrong way in the night, he'd end up smacking into the wall. Still, he cherished the setup and was thankful they had offered to open their home to him.

Though he missed his own kids terribly, Darius felt grounded here. They would come over on weekends, gathering around the fire pit, playing cards, and sharing stories. Those evenings were truly precious—a time to enjoy the stars and the peace surrounding them.

As the separation wore on, things had grown more complicated. It had only been a few weeks since they'd last met in the park, but Jessica's behavior increasingly illustrated that the marriage was over in her mind.

One afternoon, she texted to ask if he could keep their son while she went out of town. He paused, baffled. Why would their son need to come to stay with him here? Why not ask Darius to stay in their family home, where his son could sleep in his own room? Something about it didn't sit right, and he couldn't ignore the unsettling feeling that Jessica was already living as if their marriage were over.

Then she filed.

The children were devastated, reacting with confusion and grief. It wasn't what any of them wanted. Trying to hold everything together, he encouraged them to remain calm, asking them to show their mother love and support, no matter how difficult it was for them. He still loved her, and he loved their family. Even now, he held onto a thread of hope that they could find their way back to one another.

His daughter, in particular, struggled to understand his behavior.

"What do you mean, Dad? I don't understand how you can stay so calm," she said.

"Well," he replied, "I'm putting in a lot of work through counseling, this program, and by doing breathing exercises and meditation. That's what's keeping me grounded. I needed to make some changes in myself." He paused. "In the end, we all get to choose what we focus on. We can look for positives or negatives in any situation, and I'm trying to focus on the positives. This program says 15% of women who file for divorce change their minds. So there is still a chance she could change her mind."

His daughter still looked puzzled as they drove to pick up a rental car. "But, Dad," she asked, "How can you stay so hopeful? She seems so certain about her decision."

"What do you mean?" he asked gently.

"Well, she says she's prayed about it, and that this is the right thing for her," she answered.

Darius sighed. "I don't know, honey. Who's she praying to?"

"What do you mean, Dad?"

"God hates divorce. He gave it as a conciliatory measure but only when there is adultery, abandonment, or abuse. So who is she praying to?" he asked again.

His daughter looked at him. "I don't understand how you can be nice or how you are handling it this way, especially if she's cheating."

Darius looked at his daughter with a serious expression. "Jesus died on the cross for us. The ultimate sacrifice of Grace. If she doesn't need Grace now, then when does she?"

His daughter sat in silence after his rather matter-of-fact statement.

***

They had recently attended a church service where he had the chance to baptize his youngest son. It was a moving experience for him; he had now baptized all three of his children. He had prayed fervently that morning, asking God to bring a message that would bless others in the congregation, even if it wasn't meant to help him directly. After the baptism, he looked out at the church, where his family and Jessica's were sitting side by side in the pews. It seemed like a perfect moment for God to do something remarkable.

As he returned to his seat, he couldn't believe it when the minister began a sermon on marriage and divorce. It was as if his prayer had been answered right there. The minister spoke about how God's original plan was for marriages to stay intact, and how the only allowances for divorce were abuse, abandonment, or adultery. This was incredible. He glanced over at Jessica, her father, and her stepmother down the aisle; he could feel the tension, the weight of the words.

At that time, he hadn't known Jessica had already filed for divorce, though her bare finger was a telling sign. The minister continued, urging everyone to follow five steps before moving forward with a divorce. Darius realized that Jessica hadn't taken any of these steps, and he wondered if this could be God's way of opening her eyes.

Afterward, several unusual events began unfolding. The first was a vivid dream he had one night, where he saw himself moving back into the family home. When he awoke, he was startled by a voice in his mind, saying, "You need to move back into your home." The idea struck him as absurd, almost enough to make him laugh, but it wouldn't leave him. It felt unsettling, almost surreal, as if he were losing his mind. That's crazy, he thought.

In the days following the dream, he had two more promptings to return home. One was an overwhelming feeling he experienced after one of the Marriage Reset sessions: he needed to go back to his house. It seemed crazy, like a nuclear bomb would go off if he did it.

And the next morning, Andrea came up to him and said, "We need to talk."

"Sure," he said, curious.

They sat down at the table, and she looked him in the eye. "I just had the most powerful experience in prayer for you," she said. "After I finished praying, God told me that you need to go back to your house."

Darius's eyes widened. "Really?"

"Yes. Your son needs you, and with the way she's been acting, you need to be there for him. Things are only going to get stranger."

He let out a breath. "I don't know, Andrea. Part of my past struggles have always been about control, about trying to hold things together. And now I'm working hard to let go of that need. Moving back into the house feels like taking control again, and that's the opposite of what I'm supposed to be doing right now. Plus, if I do this, it could explode."

Angela nodded but replied firmly, "It may not be good, but you need to do it for your son. This isn't about control; it's about being present when he needs you most. Things are going to explode anyway."

He sighed and looked away, mulling it over. "You know what's interesting?" he finally said. "I had a dream telling me to go back home. And then, at another time, I just had this feeling that I needed to be there. Now you're saying it too."

Angela reached over and put a hand on his shoulder. "I think it's time."

Thinking about the past six weeks, it all still seemed like a bad dream. But after all this time spent in prayer, Darius felt a growing conviction that it was right. He had already packed his things. Tomorrow, he would go to the office, then return to the house and settle in the basement. He knew Jessica wouldn't take it well, but he had made up his mind. After everything, he believed that was what God had directed him to do.

Chapter 46
Back Into the Fire

The day he moved back into the house felt like the precursor to a mushroom cloud—a sudden, cataclysmic event that left unimaginable destruction in its wake. Or at least, that's how he thought of it.

The decision came after much contemplation, prayer, and deep discussions with his Brothers in Arms.

Originally, the plan, according to her, was for them to separate—for him to move out—so they could work on themselves individually before coming back together to address their relationship. That idea, however, had evaporated. Without any real effort to repair their connection or engage in meaningful interaction, she had chosen instead to file for divorce, ending everything.

Initially, he had been more than willing to leave; he loved her after all, and he wanted this to work. He'd been willing to live in the office or with friends for a time. He loved her enough to give her the space she said they needed. But now, after her decision to move forward with the divorce, it was obvious she was manipulating him.

He could no longer justify staying away. His reasons were clear: his son, his values, and their financial reality.

When he packed up the night before, it wasn't much; whatever he had taken from the house to the office and from the office to the Manns' residence. But before heading to the office that morning, he drove to the house. It was empty—she had likely taken their son to school. The dogs greeted him with wagging tails as he hauled his few belongings down to the basement.

Standing there, he looked around. This space had once been his older son's refuge—a cool, private corner of the house. It seemed ideal for a teenager. But now, at 51, moving into the basement felt far from cool. It felt like exile. His wife despised him, had nothing kind to say anymore, and, from what he understood, seemed to be involved with someone else.

"Not so cool now," he muttered. Then, with a deep breath, he shook himself out of his reverie.

"This is the right move," he reassured himself. "It's not going to be good. She's not going to be happy. There will be fallout, probably an explosion. But it doesn't matter. I've done the work and can handle it."

Over the past several months, he'd thrown himself into working on self-improvement and it had all brought him here. It wasn't about her reaction, he reminded himself. It was about being present and about doing what's right for my son and living in alignment with my values.

He hoped she might see the changes he'd made—his effort to listen, validate, and understand. Maybe she'd notice his presence, his calm, his commitment. And yet, even if she didn't, he wouldn't lose himself. He would not sink into guilt, shame, or anger. He had resolved to respond rather than react, to stay centered amidst the waves of her frustration or disdain.

I'll be the lighthouse, he thought. The coastline. Unmoved, no matter the storm.

He breathed deeply, letting the cool basement air ground him.

"This is where I am," he said aloud. "And I'm going to make the best of it."

His hope flickered, a small ember in his heart. He envisioned a future where he could cook healthy meals for his son, lead by example, and guide them both toward something better. For the first time in years, he felt medication-free, rested, and clear-headed—a remarkable shift considering how far he had come.

He stood for a moment, feeling a sense of pride—the calm before the storm. Then, with a resolute nod, he made his way out back up the stairs and out to the car, driving to the office with the certainty that he could handle whatever was to come.

***

It only took a few hours for that certainty to be put to the test.

That afternoon, reality set in, and an email arrived from Jessica—sharp and hostile. She made it clear to him that being in the basement was unacceptable. Once again, she used their son as a buffer, telling him that Ben was just now getting accustomed to the living situation and he was upsetting Ben again. Their son had expressed his feelings multiple times during their visits in North Carolina, even during their prayer times together. It was clear that his hope was for them not to get divorced. It was as if she was implying that by leaving, he had abandoned their son.

Darius shook his head, the words lingering in his mind.

You forced me out, he thought bitterly. I didn't abandon him. I moved out because I trusted you when you said we'd work on this.

He took a breath, trying to suppress his anger.

"You chose this," he whispered to himself. "I didn't."

Her accusations stung, especially when she implied that he had been irresponsible. Financially, their situation was dire. He had continued to pay for everything but he needed to start making money again. She continued to be oblivious to their financial situation, even though he kept trying to make her aware, and here she was mentioning in her email that he should just get an apartment. What did she not understand? He bit back a curse, catching himself mid-thought.

"Sorry, God," he murmured. "I'm working on it."

He shook his head, pressing his hand to his temple. His thoughts were scattered, his mind still grappling with the challenge.

The message ended with a stark reminder of how wrong he was for moving back in, and it didn't matter what he did: divorce was inevitable. She was going to reach out to her lawyer, to have them get the judge to force him out of the house. It wasn't something she wrote explicitly, but through the jargon she used, he knew what the implications were.

Darius shook his head and smiled, trying to push away the frustration. "Well, I pay for the house. I pay for everything," he muttered to himself.

More than once, people had told him to stop paying for her phone, her insurance, for everything. Maybe they were right. Maybe he was being foolish, but the truth was, he loved her. He loved his family. He didn't want to get mired in the mess of bitterness, greed, or selfishness when it came to money. But even as he held onto that, a part of him still hoped, still believed things might turn around. The business would change, he thought. He had never gone this long without making money.

He exhaled, then took a deep breath in.

He wasn't interested in fighting with her. But after she had filed, and failed to follow through with what she had promised—about working on things—he felt betrayed. If he had known she was intent on filing, he would never have moved out. Living with friends wasn't a long-term option, and they didn't have the money for him to be paying for an apartment. Regardless of how she saw it, with the tax burden hanging over their heads, the situation was dire. They had owed a substantial amount in taxes the year before and most likely would again—well over $100K.

His lawyer had been blunt. "I've had a lot of clients, but you are certainly ballsy." She laughed. "I've been getting steamrolled by your wife's lawyer over you moving back in and abandoning your son. What happened?"

"Well, you probably won't believe me," Darius said, shaking his head, "But from several different directions, I was told I needed to move back into the house."

"Told? What do you mean, who told you?"

"Well … I was given a dream that I needed to move back in. Then someone who's been praying for me said I should too." He paused. "Which didn't make sense to me, but it seemed clear that God was directing me. The Marriage Reset Program really taught me that I had to let go and stop trying to control everything. It took me a while to realize that I'd been trying to control things, even though I didn't know it at the time. But this … based on everything I was hearing, I just thought this was one of those situations where it was different."

"I would've told you not to move out at all. But based on everything you've told me, it sounds like a good thing, and I hope it helps your son," his lawyer said.

"Yeah, I hope so, too. I hope I can cook for him, spend time with him, and maybe she'll see me a little differently."

"Well, I've filed something back with the court, and it looks like … I don't know, either her lawyer talked some sense into her or maybe she realized that the judge isn't going to make you move out of a house you pay for. And even the abandonment thing doesn't really hold up. So, for now, she's taken back the request for a court hearing to try to kick you out."

"Okay, that's excellent," Darius said, relieved. "What exactly did they ask for?"

"I don't know yet," his lawyer replied. "I'll communicate with them right now. All I've received is the filing. No additional requests in terms of what they want. We'll have to go through all the assets, the information, and it'll be like ... trading horses."

"Trading horses?" Darius asked, puzzled. "I've never traded horses."

She laughed. "Well, you get my point. We'll lay everything out, like a spreadsheet. She'll probably ask for more than what makes sense, but that's how the game's played. Then we'll go back and forth until hopefully we don't have to go to court."

"I'd prefer not to go to court," Darius said. "I don't want to fight or waste money that could be going toward our son."

"I understand that, Darius," she replied. "But you have to realize that I need to do my job. If she's not reasonable, which we already know is likely, are you going to let me do my job? Especially if we have to go to court?"

Darius was silent for a moment, thinking it over. "Yes, I understand. Hopefully, we won't have to go to court, but if we do, I want you to do your job to the best of your ability."

"Good," she said. "Alright, I'll be in touch."

Hanging up the phone, he stared out the office window, feeling the weight of it all. This wasn't where he thought he'd be. Not in his marriage, not in his business. For months, everything had felt like quicksand, pulling him deeper. And yet, in the midst of it all, there was a spark—a reminder that he had something valuable to offer, even if the world couldn't yet see it.

Chapter 47
God's Plan Is Better

" How are you doing, son?" Steve asked, a broad smile lighting up his face.

Every time Darius spoke with him, he felt a measure of peace. One day, I want to feel as centered as Steve seems to be, Darius thought. This must be what it's like to have the Holy Spirit within you, which was the same feeling he got around Dr. Whitman.

Their relationship had blossomed since Darius had read *What Are the Stakes?* and then subsequently *Prayers Satan Hates* and *My Search of the Real Heaven.* Both his words and his mentorship had become instrumental in teaching Darius to personalize his prayers and be precise in what he asked of God. It was Steve who urged him to pray not only for Jessica's well-being but also for God to take off any blinders she might have due to the demonic or witchcraft.

Darius gave Steve a quick update and then with a weak smile admitted, "Yeah ... it's not good. She filed for divorce. I suspected an affair, but now it seems clear that she's in another relationship and has been for a while."

"Oh, Lord," Steve said, shaking his head. "I'm sorry, son. I know you've been through a rough year. I know you're hurting, and I know how much you love her." He paused. "You've fought hard, Darius. You've prayed, sought God, done everything you can. But ... "

"But what?" Darius asked, his voice tight.

Steve sighed. "Sometimes, God chooses to remove things from our lives, even when we don't understand why. This might be one of those times."

Darius stared at him. The words weren't a gut punch, exactly, but they hit hard. Steve was the third or fourth person in recent weeks to say this exact thing. Is God really removing Jessica from my life? Darius didn't want to believe it. He wanted a redemption arc, a miraculous answer to all his prayers—he wanted his happy ending.

"I don't want to hear that," Darius admitted. "But it seems like that's all I'm hearing lately. And I still don't understand ... half the time this year, I've felt like I'm losing my mind."

Steve nodded. "You're not alone. When God led me into this ministry, I lost friends, a lot of people I thought would always be there. You've read my books; you know the story. My wife even told me not to share the things I was learning."

They laughed, breaking some of the tension.

"I get that," Darius said. "This stuff, spiritual warfare, it's heavy stuff, man. And when you start being transparent about it, you make people uncomfortable."

"God sees your faithfulness. He sees how you're leaning into Him. But, Darius," Steve paused again, "I have to be honest with you. I think God might be closing this chapter with Jessica."

Darius looked away.

"Look back up."

He did as Steve said and held his gaze.

"Let me explain it like this," Steve said. "Think of a little boy playing outside in the mud. He's having the time of his life, splashing around, making a mess. Then his father comes out and says, 'Come inside, son. Let's get cleaned up. I have a surprise for you.' But the boy doesn't want to come in. He's upset, maybe even angry at his dad, because he's enjoying the mud too much. He has no idea that once he's cleaned up, his father wants to take him to Disneyland."

Darius smiled faintly. "Okay ... "

Steve leaned closer. "You've prayed. You've fought. You've staked out your home. But there's still free will, son. God can't force someone to choose Him. If Jessica's chosen this path, then you need to trust that God has something so much better waiting for you. Something beyond anything you can imagine."

Darius took a deep breath. "I don't want to hear that," he repeated. "But maybe I need to. I don't like it, but I do ... I understand."

Steve nodded. "Here, let me share something with you. Something that's not in my books."

Darius leaned forward, curious. Steve began recounting the tale of a young woman from the Far East raised in a Buddhist family. She had been introduced to Christianity while living with a host family in the U.S. Though curious, she didn't understand much of what she heard in church. Still, life's challenges sparked questions she needed answered before she could fully embrace faith in Christ.

"One day, she was invited to hear a presentation about spiritual warfare," Steve said.

Darius's laughter interrupted the story. "Okay, so she got invited to a church where you were presenting, right, Steve?"

"Right," Steve laughed, "So I do my presentation, and then afterwards, she comes up to me with tears in her eyes, shares her story, and then tells me that she'd never found anyone who could answer her questions."

"What happened?" Darius asked.

Steve smiled. "Her list of questions matched exactly with the chapters of my book. Every single one. The answers to her questions lined up exactly with what God had directed me to write about. She gave her life completely to Christ."

"Wow," Darius said, shaking his head. "That's incredible."

"That's God," Steve said. "His timing. His plans. They're always perfect. And Darius, I believe He has big plans for you. The enemy wouldn't be attacking you like this if you weren't destined for something extraordinary."

Moved, Darius shared his own commitment. "Once my business is back on track, your mission, your articles of faith, your work, is going to be the fifth charity my company supports."

Steve's voice was warm. "I appreciate that. I already value everything you've done so far. Are you planning to come to the charity event for the miniseries?"

"Absolutely," Darius replied. "I'll be there for sure. My oldest son is definitely coming with me, and I'm hoping to bring my younger son as well."

"That's wonderful to hear," Steve said. "I'd love to meet them. Keep your head up and keep moving forward. I promise you, God has incredible things in store for you."

Darius nodded, feeling a glimmer of hope. "Thanks, Steve. God bless you."

Chapter 48
Your Will, Not Mine

D arius sat alone in his office, staring blankly at the monitor. His left hand absently twisted the wedding ring around his finger, the motion steady, mechanical. His thoughts drifted, not anchored in anything specific. Just a fog of nothingness.

The last few weeks had been brutal. It wasn't long after their meeting in the park when she filed, and now, when he should have been dealing with the fallout, it felt like he was still in the middle of the explosion. He had hoped, believed, even, that she would change her mind. Why wouldn't he? His track record had always defied the odds. Short guy plays college sports, makes it in corporate America, starts a business, and succeeds. Why couldn't he also be one of the 15% who salvaged their marriage after one of them files for divorce?

Now the percentages were dropping, but the odds had never scared him. He'd always believed. Even now, he thought back to the guys in the Marriage Reset Program. A third of them, maybe even half, had refused to take their wedding rings off no matter what. He had been one of them. To him, the covenant, the promise he made, mattered.

Or maybe it was just arrogance.

He shook his head, unable to pin down the answer. So much had changed, so much was still changing. His beliefs, his understanding of himself, even his perception of his wife.

The signs had been there.

Recently, the three of them—he, Jessica, and their son—had met with a youth pastor at church. Jessica wasn't wearing her ring. She couldn't even look at him, not directly. It had been an odd feeling. Darius felt strangely good about the fact that he'd stayed present, hadn't let it bother him, and hadn't said a word.

Then came the tournament. Their son was playing, and they'd sat near each other in the stands. Darius wore his ring, as he always did. But Jessica? Her discomfort was palpable. She couldn't sit still, constantly shifting in her seat, her eyes darting everywhere except toward him. She looked like someone crawling in her own skin.

Later that night, he tried to communicate with her about the legal situation. His preference was not to spend money on lawyers.

But she wouldn't communicate.

When he learned about the lawyer she'd hired, he'd reached out to a couple of his own lawyer friends. The first one didn't sugarcoat it.

"Buddy," his friend had said, "I'll be honest. This isn't good. That firm she's hired? They're sharks. They usually represent clients with million-dollar assets. They're brutal. Do what they say or suffer the consequences—that's their playbook."

Another lawyer, recommended by his friend, had offered a consultation. But the call had been a nightmare. They wanted to fight fire with fire—to make things as bad for her and her team as they would likely make it for him. They warned that "it would get ugly," but even with the empty sense of hopelessness growing inside him, Darius knew that it didn't matter how bad it got for him, he wasn't going to go to "war" with her.

He understood that every blessing in his life—the properties, the trips, the abundance—was a testament to God's grace, not his own achievements. Even in his brokenness, he had faith that giving had opened the door for God's generosity. Year after year, as he gave more, he saw how God's blessings continued to flow, unearned and undeserved.

Amid his challenges, frustrations, and moments of feeling unworthy, one truth remained clear: God's kindness, forgiveness, and love were constant. Looking back, Darius could see how gracious and compassionate God had been through it all.

You can't out give God, he thought.

So much was changing within Darius. As he leaned into God, repented, and accepted his failures, he found clarity and understanding. He sought truth without anger, blame, or judgment—exactly the emotions he wanted to avoid. Remarkably, he wasn't angry, even though there were moments when his wife's actions made him think it was all some big joke. But deep down, he didn't want to harbor resentment. He wanted to grow, learn, and change.

No matter what happened, he believed life was happening for him. The lessons he'd gained from his Marriage Reset Program and his own personal work reinforced this belief. Whether his wife remained his partner or became his ex, she had given him an invaluable gift.

It was like that dinner with Barry—he wouldn't react impulsively anymore. Instead, he resolved to live by the fruits of the Spirit: love, joy, peace, patience, kindness, goodness/generosity, faithfulness, gentleness, and self-control. He would continue examining himself, striving to remove the metaphorical log from his own eye instead of focusing on others' flaws. The thought often echoed in his mind: Too often, we judge others by their actions and ourselves by our intentions.

Darius didn't want to judge anymore; he wanted to embody love, not seek it.

After considering his wife's overall behavior, he reconsidered wearing his wedding ring. What was the point? She had emotionally checked out long ago. His thoughts spiraled and soon he found himself asking: Am I wearing it to remind her of what she doesn't want? She can't even communicate with me, let alone see me as a real person. To her, I'm the *enemy*.

Sitting at his desk now, Darius felt the weight of the upcoming weekend. He was supposed to attend the International Living Conference in Denver. For years, he'd been fascinated by the possibilities of offshore investments, second passports, and expat communities. Jessica had once been part of those plans. They'd even discussed managing international properties together.

But now, everything was different.

He had planned to go, but the situation was more complicated than he first realized. For one, he could clearly see how every decision he had made in growing the business had come from a place of force, not power, from lack, not faith. Every step, whether it was acquiring additional buildings, buying the condo, or even considering international properties, it had been his decision alone. He hadn't prayed about it. He hadn't sought God's guidance. He hadn't asked God to lead.

Instead, he had taken control. He had been in charge. And look how that turned out. Everything was crumbling around him.

Now, with his wife's legal position targeting the business assets, the situation was turning uglier by the moment. Based on her attitude and lack of reason, it was unlikely this would be simple or pleasant. It could be brutal, he thought.

He couldn't help but recall her words when he told her he might not be around that weekend: "This will be as easy as you want it to be." It had a very simple translation: Bend over, take it, do everything I demand, and maybe I won't make your life a living hell.

What a joke, he thought.

That week, he had turned to prayer like never before. Over and over, he sought clarity.

"God, am I supposed to go to Denver or not? Your will, not mine. Your timing, not mine. You are the God who opens doors no one else can open. You are the God who closes doors no one else can close. You are the God of right now. I don't want to make decisions based on what I think anymore. I want to be led by the Spirit, not the flesh. Guide me, Father."

For days, he prayed with fervor, asking for direction. Now, three days before his scheduled trip to Denver, he sat in his office, absentmindedly twirling his wedding ring with his other hand.

He bowed his head once more. "Father, I ask for your deliverance, your kindness, your blessings. Please continue to lead and guide me."

As he finished, a wave of peace washed over him.

Quietly, deliberately, he slipped the ring off his finger. The same ring that had rested on his hand for over 17 years. He turned it over in his palm, then opened the drawer, placed the ring in the back, and shut it firmly.

The click of the drawer echoed in the silence.

With a sigh, Darius whispered to himself, "Your will, not mine."

Chapter 49
Destiny in Denver

D arius paused in reflection after his morning prayer, seeking discernment and peace about going to Denver. The clarity he felt afterward seemed like a blessing—a gentle assurance that this trip was the right choice. As always, he checked into his hotel, and he found himself upgraded to an enormous suite. His Marriott Titanium Elite status often afforded such perks.

The suite was undeniably beautiful, a "Royal Suite," as it was called. He surveyed the room, letting out a chuckle as he thought of Gandalf from The Lord of the Rings. "Darius the Grey continues to become Darius the White," he murmured. Yet, as stunning as the room was, he couldn't ignore the pang of solitude it triggered. Once, he would have been thrilled by such luxury, but now, all he wanted was to share it with his wife. Pushing the thought aside, he straightened. "Okay, Sir Darius, you are of royal blood, and this suite shall reflect that," he said to himself, before shaking his head. *No*, he thought with a small smile. *Just be grateful.*

The International Living Conference turned out to be captivating. At fifty-one, Darius was in good shape, with only the slightest touch of gray in his hair. Most attendees seemed older— well into their sixties, which made sense given the nature of the event. The first day was packed with sessions covering various countries, each more enlightening than the last. One talk on Indonesia and Malaysia was particularly surprising. Indonesia, with its stunning coastal homes and luxurious amenities, seemed almost too good to be true. The idea of living there for less than $2,000 a month, with access to spas and breathtaking ocean views, felt like an untapped treasure. Darius, an avid scuba diver, began to wonder if this could be a place to consider in the future. He definitely wanted to visit and dive there.

The day continued with more insights, including a fascinating introduction to minted coins as investment opportunities and even a session on oil wells. The latter seemed surreal. Investing in an oil well, Darius learned, could yield payouts for decades—something he'd never considered before. While it wasn't a fit for him right now financially, he appreciated the knowledge.

By evening, he'd had a chance meeting with the editor of International Living magazine, an attractive and friendly middle-aged woman, who was intrigued by his passion for charity. They discussed the possibility of him writing about his experiences and aspirations for a charitable foundation. It was a conversation that stayed with him as he wound down for the night, grateful for the day's discoveries.

The next morning began with prayer, breathing exercises, meditation, and Scripture, grounding him for another full day at the conference. After attending a few sessions, he wandered to a booth showcasing information about Portugal. Over the past few years, Portugal had consistently been ranked as one of the top retirement destinations for expats. The allure of affordable living, sunny weather, and accessible financing for foreigners was compelling. As Darius browsed the brochures, a young woman across the table caught his attention. She wasn't conventionally striking, but her warm energy and radiant smile were magnetic and made her very attractive.

"Hello," she said, extending a hand. "I'm Amanda."

"Hi, Amanda. I'm Darius."

They exchanged pleasantries before diving into a conversation about real estate. Amanda showed him a project she was representing and asked if he'd ever considered Portugal. Darius explained that he had once debated buying property there but had ultimately invested in Mexico instead. Curious, Amanda looked up the development he mentioned on her iPad. Her brows furrowed slightly.

"Well," she said, tilting the screen toward him, "That would have been an incredible investment."

Darius leaned closer. "How incredible are we talking?"

She hesitated. "Are you sure you want to know?"

"Probably not," he laughed, "But hit me."

Amanda exhaled. "Well, it cost around $550,000, maybe $560,000 with the discount, but that one in particular is now worth over $850,000."

Darius's jaw dropped. "Holy crap," he muttered, running a hand through his hair. It would have cost him $560k at the time he explored it. The revelation left him both amazed and slightly wistful.

As they continued chatting, Amanda revealed that she wasn't an employee of the company but a businesswoman with properties in North Carolina and several international locations. Their conversation turned to philanthropy, where they discovered a shared passion for charitable work.

"There are a few charities I support," Darius said. "One is a facility in northern Indiana that offers women alternatives to abortion. Another is a Christian school in the Dominican Republic that transforms kids' lives. Then there's a clinic in Africa, a horse ranch in North Carolina, and a new one I'm about to start supporting in Texas."

"In Africa?" she asked, her interest piqued. "I was just in Africa."

"Where?" Darius asked.

"I was in Kenya. It was amazing. For vacation."

"That's awesome! I was in Tanzania last year. It was incredible," Darius said. "The clinic I support is in Liberia—Monrovia, to be exact. I was just there this past August."

Her eyes widened. "Holy cow," she said, clearly surprised.

"What?" Darius asked, curious.

"You need to meet Chris."

"Okay ... Who's Chris?"

"He's the guy who owns this whole company and the rentals I'm working for."

"Wait. You said you're not an employee. How are you here?"

"Well," she said, "it's a long story. But we're both part of Tony Robbins' Platinum Group, and he asked me to come help him sell properties as a favor. That's why I'm here."

"Tony Robbins' Platinum Group?" Darius asked, intrigued.

"Yeah. I'll explain later. But you know who Tony Robbins is, right?"

"Yeah, I've read a couple of his books."

"Have you ever been to one of his conferences?"

"No," Darius admitted. "What conferences?"

She looked at him incredulously. "Where have you been?"

"I don't know," Darius said with a smile and a shrug.

"Well, he does all these amazing conferences. There's also this exclusive group you can join called Platinums. It comes with all kinds of privileges, incredible networking opportunities, and special events. It's hard to explain, but it's amazing."

"Okay," Darius said, nodding. "That's how you met Chris?"

"Yes. We're both in the Platinum Group, which is how I ended up helping him out here."

"Got it," Darius said.

"Chris is amazing," she continued. "He lives in Spain, sells properties in Portugal and Spain, and has a heart for charity. He even supports an orphanage in Africa."

"You're kidding."

"Nope. It's in Ghana, I believe. You're really going to want to meet him."

"Oh, absolutely," Darius said, intrigued. "I'd love to meet him."

"He's not here right now," she said, "but we'll make sure it happens."

"Sounds good," Darius replied.

They exchanged information and stood to shake hands.

"It was great meeting you," Darius said.

"You too," she replied. "I'll make sure to introduce you to Chris later."

"Looking forward to it," Darius said as they parted ways.

Later that afternoon, they crossed paths again as Darius finished another lap around the conference hall. She waved him over excitedly. "I found Chris," she shouted, her enthusiasm infectious.

She introduced him to Chris, a charismatic entrepreneur with an interesting accent, who came from England and who supported an orphanage in Ghana. The group hit it off immediately, bonding over shared values and a love for giving back. But their conversation took an unexpected turn when a woman from Chile invited them to a back room.

Darius smiled and looked at Amanda inquisitively. "Don't ask, just come on," she said with the biggest smile on her face. He smiled too, shaking his head in agreement as he followed the group into the "back room."

All of a sudden, music filled the room and the lady from Chile announced, "Who'd like to learn salsa dancing?"

Darius found himself laughing and twirling to the music, feeling like a kid again. The impromptu dance lesson was followed by a guided meditation led by Chris, who encouraged them to reflect on their lives at different stages starting at the age of 5. The exercise left Darius deeply moved, grounded by a sense of peace and gratitude.

Then it was Darius' turn. "Does anyone know who Wim Hof is?"

One person nodded but most did not. Darius had everyone lie down and they went through a full cycle. Eleven minutes later, everyone was laying relaxed on the floor, smiling.

As Darius headed back to the Conference Center, his mind kept returning to one thought: That was awesome! What an amazing group of people.

The rest of the day passed in a blur. That evening, he'd be going to dinner with the lovely editor, but plans quickly changed. Instead, he ended up going to dinner with two women he had never met before.

As he was heading to his Uber, they stopped him. "Hey, where are you going?"

"I'm going to dinner," Darius replied.

"Can we come with you?"

He hesitated, unsure of what to say. "Okay, sure," he finally agreed. Darius was trying to be less controlling and more open to being in the moment.

The dinner was ... interesting. Neither of them were someone he would typically be interested in, but there was something different about it. Darius noticed how much he had changed. He listened to them, validated their feelings, and practiced all the skills he'd been working on. It was clear that at least one of the women was interested in him, but Darius didn't even entertain the thought.

He still loved his wife, though he had accepted the marriage was most likely over. Regardless, he had no interest in being with anyone else at this point or anytime soon. He planned to keep working on himself and make sure he took the time to heal. Any advances or hints were essentially lost on him.

As they left the restaurant and made their way back to the hotel, one of the women suddenly blurted out, "You know, you're a handsome guy."

"Well, thank you," Darius said, a little taken aback. "I really appreciate that."

Then, she added, "You're incredibly fuckable."

No one had ever told him that before!

Darius wasn't sure how to respond. *You're not coming to my hotel room*, he thought.

"Thank you," he said awkwardly, shaking his head as he smiled. "You both have a good night."

With that, he turned on his heels and made his way across the street to his hotel.

What in the world? he thought again, as he stepped into the elevator. Yeah, well ... My wife is discarding me. But there we go, at least I'm fuckable. He couldn't help but laugh out loud as he entered the elevator.

***

The remainder of the International Conference was nothing short of extraordinary. Darius felt as if he had absorbed an immense amount of knowledge, met a diverse range of fascinating people, and experienced personal growth. Yet, one aspect of the trip left him unsettled—the interactions with Sarah, the editor of International Living. She was attractive and pleasant, and they had shared several conversations over the past few days. But it was the night before that lingered in his mind. They had bumped into each other by chance and ended up walking together. There was an undeniable attraction, but being with another woman was the furthest thing from his mind. Until the divorce was final—if that was the outcome—he was committed to honoring his vows and the covenant of marriage.

They had walked along the Causeway, crossing over the tower on their way back to his room, when Sarah had asked him about his divorce. He had found himself less than forthcoming, and he couldn't quite understand why. When she had asked, he found himself saying, "I've been divorced for six or seven months."

Her expression had shifted, confusion flashing across her face. "You're a nice guy," she'd said, "I don't understand."

Darius had sighed. "Look, you don't want to hear my sad story. I've made a lot of mistakes. The divorce has opened my eyes to things I needed to work on. I didn't want it. I didn't want my family to fall apart, but my wife found someone else. That's the reality."

Sarah had nodded, but the conversation felt uncomfortable. She'd turned away and started walking back across the Causeway, leaving him with his thoughts. Seven months. It had been that long since his world had been turned upside down. But they weren't divorced yet. *Why did I say that?* he wondered. It made no sense. But maybe it was because he had felt some attraction to her. She was kind, intelligent, and there was something good about her. Yet, it didn't matter. He wasn't ready and had more work to do on himself.

The final dinner before he headed back home was a wonderful experience. The group that had shared so many personal moments over the past few days went to a seafood restaurant. The energy was vibrant, and the conversation flowed effortlessly, filled with kindness, curiosity, and a genuine sense of connection. But the most unexpected part of the evening came when Chris and Amanda began discussing Tony Robbins. The way they spoke about him, the way they described the impact of his teachings, made Darius listen more intently.

"You need to go to Dallas," Chris said. "You have to be there in November. It's less than six weeks away."

Darius shook his head, feeling overwhelmed by the suggestion. "I can't go to Dallas," he said. "My business isn't doing well, I'm going through a divorce, I don't have access to any of my assets right now. My finances are a mess. It doesn't make sense for me to go to some conference. I need to focus on my work."

They wouldn't let it go, though. "What you'll gain from being there will far outweigh any time lost from your business," Amanda insisted. "You'll see the value. It will change the way you look at everything."

Darius wasn't convinced, but they were persistent. They described how being part of the Platinum group had reshaped their lives. They spoke about the growth they had experienced, how they had come to understand themselves in a deeper way, and how it had altered their perception of the world. The more they spoke, the more intrigued he became.

As the dinner came to an end, Darius felt something shift inside him. These were the kind of people he wanted to surround himself with—people who shared his desire to grow, to learn, to evolve. He thought back to how much of his life had been taken from him: his marriage, the people he once considered friends, the sense of security he had once known. It was all gone now. He had nothing but his personal growth to focus on. He had been unsure about coming to Denver, but after thoughtful prayer, had decided to come. Based on the people he had met, he knew that it had been the right decision.

God, he prayed silently. Please bring people into my life who care about truth, about growing, about evolving into the best versions of themselves, and who love you.

How could he afford it and be out of the office? How could he leave his business when it was already struggling? How in the world was he going to get to Dallas?

Chapter 50
Train to Barcelona

D arius sat on the train, Andrea dozing beside him, gazing out at the blur of countryside as the train made its way from Madrid to Barcelona. The past few days had been enjoyable, filled with new experiences in Madrid and Toledo, places he'd loved exploring. Yet, it was strange traveling without Jessica. Originally, Jessica and Andrea's husband, Rob, were meant to come along, but the unforeseen complications of their pending divorce disrupted those plans. Rob, being considerate, assumed it might be uncomfortable for Darius to have him come along so he, respectfully, bowed out. It was untrue; Darius would have welcomed his company, but he understood why Rob didn't join them.

Initially, the plan for the trip had been straightforward: spend some time in Madrid, then take the train to Barcelona for the medical device conference, and return after a few days exploring the area. Whenever he had the chance to go across the pond, he would take the chance to experience more than just business. Darius loved traveling, meeting new people, and immersing himself in different cultures. While some would simply fly in for conferences and leave without seeing more of the city, Darius wasn't among them. He valued the history, the food, the architecture, and the churches—there was so much more to life than work, and this trip affirmed that.

There were still moments when the finality of the divorce felt overwhelming. Accepting that Jessica had been having an affair and that she was in love with a woman had been difficult to grasp. He didn't like thinking about it, but there were points when it crept back into his thoughts—the sheer absurdity of it all. It was another reason why David Hawkins's work was so vitally important.

In the past, Darius struggled with "letting go" of certain thoughts; he called them "negative flow loops." He never quite understood why certain thoughts seemed to consume him, but these patterns often brought him down, making him think unkindly of himself.

Letting Go provided insight into how thoughts and emotions were linked and how failing to process them properly could lead to prolonged suffering. It explained and showed that attachments were the root of most suffering and that learning to let go was essential for emotional freedom. It was an affirmation of everything he had been learning through the Marriage Reset Program: he needed to process emotions healthily, without being a victim, and embrace a more positive mindset.

The way it spoke to him felt almost uncanny, as if the words had been written specifically for his life. It described how most people spend their lives repressing, suppressing, or escaping their feelings, never realizing the cost of doing so. That suppressed energy didn't vanish; it accumulated, seeking release through distress. It showed up as psychological struggles, physical ailments, emotional turmoil, or destructive behaviors. On the surface, it sounded simple, but the implications were incredible.

Hawkins explained that letting go of these feelings diminished dependency, a force that caused endless pain in human relationships. Dependency, Hawkins believed, was at the heart of so much suffering. By releasing those emotions, a person could climb to a higher level of consciousness, achieving a greater awareness and a richer spirituality. It wasn't just abstract talk, either—Hawkins claimed it led to tangible changes: increased happiness, contentment, peace, even joy. More than that, it brought a sense of comfort in being who you truly are. Darius found this idea liberating. He didn't want to think or live as a victim.

Hawkins offered a way out: if you could identify the emotion beneath those spiraling thoughts and surrender to it, the thoughts would stop. It was revolutionary. You didn't have to fight the thoughts or rationalize them; you just had to sit with the feeling itself, feel it fully, and let it go. The energy would naturally dissipate.

As Darius absorbed this, he couldn't help but think about his wife and the way she had treated him over the past six months. Her accusations, the way she would lash out—it all made sense now. Hawkins wrote that suppressed feelings often surfaced as projection, where a person couldn't acknowledge their own emotions and instead cast them onto someone else. She had accused him of doing things he hadn't done, things that, on reflection, she was doing herself. It was as though her mind needed a scapegoat to justify the feelings she couldn't process.

It wasn't just projection, though. Hawkins described how people tried to manage emotions in three flawed ways: suppression, expression, and escape. Suppression happened when someone was so consumed by guilt or fear about an emotion that they denied it entirely. Darius recognized this pattern too. His wife's accusations, her refusal to reflect inward, were classic signs of denial. Hawkins explained how denial is often paired with projection, creating a loop where the suppressed emotion would reinforce itself by blaming others. It wasn't personal; it was psychological mechanics at work, but it still stung.

Hawkins talked about how people think venting their emotions—yelling, lashing out, making dramatic gestures—will help them release those feelings, but the reality was the opposite. People believed they were "letting it all out," but Hawkins's research showed it didn't work that way. It simply reinforced the energy of the emotion and left the deeper feelings buried, unresolved. Hawkins suggested a different path: neutralize the emotion, process it healthily, and channel that energy into love, work, or creativity.

Escape was the last of the three, and here Hawkins struck a chord that was almost too close for comfort. Escaping feelings was practically a way of life for most people, Hawkins said. The entire entertainment and alcohol industries thrived on this. People drank to avoid their feelings, watched endless hours of TV, and filled their days with distractions—all in an effort to stay unconscious, to fill the void. It wasn't just his family; it was everyone around him. But looking back, all it had done was create more distance, more disconnection.

What hit Darius hardest was Hawkins's clarity about what to do instead. To break free from the endless loops of thoughts and distractions, you had to stop running from your feelings. Identify the emotion at the root of the thoughts. Sit with it. Surrender to it completely. Don't fight it, rationalize it, or shove it away. Just feel it. It would be uncomfortable, yes, but only for a moment. Hawkins promised that if you surrendered to the feeling, its energy would dissolve. It wouldn't last forever, and what replaced it was peace.

As the train chugged forward, he thought about the upcoming conference in Barcelona. He'd changed his approach; instead of sending initial invites and trying to push outcomes, he wanted to let things flow. He would meditate on his goals and then engage with those who resonated with him at the conference. His new mindset was about coming from a place of power, not forcing or trying to prove his worth. He was finally learning to accept that whatever happened, it was okay. His self-worth didn't depend on external validation; it came from within.

He opened his notebook and flipped through his notes. So much stress, he noted, comes from fear of loss—of things, people, identities. That was something else Hawkins talked about, something else Darius realized he'd clung to, stewing in negativity and trying to control outcomes that were never his to command. Repressed grief, guilt, or anger didn't just linger; it created self-fulfilling prophecies, pulling more of the same into one's life.

Even more astonishing was the idea that emotions emitted vibrations, transmitting energy across limitless distances. Darius couldn't shake the thought. If love attracted love and anger attracted anger, then everything—every thought, every feeling—was shaping the reality around him. It made sense now, why being in a room with someone joyful lifted your spirits, or why spending time with a pessimist dragged you down. Vibrations were real, and they mattered.

Letting go wasn't easy, though. While Darius was far from a master, he was starting to understand the technique. You had to identify the feeling, let it come up fully, and simply sit with it. No trying to fix it, no rationalizing or suppressing. Just feeling it until it ran its course.

The hardest part was giving yourself permission to feel irrational or uncomfortable emotions without guilt. Thoughts, he had written, were just the mind's way of explaining feelings—rationalizations layered over raw emotion. The real source of any feeling was the pressure beneath it, the unresolved energy stored over time.

Darius took a breath. To enjoy life without clinging to anything or anyone for happiness—wasn't that true freedom? Positive energy led to more positive outcomes, and negative energy created the opposite. He smiled.

"Be in the world, not of it," Darius said quietly out loud, thinking of John 17:14-17.

It was as if he could hear Jesus speak the words directly to him. Again, everything was coming full circle, the dots were connecting, and his eyes were opening, and his ears were listening.

He closed his notebook and gazed out the window again. He thought again about the next few days at the conference. He didn't know exactly what would unfold, but he didn't need to. He trusted the process now, trusted himself. For the first time in a long time, he felt more empowered than he ever had in his life.

Chapter 51
Spanish Vibrations

After arriving in Barcelona, Andrea and Darius took an Uber to their hotel and were relieved to check into their rooms earlier than expected. That evening, they planned to attend the conference opening dinner, which included a fireside chat. But eager to explore the city before the event, they decided to take one of Barcelona's iconic red buses and take a scenic tour of the city's landmarks. The city's vibrancy and charm left them energized for the evening ahead as well as for the energy of the upcoming conference.

The opening dinner exceeded expectations, and the next morning, Darius woke early and followed his usual routine of meditation and a cold shower (in the absence of a plunge pool). Feeling refreshed, he met Andrea in the lobby to walk to the conference venue. However, he quickly noticed she seemed distracted and flustered.

"Are you okay?" he asked, concerned.

Andrea hesitated before replying. "Yes … I'm just a little surprised."

"What's going on?" Darius pressed gently.

"I've been on the phone with Rob for over an hour," she admitted, referring to her husband.

Darius's eyebrows raised slightly. "Is everything okay?"

Andrea nodded, then paused as if collecting her thoughts. "Do you remember that book you gave him when you were staying with us? *Better Man, Better Marriage?*"

Darius smiled. "Yeah, I remember. I wasn't sure if he'd ever read it, but it had a huge impact on me."

"Well, he finally picked it up and read the whole thing. And apparently, it's had a huge impact on him too."

Darius tilted his head, intrigued. "Really? That's amazing!"

Andrea sighed. "He was talking about all these things he hadn't realized before … How many mistakes he's made, how he hasn't been the best husband to me. At one point, I got mad and told him, 'Look, I'm not a victim. I have my faults too.'"

Darius nodded thoughtfully. "I understand. But it sounds like he's had a real awakening. That's a positive thing, isn't it?"

Andrea shrugged, her expression conflicted. "He wants to talk when I get back. He says he wants to work on things. I'm just … surprised. I don't know what to say."

"Praise God," Darius said. "That's incredible news."

Andrea smiled faintly but still seemed deep in thought.

"Maybe this is an opening, a chance to share God with him in a way he hasn't seen before," Darius added.

Andrea nodded slowly. "That would be amazing."

As Darius entered the conference, he felt a new sense of anticipation. This year, he was taking a different approach than ever before. He had mapped out all the key presentations he wanted to attend and identified the executives he hoped to meet. Unlike past years, he had sent out almost no advance messages to the leadership of the companies attending, except to a few he already knew to reconnect. Reaching out to unfamiliar faces beforehand was common in the industry, where executives typically received more than a hundred messages asking for meetings. For Darius, the challenge was to balance approachability with respect for their primary purpose at the event—finding funding, networking, and building partnerships. Aggressive sales tactics or over-eager approaches were sure to backfire and create friction.

Darius was guided by a concept from *Power vs. Force* by David Hawkins. He believed that our energy, thoughts, and consciousness projected out into the world, influencing what we attracted or repelled. He planned to approach the conference at a higher state of consciousness, hoping that by focusing on growth and connection, he would draw the right opportunities to him. His strategy was simple: attend presentations, watch for confident, engaging speakers, and reach out afterward if he felt inspired. No pre-scheduled appointments. He was curious to see what would unfold.

The first day of the conference was busy and fulfilling. That evening, Darius had dinner with Sharrim, a new acquaintance and the CEO of an innovative digital med-tech company in Europe. Sharrim had been a guest on Darius's podcast, and Darius admired him for his intelligence and poise. During dinner, they caught up, shared experiences, and listened to a panel discussing the future of funding and the market. As the panelists discussed culture, Sharrim made a comment that caught Darius's attention because he used the word vibration.

"Do you mean like higher consciousness?" he asked, intrigued.

Sharrim's eyes sharpened, and he hesitated.

"Isn't that what you mean?"

"Yes, that's exactly what I'm talking about," he said with a smile. "People often speak without realizing they're coming from a lower level of consciousness. They're so fixed on their own perspective that they miss larger truths. We only have control of our own emotions. Our focus goes where our energy flows and everything has to do with energy. Just because somebody is acting that way doesn't mean we have to react to them. We can respond and we can elevate ourselves and come from a higher place of consciousness."

Darius smiled back, recognizing the shift in their conversation. "I understand. The old me would have completely missed what you said."

"What do you mean?" Sharrim asked.

Darius explained the unbelievable journey he was on, filled with challenges, divorce, self-healing, meditation, Hawkins' work, and working on himself. Sharrim seemed impressed and shared details about his own journey—meditation, cold plunges, and attending a silent meditation conference where participants refrained from speaking for long stretches.

Darius was fascinated. "That must be incredible."

Sharrim nodded. "It's powerful. It's about reaching higher states of consciousness, connecting with who you truly are, and focusing on your priorities. I want to do it every year now," he said, then shared a story of a meditation experience where he felt like he left his body.

Darius's eyes widened. "You left your body? That's remarkable," he said.

Sharrim smiled and asked, "Have you ever experienced that in your meditation?"

Darius shook his head. "Not yet, but I'm up to 25–35 minutes a day. I'm still figuring it out."

Sharrim's expression shifted to one of encouragement. "You're on your way. The work you're doing, the path you've chosen, it's clear you're not going to turn back."

Darius nodded, feeling a new sense of purpose. "When God gave me eyes to see and ears to hear, I realized how much I had been living from a place of lack, trying to force things instead of allowing them to flow. Now, my focus is on growth, healing, and reaching higher consciousness. I want to reach 540 on the scale. Unconditional love."

"That's an amazing and worthy goal, my friend."

The conversation lasted for over an hour, and as the evening ended, they embraced warmly.

"I'm glad we had this conversation," Sharrim said.

"Me too, brother. Me too," Darius replied.

That night, as Darius settled into his room, his thoughts turned to his wife and their pending divorce. Though he had hoped for reconciliation, her recent actions and her financial demands had made it clear she was moving on. Still, he reminded himself that the material possessions she sought—the house, the business assets—were just things. God had blessed him before, and he trusted that everything he needed would come again.

Sitting down, he began drafting a video message to her, wanting to express his thoughts with clarity and sincerity. After finishing a draft, he set it aside, prayed for guidance, and went to bed, ready for the new day and the opportunities it would bring.

***

The next day of the conference was another remarkable success. Darius had a packed schedule, with 10 meetings with executives scheduled only since arriving in Barcelona, and the day unfolded seamlessly. Smiling from ear to ear, the responses he received were incredible, often leading to impromptu meetings over coffee or lunch. Executives expressed genuine gratitude for his outreach and enthusiasm for collaboration.

As he walked through the bustling conference venue, Darius couldn't help but marvel at how present he felt in the moment. It hadn't always been this way. Reflecting on the past, he recalled a time when hidden anxiety loomed over him. Tasks like recording social media content, presenting at conferences, or even mingling in large groups had often felt like a grind, moments he endured with sheer determination. In those days, he frequently relied on "white-knuckling" his way through challenges, driven more by necessity than by joy.

But now, everything had changed. Whether preparing social media content or interacting with people, Darius found himself calm, focused, and confident. A task that used to take 45 minutes and multiple takes in the studio could now be accomplished in 15 minutes with a single effortless recording. His employee, Jake, had even commented on how much smoother and more relaxed Darius had become.

He recalled a presentation he had delivered before the challenges with his wife began. While the outcome was successful, the preparation had been grueling. He had rehearsed the presentation at least 40 times. He realized now that part of the anxiety was an idea from unworthiness; why would anyone want to hear what I have to say? Strange but true.

Now, however, those feelings of unworthiness, those doubting thoughts were gone. At this conference, he felt completely at ease, genuinely excited to meet new people, and eager to share his experiences.

Lunch that day was with a CEO and physician, a brilliant innovator Darius had been getting to know over several conferences. This remarkable woman, a surgeon with a big heart and an entrepreneurial spirit, had been doing groundbreaking work in South America, using nanotechnology to prevent limb amputations.

Their conversation was inspiring. Margaret shared her company's journey and the incredible potential of her technology, while Darius talked about his own mission—helping companies avoid the cost of mishires and hire more efficiently and his passion for supporting charities, including a clinic in Africa. When he described the clinic's financial challenges and their efforts to acquire much-needed equipment, her eyes lit up. "That's amazing," she said. "I'd love to help. We could potentially donate some of our products to support the clinic."

Grateful for her generosity, Darius promised to connect her with Chea, the founder, to explore the partnership further.

After a productive afternoon, Darius returned to the hotel with Andrea. They decided to wind down with a glass of wine, reflecting on the incredible conference experience. As they sat near the hotel's live band, Angela turned to Darius. "So, what's the deal with the video?" she asked.

Darius smiled faintly. "I've written out what I want to say. I'm planning to record it tonight or tomorrow morning and then send it to her."

"I'll be praying about that for you," Andrea said. "You know, Darius, you're a good man. I have said this before, but if anything ever happened between Rob and me, I could only hope he'd fight for me the way you've fought for her."

Darius looked at her, touched by her words.

"And you need to understand something," she continued. "Even though she's made this as hard as possible, you've responded with love at every turn. Someday, even if it doesn't happen now, she might look back and realize that. You have been kind instead of mean."

Darius nodded slowly. "I hope so. But thank you for saying that."

Later, in the quiet of his room, Darius recorded the video message for Jessica. He expressed his desire to avoid wasting money on legal fees, reiterating that he was willing to meet her needs directly to avoid unnecessary conflict. Calm and sincere, he ended the message with heartfelt words: "If at any point you wake up and decide you've made a mistake or want to reconsider, let me know. I love you, and I always will."

After praying over the message, he sent it off and prepared for the next day.

Chapter 52
I Am Not Sorry

T he last evening of the conference was extraordinary. A fantastic meal was accompanied by a stellar group of panelists, their discussions buzzing with insights. Darius savored the food, enjoyed a glass of wine, and immersed himself in lively conversations. As the evening progressed, he found his way to a balcony overlooking the bay in Barcelona. The ocean stretched endlessly before him, its beauty reflecting the incredible week he had just experienced.

He leaned against the railing, replaying the highlights in his mind: the memorable trip to Madrid, the train ride, the world-class speakers, and the 24 impactful meetings—18 scheduled only after arriving in Spain and six that had serendipitously unfolded. It was beyond remarkable. For Darius, this conference was a turning point. He realized he would never view professional events or, for that matter, life the same way again.

This year had been one of the most challenging in his life, yet so many miraculous moments had emerged. Healing. Awareness. Emotional intelligence. New insights into the spiritual realms, the interplay of energy, and the unseen forces shaping reality. It was as though he had lived on land his entire life and was now not only stepping into but diving into the ocean for the first time—discovering an entirely new world beneath the surface.

His thoughts wandered to the Bible, specifically 2 Kings 6:17-22, where a servant to the prophet Elijah wakes him from his sleep, panicked, as they are surrounded by enemies.

"Don't worry," Elijah had assured the man, "We outnumber them."

After the servant's confusion, Elisha prayed for the servant's eyes to be opened, and after God did, the servant saw the mountains around the town filled with an angelic army.

That story felt so real to Darius now. He was beginning to better understand the unseen forces working in his life. He smiled. Despite the uncertainty surrounding his marriage and business, he was grateful for the growth he had experienced. He wouldn't trade these insights or this journey for anything. For the first time in a long while, he felt a quiet excitement about what lay ahead.

"Hey, brother," came a familiar voice. Someone tapped his shoulder. Darius turned to see Sharrim.

"Hey, my friend," Darius said, embracing him.

"What are you doing out here?" Sharrim asked.

"Just looking out at the ocean," Darius replied, "And being grateful ... grateful for everything that's happened this year. This has been an amazing conference."

Sharrim nodded. "It's been great. But you know, about the divorce, I really am sorry."

Darius smiled. "I appreciate that."

Sharrim's face suddenly shifted. His brow furrowed, and he looked at Darius with an almost perplexed expression. "Wait a minute," Sharrim said. "Actually, I don't know why I just said that."

"Said what?" Darius asked.

"That I'm sorry," Sharrim replied. "Because, honestly, I'm not sorry. Look at you. Look at what's happening in your life. You're going to keep growing and you will be vibrating at the highest level, brother."

They both burst into laughter.

"You know what? You're right," Darius said. "There's nothing to be sorry about. She made her decision, and even though it's not what I wanted, I'm going to be grateful to her for the rest of my life. She's given me one of the greatest gifts she could have ever given me. Because of how things played out, God has awakened me in ways I never imagined. And I'm not turning back."

"No, you're not turning back," Sharrim said. "We're not turning back."

The two friends laughed again, and Sharrim clapped Darius on the shoulder. "You've come so far, my friend. I'm so glad we got to connect, but I have to go. I have a flight to catch and another presentation to give."

They embraced once more.

"Safe travels," Darius said. "Let me know if I can ever do anything for you. We are brothers now."

"Yes, indeed. And me for you, my friend."

As Sharrim departed, Darius remained on the balcony for a while longer, reflecting. This week, with all its challenges and triumphs, had left him deeply grateful. Life was taking him in a direction he could never have predicted—and he wouldn't have it any other way.

***

Before heading back "stateside," Darius and Andrea took a day trip from Barcelona to Montserrat. The journey itself was an adventure, with a scenic train ride up to the rugged mountain. Once there, they explored the quaint town, visiting shops and sampling some of the local liqueurs. But the highlight was the monastery, a site rich with history and spiritual significance.

They walked the winding paths up to the iconic cross at the mountain's peak, marveling at the breathtaking view of the monastery below and the surrounding landscape. The air was crisp, and the moment felt profound, a quiet reflection of the beauty and mystery of Montserrat.

After taking in the view, they ventured into the monastery itself. The ancient walls seemed to hold centuries of prayers and stories. Inside, they came across an area where visitors could light prayer candles, a tradition with deep meaning. It was said that people would light a candle while praying for a specific intention. If the prayer was answered, they would return to the monastery to give thanks and make a donation.

Darius purchased the largest candle available. Sitting quietly for a moment, he composed a deeply personal prayer. He prayed for his family, asking God to cover them with the blood of Jesus to protect and keep them together. Despite everything that had transpired, he prayed fervently for the covenant of his marriage. He asked God to soften her heart, to heal their brokenness, and to grant their marriage another chance. His hope was that two imperfect people could turn to God, mend what was fractured, and create a future together that was worth all the effort it would take. Twenty more years of a restored, remarkable marriage while showing their kids what commitment and true love could look like by turning to God— that was his prayer.

As Darius placed the lit candle in its spot on the wall, he felt a mix of hope and surrender. The flickering flame symbolized both his faith and his willingness to leave the outcome in God's hands.

Exiting the monastery, he found Andrea, and they began their descent back to the tram. Their next stop was a winery tour, a fitting way to wind down the day. As they rode the tram, they exchanged small talk about the beauty of Montserrat and the uniqueness of the monastery. But Darius's thoughts kept returning to the candle. He wondered, with a glimmer of hope, if life would one day bring him back to this sacred place to make that donation.

Chapter 53
Flying Eyeglasses

T he flight back to the U.S. from Spain was a reflective one for Darius. While in the past, he might have entertained himself with movies or light reading, traveling now was different for him. He didn't have a desire or need to be entertained as in the past. He wanted to read and learn with a strong focus on his Bible. For hours, he delved into Scripture, marveling at how much more it revealed to him now than ever before. It struck him as almost absurd: how could someone raised in the church, someone who had read a decent portion of the Bible, understand so little of it for so long? He wondered if he had truly grasped even 10% of it before this season of spiritual awakening.

The Old Testament, in particular, was becoming more and more remarkable to him. How it all interconnected. Now, with an evolving understanding of spiritual realms, energy, and their interplay, Darius found himself seeing its relevance in a new light. The demonic was everywhere—something he had never fully understood or recognized before, now felt undeniable. He was puzzled as to why teachings on this topic weren't more widespread.

One theme stood out to him: God's enduring love for His creation. Time and again, God laid out His expectations for humanity—love one another, be kind, avoid stealing, killing, and coveting. In return, God promised and gave blessings and protection from evil. Yet, when people turned away from Him, worshipped idols, or fell into other destructive behaviors, disaster inevitably followed. The pattern was painfully clear: those who leaned into God flourished; those who turned away suffered.

He thought about the horrifying consequences described in the Old Testament, such as idol worship leading people to commit atrocities, including sacrificing their own children. He had never understood that behind the idols were demons. God clearly stated man had to uphold the commandments and statutes because man couldn't handle the evil alone. Darius shook his head in amazement.

Prophecy was another aspect of the Bible that now captivated him. Before reading Steve Hemphill's books over the summer, Darius had little understanding of prophecy. Yet, as he studied more deeply, he was astonished to find prophetic threads woven throughout almost every book of the Old Testament, all pointing to the coming of Jesus centuries later. Isaiah, Exodus, Psalm, Zechariah; more than 300 total prophecies of His coming. The intricacy of it all was breathtaking. Even the Magi that visited Jesus at his birth was prophesied 700 years in advance.

After setting his Bible aside, Darius picked up *Letting Go*, which, by now, he was close to finishing. He was taking meticulous notes to create a summary for future reference—something he could look back on when he reread the book, and something that he could build on whenever he came across a new idea of revelation.

He loved how Hawkins talked about the benefits of continuing to grow in self-consciousness and self-awareness, in particular, the ability to be able to reevaluate where you are. Hawkins put forward the notion that life crises, as painful as they were, provided opportunities for growth, and in that idea, he asked, "Would you use the experience to hate or to forgive? Would you grow from it, or become bitter? Would you embrace hope, or succumb to discouragement?" The crisis could be used to elevate one's consciousness.

Does one want to be one of the walking wounded or to heal? Darius made a point to add this to his notes. How often had he been trapped in negative thought loops, creating unnecessary pain for himself? Probably too often.

Hawkins' perspective was that our ego clings to negativity, and this was something Dairus was learning to identify in himself. To understand those negative emotions, to confront them, and to let them go, a practice that, while not always easy, was bringing him a newfound sense of peace. It was a step forward, the next part in the process, allowing him to step away from resistance and embrace higher states of energy, like love, forgiveness, and generosity.

Darius couldn't put the book down. The insights resonated deeply with him, especially Hawkins' discussion about the origins of beliefs and the perceptions tied to them. One particular concept struck him: behind every "I can't" lies an "I won't." Hawkins argued that "I can't" is often a mask for fear, shame, or pride—a refusal to try out of fear of failure. It resonated with Darius.

Saying "I can't," Hawkins explained, is a form of self-deception, perhaps unconscious, but dishonest nonetheless. Darius thought back to how much the phrase had bothered him over the years. His wife frequently used it, and their youngest son had picked up the habit as well. It had always driven Darius crazy. Yet, as he reflected, he realized personal issues and lack of awareness didn't go well together.

Diving deeper into the Bible had revealed to him that the concept of "I can't" had no place in God's creation. In Jeremiah, God declares, "I am Yahweh. Is there anything impossible for me?" Darius also thought about Jōb, where God questions Jōb: "Where were you when I set the stars in the sky? When I commanded the seas and set their boundaries?" God, the Creator of all things, didn't create limitations; humans did.

This led Darius to an even more profound realization: lower-level emotions—fear, shame, guilt—were not just weaknesses. They were the very states that allowed negative influences to take hold. Darius was starting to firmly believe that demons feed off lower-level emotions. Hawkins stated that almost 80% of the world lived below 200 in negative emotions. If it weren't for those in higher levels of consciousness, the world would already be destroyed. A person at 400 on the scale of consciousness counteracted 800,000 people below it! Conversely, the fruits of the Spirit—peace, patience, kindness, generosity, faithfulness, gentleness, and self-control—were divine in origin. Hawkins' teachings on emotional states and their vibrations aligned perfectly with these spiritual truths. What did that say about prayer? It really was powerful!

Darius had begun practicing techniques to stop unhealthy thought patterns, identify the underlying emotion, and release it. The results were astonishing. Emotions that once lingered for days now dissipated more quickly, and his mental "reset" happened sooner. Stop the thoughts by identifying the emotion, and then just sit with it.

One of the most impactful sections in Hawkins' book was about trauma and its lingering effects. He emphasized the importance of forgiving ourselves for past emotional overwhelm, as the unconscious mind does not distinguish between past and present. Darius learned that we could choose, at any moment, to heal old wounds. The hidden gift, Hawkins explained, was that past pain provided opportunities for growth, wisdom, and deeper self-understanding.

One passage hit Darius particularly hard: "Divorce often leads to emotional crippling because of an unwillingness to let go. Bitterness reveals unhealed emotional wounds and the effort put into healing those wounds yields immense rewards."

Hawkins then asked readers to consider, "How long am I willing to pay the cost? How much blame is enough? When will I stop indulging in the secret pleasure of self-punishment?"

Darius shook his head, feeling the weight of those questions. Hawkins reminded him that emotional self-healing was a skill no one had taught him—and it was time to stop beating himself up for not knowing. It was okay to feel anger, Hawkins said, as it held more energy than apathy. Anger could be channeled into action and courage, serving as a stepping stone to higher emotional states. The key was to observe and understand the root causes, then let them go.

As Darius read further, he was fascinated by Hawkins' discussion of bioenergy fields and auras—the idea that people could influence one another through their vibrational states. The concept of "like attracts like" was a universal law: bitterness attracts bitterness, love attracts love. Josh talked about this extensively in one of the Marriage Reset Program modules.

Darius reflected on how this principle had played out in his own life, particularly in his marriage. His feelings of unworthiness and fear of losing his wife had created a cycle of attachment and insecurity. Hawkins wrote that the fear of loss often precipitates the very loss we dread, as what we hold in mind tends to manifest.

Hawkins' insights on unhealthy attachments resonated deeply. They were the root of so much suffering, including his own. Yet, Darius also saw hope. By letting go of attachments and embracing higher levels of consciousness, he could free himself from the patterns that had held him back.

He turned the page and saw the header for the final chapter of the book. It took a turn from the rest of the book, removing the focus from the reader and turning itself inward to the author. It introduced Hawkins' own self-healing journey, giving the insights and the data that he uncovered.

The chapter was a self-castigating reflection on the myriad ailments Hawkins had endured by the age of 50. Among other issues, he had used a cane due to painful gout, he had sinus issues, chronic migraines, vision challenges, all kinds of skin issues, intestinal issues, and extensive allergies. The guy had been a mess! Darius winced at the thought of it all. Hawkins described himself as unhealthy, to say the least, and many friends had wondered how much longer he would live.

But then, everything changed.

He began practicing the principles of surrender, combined with insights from *A Course in Miracles* by Helen Schucman, and discovered that suppressed guilt was underpinning his negative thoughts and feelings, which ultimately had led to all of his physical issues. Once he identified those patterns and consciously let them go, remarkable transformations began to occur.

Within days of using the technique, Hawkins experienced amazing relief, and surgeries were canceled. Chronic conditions that had plagued him for decades faded and eventually disappeared entirely. Issues in the past that would have required hospitalization were dealt with through the practice of surrender and healed on their own. Over time, the process became easier. Minor illnesses resolved quickly, while more severe conditions took up to two years—but in the end, Hawkins healed every single ailment.

Then came the story that truly astounded Darius: Hawkins' journey to heal his eyesight.

After a lecture on surrender, a student was confused about why the professor still wore glasses. Hawkins was surprised and had never considered it! He decided to discard his glasses, and one day, a profound inner peace came over him, and he felt like his surrender and faith allowed God to heal his eyes. Hawkins could read small print in poor light, read street signs, and his eyesight was flawless. As nearly blind as he had been, within six weeks, he was healed!

As Darius read this account, he sat stunned. He removed his bifocals and tossed them under his seat almost instinctively. For two years, he had depended on them for reading small print and driving at night. Yet, inspired by Hawkins' story, he resolved to heal his vision, just as he had already begun healing other aspects of his life. He was eager to dive deeper, to learn more, and to continue his transformation.

Darius closed the book, shaking his head in awe and laughing at what he had just done as everyone slept around him. Each step felt divinely guided and he was determined to order *The Course on Miracles*. He smiled, whispering to himself, "God is amazing."

Chapter 54
A Unique Fundraiser

D arius was excited about the chance to take both of his boys to a charity event in Nashville, where they would meet Steve Hemphill for the first time. He was pleasantly surprised that his youngest son would also be able to join. This opportunity was one of the few positive outcomes of his wife arranging for the family to be together at the house for his son's birthday.

Mostly, though, the birthday gathering had been awkward. His mother dominated the conversation, focusing largely on his wife, while his wife seemed to be addressing everything she said back to his mother. Meanwhile, Darius and the three kids sat around, exchanging peculiar looks in response to the comments being made. Darius listened quietly, making eye contact and focusing on the exchange without reacting to a few veiled jabs directed his way. Later, his kids confided that they didn't understand why the gathering had to happen at all and were clear they didn't want a repeat of it for the holidays.

Despite the discomfort of that event, his youngest son had shown genuine interest in attending the charity event. When Darius brought it up, his son expressed his enthusiasm and surprisingly, his wife didn't object. She simply said, "I don't care," when the idea of taking him out of school for a day and a half came up. Yet, with that, plans were set.

They drove down the night before the event and stayed in a hotel about 15 minutes from the venue. But the following morning, the boys slept in a little later than usual.

Darius, already up, had managed to get some work done and enjoy a cup of coffee before finally wrangling them out of bed around 10:00. They packed up their belongings and headed out to explore an area not far from their hotel. It had an interesting restaurant surrounded by several shops, including a cozy coffee spot. Inside, Darius asked the boys if they wanted anything before setting his plan for the day.

"I'm going to work here for a few hours," he explained, "Then when the restaurant opens, we can have lunch. Afterward, I need to take a few more calls; then we'll get ready to head to the event tonight. You'll both need to dress a bit nicer for it, alright?"

"What are you wearing, Dad?" His oldest son asked.

"A dress shirt, a jacket, and jeans," Darius replied.

"Okay, that works."

***

It was a good day. Darius made significant headway with his work while the boys entertained themselves on their phones or chatted quietly. Lunch was a pleasant affair, and after eating, they changed in the vehicle and set off for the evening's charitable event.

The venue was a sprawling mansion, or as Darius thought, more like a grand house that one of Steve's affluent supporters had recently built. Upon arrival, he noticed the multiple entrances, each adding to the grandeur of the estate. The property itself was massive, spread across several acres, although much of the landscaping was still unfinished. Gravel covered the areas where cars were parked, and as they stepped out, Darius couldn't help but admire the sheer scale and luxury of the place.

The cars pulling in were equally impressive, a clear indication that some of the attendees had significant wealth. They made their way inside, and the house proved to be just as magnificent on the inside as it was outside. The main kitchen was enormous, with food laid out in abundance. Amid the activity, Darius heard a familiar voice. Steve emerged with a broad smile, greeting him warmly. They shook hands and embraced.

"Man, it's so great you could make it," Steve said, then turned to the boys. "So nice to meet you both! Your Dad's told me a lot about you."

The boys exchanged polite smiles as Steve introduced them to various people. One man who approached caught Darius's attention—a somewhat older Hispanic man with a warm, affable demeanor.

"This is Roe. We went to college together," Steve said.

Darius shook Roe's hand. "Nice to meet you."

"And you as well," Roe replied with a genuine smile that reminded Darius of Steve.

As Steve excused himself to tend to other guests, Darius and Roe began talking. They quickly found a conversational rhythm, with Roe asking about Darius's connection to Steve. Hesitating for a moment, Darius shared his story. "Let's just say the last year of my life has been challenging, filled with one difficult event after another—kind of Jōb-like," he began. "The final straw was my wife of 17 years telling me she didn't want to be married anymore. It wasn't long after that a friend suggested I read Steve's book, *What Are the Stakes?*, and that's how I got connected with him."

Roe nodded sympathetically. "I understand. There's a lot of darkness in this world that most people don't even realize."

Their conversation continued, flowing naturally into deeper topics about faith and resilience. When Roe revealed he was an artist and would be painting live for the auction that evening, Darius was intrigued. "You're going to paint it here tonight?"

Roe nodded with a smile. "Yes, I'll finish it during the event. I don't really have something in mind, but it's always exciting to see how it comes together."

Later, as Darius mingled, he couldn't help but admire how Steve managed the room. He moved effortlessly, speaking to everyone while also orchestrating the evening's logistics. When Steve found a moment to pull Darius aside, he expressed his gratitude: "I know you've been through a lot, and I'm thankful for your support," Steve said earnestly. "Your contributions have already made a difference."

Darius shook his head. "It's my pleasure, Steve. Honestly, your work has been a blessing to me. Your books have given me a better understanding of faith, prophecy, and spiritual warfare. I've shared them with so many people."

Steve's face lit up. "That means the world to me, Darius. It's not an easy path to take, but hearing stories like yours makes it all worth it."

Darius looked at Steve. "When I first started this journey, it was remarkable. I may have ... overdone it at times in sharing transparently. People will think you're crazy when you talk about the demonic, but how do you not share the truth when you know it? Spiritual warfare, the demonic ... I didn't have any understanding of it until reading your book, and it's all over the Bible. Everywhere. I never expected this. Some people look at you like you're crazy."

Steve nodded. "I've had people distance themselves, people who didn't want to be my friend anymore, didn't want anything to do with us. Even my beautiful wife wasn't exactly thrilled when this was the path God led me down. But it's making a difference in people's lives. When you hear the stories in the book—and there are so many more—I could write several other books on just that topic. People are being blessed, lives are changing because we're staking out the land and giving it to God."

"Yeah, I have had multiple friends benefit from staking their homes out already," Darius replied, nodding his head. "It's something that needs more awareness. When my business picks up again, I want to support you financially, just like I do with other charities."

Steve slapped Darius on the arm. "I'm really grateful for your contribution to this event. The fact that you're here, despite everything you've been through, means a lot. Just remember: God loves you, and He'll get you through this. I know it's not the way you wanted things to go, that you wanted to keep your marriage intact but don't stop trusting Him. Even if things don't work out the way you hope, He has something better in store for you. Steve then shook his head, a somber expression crossing his face. "Have there been any changes?"

Darius sighed. "No, not really. Since we last spoke before I went to Denver, I've kept up with the advice you gave me. I've been customizing my prayers."

Steve nodded. "You have to pray that God will give her what He knows she needs."

"I've been doing that," Darius confirmed. "The book *Prayers that Satan Hates* has been a real blessing in that regard."

Steve smiled, but his expression turned even more serious. "But no changes?"

Darius shook his head. "After she filed, she's pretty much been acting like we're already divorced. I suspected she was having an affair, but it seems she's with a woman."

Steve looked at him, concern etched on his face. "That's really unfortunate," he said. "But it does explain a few things. Keep praying for her, though."

"I will," Darius replied, his voice steady. "I'm still hopeful, but it's not looking good. Regardless of what happens, I have to focus on my personal growth and keep leaning into God, changing the things I need to change."

"That's smart," Steve said. "Okay, I have to go help with some other things—"

"Before things get crazy," Darius quickly said, "Can I get a picture with you and my boys?"

"Absolutely," Steve smiled.

They walked to an area near the pool, which was absolutely gorgeous, and took some pictures together.

"Thank you," Darius said as they quickly embraced.

"You're more than welcome, Darius. I appreciate your support, and I'm glad to know you. I'm honored to call you a friend."

"I hope we'll know each other for a long time," Darius replied. "And I plan to support you and your work as much as I can, especially when my business picks up financially."

"That's awesome," Steve said, smiling at the boys. "Alright, there are plenty of snacks and hors d'oeuvres. Help yourselves to whatever you want. And if you want any books or anything from the Act of Faith collection to take for someone, feel free. Enjoy the show!"

Darius and his boys made their way around the room, meeting different people, snacking, and waiting for the event to begin. But then, out of nowhere, he was face-to-face with the producers of

"God's Not Dead" and "Nefarious," Cary Solomon and Chuck Konzelman.

For a moment, he couldn't believe his eyes. Chuck was tall, somewhat imposing at first glance because of his size, but after spending a few seconds with him, it was clear he was anything but intimidating. His smile was infectious, and kindness radiated from him. Cary was shorter, wearing glasses and sporting a mustache. They were an interesting pair, childhood friends from New Jersey, Darius recalled.

He stepped forward and quickly introduced himself. "Very nice to meet you."

"Likewise," they said in unison, shaking his hand.

"I loved your work. I just watched Nefarious over the summer. It was remarkable."

"Thank you," they both replied, smiling.

Darius smiled and introduced his boys. "It's great to meet you."

He shared how, earlier in the year, he'd watched a 30-minute documentary about the making of Nefarious and remembered the producers talking about how the film cameras had failed, and how, after a priest had blessed the set, the film started working again. He also recalled the stories about hearing demonic voices while filming in a prison.

"Oh, yeah," Cary said, shaking his head. "There were times during filming that we weren't sure we were supposed to make the movie. We weren't even sure if we'd be allowed to finish it."

"What do you mean?" Darius asked.

The two producers exchanged a glance. "If you knew the challenges we faced ... " Chuck began, shaking his head. "We almost didn't get 'Nefarious' made."

Cary jumped in. "After growing up in New Jersey, we moved to Hollywood, and now, by God's direction, we're in Texas and

Nashville. We've had some difficult moments in this industry, but we've been able to get films made. And, of course, God's blessed our work."

Chuck continued. "With 'Nefarious,' we had three major stakeholders nearly killed in the span of four weeks while we were working on the film. One of our key people went to get something from the car but forgot something in the office. When he turned back, a drunk driver slammed into the car. If he had been just seconds earlier, he would have been killed."

Darius's eyes widened. "That's scary," he said.

"Oh, yeah," Chuck replied. "The demonic is no joke, and there were other examples. They're active, and they're real. Half the world doesn't even believe the devil and the demonic exist, but they are out there, and they hate us because of the work we do to expose the truth."

"There was a moment when all six of us, the major stakeholders for 'Nefarious,' gathered and wondered if we should stop. The enemy was trying to stop us, but we prayed on it," Cary said. "God said do not be afraid. We put it in God's hands, and look where we are now."

Darius nodded, his mind racing. "That guy who plays the prisoner, the one who flips between being the prisoner and the demon, he did an incredible job. I've never even heard of him before."

"Yeah, he was a blessing," Chuck agreed. "One of the most remarkable performances I've ever seen."

Darius smiled. "In that video I saw, it talks about the things that happened at the actual prison: the voices, the strange occurrences—like at certain hours in areas that were shut down. It's mind-blowing."

Cary nodded. "Yeah, and we even talked to the guards and people who worked there. There's a part of the prison that's been inactive for decades, but people have seen and heard things there."

"It's phenomenal," Darius said. "But it's real. That darkness, it's real. I have encountered it myself, which is how I met Steve."

The conversation shifted to their upcoming projects, and Cary shared a script for a new movie about a former college basketball coach who falls from the peak of success to rock bottom. As he struggles with alcoholism and his failing life, he discovers faith and faces choices that will either lead him toward redemption or deeper into despair.

"That sounds amazing," Darius said.

"Our projects do really well for everyone. 'God's Not Dead' cost $2M to make and grossed $64.7 million," Cary explained. "And actually, we're looking for investors and actors for some parts. You know anyone?"

His youngest son, standing nearby, piped up, "Well, my Dad's a coach, and he knows how to yell."

Everyone laughed. Darius grinned. "Yeah, you could say the older version of me was a pretty vociferous coach."

"I'd love to get a picture with you guys if that's okay," Darius said.

"Absolutely," they replied.

After taking some photos and exchanging contact information, Darius said, "I'll definitely send you an email. I'd love to stay in touch and learn more about what you're doing."

Chapter 55
The Bidding War

S uddenly, an announcement echoed through the room that the auction was about to begin. Darius, eager to see Roe's painting unfold, found a seat right in front of the stage, positioning himself perfectly for the event. The moment Roe began setting up, the crowd grew quiet as Steve took the stage. With a warm smile, he thanked everyone for coming and spoke about how blessed he had been in his life, reflecting on how he'd never imagined he'd become an author. He shared a touching story about how God gave him the chapters for his first book in a way that still amazed him. Then Steve introduced David, an award-winning pianist who would be playing throughout the evening. Darius thought back to meeting David earlier in the day, completely unaware that he was the pianist. As the music began to fill the room, Darius's excitement grew. He realized that the night was about to unfold in ways he hadn't expected.

As the hauntingly beautiful music played, Roe began his live painting, his movements both swift and deliberate. Darius watched, fascinated by the artist's method: how Roe used brushes, his fingers, and a towel to blend and manipulate the paint, creating something from nothing in mere minutes. The precision with which Roe worked left Darius in awe, joking to himself that his artistic ability was limited to stick figures. The energy in the room was electric, and as the painting took shape, Darius's boys were just as captivated. They snapped photos and recorded videos, amazed by the artist's process. In about 35 minutes, Roe had finished his masterpiece, and the crowd stood to give him a well-deserved standing ovation.

Roe, humbled by the response, took the mic and expressed his gratitude. He spoke about his friendship with Steve, how they had met in college, and how proud he was to support Steve's vision for Active Faith. He also mentioned that the auction would raise funds to turn *What Are the Stakes?* into a miniseries. Roe announced that if the painting sold for over $10,000, he would visit the winning bidder's home to paint another piece and host a dinner for their guests. Darius, impressed by the gesture, thought to himself, If only I could afford to win this and have a Roe original at my house.

The auction began with an opening bid of $1,000. The price quickly jumped to $1,500, then $2,000, but strangely, it stalled at $2,500. Darius couldn't believe it—he knew Roe's paintings could sell for anywhere from $5,000 to $15,000, and with the room full of well-off guests, the low bid made no sense. As the auctioneer called out:

"Going once."

"Going twice."

Darius's hand shot up. "$3,000!"

"$3,000 bid, thank you, sir!"

Immediately, he regretted it. "What am I doing? What am I doing? I shouldn't spend that kind of money with the business issues," he thought, but he convinced himself that it was for a good cause.

Thankfully, the bidding continued: $3,500, $4,000, $4,500. Darius felt the weight of everyone's eyes on him. He glanced around the room and saw his sons shaking their heads, smiling at the spectacle. His pulse raced as the auction climbed higher—$5,000, $5,500, and then $6,000, $7,000, and finally, $8,000. The tension in the room was palpable, heightened by the haunting music still playing in the background.

When the bid hit $10,000, Darius realized the other bidder was still in the running. He looked at the room full of people and, after a deep breath, said, "I'm out. Congratulations." The crowd erupted into applause, and Darius made his way to the kitchen to escape the heat of the moment.

As he stood there, trying to process what had just happened, his son appeared beside him. "Dad, what were you thinking?" His son asked with a grin. "I didn't know it was you until it hit $8,000. What would you have done if you'd won?"

Darius laughed. "I don't know. I was just trying to drive the price up. Maybe if I had won, I'd pray for some business miracles to help pay for it."

A few minutes later, Darius felt a tap on his shoulder. It was Roe. "Brother, you're awesome," Roe said, his gratitude shining through. "I can't thank you enough for what you did."

"What did I do?" Darius said, smiling sheepishly.

Roe laughed. "You got the room moving, and without that, the painting wouldn't have sold for what it did. So thank you, man."

Darius chuckled. "I just couldn't sit there and watch it go for $2,500. I had to do something."

Roe nodded, lowering his voice to make sure no one else could hear. "There are people in this room who could easily pay $10,000 for that painting, but they were just sitting there. You got them involved. That's how we reached that price."

Darius smiled, feeling a sense of satisfaction. The conversation shifted to their mutual appreciation for art and faith, and Roe invited him to look him up if he ever found himself in Dallas. They exchanged contact information, and as they parted, Darius felt a renewed sense of connection to the people around him.

As the event came to a close, Darius thanked Steve for the invitation, feeling grateful for the experience. He turned to his sons. "Well, boys, what did you think of that?"

They just shook their heads, still processing the night's events. "Wild," one of them said.

Darius, smiling to himself, couldn't help but agree. "Wild" didn't even begin to describe how his life had changed since May.

Chapter 56
A Basement in Darkness

The morning began like every other since Darius had moved into the basement. He woke in complete darkness as there were no windows in the basement, which added to the tomb-like feel, his body aching from the cold, hard mattress. Shaking off the lingering stiffness, he started his day the same-always with Scripture first, prayer, meditation, his cold plunge, and then a workout. The familiar routine brought a semblance of normalcy, though his life was anything but normal.

Climbing the stairs, he found his wife and son in the kitchen. Her face was twisted, furious and full of anger, but his son greeted him with a smile, a small spark of warmth in the tense air.

"Good morning," Darius said as he passed through.

"Morning, Dad," his son replied cheerfully.

Without another word, he moved to the spare bathroom—now shared with his son—to shower and prepare for the day.

By the time he got dressed and left for the office, the weight of the morning had settled in his chest. The days passed with an uncomfortable rhythm. For nearly a week, tension hummed between him and his wife, a thin thread stretched taut but unbroken. It wasn't until communication with the lawyers picked up that her demeanor began to shift. The sharp edge of her fury dulled into curt indifference.

Their exchanges remained brief, almost mechanical. Darius, committed to an all-organic diet, cooked his meals alone. He'd return from the office around 5:30, take over the kitchen, and if she came home, he would ask her about her day. Her responses were short, but no longer laced with venom. She spent most evenings retreating to what had once been their bedroom, emerging only briefly before heading out, leaving Darius to wonder where she was spending her evenings.

Then, one evening, as he chopped vegetables for dinner, she returned home earlier than usual. The slamming of the front door signaled her arrival, followed by the sharp click of her heels on the hardwood floor. Darius glanced up as she entered the kitchen.

"How was your day?" he asked.

Her response came in a torrent. "Awful. Michelle has made everything impossible. I told her she'd better keep my fucking name out of her mouth. I'm done with her games!"

Darius froze, knife poised mid-chop. He forced himself to keep a neutral expression. Michelle was her business partner, the one at the center of the escalating breakup of their company.

"I mean, the nerve of her! I hate her!" she continued, her voice rising. "She's trying to sabotage everything. But I told her I won't put up with her shit anymore." She shook her hands in frustration before storming off to the bedroom, her anger echoing down the hall.

That evening lingered in Darius's mind long after she had left. It had become her routine—coming home for just fifteen or twenty minutes, avoiding any real interaction with him, then leaving again. She wouldn't return until later in the night. Her behavior was a constant reminder of the distance between them, and yet, it gnawed at him in ways he couldn't quite shake.

As he cooked dinner that night, he thought about her words, the way she had expressed anger and hate. It wasn't like her. He couldn't let it go, so he prayed, searching for clarity and peace. Later, compelled by a mixture of care and hope, he decided to send her a message.

> *You know, I understand that you're going through a difficult time and that you're angry. But you saying that you hate someone? That's not the Jessica I know. I just wanted to send you this text. I pray that God will give you peace and help you through the situation.*

He hesitated before pressing send, wondering if his words would be received in the spirit he intended. He didn't want to provoke or patronize her, only to remind her of the person he remembered—the person he still believed she could be.

Later, his phone buzzed with her response.

> *Thank you. I don't want to ever hate anybody. You're right when I think about it. Thank you.*

For a moment, Darius felt a flicker of hope. It wasn't much, but it was something—a glimpse of the woman he once knew, maybe even a small step toward healing. He sighed, letting the moment settle, and silently prayed that it wouldn't be the last.

***

Weeks blurred together in the silence of the house, growing more and more strange with each passing day. Darius sat in the office, his refuge since moving back into the house in late August. The weekends, especially, had become a time for solitude—meditation, contemplation, and wrestling with the chaos his life had become. This past week had been particularly heavy. The lingering suspicion that Jessica was having an affair still haunted him, though he clung to hope, praying fervently that he was wrong.

Most evenings were the same: a few brief, cold interactions in the morning, hours spent at work, and his return to an empty home. Jessica barely stayed long enough to exchange pleasantries before vanishing into the night. But that week, something was different.

He had worked late one evening and came home to find Jessica sitting on the couch. She was in pajamas, impossibly close to a colleague from her office. There they sat, inches apart, as if no one else existed. Across the couch, their son sat awkwardly, seemingly oblivious to the tension thickening the room.

Darius froze in the doorway, an unpleasant feeling in his stomach. He walked into the kitchen, fumbling for normalcy. He was aware of their backs to him as they sat on the couch. The realization hit him hard: all the rumors and things that he had been told were true. It was obvious his wife was in a relationship with her lesbian colleague. The proximity, the comfort—they weren't hiding it anymore or they thought everyone was dumb.

The house felt suffocating. He couldn't stay. Grabbing his phone, he queued up a Tony Robbins walking meditation, slipped in his earbuds, and stepped out into the cold night air. The words of the meditation echoed in his head, "Everything I need is within me now." He walked briskly, repeating the mantra aloud as Tony kept repeating the mantra changing the emphasis on a different word with each repetition. "Everything I need is within me now." The chill of the night bit at his skin, but the rhythm of his steps and the strength of his voice steadied him. He needed to adjust his mind, to process the truth he could no longer deny.

The revelation didn't end there. Weeks later, his office manager, Andrea, pulled him aside. "Darius, we need to talk," she said, her tone cautious but firm.

"Okay," he said, trying to brace himself. "Have I not been an open book? You can tell me anything."

"It's not about that," Andrea said, shaking her head. "This isn't gossip. This is important. I've heard things that I haven't told you. And ... Well, I didn't want to bring this to you, but I think you need to know."

Darius sat down, his chest tightening. "Go on."

"I don't agree with how everything's been handled," Andrea began, "but I've heard from several sources that Jessica is having an affair. And not just rumors ... people have seen her and Ash together. It's public now."

Darius inhaled sharply. Ash. He'd been right. The name felt like a knife twisting in his gut.

"That's not all," Andrea continued. "Jessica and Ash are using the same lawyer. Ash is divorcing her wife, and now it looks like they're coming for the business, too."

He stared at her, speechless. "The same lawyer?" He finally managed.

"Yes," Andrea confirmed, her voice heavy with concern. "Look, Darius, I care about you as a person, and I know how much you've been through. But I thought you needed to know. This isn't just about you—it affects all of us."

Darius lowered his gaze, his mind racing. The betrayal was no longer just personal; it was entangled in every part of his life—his family, his finances, his work. He nodded slowly, forcing himself to breathe.

"Thank you … for telling me," he said quietly.

As Andrea left the room, Darius remained seated, staring at the floor. He had hoped to avoid conflict, to salvage something from the wreckage of his marriage. But now, it seemed, the battle was unavoidable.

Chapter 57
Nothing Stays Hidden

Darius sat in the conference room with Andrea, Jake, and his older son, conducting a training session. The office had grown quiet in recent months, with only Andrea and the three of them remaining on staff. As the training video played on the screen, a knock interrupted the session. Andrea stood to answer the door, leaving Darius focused on the presentation.

A moment later, Andrea returned and tapped Darius on the shoulder. "It's for you," she said.

Darius glanced over to see a woman standing in the doorway, peering in. He didn't recognize her immediately. "What does she want?" he asked Andrea.

"I don't know, but she says she needs to talk to you."

Darius got up and walked over, unsure of what to expect. He opened the door further, looking at the woman on the other side of the threshold, and asked, "You wanted to see me? How can I help you?"

"I'd like to talk to you," she said, her tone serious.

"Alright," he replied, leading her to a separate room. Closing the door, he turned to face her. "What can I do for you?"

"Do you know who I am?" she asked.

He studied her face, searching for familiarity. "I don't think so," he said, shaking his head.

"I'm Ash's wife," she revealed.

Darius's expression shifted, his brows lifting as realization set in. "Okay ... But what can I do for you?" he repeated.

She wasted no time. "Do you know how long they've been together?"

Darius took a measured breath, his mind recalling the tools he'd been practicing. Pause. Validate. Respond. "You want to know if I know how long they've been together," he said, his voice calm.

"Yes," she replied.

He shook his head.

"They've been together since February."

Darius stood there calmly taking it in as his worst fears for so long had just been affirmed. "I'm no fool," he admitted, "I've suspected it for a while. But how do you know that?"

"Because. I've been keeping track of her. There have been multiple times that she was supposed to be home and wasn't. I would track her phone and she would be at the office—one time I went to the office and they were there together."

"That doesn't necessarily mean they were in a relationship at that time," Darius replied, attempting to remain objective.

"Oh, come on," she snapped. "Do you also know your wife is paying for Ash's lawyer?"

Darius tilted his head, his eyebrow arching. "How do you know that?"

"Because we don't have any money," she explained. "Ash doesn't have the money for a lawyer like that. And I know how expensive her lawyer is."

Darius paused, considering her words. She wasn't wrong about the costs—Jessica's lawyer was top-tier, the kind of attorney who represented millionaires and professional athletes. His own lawyer charged less than half that rate. But the idea that Jessica might be funding someone else's legal fees left him unsettled.

"How do you know that?"

"I don't know how that could be possible," he said carefully. "Jessica doesn't have much money either, as far as I'm aware."

"She's getting it from somewhere," the woman pressed.

Darius wondered if it was coming from Jessica's parents as he sighed, keeping his tone measured. "Look, I'm really sorry for the situation you're in. What is it you're hoping to get from me?"

"I'd like to compare notes," she said. "Maybe we can support each other, help our lawyers understand the situation better, and then maybe—"

Darius raised a hand, stopping her mid-sentence. "I'm sorry," he said. "I really am. But I can't help you. I love my wife. I love my children. This isn't what I wanted, but I'm not going to involve myself in your court proceedings."

Her shoulders slumped. "I hate this for our children," she said quietly. "It's horrible what they are doing to them."

"Yes, it is," Darius agreed. "This isn't what I wanted for my family either."

She hesitated before continuing. "Did you know she's filed on me twice?"

Darius shook his head. "No, I didn't."

"Well, she filed, but then she stopped. Because of the video you sent to your wife—"

"How do you know about that?" Darius asked.

"Because I saw it," she stated. "After that, she thought Jessica was going to reconcile with you."

While in Barcelona, Darius had recorded a heartfelt video for his wife. In it, he expressed his deep love for her and their family, emphasizing how hard he had been working and how much he wanted to mend their relationship. Despite the challenges, he had made it clear that a divorce was not what he desired. His intention was to show vulnerability, to open a door to reconciliation even after Jessica had initiated the divorce proceedings.

Now, as he listened to Ash's wife recount what she knew, his eyebrow lifted in surprise. The private moment he had shared with Jessica was something he had never expected to surface in another context.

The weight of her words settled over Darius. For a moment, hope flickered—a sign that Jessica might have hesitated, and reconsidered the path they were on. But as quickly as it came, the hope faded. Whatever momentary pause there had been in the divorce process, Jessica had shown no sign of changing course since then. Instead, she had remained resolute, her actions pointing to an entirely different future than the one Darius had envisioned.

Whatever chance there might have been to repair their marriage seemed long gone now.

"I don't know what to say to that," he admitted. "Yes, I made a video for Jessica when I was away, telling her I wanted to work on our marriage. But she hasn't given any indication since then that she's reconsidering the divorce."

The woman looked at him intently as though searching for some hidden truth. "I thought you should know," she said finally.

"I appreciate you coming to me," Darius replied. "But I can't help you. I'm sorry."

He opened the door, signaling the conversation was over. She hesitated again, shaking her head before stepping into the front of the office. Darius walked her to the front door, holding it open as she left. She turned back one last time, as if to say something, then thought better of it and walked away.

Darius closed the door and leaned against it, exhaling deeply. The conversation replayed in his mind, confirming what he had long suspected but hadn't wanted to admit. Even his children had noticed the signs—two of them had openly suggested their mother was having an affair, and both believed it was with Ash. He had always cautioned them to avoid jumping to conclusions, urging them to pray for Jessica and support her. But now, the evidence was mounting. It wouldn't be long before everything came to light.

Darius thought about multiple Bible verses; everything done in the dark will be brought to the light. He had just read 2 Samuel and thought of David's sin with Bathsheba. He not only committed adultery but then sent her husband off to his death to be murdered so he could marry her. God then sent the prophet Nathan to reprimand David, stating in 2 Samuel 12:12: ***"Though you did this in secret, I will do this thing before all of Israel in broad daylight!"***

"Lies never stay hidden," Darius thought. The truth always comes out.

Chapter 58
Pirates & Jesters

H e had not long arrived home, but here he was, staring out the airplane window once again, the sprawling clouds beneath him offering a strange sense of calm. The flight to Dallas wasn't long, but it was enough time to reflect. He still marveled at how he'd ended up here, invited by Amanda and Chris after the International Living Conference in Denver. Their enthusiasm had been infectious:

"You have to come. You just have to."

Now, he wasn't just attending Tony Robbins' "Unleash the Power Within" as Amanda's guest but had also arranged to reconnect with Roe Garcia, a meeting that excited him nearly as much as the event itself.

Darius was grateful for having met Roe at Steve's Fundraiser and striking up a friendship with the passionate artist and musician. Roe had insisted, "If you're ever in Dallas, you've got to look me up." True to his word, when Darius reached out, Roe responded immediately, even offering to pick him up from the airport.

After the plane landed, Darius collected his suitcase and checked his phone. Roe's text was waiting: *I'm outside in the cell phone area. Let me know when you're ready.* Making his way to the curb, Darius spotted Roe's small pickup truck approaching. The man climbed out, grinning broadly, his distinct Cuban accent cutting through the din of the airport as he exclaimed, "Hey, brother!" Pulling Darius into a firm hug, Roe took the suitcase and tossed it into the truck bed.

"How was the flight?" Roe asked as they climbed in.

"They didn't let me fly the plane, so it was smooth," Darius replied.

They both laughed.

As the truck pulled onto the highway, Roe launched into updates about an upcoming event he was hosting. "It's an art showing," he said. "The new series is called 'Pirates and Jesters.'"

Darius raised an eyebrow. "Pirates and Jesters? That's a combination I wasn't expecting."

Roe chuckled. "It's a political parody. The pirates—well, they want to take everything you've got. And the jesters? They're so ridiculous it's hard to take them seriously. Together, they're perfect for this mess we call politics."

Darius laughed. "That's both clever and painfully accurate."

Roe smiled but grew more serious. "I'm trying to bring some levity to the chaos, you know? Through art and culture. But it's rooted in truth, the ways we've drifted so far from biblical principles."

The conversation ebbed and flowed as they drove, touching on politics, faith, and art. Darius was fascinated by Roe's multifaceted life.

The cityscape of Dallas unfolded before them, sunlight glinting off the buildings as Roe shifted the subject. "Enough about me. How are you, Darius? Really?"

Darius hesitated, unsure how much to reveal. Eventually, he sighed. "I'm doing better than I thought I'd be. But it's not where I wanted to be. I hoped ... Well, I thought there was a chance to fix things with my wife. But after living in the house with her again, it's clear she's already moved on."

Roe shot him a concerned glance. "That's hard, man. I'm sorry."

"Well, there's another twist to it," Darius said.

"What's that?" Roe asked.

"Well, it's a woman," Darius replied.

"Oh, man, you've got to be kidding!" Roe exclaimed.

"No, I'm not kidding. It's pretty much what I had suspected, even though I've been continuing to pray that I was wrong," Darius continued.

"There's no doubt about it," Roe added, shaking his head. "From that standpoint, a married mother with a family, after all these years together, that's quite the surprise, and not a good one either."

"Yeah," Darius said, nodding. "So, anyway, I moved back in—"

"You moved back in?" Roe asked in surprise.

"Yeah. There were just too many things happening that were ... a problem," Darius explained. "I was fine with moving into the office because, well, I love her."

Roe paused. "Loved her."

"No, man," Darius said, his voice soft. "I still love her. Even with this. What's amazing to me is, I'm still not angry. I feel sad for her. I feel sad for our family. And yeah, I definitely feel sad for myself sometimes, but ... I still forgive her."

Roe nodded solemnly. "That's a big heart you've got, brother."

The weight of the conversation hung in the air as Roe asked about what life was like back in the house. Describing it as "crazy" didn't do any of it justice, and now, with the added financial strain, things were only going from bad to worse. Roe listened intently as Darius updated him.

"It's the Twilight Zone. Man, it feels like I am living in a tomb," Darius stated. "You can ... feel the heaviness."

Soon, they arrived at Roe's studio, an unassuming building tucked into a vibrant part of the city.

"This is where we're going to park," Roe said, pulling into a small lot. "My studio is in the basement of the building. Unusual maybe, but I figured I'd show you around, show you where the band plays and everything."

Darius raised an eyebrow. "You're in a band now?"

Roe chuckled. "Well, I've been in a band, off and on, for a long time. Do you remember the guy playing piano at Steve's event?"

"Oh yeah, he was phenomenal," Darius replied.

"Well, David and I were in a band together before he got married. We still play occasionally. When I have events, especially when I release new art collections. We usually have music, food, drinks, and a gathering at the gallery. It's a great time."

"I had no idea you and David were bandmates! He's amazing on the piano!"

"Yeah, man, I've known him forever. That guy ... " Roe shook his head, laughing. "He's always had women throwing themselves at him."

Darius laughed along. "I can imagine. Talented musicians have that effect."

"True, but David's had quite the journey. He grew up knowing the Lord, drifted away for a while, blamed the music industry, and then found his way back. He got married, had kids, and turned his life around completely."

"That's incredible."

As they got out of the car, Roe gestured toward the building. "Come on, I'll show you the studio."

Inside, they took the elevator down to the studio. As Roe unlocked the door, Darius stepped inside and immediately noticed the vibrant energy of the space. Artwork was everywhere—on the walls, stacked on the floor, and framed on shelves. Instruments were carefully displayed alongside books and art supplies. The air buzzed with creativity.

"This is incredible," Darius said, spinning slowly to take it all in.

Roe grinned. "You haven't seen anything yet."

Roe led him through the studio, pointing out different sections. One area featured a mural above the entrance. "I painted that," he said proudly.

"That's phenomenal work," Darius replied.

"Thanks, man. Means a lot."

Roe opened another door, revealing a larger gallery area. Darius's jaw dropped as he took in the paintings—large, vivid canvases depicting everything from mythical creatures to historical figures. One side of the studio had a gallery showing the "Pirates and Jesters" work.

"Go ahead," Roe announced, "Pick a painting—anyone you want. It's yours. Well, anyone except for the Four Horsemen series. Those are ... Let's just say they're spoken for."

Darius froze, his disbelief apparent. "What? Roe, I can't—"

"You can, and you will," Roe interrupted. "It's my gift to you. You've done a lot for Steve's causes, raising money for good work. Let me do this for you."

Darius wandered through the studio, marveling at Roe's vibrant, thought-provoking pieces. Then, one painting stopped him in his tracks. It depicted a serene Madonna cradling a child, surrounded by tall, imposing columns. Hidden among the trees in the background, a beast's eyes glinted with menace, its presence both subtle and chilling.

"What is this one called?" Darius asked, unable to look away.

Roe joined him, his voice soft. "The Garden of Good and Evil. It's about the Virgin Mary and baby Jesus. The beast symbolizes Satan's hunt for the child through Herod."

Darius stared at the painting; his breath caught. "This is it. This is the one I'm supposed to take."

Roe smiled. "I'm glad it found you. It's been here for years, waiting for the right person."

Well," Darius said, turning to Roe with a grateful smile, "I don't have to think about it. This is the one."

Roe clapped him on the back. "It's yours, brother."

Chapter 59
Seeds of Evil

A fter Roe sang two amazingly beautiful songs for Darius, they locked up the studio and headed to eat. Darius asked, "You've never been married, right?"

Roe shook his head, his voice soft. "No, no, brother. Never married. Came close once, but ... I just knew it wasn't meant for me. Family, kids ... it's something I always wanted, but yeah ... It just wasn't in the cards for me."

"Why's that?"

"We'll talk about it over lunch," Roe said, trying to manage a laugh.

They crossed the street and walked around the back entrance of a rather unique-looking hotel. Going in through a side door into a little restaurant, Roe waved to the bartender, who waved back with a smile. Obviously, Darius was the only stranger here. They sat at a table in the corner, and the waiter came over to take their order. Darius had already seen what he wanted on the specials board behind the bar.

"Can I get you something to drink? Beer, wine, we have a good selection."

Roe shook his head. "No alcohol for me. Just tonic water, maybe with some lemon."

"I'll have water," Darius said.

"And for food?"

"The special burger? The one with the curry cheese, sautéed onions, garlic aioli mayo, and a side of sweet potato fries?"

Roe grinned, excited. "Oh, man. That sounds good, make it two."

The waiter nodded and moved back to the bar.

Roe's tone turned serious. "Do you know how I ended up here in the United States?"

Darius nodded. "You mentioned in Nashville that you were from Cuba and came over when Castro took power, right?"

"Yeah," Roe replied. "My family, my father, owned a coffee farm. He was a businessman. We lived well, had servants, a beautiful home, and lots of land. But then Castro came and took everything. Confiscated it all." He paused, the weight of the words settling in. "I don't know how much you know about that time."

Darius shrugged. "I've never been there, but I've read a lot of books. About the Bay of Pigs, the Cuban missile crisis, Che Guevara. I've always been a history buff; my Dad was big into military stuff. I've got a lot of respect for the military. I just try to understand communism, how it works, how the United States interacts with it. And the Kennedy assassinations, both JFK and Bobby, were just remarkable, all of it. So, yeah, I have a perspective on Castro. And it's not positive."

Roe's expression hardened. "No, he's a monster. People who don't understand communism, who don't get what it really is, haven't lived through it. I can't get behind a Party that supports those ideas. It just leads to disaster, you know?"

"Yeah, capitalism has its flaws too, but free enterprise, competition, it's good for everyone."

"It was so bad," Roe continued. "On top of stealing everything, they ran my father's business into the ground. Then they tried to force him to run it for them, and he refused. In the end, I was sent over here on one of those boats with the kids fleeing the country. Ended up in an orphanage in Denver, then later, Florida." He paused, gathering himself.

Darius's voice softened. "Man, that had to be terrifying. To be so young, leaving everything behind."

"Yeah, brother, you have no idea. Then the orphanage ... It was tough. Kids picked on me. It was hard. And not seeing your family again? It was the worst." He sighed deeply, then looked at Darius, quiet for a moment. "You asked about family, about having kids, well, it was never really in the cards for me. I'm just not built for it. I've seen too much pain." He trailed off, the weight of his past hanging in the air.

Darius, sensing his pain, asked quietly, "You ever talk about all this? I mean, what happened back then?"

Roe hesitated, looking down into his drink for a long moment before meeting Darius's eyes. "Not often. But ... My family had a servant, a man who helped out around the house. Took care of things for my father. He molested me. Many times when I was a boy."

"Oh man," Darius whispered. "I'm so sorry."

Roe's voice was low, almost detached. "I didn't know how to deal with it. Didn't even know how bad it affected me until later. I had relationships, tried to settle down, and thought I could marry once. Was with a woman for three years, loved her ... But I knew it wouldn't work. I broke it off. She wanted things I couldn't give her.

There were things I just couldn't do. Things he—" He paused, the weight of the memory hanging heavy for a moment. "It haunted me for years. I didn't understand it then, but I do now. Relationships were difficult. I knew I couldn't be the husband or father I needed to be because of those scars. And in the end, it feels like that was taken from me." Roe looked away, then, with a bitter edge, he said, "He ruined my life."

Darius's expression softened, pain evident. "I understand, man, more than you know. Maybe not all of it, but through a lot of the work I've been doing, I've made my own discoveries. I didn't realize it when it happened, but, you know, I was molested twice."

"I'm so sorry, man."

"What's crazy? I didn't remember any of it, not until I started this journey. When I started working on myself, emotional trauma therapy, meditation, counseling, it came back. The first time I did heart wall therapy, it all came flooding back the next morning after I meditated."

Roe raised an eyebrow. "Heart wall therapy?

"Yeah, that's what they call it," Darius explained. "It's about releasing emotional trauma that is trapped in the body. The body holds onto emotions, especially trauma. That's how it stays stuck. And if it's not dealt with, it keeps festering, you know? But this therapy helps you heal. And it really helped me."

Roe listened intently, his curiosity piqued. "You've been working through a lot."

Darius nodded slowly. "I've learned a lot. Like energy work, understanding muscle testing. You wouldn't believe how much you can learn about yourself by testing the energy your body holds. It's crazy."

Roe's eyes widened. "Wait, muscle testing? What's that about?"

Darius explained about first meeting Larissa, then Dr. Whitman and their use of muscle testing. "It's all about how the body reacts to different things, foods, chemicals, emotions. It's wild. I've been studying David Hawkins, his work on consciousness, energy levels ... it all ties together. You can actually determine if anything from the past is true or false."

Roe was silent for a moment, taking it all in. "That's fascinating. But man, it sounds like you're going through something intense with your health. The meds, the heart stuff ... "

Darius nodded. "Yeah, I had a heart scare, and it was tied to everything. The therapy, I can't even explain it. My heart was 85% 'dead,' energy-wise, but after just one session, it was 90% healed. And now? I'm off all my medications."

Roe looked at him in disbelief. "No way."

"Yeah, way," Darius laughed. "Meditation, cold plunges, breathing exercises ... I check my blood pressure regularly now. It's normal. And when it's not, I can fix it just by doing a focused breathing exercise."

Roe stared at him, impressed. "That's amazing. I need to learn that."

Darius smiled, a bit of assurance in his voice. "I'll share it with you. It's been life-changing."

The drinks had been set on the table, and neither of them had noticed, but they could smell the food before they could see it. Its arrival signed an end to their conversation, if only for a short while, as both of them devoured their burgers. They sat in silence for a few minutes.

"Man, that was one good burger," Darius said.

"Yeah, the food here is always good. Never an issue."

When the check came, Darius instinctively reached for it. Roe laughed, and quickly snatched it over to his side of the table.

"No, no, no, I got this."

"Are you sure?"

"Yeah, man, you got enough stuff to deal with right now. It's my pleasure. You can get it next time, alright?"

As they left the restaurant, the weight of the previous conversation lingered, and they turned to the topic of God and faith.

"The more you search for it, the more it finds you," Roe said quietly. "The more you see, the more it reveals itself to you. There's evil in this world, man. It corrupts everything."

Darius nodded. "Now that I have encountered it. You can't … unlearn certain things."

"What do you mean?" Roe asked, a flicker of curiosity in his voice.

"Since May, I have had multiple experiences with the demonic. Steve's work and the Bible have opened my eyes to a lot. I don't think anyone who commits evil acts does so without demonic influence. I have read that those who do those acts oftentimes have had it done to them. I think the demonic plants seeds of darkness and access when it happens," Darius replied. He explained the demonic chord experience.

Roe stared briefly at him, thoughtful. "Yeah, I think you're right. It's something I've battled my whole life." He shook his head slowly. "It's a horrible thing to deal with."

"I think about certain things I've done, and it's like … Why the hell did I act like that? Not that I'm blaming all my mistakes on some demon, but when I look back, I don't always understand why I did what I did. Why I hurt people … or myself. It's like there's a fog, and only now, looking back, things start to make sense." He paused. "Those demonic forces are territorial. I have realized now that Jesus never once said let's go over there and exorcise a demon. They just manifested everywhere he went. They're constantly at work around us, even if we can't see it. Most of us are blind to other realms, to other layers of existence … But now, with what I am learning about energy and consciousness along with Scripture, it starts to make sense."

"Yeah," Roe agreed. "They're real, no question ... The woman I told you about, the one I almost married."

Darius looked at him curiously. "Yeah?"

"We're still friends," Roe said. "I still talk to her, and I know her husband too. She's got a good life now, and we actually talked about how it was for the best that we didn't get married."

Darius nodded, a quiet understanding passing between them. "Yeah, I get that. It wasn't meant to be, but she's happy now."

"I think, for me, it was the right choice, too," Roe admitted. "You know, I went back to Cuba to film a documentary, and while there, I confronted the man who molested me."

Darius turned sharply to look at him. "You met him?"

"Yeah," Roe said. "When they did the documentary on me, I went back to the house my family used to own. He was still living there, an old man now. I knocked on the door, introduced myself, and when he let me in, I told him everything."

Darius's eyes widened. "What did you say?"

"I told him he ruined my life," Roe said, his voice steady but thick with emotion. "I told him how much I had hated him for what he did to me, but that God had helped me through it. And I needed him to know what he'd done, to hear it from me."

"What did he do?"

Roe shook his head. "He didn't do anything, didn't even say a word. He just sat there. I told him everything I needed to say, and then ... I just walked out."

There was quiet for a long while before Darius finally broke the silence. "Man, that's ... That's incredible."

"It was," Roe said softly, his gaze distant. "Emotionally draining, but something I knew I had to do."

The moment lingered, the weight of shared experience holding them in a space of mutual understanding. They arrived at the hotel, and Darius stepped out of the car. Roe followed, grabbing his bag for him.

"Brother, that was an amazing day," Darius said. "I can't thank you enough. And I can't thank you enough for the painting, the songs, and your time."

Roe smiled, his heart lighter. "The pleasure's all mine. Let me know when you're done with everything, and I'll come back. We'll grab some food, and I'll take you to the airport."

"Deal," Darius said, pulling him into a hug. "Love you, man."

"Love you too, brother," Roe replied as Darius turned toward the hotel lobby and retired for the night.

Chapter 60
Platinum With Tony

D arius scanned the stadium in Dallas, his eyes wide with disbelief. He had just walked a mile from his hotel to meet Amanda for registration for Unleash the Power Within (UPW). The events of the day still felt surreal. It had been amazing to meet with Roe and to receive the surprise painting, but the most remarkable part of it all was how he had ended up here, standing in the middle of this buzzing crowd.

It had started in Denver, at the International Living Conference. There, he'd met Amanda, another platinum member of the Tony Robbins community. At the time, Darius had been adamant. "I can't go to this. There's too much going on. My business isn't doing well. I just can't." But she had been persistent and offered him her platinum pass, and after praying about it, he had felt a clear nudge that he was supposed to go.

That was one thing that had changed dramatically in his life. *Well, a lot had changed*, he thought. Before, when he was buying properties, even considering international investments, he hadn't been seeking God's direction. He hadn't been praying about it; he was just doing what he thought was best. But now? Now, it was different. The only thing I do without asking God for direction is go to the bathroom, he thought with a slight chuckle.

He looked around, trying to take it all in. Darius had been to a lot of big events—amusement parks, concerts, conferences—but this? This was something different. The energy in the stadium was palpable. You could feel it buzzing in the air, alive and electric. People were everywhere, laughing, talking, high-fiving, hugging. The volunteers wore wide smiles and moved through the crowd with ease. Music played overhead, adding to the atmosphere. Darius had never experienced anything quite like it.

As he texted back and forth with Amanda, he tried to explain where he was.

It's a long, long line to get in to register.

Are you in the platinum line?

I have no clue. I don't really see a difference in the lines, but I got us a spot.

Okay. I'll let you know when I get there.

He continued people-watching, amazed by the variety in the crowd. People of all ages, ethnicities, and styles were here, all sharing one thing in common: a positive energy that seemed to infect everyone around them. Smiles everywhere. The vibe was electric.

After a short time, his phone buzzed again.

Where did you come in?

I came in through the main entrance, went up the escalators, and then the doors were to the left. It's a long walk because the line is really long.

Okay, come back to the escalators. Head toward those doors. That's where I'm at.

Okay, on my way.

As he started the long walk back toward the escalators, a thought crossed his mind: Are we just going to have to come back to the end of the line?

When he finally spotted her, Amanda waved him down and smiled.

"Come on, where are we going?" Darius asked.

She grinned. "Man, we're platinum! You're a platinum member. We don't wait in line."

Darius smiled back as they hugged. She was just as he remembered her—happy, pleasant, and full of an incredible spirit. She radiated warmth, a sense that she was someone who genuinely loved people and loved God. Darius couldn't help but feel that he was in good company.

They headed toward the security checkpoint, where Amanda showed a form that identified her as a platinum member. "He's with me," she said to the staff, and just like that, they bypassed the long line.

Darius couldn't help but be amazed.

As they breezed through the security check, Amanda lightly smacked him on the chest with the palm of her hand.

"Yeah, this is how you roll with platinum," she said, her smile wide.

Darius laughed. "Okay, I could get used to this."

As Darius and Amanda walked through the doors and into the vast facility, his eyes widened in awe. The energy in the room was palpable, the music thumping in the air, and people were already dancing, caught up in the excitement. The atmosphere was buzzing with intensity. There were thousands of people here, the space enormous, with massive screens hanging from the rafters.

"This is it," Amanda said, leading him through the crowd. She carried a bag over her shoulder. "We're sitting right at the front. About 20 rows back from the stage."

Darius could barely take it all in. "This is where the platinum members sit," she continued, grinning. "This is where you feel all the energy, where you see everything up close. This is the place to be."

As they settled into their seats, Amanda started introducing him to people. The variety of attendees amazed him. There were successful investors in international real estate, owners of fitness centers, a guy who owned a chain of hospital clinics, and another who owned multiple hotels. It was a remarkable mix, each person brimming with energy, and the vibe was electric.

Darius soaked it all in as he took in the scene. The anticipation in the air was building. Suddenly, the entire room was alive with energy—people jumping, dancing, and high-fiving. An Australian voice boomed over the speakers, announcing it was time to "prime." And with that, the crowd erupted into motion, the collective energy spilling over. Darius didn't miss a beat. He jumped right in, dancing and having a blast, feeling more alive than he had in days.

After a while, Tony Robbins appeared on stage, and the crowd went absolutely wild. The energy in the room intensified as Tony began his introduction, sharing his story. He spoke of his journey, of how he had built his career, and how he had managed to connect with people in over 100 countries, speaking to them in their own languages.

He went on to explain how, despite cultural differences, people all over the world were driven by similar core principles. Those shared human experiences were what enabled his success and why the message he teaches resonates universally.

Then, Tony shifted the tone, asking, "Why are you here? What brought you to this event?"

"Every life," he said, "is either a warning or an example."

He began to tell the story of Robin Williams—one of the most successful TV stars in the world, an iconic comedian, and a beloved actor who had achieved everything anyone could dream of. He painted the picture of Williams's extraordinary career, building it up with dramatic flair. But then Tony became serious. "But here's the thing," he said, pausing for effect. "How successful was he really?"

The room fell silent. Tony continued, "He made everyone happy but himself."

He talked about Williams's death, the tragic reality of a life that, despite all outward success, ended in despair. The mood in the room shifted.

"Take out your notebooks," Tony instructed. "We're going to focus on the emotional home, the emotions that empower you and those that disempower you."

Darius pulled out his notebook and began writing.

Under Empowering Emotions, he wrote: *"Love, Excitement. Then, he listed the fruits of the Spirit and added Empathy, Gratitude, Boldness, Curiosity, and Courage."*

"What are your top two empowering emotions?" Tony asked.

Darius thought for a moment. He wrote: *"Gratitude. Love. He made a note beside Love: Curiosity and Self-control."*

Next was something Darius had confronted a lot in the past few months. "List your disempowering emotions." Darius wrote: *"Fear, Sadness, Unworthiness, Anger, Guilt."* He drew a line through Anger with a note: *"Used to, no longer,"* then put an asterisk beside Guilt and Unworthiness. These are my two biggest, he thought.

Tony continued. "What emotions do you want to live by? The ones that will guide your life?" He emphasized that there were no victims—only volunteers. "Where your focus goes, your energy flows."

He spoke about changing your state at will, about choosing the dominant emotional state you wanted to be in. "Don't stay in a negative state for any longer than you need to. You can choose your state," Tony declared.

Darius wrote: *"Dominant State: Positive, Joyful, Enjoying Life."* He made a note to eliminate Fear, Guilt, Sadness, and Unworthiness from his mindset.

"You get what you tolerate," Tony said. "From your emotions, physiology, and focus, you create your life. In every area—business, love, health. You have to understand what you want."

1. *Know what you want* – and make it specific and measurable.

2. *Find and face the truth* – be honest with yourself. If you don't, you're screwed.

3. *Close the gap* – figure out what's holding you back, whether it's fear, limiting beliefs, or poor habits.

4. *Do what's hard* – take massive action. Change what needs to be changed.

5. *Develop a daily practice* – condition the change you want.

6. *Raise your standard* – don't be lazy. Don't settle for less than you deserve.

7. *Celebrate life* – life is a gift. Celebrate it.

Seven different areas Darius could begin to focus on and transform, but which one was the one he had neglected the most?

"Celebrate life"—he wrote it down, underlined it. He couldn't help but think about how much he had missed not celebrating the small things, including in his marriage. He had never had any

qualms about beating himself up, but he wanted to celebrate more, particularly the small, daily positives.

If you're not taking care of the small things, then how much do the big things really matter?

***

They took a break, and a group of dancers stepped onto the stage, all wearing matching outfits.

"Here come the energy dancers," Amanda said with a grin.

Darius laughed, watching in awe. "This is remarkable."

"Let's go!" Amanda said, already moving toward the open space.

"Where are we going?" Darius asked, following her.

"We're going to dance!" She replied, pulling him along. "There's more room out there. It's way more fun."

"Do they do this a lot?" Darius asked, curious.

"Oh, heck yes," she laughed. "Let me tell you something—you're going to be jumping, dancing, and moving a lot, so I hope you like it."

"I love to dance," Darius said, grinning.

Amanda nodded. "That's exactly what I wanted to hear."

***

"You want to live life on your own terms. Freedom without guilt, but with gratitude and curiosity."

Darius took out his notebook and started writing down what an extraordinary life would look like for him. Financial freedom was at the top of his list. He circled it but with a thought: the divorce might change things, depending on how painful it was and when he would be able to start earning again. His financial situation was still uncertain.

He wrote down other goals, too: *"feeding people from a charitable perspective, getting more involved locally, and traveling freely. I want to fly anywhere, whenever I want, with whoever I want, and give to charities however I choose."* He added a note beneath: *"All God's Children"*—a vision for the charity he hoped to start.

He then wrote: *"Next year: Solve all current financial issues, generate $3 million in revenue, give $400,000 to charity, and get the charity started."*

There was more. He wanted to continue improving his health, stay off medications, sleep well every night (a first for him), and spend more time with his kids, ensuring it was meaningful time. He also longed to be around incredible, impactful people—those who were doing things that mattered and could help him become a better man.

Lastly, with a smile on his face, he wrote: *"Dancing and Cooking classes."*

There it was, right in front of him, the life he *wanted* to live. So why wasn't he living it?

He thought about it and wrote down: *"lack of joy, unworthiness, fear, and guilt, leading to pride."* He circled pride. And then circled it again for good measure. He acknowledged that he had been viewing life through the "wrong lens," missing the joy in the process. Poor defense mechanisms.

He continued writing, reflecting on stress-inducing thoughts, particularly things he couldn't control. Tony's reminder echoed in his mind: **Life is happening for you, not to you.** He drew a line from fear, guilt, and pride to the idea that life was happening for him as an arrow, pushing him forward.

Then Tony shared a personal story about his mother's challenges and how that had shaped his life choices, particularly his decision to stay sober. Darius, intrigued, thought about his own experiences. Darius had started doing cold plunges after learning about Wim Hof, starting with cold showers and now the stream every day. Tony shared he jumped into 42-degree water and found it to be the hardest thing he'd do in the morning, but it set the tone for the rest of his day. Tony emphasized how important it was to embrace such discomfort, as it made everything else seem easier.

"So, what do *you* need to change now to make life happen on your terms?"

Darius wrote in bold, scoring the page several times over: *"Focus on gratefulness,"* followed by *"Love myself,"* then finally, *"Set healthy boundaries,"* a practice he had learned in the Marriage Reset Program. He also wrote: *"Curiosity"* and underlined it; his counselor, Kristen, told him to approach life *with* curiosity and *without* judgment, and that resonated.

He also noted: *"Give, expect nothing in return, volunteer, charity. Strong routines and consistency."*

Tony explained that if you succeed in life but remain unhappy, then you've failed. Darius wanted both, so beneath all of this, he wrote an affirmation: *"Self-love. I am worthy. Manifest destiny."*

His deepest fear, which he hadn't fully understood until now, was that he wasn't lovable and didn't deserve anything. Tony spoke to this fear, explaining that most people's deepest fear is that they won't be enough and, as a result, won't be loved.

"Love is the oxygen of life," Tony said with power. "You have to create your own culture, give love, and give it unconditionally."

Darius reflected on his journey. He had been learning so much over the past few months—reading books, working through emotional trauma therapy, and now, in this moment, everything felt like it was aligning. It was as if UPW was going to be five days of immersion around the things he had been working on for five months in the Marriage Reset Program.

This was his chance to break away and escape his state of suffering and finally tap into his "beautiful state," and if that was the case, he'd make sure he was tapping into that high energy state each and every day. He just had to eliminate that fear.

Darius had been working on letting go of fear and negative thoughts, particularly through David Hawkins' methods. He wrote down:

1. *Because God loves me, I'm special and worthy of a beautiful state.*

2. *Why will I transform? My mental, physical, and spiritual health depend on it.*

3. *How will it transform my life? Everything will improve. My business, charity, relationships—all will flourish.*

"*Divorce, assets, I can't control it. Why waste time suffering over it?*"

He was determined to focus on higher-level emotions, continuing his practice of gratitude and meditation. Darius knew he had to keep progressing. His goal now was to reach the level of 540—unconditional love. Beneath it all, circled and underlined, Darius wrote: "*Live life, dance, laugh, and love.*"

Change the conversation, change your state. That was the whole theme of the day.

Darius laughed. He could already see how he could use the strategies to change his perspective, thus changing the experience. Tony had shared a humorous moment, talking about how people who deny the existence of God sometimes find themselves questioning their beliefs. Tony laughed, "There is a God. He just doesn't want to come down and hang out with you because you *bitch* too much," and the room erupted in laughter as Tony emphasized the swear word.

Darius high-fived Amanda, appreciating how much he was learning.

Later, Tony discussed the six human needs that drive us: certainty (avoiding pain), uncertainty (variety), significance, love/connection, growth, and contribution. Darius thought about his own life and how each need had played a role. After a few minutes, it seemed obvious that Significance was his number 1 and Certainty number 2. Ouch, he thought.

He listed the positives and negatives from their positioning. Positives: exercise routine, financial success, travel, persistence. Negatives: alcohol, self-inflicted stress, overbearing for others, unconscious habits, judging himself and others.

He finished the exercise by considering his top two needs. For so long, Significance and Certainty had been at the top. Tony had made it clear: If your primary needs are Significance or Certainty, you'll never find lasting happiness.

Thanks, Tony ... Where were you 20 years ago before I made this mess!?

Darius stopped and thought about what he wanted his new primary drivers to be. *"Contribution and Growth."* What would change with your new drivers? Darius wrote: *"Love would find me because I'm giving it freely. My connections would be more significant. I'd be more fulfilled."*

This journey, Darius realized, was just the beginning of something transformative. He was already abuzz, his body and soul vibrating. He was ready to keep growing, embracing the change in mindset with open arms.

Chapter 61
Changing Stories

D arius woke up early the next morning, his mind already racing. Man, she wasn't kidding about these events, he thought. They're non-stop, always keeping you on the go.

He quickly realized that sleep was going to be scarce—and with it, his usual morning routine would be on hold. But that was okay; he skipped working out and meditation while continuing to start the day with Scripture. He was here to immerse himself, to learn, to change, and to grow.

Had Josh worked for Tony Robbins in the past? Darius wondered. The Marriage Reset Program had so much in common with the first day and a half of Tony Robbins' teachings.

As he got ready for the day, he grabbed his water container and bag. He headed to the concierge lounge for a quick breakfast. The place was packed, but Darius managed to grab something light, took his organic cleansing pills, and filled his water bottle with three glasses of water. Then, he set off for his mile-long walk to the event.

Upon arriving, the usual routine kicked in: waiting in line for a seat. He met up with Amanda and found their spots. From there, it was more high-energy dancing, jumping, and motivational talks. The day began with a deep dive into the power of beliefs and steps to lasting change. A new speaker took the stage. He was amazing.

Sharing his wisdom on the importance of exercise and change, urging the audience not to beat themselves up, he joked about them all being in the "club of kicking your own ass." Stop criticizing yourself. That was the message he had for the room.

"You wouldn't let a two-year-old finally start walking and then criticize them, would you?" he asked the audience. "No, you'd praise them!"

Emotion drives action, and once you're in motion with emotion, it propels you toward your goals. The conversation then shifted to the science of motivation, and he nailed home a key point: hesitation equals failure. Avoid making decisions, and you avoid growth.

Darius reflected on his own journey. Making decisions wasn't an issue but he needed to make them from a higher level of consciousness moving forward and be nicer to himself.

He thought back to his initial $70,000 investment in himself and his business. Despite all the mistakes, he had built something impressive and had made it almost nine years against the odds. Regardless of the divorce and even if he lost everything, he was proud of how far he'd come. He'd started with nothing and grown it into nearly $6 million accumulative. And if it crumbled, he knew he could rebuild.

But then he remembered something else and laughed quietly. His memory took him back to his time playing college basketball. He was only 5'10"—not good enough to play Division I—but playing taught him perseverance, the need to push hard even when the odds were stacked against him. He also reflected on his clinical work, a field where life and death were constant realities. That experience had shaped his ability to perform under pressure and understand how precious life is.

Starting his company had been the hardest thing he'd ever done, but he had done it. He had built something from scratch. *"I will survive,"* Darius wrote in his notebook. He was committed to making two key decisions: first, to love himself, and second, to start his charity.

For the first time in a long time, he felt truly present. The journey of self-discovery was difficult but beautiful.

Then came a deep dive into the Wheel of Life. He reflected on his physical health, emotions, relationships, and work-life balance. He'd made great strides in each area. He was healthier than ever, emotionally more stable, and focused on what really mattered in life. He stared at the relationship section with a frown. Amanda noticed and asked if he was okay.

Darius smiled. "I mean, I am going through a divorce, right? Having a relationship isn't high on the list to work on! I don't see dating anytime soon."

Amanda was single herself and recently out of a serious relationship. "Yeah, Darius," she said. "It's okay for us not to work on every section of the wheel. We can let that one sit for now."

They followed it with a high five of agreement.

After Tony walked them through the ability to change their state, they all headed outside for the famous firewalk. Darius was excited with a tinge of fear, but hey, if thousands had done it, he would make it work. An attractive woman followed him and struck up a conversation. She wasn't going to do it but would go watch. Darius encouraged her to give it a try. As he got to the beginning of the lengthy fire walk, he thought about the directions. There was music, lights, cheers of encouragement, and motion all around as there were multiple fire walks set up.

Darius quickly cleared his mind, went into his "move" as he took both hands and pounded them on his chest and then into the air ala a Gladiator pose and immediately started walking across the burning hot coals. Suddenly, he was grabbed by someone and led to a cooling mat, as his eyes came back into focus. Wow! He had done it, and his feet hadn't felt a thing! Amazing, he thought.

Suddenly, he was being hugged; his new friend had decided to do it and was yelling with triumph at her success. They embraced, high-fived, and headed back, talking excitedly. After the firewalk, the energy in the room was electric. People were energized, excited, and having a blast. No alcohol. Just pure, unfiltered joy.

The day had been a whirlwind of inspiration and exercises, and through it all, Darius had felt something shifting deep inside him. He thought of Tony's words, "The secret to living is giving." For the first time, Darius felt like he was on the right path—not just for himself but for others as well. The journey wasn't over, but he was ready for whatever came next.

That night, nobody got much sleep, but it didn't matter. As he walked toward the venue the next morning, Darius felt the pulse of something bigger happening. The vibe was infectious.

Once inside, he met up with his new friends, including Amanda, and they decided to partake in a session of energy stimulation therapy at the biocharger before the event started. As they chatted, Darius found himself talking to one of the original founders of the biocharger, who shared how people were using it in business to set up centers and make money. The idea intrigued Darius. Maybe he could get one for the office and integrate it into the company's health program. The conversation shifted when a sales rep brought up someone else.

"Have you heard of Joe Dispenza?" They asked.

"Joe Dispenza?" Darius repeated, unsure.

"Yeah, he's amazing. Thirty years ago, he was hit by a car during a triathlon. His back was crushed, and doctors said surgery would leave him immobilized. He refused and healed himself in six months through meditation. Can you imagine?"

Darius blinked in disbelief. "Six months through meditation? No way. That's incredible."

"Yeah, now he writes books and does life-changing events on meditation. One of our sales offices did his 'Tuning into New Potentials' meditation along with the abundance recipe on the biocharger and their sales increased by 30% in four to six months."

Darius nodded slowly. "I'm not sure I see the connection."

"Well, Dispenza talks a lot about abundance, being present, and manifesting. His work taps into some deep stuff, including self-healing."

Darius considered this. He had been on a journey of self-healing for a while and had made significant progress. He definitely needed to learn more about Dispenza.

After the biocharge session, they headed back to the main event area. More dancing, high-fives, and hugs. Always so many high-fives and hugs, Darius thought. It didn't bother him. In fact, it felt refreshing. He hadn't been hugged this much by women in a long time.

As the day progressed, Darius began to realize something: he had felt different for a while, but now it was clear. His chances of reconciling with his wife were slim, and he was at peace with that. But here he was in a new world, surrounded by successful, attractive, and single women. More than once, women approached him, drawn to his energy. He was no longer the person he used to be. He didn't feel needy. He didn't feel unworthy. In fact, for the first time in his life, he liked himself and was working toward love.

He had originally desired to save his marriage but a lot had changed in him; what mattered most to him now was growth. Healing. Becoming the best version of himself. He wanted to increase his level of consciousness, give others grace, judge less, and embrace unconditional love.

Tony encouraged them at every point to think about what was stopping them. If they wanted to live a truly extraordinary life, why weren't they? Everyone in the room, including Darius, was more than determined to push beyond their limits and achieve something incredible, so what was stopping them? What was stopping *him?*

Darius sat down and reflected, focusing on that question and uncovering some of his major limiting beliefs.

- **Belief #1: "I am not worthy, not good enough."**

Negative consequences: Self-sabotage. Drinking too much. Always needing to be right. These traits had destroyed his ability to have fruitful relationships and stifled his overall success.

- **Belief #2: "I'm not lovable."**

Negative consequences: Guilt, shame, never fully present. Always rushing through things.

- **Belief #3: "Women are nuts."**

Negative consequences: How could he have strong relationships with any female if that was his default perspective? Maybe it was more about his inability to attract the higher value female due to a lower level of consciousness? He wanted to have the best possible relationship with his daughter; how would that perspective contribute positively?

Darius rewrote these beliefs, framing them from his new perspective:

- ***For Belief #1:*** *I am outstandingly worthy and blessed, and my future success is guaranteed by my Creator.*

- *For Belief #2: Everyone who meets me loves me and wants to spend more time with me because of my level of consciousness and the positive energy that I bring.*

- *For Belief #3: All women are a blessing from God, and the world is a better place because of their beautiful feminine energy.*

As the session ended, they went through mantras. Darius repeated, "I am the voice. I will lead, not follow. I will believe, not doubt. I will create, not destroy. I am a force for good. I am a force for God. I am a leader. I set a new standard. I will step up."

The room erupted with energy. What a day. The rest of the evening was filled with deep conversations about their dreams, beliefs, and the changes they were experiencing.

Darius couldn't help but think, Where has this been my whole life?

***

The group decided to head out for dinner, one of the few breaks they'd been given. As they sat down to eat, the conversation turned to all that had transpired so far—their dreams, beliefs, and the changes they were experiencing. It was, once again, a remarkable group of people. I don't want to miss out on this journey.

After dinner, they hugged and agreed to meet back in the morning to find seats. Darius walked the mile back to his hotel, feeling a deep sense of satisfaction, fulfillment, and gratitude.

As he crossed the street toward his hotel, a loud noise caught his attention. Looking up, he saw a white SUV peeling out of a garage. His heart skipped a beat as the vehicle suddenly stopped, the side door flying open. To his horror, a woman was shoved out onto the street, shouting as she fell to the pavement. A purse was thrown on top of her, and the door slammed shut. The SUV's tires squealed as it appeared to run her over and then sped off.

Darius couldn't believe what he was witnessing. It was 12:30 AM, and the street was nearly empty—only a few people lingered near the entrance of his hotel. The car sped away as the woman began to crawl across the street. Darius didn't hesitate as he immediately started running toward her to see if he could help.

When he reached her, the car had already gone about a thousand yards. He asked if she was okay. Her pants were ripped, blood stained her jeans, and she was gasping, tears streaming down her face.

"I think my leg is broken," she gasped.

"Do you want me to call an ambulance? 911?" Darius asked.

"No ... please, don't call 911," she pleaded. "I just want to get to my car."

Suddenly, the white SUV roared into reverse, speeding back toward them. The vehicle stopped, and a bald man got out. Darius could feel the tension and a darkness in the air—whatever was going to happen, it wasn't going to be good.

The woman looked terrified, her eyes wide with panic as the man approached. Darius could see the man's eyes—fiery red, full of rage—and he could tell this wasn't just anger; it was something darker. Just like his previous experiences in his car, the house, and in D.C. during the summer, when he had felt the demonic. His only thought was, I hope I don't get shot.

The man came within six feet of them, glaring at Darius before turning his rage onto the woman.

"See what you do? See what you make me do? You're pathetic!" he screamed.

"Just leave me alone!" she wailed. "Please, leave me alone!"

The man's anger boiled over. "Everything's always about you, woman!" He glared at Darius and took another step forward.

Darius stood tall, maintaining a strong, masculine frame. "You need to stop," he said, his voice firm. "You know this is wrong."

The man became enraged and turned his attention toward Darius and started to move toward him.

"Jesus is Lord," Darius exclaimed loudly.

The man froze after Darius made the statement, his eyes narrowing as he processed the words. Darius sensed that he was either drunk or on something.

"Look at what you're doing," Darius said, pointing at the woman. "You ran over her leg. Your behavior is not okay. It's not okay in the eyes of God, and you know it."

The man sputtered, his words failing him. He stared at Darius with confusion, his anger faltering as Darius started to profess Ephesians 6:10-13 in his mind to exorcise evil spirits. Without another word, the man jumped into the SUV and sped off.

Darius stood on the sidewalk, shocked. He couldn't quite believe what had just happened. Shaking his head, Darius turned back to the woman. "Ma'am, this doesn't look good. You need help. I can get you an ambulance, or we can get you to a hospital."

"No," she said weakly, shaking her head. "I'm not going to a hospital."

She struggled to get up and began staggering across the street. Darius walked beside her, offering his assistance, but she refused.

"Please," she said, "I appreciate your kindness, but no."

She headed toward a nearby parking garage, where her car was. Darius watched her disappear around the corner, his heart heavy with concern. He shook his head, knowing there was nothing more he could do.

He crossed the street again and entered his hotel, heading up to his suite. Just like in Denver, he had been upgraded. It seemed a bit over the top as he had his own boardroom, a separate bedroom, and a luxurious bathroom.

Darius lay on the bed, taking a deep breath. What the hell had just happened? he thought, still reeling from the events of the night. The encounter had shaken him. He'd seen something truly dark tonight and wasn't sure if his own response surprised him or not. He had remembered Steve talking about it in his books on multiple occasions, and it had … just come out. It was a reminder of how real the spiritual battle was.

As Darius lay there with his mind racing, he thought the same thing he had thought many times since he had called Larissa on the lawn mower months ago. He would never be the same.

Chapter 62
New Perspectives

Darius got up, gathered himself, did a short meditation, and dove into the Scriptures. After cleaning up, he made his way to meet Jonathan. Jonathan lived in Dallas but they had met through and supported each other in the Marriage Reset Program. Jonathan had struck Darius as incredibly smart. He was a musician by trade, was incredibly measured, and came across as genuinely likable during their group sessions. Both men appreciated each other's perspective in the group counseling sessions and posts on the group page. When he noticed Darius would be in Dallas for UPW, Jonathan insisted they had to meet in person.

They embraced before heading upstairs to the concierge lounge to grab some food. As they ate, they chatted about UPW. Jonathan had never attended a Tony Robbins event, but he had heard amazing things about it. Darius shared how transformative the experience had been—an immersive five-day deep dive into self-improvement with like-minded people. He explained it was a perfect complement to everything they were doing in the Marriage

Reset Program. A perfect complement but with an energy and experience that couldn't be duplicated remotely.

Jonathan could feel his excitement. "Man, that's awesome," he said, genuinely impressed.

Their conversation shifted to the Marriage Reset Program. They spoke about the men they both knew, some closer friends, others not as much. Jonathan, like Darius, believed in God, and his faith was important to him. Darius shared a memorable exchange he had had with one of their friends recently. This mutual friend, who they loved and respected, was an atheist, but they had had great conversations with him despite their differing beliefs.

"Yeah," Darius began, "He didn't really seem to like one of my recent posts that included Scripture, so he messaged me privately. He said, 'Hey, I liked your post, but just so you know, Jesus was just a man.' Then he said he didn't want to argue about it but shared he had researched religion, and while Jesus did amazing things, he was just a man."

Jonathan chuckled. "Oh, wow, that's interesting. How'd you handle that?"

Darius grinned. "Well, I prayed about it and then responded versus reacting. I told him, 'I appreciate your message and have great respect for you. Isn't it interesting that you are reaching out to me to tell me my perspective is wrong, though you don't really want to discuss it?'"

Jonathan raised an eyebrow. "What did he say?"

"Well," Darius continued, "He replied, saying, 'I don't want to get too deep into this. I've had bad experiences and don't need to be preached to or converted.'"

Jonathan laughed. "And how did you respond to that?"

"I told him, 'Brother, I love you. You reached out to me, not the other way around. I'm not here to preach to you or convince you of anything. But I will tell you, with all respect, that your position is incredibly weak and not worthy of you.'"

Jonathan's eyes widened. "You said that?"

Darius nodded. "I did. He came back saying, 'Excuse me, what exactly are you trying to say?' So I explained, 'I understand that you've done your research and believe God doesn't exist, that Jesus was just a man. But I'd suggest there's more research you need to do because your position is weak. Jesus was either the Son of God or a madman. He said it Himself, time and time again. He was God in human form. And over 500 witnesses saw Him after He was resurrected. To say He was just a man is weak. You would have to instead say he was a madman if he wasn't really God in human form.'"

Jonathan leaned back, astonished. "What did he say to that?"

"Well, he came back and said, 'Wow, I've never heard it put like that before. Nobody's ever framed it that way.'"

Jonathan grinned. "So, how did it end?"

"Honestly, it ended really well," Darius said. "He appreciated my response. I told him that I loved him, respected him, and that he'd helped me through the program. So, all in all, it was a good exchange, and maybe I planted a positive seed."

Jonathan laughed. "Sounds like a Marriage Reset lovefest."

"Exactly." Darius chuckled.

They laughed and shifted the conversation to their personal lives. Jonathan spoke about the woman he was dating, how well it was going, and how often she complimented him on his awareness, communication, and presence.

"That's awesome," Darius said, genuinely happy for him.

"What about you?"

He sighed, his expression shifting. "Well, it's not good. I had hoped things would work out, but my wife filed. I had hoped I'd be part of the 15% who can turn things around, but I'm starting to see that's not likely. She's just not the same person anymore, and my perspective continues to change, as well."

Jonathan looked concerned. "Your perspective? Do you want her back? Do you still want to fix it?"

Darius paused, grappling with the complexity of his feelings. "I have to admit the old me would've been desperate to save the marriage, to fight for the family. But I've done the work; I don't need the marriage to last. Letting go of her was the first step. But letting go of the marriage was a little harder. At this point, I wouldn't want to go back."

Jonathan nodded, understanding. "But you'd still be open to being together if that's what God wants, right?"

"If she changed her mind and worked on herself, it's possible," Darius said. "But I don't want the old marriage back, and I honestly wouldn't want the old version of her or this ugly new version she's turned into. I'm grateful for the person I am becoming through this journey. I want to keep growing and moving forward."

Jonathan smiled. "Man, that's powerful. I'm really proud of you."

Darius smiled back, appreciative of Jonathan's support. "Thanks, brother."

"You know," Jonathan said, "this work we're doing? It's making us so much more attractive than we ever were before. We're like the 1% of men. Wait till you start dating, and you'll see what I mean. Women really resonate with this stuff because it's genuine and a higher awareness. I'm telling you, my gal, not only is she amazing, she 100% appreciates everything I'm doing, for her and for myself."

Darius chuckled. "I get it, man. But honestly, I'm not ready for dating yet. Not for another year, at least. And definitely not through online dating."

"Man, how are you gonna meet anyone if you don't do online dating?" Jonathan laughed.

"I don't know," Darius said with a shrug. "I'm just really focused on my spiritual growth right now. There's a lot of growth and healing I still need to do. But the one thing I know for sure is that I don't want to fall back into sin. I don't want to be that old version of myself anymore. I want to do what God wants me to do."

"I get it, man," Jonathan said, nodding.

After a while, the time came for Darius to head to the conference. He said goodbye to Jonathan and walked toward the center. As Darius walked, his thoughts drifted back to the week he had just experienced—it was overwhelming in a positive fashion. He felt deeply grateful. Then he thought of the unexpected and intense encounter the night before with the woman who had been run over. Another direct encounter with the demonic. He frowned, shaking his head and sighed. Crazy ... Who would believe him outside of a select few?

He also thought about the woman from the firewalk that he had met up with after dinner—a beautiful woman who had shown significant interest in him during the conference. He'd mostly kept his distance, though. There had been others who'd shown similar interest, but Darius hadn't reciprocated. He still believed in the covenant of his marriage, despite the storm he was going through. He wasn't ready for a new relationship, and he knew that if he got involved with someone while still married, it would be adultery. He hadn't had an issue with sex outside of marriage before but he couldn't lie to himself anymore when the Bible was perfectly clear on the subject. Particularly now that he understood the truth of the demonic and the consequences.

But then, after dinner, they'd stepped outside and shared an impromptu kiss. It had been natural and pleasant, and Darius had enjoyed it. As he walked back to his hotel, however, doubt crept in.

Did I just make a huge mistake? he thought.

He prayed, repented, and by morning, he found peace. It was just a kiss—nothing more. He hadn't been touched in months. The rejection he'd faced from his wife, including questioning his sanity, the email calling him a horrible husband and father, and the lack of any kindness or respect for all he had done over the years—it had all left its mark. But now, he decided to see the kiss as a gift. He wasn't ready for a relationship, but it had been nice to feel desired. There were people out there who saw him as worthy of attention, and he decided to just be grateful.

The last day of the conference was filled with amazing insights on health and wellness. They discussed proper hydration—living water—and the dangers of chemicals and pesticides in food. Darius was already ahead of the game. Much of what was discussed, like the impact of dairy on skin and weight, was information he had already learned. They talked about clean eating, free-range, grass-fed, organic foods, and Darius thought: Check, check, check. I'm already on top of this. And when they covered the importance of greens, Darius nodded along, already familiar with the benefits. Thank you, Dr. Whitman!

Then Joseph returned. The man was hilarious. He walked everyone through vital breathing exercises and lymphatic health, and Darius was once again ahead of the curve. They even discussed specific breathing techniques: inhale for 8 seconds, hold for 32, and exhale for 16 and showed a video from his favorite in breathing—Wim Hof!

As the day drew to a close, Darius knew his flight was in three hours. Roe was picking him up to take him to the airport, and they were going to grab a meal together before he left. Darius was excited to see him again. He said goodbye to Amanda and some of the friends he had made, agreeing to keep in touch. He grabbed his bag from the hotel and walked outside just in time for Roe to pull up.

"Your Uber's here!" Roe called, laughing as he stepped out of the car. Darius chuckled and embraced him. Roe was one of the most loving people he knew, the Holy Spirit radiating from him. Steve,

Larissa, Dr. Whitman, and now Roe. These were the type of people he needed more of in his life.

They got in the car and began chatting about the conference and their week. Darius shared the crazy experience with the lady who was run over and what happened.

"Woah, Man, that's crazy," Roe said, shaking his head with eyes wide.

As they pulled into a Mexican restaurant parking lot near the airport, Roe leaned over and said:

"Let me see a picture of her. Of Jessica"

Darius showed him a photo of Jessica.

"She's gorgeous," Roe said.

Darius smiled, nodding. "Yeah, she is."

"Yeah, that's the kind of woman the demonic world would want to corrupt to destroy a family," Roe added, his voice serious. "The attacks on the family, on the kids, it's all part of the enemy's plan to destroy what God holds sacred."

They walked into the restaurant and sat down to eat. As they ordered, Roe suddenly stood up. "Hold on, I've got to take care of something," he said, pointing toward a wall of picture frames. "Those are off."

Darius looked over, confused. "What do you mean?"

"They're not the right height," Roe explained. "They're not aligned properly."

Darius chuckled. "I wouldn't even know."

Roe walked over to the server and had a brief conversation with him. A few minutes later, some of the staff rearranged the frames on the wall.

"Thanks, guys," Roe said as they returned to their table. "They're better now."

"Really?" Darius laughed. "I had no idea they were off."

"Well, you know, I'm an artist," Roe said with a grin. "What can I say?"

As they finished their meal and got the check, Darius reached to pay and was rebuked again. "I meant the next time you are in town, brother!" Roe exclaimed as Darius grumbled.

Darius put his hands up in surrender. "I'll get you back, my friend," he said.

After they pulled into the terminal, Roe got out of the truck, got into the back, and handed Darius the painting he had picked the day he visited the studio—wrapped and ready for transit.

"Here you go, man," Roe said. "It's got the label and the letter of authentication."

Darius was filled with excitement. "How do I frame it?"

"Regular frame, or you can stretch it on canvas," Roe suggested. "That's probably what I'd do. See how it looks first, then frame it later."

Darius admired the piece. "I love it, man. It's amazing."

"Oh, you're too kind," Roe said, waving it off.

"No, you're too kind," Darius replied. "I can't thank you enough for letting me see your studio, for sharing your gift with me. I'm so grateful."

"It's my pleasure, brother," Roe said warmly. "God has blessed you in so many ways. Stay strong; you'll come through this in amazing fashion. Just keep leaning into Him."

They embraced, and Roe drove off, leaving Darius at the airport. Darius made his way through security, preparing to fly back home. What an amazing week, he thought.

Chapter 63
Positive Masculine Energy

D arius stepped into the gym, unsure of what to expect. The place was called Dragonfly Elite, and the artwork on the walls intrigued him. He'd scouted a few gyms nearby—jujitsu, karate, Muay Thai, boxing—and landed here without a clear reason. Maybe it was the proximity—just a mile from home—or perhaps the energy of the place. Whatever it was, it felt right.

Inside, the scene was lively. A group of people were sparring, clad in what he supposed might be called robes, though the proper term escaped him. He'd dabbled in karate during college, so he remembered uniforms and belts. These folks were grappling, pulling, throwing each other to the mat. Arms, legs, feet, faces—it was all chaos, the kind of rough-and-tumble that made Darius smile.

He'd signed up for an introductory trial in Muay Thai—Thai kickboxing—though the gym also offered jiu-jitsu and boxing. Jiu-jitsu was tempting; he could see the advantages in learning leverage and control, gaining the upper hand in a fight. But the thought of ending up with someone's foot—or worse—in his face held him back. Muay Thai seemed like a better fit.

What was he doing here, anyway? he thought to himself as he approached the counter. That was the real question. Behind it was the woman he'd spoken with on the phone, busy with another customer.

It all started at UPW in Dallas. On the second day of the event, he'd met one of the volunteers during the walk back to the hotel. They'd hit it off, swapping stories. Darius had shared the messy highlights of his last six months—the divorce, the turbulent year at work, and everything in between. The young man, after listening intently, said, "I need to introduce you to my friend Roberto."

Roberto was part of the security team for the Tony Robbins events. His story, Darius had learned, mirrored his own in some ways. Roberto had been through the wringer, handling a similar divorce and struggling with the same emotional pitfalls—needy behavior, a scarcity mindset, and a lack of confidence.

***

Darius leaned back in his chair, listening intently as Roberto shared his story. The two had been introduced the day before, and now they were deep in conversation. Roberto's tone was open, almost confessional, as he recounted what had happened in his marriage.

"My wife had been having an affair," Roberto said. "When I found out, I completely lost it. I mean, meltdown-level lost it."

Darius nodded, feeling an unsettling familiarity with the story. "Yeah, that sounds familiar."

"I was a mess," Roberto continued. "Needy, desperate ... showing all the worst kinds of negative masculine behaviors. It wasn't good."

Darius leaned in. "What happened after that?"

"Well, someone on Tony's team found out about the situation and told him. The next thing I know, Tony himself intervenes. I'm thinking, wait, I'm just security here, but Tony thought I was important enough to speak with me personally. Talk about *humbling*."

Darius blinked in disbelief. "Wait, what?!?"

Roberto laughed, the memory a mix of humor and awe. "Yeah, no joke. He sat me down and didn't sugarcoat a thing. Told me to cut the crap. Said I couldn't keep acting like this."

"Yeah. He told me that she had made her choices, but that I had to take responsibility for how I was leading, that I needed to get into a positive masculine frame. He was blunt, man. Told me to take my focus off her, stop acting like a victim, and start working on myself."

Darius sat back, taking it all in. He thought about everything he had been learning about polarity and masculine energy this year. "Man," he said, shaking his head, "It's wild how much of this stuff we don't know until we're forced to face it. I had no understanding."

"Exactly," Roberto said. "Tony put me on a path. Had me start reading, working on myself, and, most importantly, getting into a gym, a dojo, actually, for at least a year."

Darius smiled. "So he wanted you to surround yourself with positive masculine energy?"

"Exactly," Roberto said. "It wasn't just about learning to fight. It was about confidence, discipline, and being in an environment where I could grow."

Darius thought back to his own struggles. "Yeah, I've realized how many negative masculine traits I displayed and how I was coming from a place of neediness, lack, and insecurity. It's humbling."

Roberto nodded, a knowing smile on his face. "It is, but it's worth it. Once I started doing the work, mentally, emotionally, *and* physically, everything began to change."

Darius couldn't help but laugh at the absurdity of it all. "Man, imagine having Tony Robbins telling you to get your act together."

"Right!?" Roberto laughed. "And it wasn't just about her anymore. I was growing for me."

Darius leaned forward. "So, where are things now?"

"Well," Roberto said, "We got divorced. She wanted to come back after the affair fizzled, but I wasn't interested. She hasn't done the work on herself, and honestly, she's a mess. I've moved on. I'm dating someone who's kind, confident, and appreciates me for who I am."

Darius nodded slowly. "Yeah, I still love my wife, always have, but she's been having an affair. And she's ... anything but kind. I've been doing all this work, though, and it's been changing me. Have you heard of David Hawkins?"

"No," Roberto said. "Who's that?"

"Man, his work is transformative. You should check him out. It's been a game-changer for me. Same as the breathing exercises, meditation, even cold submersion. Have you heard of Wim Hof?"

"You mean the cold guy?" Roberto laughed.

"Yeah, the Iceman!" Darius said, laughing too. "It's been incredible. Between that, an all-organic diet, and everything else I've been learning, I'm off all medications now. Haven't taken a pill since August."

"Man," Roberto said, shaking his head, "That's remarkable."

"It's been a journey," Darius admitted. "But the more I learn about healing, energy, polarity, and levels of consciousness, the more I realize how much I didn't know. And there's still so much more to understand."

"What do you mean?"

Darius nodded, his enthusiasm unmistakable. "I've been diving into his methods and studying his books. So far, I've read three and am about to start the fourth. He talks about things like muscle testing and self-healing. It's life-changing."

"Muscle testing?" Roberto asked, leaning forward.

Darius grinned. "Exactly. It's a way to tap into energy and truth. Everything is energy and leaves a trail so to speak. It's wild at first, but once you understand it, it makes sense. For example, I've done tests with my kids and even my employees. You hold something organic, like an orange, near your navel and then resist pressure on your arm. Your muscles stay strong. But if you hold something synthetic, like a packet of sweetener, your muscles weaken immediately."

Roberto blinked, astonished. "You're serious? Your muscles just … give out?"

"Absolutely. I know it sounds strange, but I've seen it work time and time again and have been calibrating scenarios. The body's energy doesn't lie if done correctly and without bias. Hawkins explains this in detail, but it's all about calibrating truth versus falsehood and understanding positive versus negative energy."

"And you're doing this on your own now?"

"Yeah," Darius admitted with a sheepish smile. "I've been practicing for a couple of months. But it's not just about the mechanics. Intent and the person's level of consciousness are critical. Someone trying to prove a preconceived notion will get false reads, so you have to be careful. I am careful to do calibrations up front and to make sure I am seeking truth versus validating my own bias. Then, there are some things I don't want to know."

Roberto nodded slowly. "So, what's the kicker for you? What made you believe this could actually work and start trying to learn muscle testing?"

Darius leaned back, a nostalgic grin spreading across his face. "Let me tell you a story. I was on a flight back from Madrid earlier this year, finishing *Letting Go*. The last chapter is all about self-healing. Hawkins shares how he wore glasses for over 20 years because of glaucoma. One day, one of his students challenged him, saying, 'You've healed from cancer, why not your eyesight?' It hit him like a ton of bricks. The next day, he stopped wearing glasses. Within weeks, he completely healed."

Roberto sat back, his jaw slack. "You're kidding."

"Not at all. So, on that flight, I decided to test it myself. I'd been wearing reading glasses for two years. After finishing that chapter, I took my glasses off, tossed them under the seat, and thought, 'If Hawkins can heal, why can't I?' Four weeks later, my sight came back clearly like it was before I started using them."

"Unbelievable." Roberto shook his head, a wide smile breaking across his face.

"It's the truth," Darius said, chuckling. "Now that I know, I share it with anyone who's interested so it can help them."

Roberto clapped him on the back, his enthusiasm matching Darius's. "Man, that's amazing. I've got to check this out."

***

Smiling, Darius found himself filling out paperwork to join Dragonfly Elite—this was another new chapter in his life. He'd barely completed it when Kenny, the owner, introduced himself. Kenny was ex-military, with a commanding presence and an undeniable air of confidence. A photo on the wall showed him in full Navy SEAL gear. Watching Kenny demonstrate moves during a sparring session, Darius couldn't help but admire the man's skill and poise. He was ... a badass, not someone you would want to mess with.

After the session, Kenny approached him. "So, what brings you here?"

Darius hesitated, then spoke honestly. "I've been going through a rough time, and I've realized there's a lot about myself I need to change. I'm working on taking responsibility and letting go of the victim mentality."

Kenny nodded. "That takes guts to admit. What are you looking to get out of this?"

"I want to be part of a positive, masculine environment. I've always worked out, but this is about more than just fitness. It's about cultivating strength, not just physically but mentally and emotionally. I want to learn how to better protect myself, improve my discipline, and be in a setting that has positive masculine energy.

Kenny grinned. "You're in the right place, brother. This is about learning how to be strong, how to protect yourself, and how to move through life with confidence and integrity. Yeah, you will learn how to fuck someone up but it starts with self-defense, and it's all grounded in positivity. We're here to lift each other up, not tear anyone down."

Darius nodded, already feeling a sense of belonging. "That's exactly what I'm looking for."

Chapter 64
A Wim & a Prayer

Darius woke at 5:00 AM, feeling refreshed after a great night's sleep. His morning routine had become a cornerstone of his day—a consistent, uplifting practice that provided a sense of clarity in all of the chaos. While he'd always considered himself disciplined, Darius realized that much of his past efforts had been driven by force rather than power, and it was through David Hawkins' work that he was beginning to grasp the distinction.

Each morning, Darius would take a moment to pray, asking his Creator for guidance.

"Through the redemptive blood of your Son, Jesus," he would pray, "bless my efforts today. Help me to hear your voice, clear my mind of distractions, and focus on positivity, grace, and goodness. Tie me tightly to the vine of your son Jesus, so I have access to your power, your protection, your wisdom, and your direction."

Then, his routine would really begin. He'd settle onto a couch, open his phone, and start a meditation—usually one by Dr. Joe Dispenza or Tony Robbins. He would immerse himself in these meditations, focusing deeply on aligning his thoughts and emotions with the principles he was learning. Once finished, he'd reach for his phone again, opening that day's Scripture, and then close with another prayer.

After finishing his morning prayer and meditation, Darius would slip into swim trunks, put on a pair of tennis shoes, and throw on a sweatshirt. He'd grab a towel, head out to the car, and drive to the local park, which had a stream running through it. He had scoped out a spot beneath a bridge where he performed his daily cold plunge.

When he first learned about the Iceman and the benefits of cold therapy, Darius had scoffed at the idea. This breathing is great, he'd thought, but there's no way I'm doing that cold-water stuff. Now, he shook his head and laughed at his past self. So much had changed, and so much kept changing. No arrival date.

After months of doing Wim Hof's breathing exercises and experiencing their physical and emotional benefits, combined with Dr. Whitman's program to reset his body and heal, he decided to look more seriously into cold therapy. Dr. Whitman often emphasized that 70% of illnesses stem from the gut, with inflammation being a major culprit of all disease and illness—whether from emotional, chemical, or physical factors ... and spiritual too, he would often add.

But his first foray into cold therapy had been five-minute cold showers while living at the Mann's household. It had been rough at first, but within a few weeks, he adapted. Soon, he found himself looking forward to the clear-headed, invigorating feeling it gave him, especially when combined with his workout and meditation routine. He also noticed a steady improvement in his blood pressure and getting off the HTN medications was a priority. Now, testing it three times daily, he consistently saw readings of around 100–110/70—well within a healthy range.

When September arrived and the weather turned colder, he decided to take the next step. He began doing daily plunges in the stream, and by late November, it had become a non-negotiable part of his morning.

On this particular Thursday, as he pulled into the carpark, the temperature hovered around 30°F, and snow had already dusted the area. As he parked, he smiled, remembering how he used to sit in the car debating whether he really wanted to go through with it.

"Man, I do not want to do this," he used to say to himself. But lately, the hesitation faded. Like Tony Robbins said, "If you get into cold water every morning, the rest of the day is a piece of cake."

Darius marveled at how much stronger he had become mentally—not through sheer force, but through a healthier, more grounded perspective. He was beginning to grasp the concept of power, as it related to levels of consciousness, spiritual realms, and biblical truths. He was fascinated by what he was learning about muscle testing and how it revealed the principles of truth and falsehood. Remarkably, it all seemed to tie together with his spiritual understanding, leaving him in awe of God's intricate design around the body and energy.

As the days grew colder, his routine adjusted. Earlier in the season, he could stay in the icy stream for 10 to 15 minutes. Now, plunges lasted five to six minutes; he felt that was the sweet spot. When the air temperature dropped below 30°F, and the water grew even colder, it somctimes took his body a few minutes to stop shivering. His teeth would chatter, and the cold would cut through him, but he noticed his body adapting over time. The shaking and teeth-chattering became less frequent, and his body began warming itself more efficiently after each plunge.

Darius pulled off his sweatshirt, took off his shoes, grabbed his towel, and got out to the car. Walking barefoot to the trunk, he retrieved a trash bag and his water shoes, a purchase he had made for a family trip he had planned to Alaska. They had become his go-to footwear for his plunges.

From the moment he exited the car, Darius was in prayer. As he walked the wooded trail leading down to the streambed, he focused on connecting with God. In the breaks between his thoughts and prayers, he listened to the world around him. The morning, as he'd grown used to, was quiet and still; there was not another soul in the park, but he wasn't alone. He could hear the birds and animals waking and starting their day; he could feel the wind, cold but gentle, blowing up from the stream; and he could sense His presence all around him as he basked in the beauty of His creations.

Once he reached the stream, he placed the trash bag on the rocks to keep his phone and keys dry, laid his towel and sweatshirt aside, and prepared for the plunge.

Without hesitation, Darius started the timer on his phone and headed straight for the water—no second-guessing, no delays. The spot he had chosen, beneath the bridge, was typically two to three feet deep, depending on the water level. Wading in until the water reached his waist, he'd sit down, submerging himself to his neck. His hands spread out for balance, his feet stretched forward just grazing the riverbed, he began his prayers.

He always began by praying for his family, blessing his children, and asking God to break any generational curses while blessing as the Scripture stated to the thousandth generation those that love Him. He prayed for their protection, guidance, and for God to bring people into their lives who would lead them into a closer relationship with Him. He no longer prayed for the restoration of his marriage, but he still prayed daily for Jessica, as well as for those who had wronged or persecuted him.

By name, he lifted up his mother, the employees suing him, the one who started a competing business, and others who had caused him pain. His prayers were filled with love, not resentment:

"God, bless those who have wounded me. Fill their hearts, minds, and souls with the Holy Spirit. Bring people into their lives who will help them know You. Protect them with your angels, and bless their futures."

He also prayed daily for the men in his Marriage Reset group. Months earlier, he and his Brother in Arms, Jeff, had started a prayer list for men seeking strength in their marriages and families. The list had grown to 65 names, and Darius prayed for those men daily.

"Father, bring the Holy Spirit into their homes. Bless their efforts, decrease their pride, and grant them humility. Help them to grow into the best versions of themselves. Bless the covenant of their marriages and Soften the hearts of their wives if it be your will. Bless their children for the work they are doing. By the blood of Jesus, strengthen them to do the work they need to do to improve and most importantly to forgive their wives."

He ended each time with the passage from Jōb 42:10: ***"After Jōb had prayed for his friends, the Lord restored his fortunes and gave him twice as much as he had before."***

Darius often thought of Jōb from the Bible, who had prayed for his friends and was rewarded with restoration—double of all he had lost. Unlike Jōb, Darius was nowhere near to being the most righteous man in the world, but he felt a kinship to Jōb's trials and prayed to endure them as well—he felt a kinship in enduring trials.

After finishing his prayers, he recited the Lord's Prayer or spent the final two minutes simply meditating in the water. By then, his body felt strong and invigorated, and the cold had washed away any aches or tension.

Once he left the water, he climbed back to the bank, dried off, and put his sweatshirt back on. His body was shivering, but he didn't mind. He walked back to the car, taking in the beauty around him. The quiet still of the park that early in the morning personified what it meant to be at peace, surrounded by God's love. He watched the ducks take their own plunge in the stream not far from where he just was, and for a moment, before he headed back to the trailhead, he stopped and watched them.

Walking back to the car, his body was buzzing with energy. He no longer needed to run the heater for warmth. He put his keys in the ignition, started the engine, and began the drive home—heating up as the car did. And by the time he drove the mile from the park, he had stopped shivering entirely.

Chapter 65
A Father's Confession

Darius had invited his children over to the house for Thanksgiving dinner. Moving back into the house hadn't been what he had hoped for, and the situation seemed to be getting darker, but he was excited to enjoy the rare opportunity to have his kids together. He had no idea where Jessica was, but since her relationship had come out, she wasn't home often.

His oldest daughter and son arrived first, followed by his youngest son. A little later, his daughter's boyfriend, Allen, showed up. He and his daughter had been dating for around nine months, and despite having a challenging home life, he was polite, hardworking, and well-liked by Darius and his kids.

Darius's middle son opened a bottle of wine and poured a glass of Cabernet for each of them, while Darius started cooking. His daughter put some music on, and the others started playing cards. They laughed and caught up, enjoying the time together.

After a little while, his daughter walked over from where she'd been sitting at the counter and approached Darius at the stove. She put her arms around him, and they shared a warm hug.

"How are you doing, Dad?" she asked with concern on her face.

"I'm good, honey," he replied.

"Dad, really, how are you?" she asked.

"Yes, honey it's frustrating, what's happening, but as Tony Robbins says, 'Where focus goes, energy flows.' So I can either focus on growing and learning from the situation or I can—"

"I don't understand," Alexandra interrupted. "How are you handling it all so well? Why aren't you mad?"

"Well, I could be angry, sure. The old me probably would've been, but that wouldn't have gotten me anywhere. Mostly, anger is a wasted emotion. I've chosen to focus on what I can control, what I can learn from this situation, and really just give grace. It's not what I wanted but I can only control how I respond."

Alexandra frowned, clearly still frustrated. "But, Dad ... How can you forgive her?"

"As much as I would not have chosen it for myself, it's given me a great opportunity to heal and to find the tools and resources to change. And there's so many men in the program that I'm in who were or are in the same boat, and I'm grateful for all of the people that God has now put into my life."

"I don't want to be around her or her creepy girlfriend. It's weird."

"I understand, Alex," Darius said, gently interjecting. "But here's the thing: regardless of the situation, she loves you, she loves all of you, and she's not going to stop loving you. I don't want any of you kids to have an issue with your mom or not have a relationship with your mom because of me. It shouldn't have anything to do with me. I've learned that God is all about love, grace, and forgiveness."

Alexandra stepped back, thinking about what he said.

Darius smiled, his voice soft but firm. "Well, come on, let me explain something to all of you. I was going to wait until after dinner, but the steaks are almost done. Let me pull them out and let the food cool for a minute, and then I'll share something important with all of you."

As Darius turned off the stove and checked on the veggies, his kids gathered in the kitchen. Allen lingered in the background, having heard the topic of conversation and feeling the weight in the air.

"Do I need to leave?" he asked.

Darius paused, wiping his hands with the kitchen towel. "No, Allen. You're welcome to stay. I know your family's had its own challenges, and you haven't had a father figure around much. I wish I knew these things when I was your age. I wish someone had been there to tell me, so you might need to hear what I have to say too."

Allen nodded silently.

Darius smiled. "Come on, let's sit at the table."

They all sat down, and Darius pulled up a stool from the bar to join them. He looked down the table at the faces staring back at him; each was awash with curiosity and concern.

"I love all of you, and I want you to understand this. Jesus died on the cross for us. God sent His only son to die for all our sins because He loved us so much. That's the ultimate grace. Life isn't easy but we can choose to give each other grace."

Alexandra lowered her head, deep in thought.

Darius continued, looking at each of them in turn. "I've made many mistakes in my life. I've failed in ways I'm not proud of. But I want you all to know something. I don't want you to reach my age and still be lost, still unsure of your purpose. I don't want you to wait until you're 51 years old before figuring out where your value comes from. I've tried to be the best father I could be. I've always wanted to be involved in your lives. That's why I coached your sports teams, volunteered at school, and tried to show up when it mattered. But I realize now that there were things I didn't understand, things I was missing."

"Dad—"

"Please, let me finish," Darius insisted, finding himself staring into the distance.

The table fell silent again, giving him the space he needed to reflect.

"When I was growing up, I thought my childhood was good, but as I've gone through therapy and self-reflection, I've realized it was filled with anger and a lot of judgment. It was a tough environment and I am not blaming my parents as I am sure they did the best they could. I don't want you to think that I'm excusing that, but I want you to understand that it shaped me. In hindsight, I was too quick to anger, too quick to lash out. And if I'd known all of this sooner, well, I might have handled things differently. I could've been slower to anger. I could've been more patient, more loving. I am sorry and I hope you can forgive me for the times I was too quick to anger. But that's something I've learned, and I'm sharing it with you now, so you don't make the same mistakes."

He looked at them all, his voice filled with vulnerability.

"Most of my life, I haven't liked myself. I set impossible standards for myself and for you and for your mom as well. I tried to find my value in achievements, in getting recognition from others, but that's exhausting. I was always seeking validation, trying to prove I was worthy. But the truth is, I wasn't being true to myself. I didn't understand where my value came from."

His middle son spoke up. "Yeah, Dad, I get that. But look at you now. You're handling everything with grace. You've been through so much, and yet you're still here, still caring about us. You don't need to apologize for anything. You have been a great Dad."

Darius nodded. "I'm grateful for that. But the main thing I want to share with you is this: You don't have to go through life like I did, searching for your worth in all the wrong places. You don't need to seek validation from others. Your value comes from your Creator. I've learned that now, but I'm 51 years old. You know, at the Tony Robbins conference, they talked about the core drivers of human behavior." He paused, thinking back to the energy he felt while in Dallas. He smiled. "They are universal. They're the reason why Tony can go to different countries, work with people from all walks of life, and still have his material resonate. Sure, cultures, languages, and even values differ, but the things that drive people? Those are fundamentally the same."

His daughter leaned forward, intrigued. "What are they, Dad?"

"There are six," he replied, holding up his fingers one by one. "Significance, certainty, variety, love, growth, and contribution. And when we better understand these, we better understand ourselves."

Darius paused, his tone shifting to something more personal. "I want you all to understand this because I've been working hard on myself lately, on changing the way I think. I used to be so hard on myself, constantly filling my mind with negativity. 'That was stupid.' 'Why did you do that?' 'You're an idiot.' Things like that. My internal voice was relentless. I never felt worthy. I never felt good enough."

Sheehan's brow furrowed. "That's hard to imagine, Dad."

He smiled faintly. "It's true. The men's marriage group I joined has been amazing but the conference in Dallas, UPW, was a game changer. We worked on reframing our self-talk, breaking the cycle of negativity. One of the key exercises was identifying the beliefs that hold us back, then turning them into positive affirmations."

"Like what?" Sheehan asked, leaning closer.

"Well," Darius said, "For me, it was about worthiness. I've always struggled with feeling like I wasn't enough. Now, every morning during my meditation, I repeat this incantation with positive emotion: 'I am outstandingly worthy and blessed. My future success is guaranteed and ordained by my Creator.' Anytime I start to doubt myself, I replace the negative thoughts with that affirmation or other positives."

"Wow," Sheehan murmured. "That's ... powerful."

Darius nodded. "Another big one for me was love. I never felt truly loved, not because of you all, but because of unhealthy mental patterns I built as defense mechanisms. Now, I'm working to reprogram that belief, too. When I think about love, I remind myself: Everyone who meets me loves me and wants to spend more time around me because of my positive attitude and energy. It's a complete shift in perspective."

"Does it really work?" Alexandra asked, a touch of admiration seeping through her skepticism.

"It does," Darius said earnestly. "It doesn't mean life's perfect, but it means I'm approaching it differently, more intentionally."

He looked at all his children, his expression softening. "The main thing I want you to understand is to think about what truly matters to you. Know your Creator, because that's where your value comes from."

"How do you figure out your purpose, though?" Ben asked.

"If you're connected to your Creator and reflecting on the talents and skills He's given you, your purpose will start to become clear," Darius replied. "For me, it's about raising my level of consciousness and using my gifts to bless others. I want to give unconditional love and contribute more charity to the world. That's my purpose."

A knowing smile crept across his daughter's face. "Let me guess, you wrote that down at the conference."

Darius laughed, raising his hands. "Guilty as charged! But it's true. For a man especially, if you're not using your gifts to help others, you'll never feel satisfied."

He shifted in his seat, his voice growing more serious. "That's why I've been sharing what I've learned about emotional intelligence, levels of consciousness, and polarity. I want all of you to be happy, healthy, and successful. I want you to have relationships filled with positive polarity, where you bring out the best in each other, where you complement each other's energy. I don't want any of you to go through the pain of broken families or divorce. I love you all so much, and I'd do anything for you."

They all stood and embraced, the warmth of their love filling the room. It was a moment Darius would cherish, one of connection and hope. Afterward, they shared an amazing dinner, filled with laughter and conversation, and ended the evening playing cards. For the first time in a while, the house buzzed with joy.

As Darius cleaned up, he reflected on the journey he'd been on. If only he had known these lessons years ago, how different might things have been?

But he reminded himself of an important truth he'd learned through the marriage program and the Tony Robbins conference: he had done his best with what he knew at the time. He couldn't carry the burden of blame for past mistakes. Instead, as David Hawkins taught, he had the tools now: the ability to forgive, to let go, and to keep moving forward. And with that, he was determined to create a beautiful future—not just for himself but for his family. It was a lesson worth imparting, and one he was grateful to have shared as part of an incredible night.

Chapter 66
Destiny's Date With Darius

Darius couldn't quite believe where he was. As the plane touched down in Florida, the realization began to sink in—he was about to attend his second Tony Robbins event: Date with Destiny (DWD). Just a few months ago, he had been in Dallas for UPW, an experience that Amanda had insisted he couldn't miss. "You have to go," she'd urged relentlessly. When she finally offered to host him as her guest on her Platinum Pass, how could he refuse?

Dallas had been nothing short of life-changing. The six-day immersion was beyond explanation; it made him feel alive in ways he hadn't in years. At 51, after a lifetime of focusing on the wrong things and struggling with scarcity, his life was changing for the positive.

But the idea of joining Tony's Platinum Partners program had initially seemed laughable, given his financial situation. But then, how could he not? The community, the mentorship—it was calling to him. His plan had been to start the following year, but, just like Dallas, Amanda had other ideas.

"You've got to go to DWD," she'd said. He'd protested, citing work commitments and business obligations, but Amanda—and others—were adamant. "No excuses. You need to be there."

Reluctantly, Darius agreed, planning his trip with the intention of returning on Thursday, right after the event ended, but she even had something to say about that.

"Oh no, you can't leave on Thursday," Amanda said. "You have to stay for the Friday night after-party!"

He rolled his eyes and texted: *Do you People ever work??!*

Her response was cheeky:

LOL.

Welcome to our world! You're going to have to figure out how to create more passive income and build systems so you can work on your business, not in it.

Darius laughed while shaking his head. If only it were that simple as he decided to stay the extra day. He'd made his fair share of mistakes in business—hiring the wrong people, juggling too many projects, and not focusing on what mattered. But thanks to the work he had been doing and the insights from UPW, he now saw a better path forward. With a new attitude and tools for transformation, he was determined to not just survive but thrive for another decade.

When it came to lodging, Darius initially booked a hotel room near the event venue using his Marriott points. But in a group chat, an Australian participant named Chris mentioned he and a friend were looking for a "mate" after someone had backed out. Intrigued, Darius messaged Chris for details. They had rented a small house about a 10–15 minute walk from the venue, complete with a pool and private bedrooms. It would cost $500—a fraction of the cost of the hotel. Darius decided to go for it. It seemed like the perfect opportunity to connect more deeply with others in the Tony Robbins community.

He took an Uber from the airport, and upon arriving at the house, retrieved the key from the lockbox, and stepped inside. It was cozy and private, with a charming backyard and a small pool surrounded by lush greenery. Someone had already claimed one of the bedrooms, so Darius, wanting to be courteous, set his belongings on the kitchen table and spent a couple of hours working on his laptop before heading to the venue to register.

The walk to the facility was pleasant, winding through quiet neighborhoods. At registration, Darius exchanged pleasantries with a few attendees, though none were familiar faces. With his lanyard in hand, he returned to the house, where he met Chris and James—his Australian housemates. Both were lean and fit, with Chris sporting a balding head and James boasting a thick shock of hair.

"Hey mate, what's up?" They greeted him warmly. The three shook hands, exchanged brief hugs, and sat down to chat. Both Chris and James had grown up in the UK before relocating to Australia, and like Darius, they were relatively new to Tony Robbins' world. They shared their hopes for the event and the areas of life they wanted to improve.

"What time do you usually get up?" Chris asked.

"I'm an early riser," Darius replied. "I like to read Scripture, meditate, work out, and do the Tony Robbins active meditation."

"Ah, the one where you focus on emotions and flood your heart with positivity?" James asked.

"That's the one! I got a copy of it in Dallas. It's phenomenal; I do it almost every morning. It moves me to tears, but it fills me with so much joy."

Both men nodded enthusiastically. "It's amazing," Chris said.

"Lately, I've been alternating between that and a morning meditation by Dr. Joe Dispenza," Darius added.

"Dispenza?" James asked. "I've heard a little about him."

"Yeah," Darius explained. "Someone at the biocharger station told me about his work, and I've been experimenting with his meditations. I like it. It's a nice change of pace."

"Sounds interesting," James said. "Let's all plan to get up early, work out, meditate, and pump up the energy with some music before heading to the event."

"Sounds good to me," Darius agreed, feeling a growing sense of camaraderie with his new housemates.

***

The morning started early—5:00 AM, to be exact—with everyone working out. The house buzzed with energy, ACDC blasting through the speakers. Chris, in particular, loved TNT, so it was practically on repeat. The very house itself felt alive, energizing them for the day ahead. Afterward, they got cleaned up and prepared for DWD. They wouldn't be sitting together for the event, but they all agreed to regroup later that evening.

When they arrived, attendees were ushered through lines and eventually sorted into color-coded groups. Darius found himself in the yellow group, where introductions were made, and a few group members explained the week's agenda. It was all about transforming how they thought, building empowering mantras, and shifting mindsets.

Inside the stadium, the atmosphere reminded him of UPW. That event had included participants from over 70 countries, with even more joining virtually. DWD had a similar global vibe but was much smaller with around 2,000 attendees, but Darius couldn't shake the thought: Is this really that different? He remained curious, flipping through the workbook handed out to participants.

"The future has several names. For the weak, it is impossible.

For the fainthearted, it is unknown. For the thoughtful and valiant, it is ideal."

Darius smiled to himself. Alright, that works for me, he thought, as music blared and the energy in the room reached a fever pitch. People jumped, high-fived, and danced as the event's team pumped up the crowd. Soon, Scott Harris took the stage.

"When new beliefs hit you," he shouted, "They change everything."

Darius couldn't help but compare it to lessons he'd been absorbing from Dr. Joe Dispenza, particularly the emphasis on combining intention with emotion.

A recurring theme surfaced: **Your mind is your biggest challenge**. Two limiting beliefs stood out to Darius:

1. I'm not good enough.

2. If I'm not good enough, I won't be loved.

Now, they delved into triggers and how resisting problems often makes them persist.

"Problems need energy to survive," Darius wrote in his notes.

After a brief break, the music resumed, and the dancers returned, amping up the crowd before Tony Robbins himself took the stage. His first declaration: "Love is a process, it's not a verb. Either you are being loving or you are not."

Spot on, Darius thought.

Tony explained how people distort, delete, and generalize their experiences. "You don't experience life," he said. "You experience the life you focus on."

Darius scribbled furiously in his notebook, reflecting on how much he'd grown since May. Despite going through a divorce and the financial strain it brought, he was sleeping better, eating healthier, and feeling more balanced than ever. For the first time, he felt grounded—even as his life was being uprooted.

When asked to write down what was great in his life, Darius noted:

- *His health was improving.*
- *He was off medication.*
- *He had new friendships and was learning more about spirituality through Bible study.*

But when asked to consider what was missing, he had to confront some hard truths:

- No love life.
- Financial instability in his business.

He wrote down a plan: *"Fix the finances. Make money again! Get divorced already!"* He laughed as he wrote it.

"Change isn't about ability," Tony said. "It's about motivation. Problems are like drugs. People use them to justify why they're not okay. Leaders, though, see problems differently. They transform their thinking."

Then he dived into something that Darius couldn't not pay attention to. They delved deeper into relationship dynamics—why opposites often attract. Tony explained that one of the challenges in relationships is not understanding why you're attracted to certain people and how your differences, based on these personality traits, can affect the relationship. The truth is, people are often drawn to traits that they are weaker in. This concept is also part of polarity, which Darius had never fully understood, but made sense based on the work he had been doing. Every man in the Marriage Reset Program, Darius thought, was dealing with issues of polarity in their marriage, where it had either been destroyed or was greatly suffering.

Tony continued, explaining that when you're in a relationship, if you don't understand your own strengths and weaknesses, or what traits you have and lack, it will be difficult to manage the relationship effectively. If you're not building the relationship together and making it grow, it will slowly decay. But typically, without recognizing your own complexity, you won't take the time to understand the areas where you are weak. This lack of self-awareness leads to a lack of appreciation for your partner's strengths, and over time, you'll start resenting them for being strong in areas where you are weak.

Darius thought about this and wrote down, *"I did not take on and appreciate her positive traits, so I began to resent her."* He shook his head, acknowledging the truth of it.

Tony suddenly directed his speech to the men in the room, asking, "How many men here in the last week have felt unsafe?" Darius chuckled, looking at Antonio sitting next to him, who smiled and shook his head. No hands went up, except for one or two in the back. But then, Tony then turned the question around: "How many women here in the last week have felt unsafe?"

Darius was shocked as every woman's hand went up. You've got to be kidding, he thought.

Tony then explained that women are the bravest people in the world because, every time they go on a date, they are essentially going out with the person who is most likely to kill them. Darius couldn't even wrap his head around that idea. Looking around, he saw that many of the women were nodding in agreement.

The day continued with exercises in gratitude, effective blaming, and understanding conflict through a lens of appreciation. Tony reminded them: "If you're going to blame someone for the bad, you have to blame them for the good too."

Darius took a deep breath, his pen moving steadily across the page. This was just the beginning, but already, the lessons were striking nerves.

The room fell quiet, an unusual occurrence considering how rarely you could hear a pin drop. But when Tony started speaking—when he shared his insights and stories—the atmosphere shifted. The silence was palpable.

Tony began by sharing a raw piece of his past: his childhood, the chaos of his mother, how she chased him out of the house with a knife. He spoke of the many challenges he faced with her, but he had come to a powerful realization early on. If he was going to be angry at her for her flaws, he also had to acknowledge that her actions had shaped him into who he was. The Tony Robbins he'd become wouldn't exist without that upbringing. He had learned that if he hadn't gone hungry, he might never have developed a deep desire to help feed others.

He then gave the group their assignment for the evening: to write a letter to someone in their life who had hurt them deeply. Someone they were angry with. It could be a letter sent, a phone call made, or even a text.

Darius felt a weight settle in his stomach. Earlier in the afternoon, his flatmate James had moved closer to him, and now, as they sat together, James noticed his unease.

"What's up?" James asked.

Darius hesitated, glancing at him and then away, shaking his head.

"What are you thinking, mate?" James pressed.

Darius swallowed hard. "I know who I need to write this to … but I don't want to."

"Why not?" James asked.

"Because it'll just get smacked right back in my face," Darius replied, frustration creeping into his voice.

James leaned in, putting a comforting arm around his shoulders. "Just do it, mate. It's not for them; it's for you. Write it out. You need to do it."

Darius let out a deep sigh. "Okay, I'll think about it … but I don't think I can call her. I'll write a letter, or maybe text it."

"Either way, mate, whatever you do, just do it. Remember, it's for you."

Darius nodded slowly, trying to absorb the advice. The room fell back into focus as Tony began discussing human needs, revisiting many of the concepts from UPW. Darius checked out momentarily, his mind swirling with excitement. This event was already amazing, and it had just begun.

Tony then spoke about the 21 ways to get stuck—or unstuck. Darius leaned in, listening closely.

"The more rules you have in life, the unhappier you'll be," Tony said. "The more difficult it will be to find happiness. You have to get comfortable with uncertainty. The more comfortable you are with it, the happier your life will be."

This struck a chord with Darius. He realized that being stuck in rigid expectations or ideals kept him from appreciating what he already had. Rules, he realized, were just a form of conditioning. And if he could break free of that conditioning, he could free himself.

Tony went on. "Don't get stuck in your head versus your heart," he said. Darius appreciated this more than he expected. If you're in your head, you're dead. That resonated deeply. In relationships, especially, never approach a difficult conversation from your head— always from the heart.

Darius could feel these truths sinking in. He knew there was still much to understand, but the work he'd been doing with meditation, David Hawkins, and now starting to learn from Dr. Joe Dispenza helped everything make more sense. Tony emphasized another key point: never focus on what you don't have. Instead, stack the positives, one on top of the other. By the time you get to the end of the day, you'll have built a foundation of emotional bliss.

Don't focus on what you can't control. Focus on what you can. Stop worrying about being right or wrong. Tony's advice was simple: Do you want to be right, or do you want to be in love?

Darius shook his head. That had always been an issue. His and Jessica's need to be right had caused more stress than he cared to admit.

Then, Tony introduced the five givens of life:

1. *Everything changes and ends* – Life moves in cycles, renewing itself as it evolves.

2. *Life is not always fair* – But within us, there's a deep commitment to fairness. Resisting this fairness only keeps you in a miserable place.

3. *Things don't always go according to plan* – But sometimes, the unexpected leads to a greater plan, one shaped by synchronicity and larger possibilities.

4. *Pain is part of life* – But suffering is optional. *There are no victims, only volunteers.* Darius circled this point, deeply moved. Life's pain could be dealt with, and through it, one could gain the strength to help others.

5. *People are not loyal and loving all the time* – *No kidding.* But even then, it's essential to keep acting with kindness and love. No human action can take away someone's ability to love.

He encouraged them to stop seeking to be understood before understanding themselves. You must first seek to understand, then, once you've done that, you can worry about being understood. Darius reflected on this. *You probably don't even understand yourself.* That truth stung, but it was undeniable based on his new awareness.

The first day wrapped up in a remarkable way. It was nearly 2 AM when he finally crawled into bed, reflecting on the day's events, the people he'd met, and the incredible experience he had just begun.

And he couldn't help but feel that, somehow, it was only going to get better.

Chapter 67
The Story of My Life

"It's not the events that shape my life, that determine how I feel and act.

Rather, it's the way I interpret and evaluate my life experiences."

Today's going to be interesting, Darius thought.

Arriving at the stadium, the room was on fire again. He got to his seat and said hello to some of the familiar faces around him. He couldn't keep track of all the names. What mattered was the energy in the room: high-fives, music, dancing, hugs.

When Tony got on stage and the room settled, Darius listened intently, scribbling furiously in his notebook, absorbing every word. Tony was outlining the seasons of life, a concept Darius remembered from Dallas.

"Your deepest desires, your journey ... so many of them are manufactured by others," he said, warning the crowd to be careful about what they wanted, and why they wanted it. "Being successful and miserable? You're screwed. When everything in your life is predictable, it's boring. Winter, spring, summer, fall. Life's seasons, they reveal who you really are."

Winter, spring, summer, and fall ... Darius thought about the time frame Tony mentioned—20 to 25 years per season, psychologically speaking. He paused. "No winter lasts forever," Tony had said. It was something that let his mind wander, wander away from the stadium and back home. He thought of Jessica, of his kids, of the divorce, he even thought of the business. He was certainly in his winter, but maybe it was starting to come to an end?

"What you get will never make you happy," he heard Tony, being pulled back into the energy of the room. "Two of the biggest fears are not getting what you want or losing what you already have. But you can't live in fear. You don't want to live like that. Remember, where focus goes, energy flows. There were patterns to everything, especially life's seasons. If you understand the patterns, you can predict them. And if you can predict them, you can succeed."

Tony kept going: power versus force, familiarity, comfortability, repetition, emotional mastery, physical mastery, truth, simplicity, the importance of being consistent with your actions ... It was a download and an overload all in one.

Darius recalled hearing "complexity is the enemy of execution" back in Dallas. He'd thought he understood it then, but now, reflecting on his own mistakes, he realized how true it was.

Last year, he'd created a complicated business development plan that seemed brilliant at the time—only to realize it was too complex for anyone else on his team to follow. The process, while unique, had made things harder, not easier.

It seems so obvious now, Darius thought.

Tony's framework for mastery—cognitive, emotional, physical— was sinking in. "Knowing it isn't enough; you have to feel it, embody it, and make it your identity." He jotted it down as a note in his book.

Tony shifted the focus to the power of meaning. "How often do we judge others—or even ourselves?" He asked. "What if everything is a blessing and we gave up on blaming? What if the worst thing that ever happened to you was actually the best thing that ever happened to you?"

Darius smiled, knowing strongly that this was going to be true for him. This was exactly what David Hawkins and Dr. Joe said, as well.

What if the worst thing that ever happened to me was the best thing that ever happened to me? Darius wondered, his thoughts swirling. Since June, his life had been a whirlwind of change. On the surface, everything seemed to be falling apart. But beneath the chaos, something truly incredible was happening. He was healing. He was learning to take accountability, to forgive, and to love unconditionally—without judgment or expectation.

Tony then said something that connected with everything Darius had been experiencing since that night in Mexico. "Faith is seeing the future and developing a healthy certainty—one that serves you. One that leaves behind suffering and pain, but the ego," he said, "is nothing but fear. No matter how you look at it, slice it, or analyze it—it all comes back to fear."

Darius had once been living in his ego, that was all too clear to him now, but since everything happened—since everything only seemed to escalate—he had surrendered completely to his faith.

One of the exercises was about identifying your primary question—the question that silently drives your thoughts, actions, and emotions. Tony shared a personal example, recounting how one of his business partners had stolen from him, leading him to bankruptcy. That wasn't the only time he had dealt with bankruptcy either as his divorce has cost him millions. Despite his immense success—owning over 100 businesses and being respected globally—Tony had faced extreme challenges.

Darius felt both inspired and introspective. He thought about his own life and the recurring question that had driven him for years. He realized it was always: *How do I get to the next level?* The revelation was bittersweet. While this question had fueled his ambition, it was rooted in insecurity—a fear of not being good enough.

It's the same old story, Darius thought. It was the narrative of his life. The pursuit of success had consumed him, leaving little room to appreciate the blessings he already had.

For Darius, it was time to rewrite that narrative. He chose a new primary question: How do I appreciate and enjoy more of God's blessings and abundance in this situation? It was a monumental shift.

For so long, he had carried the weight of asking, "Why am I not good enough?" or "What is wrong with me?" Now, he wanted to change his wiring and thought process to know God made him, his value came completely from God, and he was more than enough. He was worthy and he would be grateful—for what he had, for where he was, and for the opportunities ahead.

You either get stronger, or you die—that was the root of what he was saying.

Most people weren't wired to handle the hardships of winter, but if you understood the cycles, you'd always find a way to thrive. You could control your thoughts, your emotions, and ultimately, your actions.

Every thought, every feeling, every action stemmed from values and beliefs. That's why Tony's work was focused on mastering the inner world—if you could control that, you could influence the *outer world*. He emphasized, "You have to master your inner world before you can have the life you really want."

Suddenly, Darius had an epiphany thinking of Scripture. He thought of Ephesians and Corinthians—while we live in the flesh, we don't war against the flesh, and we must take every thought captive to the obedience of Christ. He felt Tony was describing this truth beautifully. What really mattered? Relationships, contribution, love? His spheres of influence, he realized, had been misaligned and misguided. Instead of placing significance and certainty at the core of his world, he would work to shift his focus to relationships, growth, and contribution. He smiled.

As the music blared and the dancers took the stage again, Darius sat back, feeling a shift within himself. *"If you focus on relationships, giving love, and contributing to others, everything else will follow."* He wrote it down and underlined it several times. He took a deep breath, and thought about it again.

***

What's the story of my life? Darius wondered.

A sad drama.

That was his life, if he had to sum it up in a limited way.

Divorces. So many missed opportunities. Sadness. Frustration. *Rarely in the moment. A lot of drama ...*

I've never had peace in my life, he thought before catching himself. "Until now," he said. Even while everything was crumbling around him, or at least, that was how it appeared.

Darius closed his eyes, took another deep breath. "Okay. What's the story of your life?" He muttered.

He let it flow. *"Life was about being successful,"* he wrote. *"Life was trying to be loved. It was full of anger—with a limiting belief of not being worthy. I was a victim. I wanted to be a knight but was mostly a sarcastic jester. Desiring significance, I sought to feel worthy and to be loved. I battled with my family—my wife—and sadly, mostly myself."*

"I never appreciated the blessings right in front of me," he added, sighing. "I made others feel like they weren't enough. I was never good enough, and somehow, with all those blessings around me, I was still lonely. Self-inflicted loneliness. My behaviors made others uneasy, on edge."

He stopped, reading over what he had written.

"Okay, Darius, what do you want the new story to be?" He asked himself.

He thought back to Tony's talk about tragedies and dramas. Darius had always seen his life as a sad drama. But now, what did he want it to be? A comedy? A romance? An adventure? He could keep it as it was before—horror, action, a flick filled with tension— or he could let his spirit lead him to something new. What had God meant for him to do? Be? Share? Love? Inspire?

Darius let his heart open. The words flowed once again:

A HEROIC ADVENTURE

"A knight crowned a king. He knows his value. He is honorable. He knows his purpose. He is a Godly man—loving, compassionate, kind, patient, playful. He is confident, loyal, and a loving force for good. His life is directed by power versus lack or force. He is a smart businessman, focused on giving and expanding charity. This man—this new man—is outstandingly worthy, blessed, and his success is guaranteed, ordained by his Creator. Everyone who meets him, everyone who knows him, loves him. They feel the incredible positive energy he brings into their life."

Yes, Darius thought, reading over the words. Yes, that's what I want the movie of my life to be.

What emotions would dominate this new life? Love. Grace. Compassion. Playfulness. Fun. Passion. Gratefulness. Why not one more? Curiosity.

And then he added the final touch, the grand finale, the cherry on top. He rewrote the ending:

"Because he gives love freely from a place of power, love finds him. He heals and connects people as a force for good, and because he gives love freely, love is always present in his life moving forward."

He smiled.

With that, the first day ended and the music exploded again. Before Darius knew it, he was on his feet, dancing and singing with joy. Tears streamed down his face—tears of joy.

Chapter 68
Reimagining Oneself

A lready, in less than two days, he felt like he'd been blessed. The energy was overwhelming. They'd said this was better than UPW ... How could it possibly get any better?

Chris, James, and Darius, after their morning activities and freshening up, sat down together to enjoy breakfast. They discussed a few different things, but the focus was on DWD and the remarkable experiences they had already had during the first few days. They marveled at the new insights and relationships they were discovering, all of them feeling truly amazed by how much they had already learned.

After breakfast, they walked over to the facility together, heading for their designated areas. As they entered, high-fives and hugs were exchanged, and they split off to their separate groups. Darius made his way to his seat, pausing to greet a few new faces he had met over the last few days. Then, he spotted Tamara. Their friendship was evolving, and as they shared a warm hug, Darius couldn't help but notice how much she had changed in just a few days. She seemed more relaxed now, less guarded.

When he had first met her, she seemed closed, a little rude, slightly entitled—she seemed almost trapped in her masculine energy, but now, there was a softness, a shift toward her positive feminine traits. It was fascinating to witness, and Darius was intrigued by her growth. Like many of the people around him, she was clearly enjoying the process of self-discovery.

The Hawaiian meditation they had done the day before had been deeply revealing—an intimate, beautiful bonding experience. Darius could see how the exercise had affected them both. During it, they had been required to stand face-to-face, staring into each other's eyes while placing their hands on their hearts and repeating an incantation. The whole experience was intense, but for Darius, staring into Tamara's eyes had been eye-opening. He had seen the strength in her—she had clearly faced many challenges, and her walls were still there, protecting her heart.

Later that day, they found time to talk. Tamara opened up about her past, including the struggles of her previous marriage. She shared how her husband had been an alcoholic, how they had grown disconnected, and how their impending divorce had been followed by his death. Darius felt his heart ache for her as she spoke, especially as she described the guilt that often comes with divorce, and the added burden of losing someone after making that decision. Tamara also explained how different they had been in every aspect of life—her commitment to self-improvement, her focus on physical health—while he had been consumed by his addiction. Darius could understand the walls she had built in response to such pain.

After sharing her story, Tamara turned the conversation toward Darius. She asked him about his own journey, and he shared some of his struggles, admitting that he was undergoing a major transformation. He explained that he had realized how much work he still had to do to become a better version of himself. Tamara listened intently, then looked him in the eyes and said, "Can I tell you something?"

"Of course," Darius responded.

"I know that when we did that exercise, I saw into your soul," she said, her gaze unwavering. "I saw into the depths of your heart."

Darius met her eyes and nodded slowly. "I felt the same way about you."

Tamara hesitated, then said, "Darius, you are an incredibly good man."

Darius smiled weakly.

"I also saw that you are in a lot of pain," she added.

Darius remained still, processing her words, then responded, "Thank you. I receive that. One of the things I've always struggled with is accepting compliments, but I know I have work to do in that area. So, thank you."

She smiled warmly, and Darius continued. "I've made many mistakes, focused on the wrong things. I sought love and I was driven by a need for significance and certainty, as Tony would say, traits that exhaust those around you. But now, I have a new perspective. I want to focus on contribution, growth, and being present. I need to learn to receive love and give it freely. Yes, I've been in pain, but that pain has been a gift in many ways. It's helped me wake up and make changes I desperately needed. I've been blessed, even though there's still healing to do. I'm confident I'll get there."

They hugged. It was a beautiful moment of connection between two people who had only known each other for a few days; a testament to the relationships that were beginning to form in this incredible space. Darius felt a deep sense of gratitude for the new people God was bringing into his life.

Once again, Darius wondered how it could get any better than this, and yet, he also had to remind himself that every day seemed to surpass the last.

Today was a deep dive into the stages of spiritual development and the different levels of consciousness as Tony defined them. Darius was eager to learn but also curious about how this new framework of Clare Graves would compare to the teachings of David Hawkins, which had already profoundly influenced him.

Darius felt a mix of anticipation and skepticism. The concepts seemed different from what he had been exploring, but he would focus on being curious. Over the past seven months, he had encountered countless ideas that, while initially distinct, often revealed surprising connections.

As the energy in the stadium died down just a little bit, Darius readied his notebook to take detailed notes. Tony began by discussing the importance of motives, emphasizing that while serving your own needs is natural, true breakthroughs come when your actions benefit others—the more you give, the more you receive. Darius thought of one of his favorite verses, and the one he wanted to be the key verse for the charitable foundation, Luke 6:38:

"Give, and it will be given to you, a good measure—pressed down, shaken, overflowing—they will pour out into your lap. For with the measure by which you measure out, it will be measured out to you in return."

The discussion shifted to consciousness and the role of the ego in shaping perception. Tony explained how the ego often creates problems by preventing people from appreciating what they already have. Growth isn't just personal—it allows you to give more to others. "Consciousness equals caring," he remarked.

The idea that higher consciousness doesn't just elevate the individual but also positively influences those around them—it had appeared time and time again, and here it was again. The sudden realization filled him with awe. Someone operating at a high level of consciousness could counterbalance the negativity of hundreds of thousands of people. He thought of this relevant to Scripture and Hawkins' work showing that a person at 400 on the scale of consciousness counteracted 800,000 negative people.

Letting that connection sink in, he couldn't help but utter, *"Wow."*

Tony then introduced the levels of consciousness, each representing a distinct worldview and set of values. The foundational level, survival and instinct, focused on basic needs like safety and was often seen in tribal settings where rituals and leaders played key roles. The next level, associated with power and dominance, centered on individuals who sought control without regard for consequences. Tony used examples like rock stars, warlords, and celebrities to illustrate this stage.

Darius grimaced, recognizing his own drivers—certainty and significance—might place him in this category, but as Tony continued, he actually found himself somewhere in the middle. It wasn't much better, he would have hoped, even thought, that he was living with a higher level of consciousness. But as Tony explained, he realized how long he still had to go before he would get anywhere close to the highest levels.

There was, however, hope. Tony explained that problems couldn't be solved at the same level of consciousness that created them. It meant that so long as Darius was moving and solving, he was climbing. He realized he couldn't see many of the past issues until he had worked to raise his consciousness or awareness, and in that, Darius recognized himself as an achiever, thriving in the drive for growth and success. But he also noticed that in times of stress, he tended to slip into rigid thinking, seeking certainty and rules, especially in personal relationships. This self-awareness prompted him to jot down a note: "Acting self-righteous, like his mother tended to do."

Darius began to see how viewing others through another lens, through another level of consciousness, could help him communicate with more understanding and empathy. Growth, he realized, required a willingness to rise above old habits and see things differently.

As Darius reflected on the session, he saw an opportunity for himself. While he identified strongly with the achiever's mindset, the idea of integrating lessons from other levels—particularly connection and love—was compelling. He envisioned himself becoming a bridge, someone who could unite different perspectives and foster greater understanding. That would be an incredible goal.

***

As things settled down, the conversation shifted back to the work they'd been doing—discovering personal values and beginning to talk about the rules that governed them. This, Darius thought, was going to be crucial for him. He had an intuitive sense that his own rules were not serving him. He was fairly certain they were unhealthy and hindering his growth.

Again Tony brought the ego. He delved into the importance of boundaries, the differences between masculine and feminine energies, and the fact that "safe spaces" were absurd, another psychological buzzword, like narcissism, that was overused and had lost its true meaning. "You're not really broken. You just didn't know the truth or have the right tools," he insisted.

Darius muttered, "fucking A," suddenly thinking of their old counselor, Sharon, and how she had planted the seed to his wife that he was a narcissist. It was true, as Tony put it, that he had likely been living in a self-suffering cycle, beating himself up whenever he could, but he wasn't a narcissist, he wasn't broken, he just wasn't as equipped as he should have been—as equipped as he was now.

He had been actively working on changing how he spoke to himself—how he viewed himself—and he could already feel the difference. He was working to set healthy boundaries for himself for the first time in his life. And this was giving him the right tools to move into the person he was always meant to be.

But then he heard what Tony had to say next:

"You can't focus on yourself," he said. "You have to find a standard for how you interact with others. It wasn't just about you; it was about a code of conduct that guided your behavior. When you're unhappy with those closest to you, listen. Be kinder. Don't make yourself a victim. It's too easy to fall into that trap, and when you do, you end up hypnotizing yourself into making everything about significance."

Ouch, Darius thought. I'm *trying* ...

"Trying is a bullshit word," Tony declared, as if he could hear Darius's thoughts and called him out directly. "Language and beliefs shape our lives. We get the life we focus on. If we focus on creating suffering, we can do that—it's easy, but it's also limiting and destructive. If we choose to focus on connection, growth, and honoring others, however, we shift our focus away from ourselves and toward something greater. Life doesn't wait for us to be ready to give us challenges; it gives us challenges so we can grow. How we respond to them determines everything."

Darius shook his head, grinning an ear-to-ear grin. "Okay," he muttered, "No more '*try.*' Got it."

The discussion shifted to the power of consciousness in shaping our lives.

"Many people chase after things they think they want, only to realize that their values are misaligned. Values are the emotional states we prioritize, either those we strive to experience or those we try to avoid. Life becomes much more fulfilling when you identify what you truly value and pursue it with passion, excitement, love, and gratitude. So what do you want?" Tony asked, his tone direct.

"Adventure? Success? Love? All decisions come down to value clarification."

Darius began jotting down emotions he wanted to move away from—anger, rejection, loneliness, failure, and depression. Darius understood that the emphasis was that most people are more motivated by a desire to avoid pain than to seek pleasure. That struck a chord with him because he recognized how his fear of failure and rejection had often driven him. While it had fueled his achievements, he saw how it wasn't a healthy or sustainable source of motivation.

"What rules do you have around success or rejection?"

The question suddenly caught Darius off guard. He didn't want to be rejected, and if he wasn't rejected, then he was successful, right? Was that really how he thought? Was his happiness really tied that tightly to his external ambition and acceptance?

"If your happiness depends on someone else's actions, you'll never be satisfied," Tony warned. "You'll burn yourself out—and burn others out, too." Trying to be perfect, he explained, is an exhausting pursuit that often leads to misery.

It was an echo of everything he had been learning. Master Co and David Hawkins had it plastered all over their philosophies. Though both took it a step further: You are not your thoughts, your feelings, or your body. You are the soul. So why had he been allowing himself to live in his thoughts, inside his feelings and judgments?

Again, it was like Tony was calling him out in front of everyone.

"Stop making rules that make it hard to feel good," Tony urged. "Too many of you unconsciously choose rules that make you feel miserable. But now, you have the power to consciously choose rules that allow you to grow and feel good more often. Remember, love is not a noun or a verb. It's a process. You're either being loving, or you're not."

Could love really be so straightforward?

Darius recalled David Hawkins' teachings, where unconditional love corresponded to 520 on his scale of consciousness. For him, this was an aspiration: to love without expectations and to feel secure in his purpose, free from the pains and wounds of his past.

From his time in therapy, he wanted and needed to keep working to meet people where they were. Whether it be humbling himself or to rise to a higher level of consciousness to engage at their level.

"I don't mean to sound uncompassionate," Tony said carefully, "But every 24 months, your body completely regenerates. Every cell is replaced. Physically, you're a new person." His point wasn't to diminish the reality of trauma but to emphasize the need to break free from replaying the same painful memories. "Don't let the same negative movie play in your mind a thousand times," he urged. "You're not defined by what happened to you. Instead, figure out what you truly want, create rules that empower you, and align your life with your values."

Darius thought about how Scripture stated we needed to renew our minds daily and put on the armor of God daily. He thought of everything he had experienced, was learning, and the sermon in Africa on how evil can influence us.

The discussion then focused on the nature of true love versus transactional love. Too often, people give love with an unconscious expectation of receiving something in return—what Tony called "bartering." Real love, however, is about consistently putting the needs of others before your own without expecting anything back. It's about being a generous lover, giving freely, and stepping into the person you were always meant to be.

"Every time you step into the unknown, it will reward you," Tony said.

Darius sat staring forward. Dear Lord, please help me keep changing.

Chapter 69
Relationship Day

T he following day brought a rush of mixed emotions for Darius. His relationship, as far as he could tell, was over. It had been the cornerstone of his life for almost two decades. He hadn't been with another woman, hadn't loved anyone else. Although he'd done a lot of healing, learned so much, and accepted a great deal, spending an entire day focused on relationships didn't sound like it would be much fun. He had no idea what was in store for him.

But as the day unfolded, it was both painful and healing, as well as profoundly insightful. What was the purpose of relationships? What shapes them in state and meaning? Despite the newfound clarity, Darius sat in deep discomfort.

Tony asked the crowd to think about when they last felt like they were truly, fully, and freely in love. He asked them to think about what it *felt* like, asking the question two or three times, each time adding more emphasis on the word.

What did it *feel* like?

Darius opened to a fresh page and wrote down: *"Attentive. Carefree. Less judgmental. Loving. Unselfish. Caressing. Kinder. Gentler. We were* **connected**.*"*

Then Tony asked, "What would you be willing to do to experience these moments consistently? What would you do differently, or what would you be willing to let go of?"

For Darius, this wasn't hard to answer—he'd been doing the work for months leading up to this day. Anything healthy and within boundaries—that was the key. He wrote:

"I would lead with my heart and get out of my head. I would kill the ego and the small self, as Hawkins calls it. I would listen, validate, and ask questions from a place of curiosity. I would be more loving, more open, expecting nothing in return. I would let go of being right, stop being judgmental, and stop seeking love. What I truly understand now is I need to lead in all areas. I will work hard to create experiences daily. I would be vulnerable and honest, understanding where my value comes from, and I would identify opportunities to lead my lover into her feminine energy because she feels safe."

That last part made Darius smile in surprise, even as he wrote it. Leading a woman into her feminine energy? It was a concept he'd never understood at all until the past year—a result of reading G.S. Youngblood's *The Masculine in Relationship*. While he was anything but an expert, he was learning to identify and connect with a woman's emotions, understand what she was feeling, and help her feel safe and loved, giving her the space to be more carefree. It started with controlling your own emotions first, though, by being in a positive masculine frame.

The discussion shifted to forgiveness. Tony quoted Nelson Mandela, who said that holding onto resentment is like drinking poison and expecting the other person to die. Darius knew this to be true. He had come a long way in the past year. A few years ago, he might have been consumed with anger and resentment over his marriage, but now, by leaning into God, he was learning not to judge or hold onto negative emotions. Stop the thoughts, identify the emotion, and let it go, he thought.

He closed his eyes, rubbed his face, and thought about what needed to change. Suddenly, he felt a weight on his shoulders. His feeling of unworthiness. His ego. His neglect. His inability to see and cherish the differences between him and Jessica ... So much negativity had been in control for so long. A tear slipped down his cheek

Darius shook his head, feeling the weight of it all. Turning the page, he wrote: *"I have to kill the victim mindset for the rest of my life. I've made so many strides, and I know my value and purpose. There's more healing to do, but I want to keep growing. I will be strong in my worth and honor the feminine energy in the women I interact with going forward ... and in whoever my beloved will be."*

He paused, considering the possibility that he might never be with anyone again. If that's what's meant to be, then it's okay. The conversation from years ago with his wife came to mind—her telling him that he could never be alone, that if something happened to her, he would find someone else in a heartbeat. Then, she'd told him that she would never get married again. That conversation seemed like a warning now—a clue he hadn't understood back then.

In reflection, how interesting it was now that she had been in a relationship for months and he had no interest in dating. He just wanted to keep healing so when the time was right, he wasn't trying to find something in another that was missing in himself. Now, with the distance between them, he could see it more clearly.

He thought about his changing perspective on relationships. For years, he had believed that sex outside of marriage was just a part of life, something acceptable. But now, after immersing himself in the Bible and exploring deeper spiritual truths, his beliefs had shifted. The Bible was clear on the topic. He was deceiving himself previously based on what he wanted. He had seen things from a new perspective, especially with what he'd learned about the spiritual implications of relationships and the doors opened through them. He was starting to believe that each sin listed in Romans or Galatians wasn't just an act or sin; those sins opened up doors and there were evil spirits behind them influencing people through the emotions in the lower levels of consciousness.

He went back to the exercise, determined to find beauty and love in all situations. His goals were clear:

"I want to never stay in a state of suffering for more than 90 seconds. I want to identify what my love needs and help her defuse negative energy so she can feel safe and loved in her feminine. I want whoever I'm with in the future to feel cherished. Connection, laughter, passion, and joy—those are paramount."

He smiled at the thought of what he had to work toward. But then he was introduced to the relationship pyramid. At the top was "Select and Connect," with the middle focusing on giving so much to your partner that they become a raving fan. It was about devotion— total commitment to another person.

Darius, feeling a little numb, listened attentively. He knew this was all important, even if it didn't feel fun. Tony emphasized that the key to lasting love, passion, and fulfillment was becoming addicted to pleasuring your partner.

"If you have more rules, you'll have less love," Tony asserted. "Do you want to be in love, or do you want to be right?"

Oh, how I loved my rules, Darius thought, putting a hand over his face.

"If your spouse or partner doesn't feel like the most important thing in your life, you're in trouble."

Darius heard the words and felt their weight. He knew he had failed in many ways.

As Tony continued explaining the six positions in a relationship, Darius grimaced. In his notes, he circled position five: You are not in a relationship, but you want to be. He added a small asterisk next to it. Not anytime soon, but at some point, yeah, that would be him. The irony of it hit him hard. He was healthier than he had ever been. Physically fit. Emotionally healing, but how much more did he have to go? He sensed there was a lot more healing to do. Yet, he was alone. And likely would be for a while.

Delving deeper into the topic of polarity, something Darius had learned to appreciate over the past year, Tony explained how opposite energies create attraction and how pressure could shift a person's natural polarity. Men, under pressure, could start taking on negative masculine or feminine traits, while women could do the same. Darius knew he had a lot more to learn and wanted to become adept at understanding polarity.

What shuts down intimacy? Tony explained emotional disconnection that leads to the death of a relationship. Irritation, frustration, emotional stacking, stonewalling, and ultimately, the loss of intimacy ... Staring at his notes, Darius was stunned.

The framework of relationships Tony described felt like a road map of his own marriage's downfall. Each phase resonated with painful precision, revealing how the bond he once shared with his wife had unraveled over the years. The realization was staggering.

The concepts of polarity and energy in relationships struck a chord. Tony's assertion that relationships are either growing or dying mirrored Darius's own philosophy about life. Yet, the truth of how their focus on self over partnership had contributed to the deterioration of their marriage was difficult to bear. He had failed to make his wife feel seen, heard, and understood. She had closed off, and the connection they once had gave way to criticism, control, and ultimately, distance.

As Tony continued, Darius saw how their love had succumbed to cycles of power struggles. Miscommunication had driven them to blame rather than take ownership, and over time, the resentment stacked. By the time rejection set in, it was too late. The tone of their interactions had shifted from love to contempt. Words were spoken that couldn't be unsaid, further pushing them apart until all that remained was repression—the death knell of intimacy. He could clearly see how both of their actions had slowly destroyed their marriage.

Darius's heart ached as he thought about his wife of 17 years and his children. The life they had built together was now irretrievably broken. He reflected on the final blows: the revelation that her affair was with a woman and their family fractured. What would the repercussions be on their family, and for how long?

As the weight of these truths bore down on him, tears began to flow. Darius bowed his head, overcome by grief, regret, and shame. He mourned not only the end of the relationship but also the man he hadn't been—the partner who could have made her feel more loved and safe. If only they had learned these lessons previously together, what type of marriage might they have had?

As his shoulders shook with silent sobs, Darius felt hands on his knees. He opened his tear-blurred eyes to see Sarah, Antonio's partner, kneeling before him, her own eyes glistening with empathy. She reached out and embraced him, holding him with kindness and compassion. Beside him, Antonio placed a steady hand on his shoulder, silently offering support.

"It's okay," Sarah whispered, her voice gentle and sincere. "We're here for you."

Darius leaned into the embrace, grateful for the unexpected kindness. In that moment, being seen, being heard, and being held brought a flicker of solace amidst the overwhelming grief. In that moment, he felt healing, forgiveness, and the letting go of his marriage and the past.

He reflected on the journey of the last year. Painful as it had been, it had also been eye-opening. The insights he had gained about himself, relationships, and love were priceless. He couldn't change the past, but he could honor the lessons it had taught him and carry them forward.

He could lean into gratitude for the growth, for the awareness, for the opportunity to rebuild himself. The lessons and a higher awareness could help him continue to transform and share love in the future that hadn't been an option for him in the past.

This moment of connection—with Sarah, Antonio, and himself—was one he would carry with him as a reminder of his capacity to heal, to forgive, and to move forward with grace. Painful as it was, this was the start of something new and he would forever be grateful.

***

Darius wasn't sure how long it had been since Sarah embraced him, nor how long he had wept. His tears eventually subsided, he stood up, and they held each other in silence. Antonio stood up and joined the embrace, offering his own support.

Tony's voice called out to the crowd. "What is your vision for an ideal relationship?"

It was a confusing question to be asked, one Darius found difficult to imagine but knew he needed to embrace the question. He closed his eyes, folded his hands, and took a deep breath, offering a silent prayer. Then he turned his mind to the exercise. What would an ideal relationship look like? What impact would it have? Who would it serve? What would it inspire? These were challenging questions, but as he pondered them, he realized something.

He began to write. *"Trust"* was the first word that came to him. Incredible shared outcomes—that was what he wanted. This was his vision of love. He wanted to be his partner's biggest cheerleader, to be the person she could turn to for anything, to be someone who made her feel safe, cherished, and loved. He imagined a relationship where both partners could share their dreams, their fears, their deepest selves, without judgment.

I WILL HEAR YOU

"I will destroy your fears with love. He paused for a moment, feeling a wave of emotion as he thought about how he had fallen short in his past relationship, how he had failed at times to be the cheerleader his wife might have needed. He carried a deep sense of guilt for the disconnect that had grown between them over the years, the lack of shared information, and how both of them had withdrawn into their own worlds."

In his next relationship, however, he would validate, to connect. He would listen with sincerity and love. He would be the first person she turned to when she needed someone to share her dreams and fears with.

He continued to write: *"When you feel out of balance, overly emotional, or 'crazy,' I will be your shoreline. I will be your lighthouse."* He smiled as he wrote that. He had learned this year while cleaning out unhealthy emotions from the past through his sessions with Larissa. He was committed to continuing working so that never again would he allow others to determine his emotional state.

The more he wrote, the more clarity he gained. He would protect the polarity between them, encourage her to relax into her feminine energy, and make sure she felt safe. Their love-making would be filled with passion and intimacy, and their life would focus on adventure, giving, and faith in God.

Darius looked up from the page, wiping a tear from his eye. How many times had he asked himself how much a man could cry? As he sat there reflecting, he realized that all these tears were part of his healing. He had a lot to purge, and through the tears, he was doing just that in an honest and transparent way.

As Darius finished his writing, he thought back to the past few months since everything had fallen apart at the end of May. He couldn't stop now. He had learned too much. He could never stop— he would keep working on himself, manifesting the life he wanted, because now that he had the eyes to see and the ears to hear, there was no turning back.

The room grew quiet as *Braveheart* appeared on the screen. "What would you give for one day of freedom?" Gibson's voice echoed. Then the music began to swell, blaring as Tony urged them to do whatever felt natural when they were called to.

Suddenly, Mel Gibson's voice yelled out, "Freedom!" and something remarkable happened. Darius found himself standing, his left arm raised high, his right fist pounding his chest. "Freedom!" he yelled. And he wasn't the only one. Around him, every man stood, repeating the words, mirroring the energy. The room vibrated with positive masculine energy. Darius could feel it in every fiber of his being.

It went on for what seemed like an eternity, though it was only five to ten minutes. When it ended, the room was still. The men stood tall, proud. There were no words to describe it, only a profound energy filling the room. The women in the audience stared in awe, eyes wide open.

Then it was the women's turn. Tony began by touching on that beautiful contrast between the masculine and the feminine. He discussed how beautiful, healing, and freeing feminine energy was and asked those aligned with that energy to express themselves, just as the men had done.

As the music started, Tony encouraged the women to step into the aisles, to let go of self-consciousness, and to move naturally and freely. "Don't worry about the men watching," he said. "This is for you, just feel what's inside you and let it flow."

Sarah glanced at Antonio and Darius, hesitating before shrugging and deciding to stay in her spot. What followed was unlike anything Darius had ever witnessed. Women all around the room began to dance, some closing their eyes, others leaving them open. Their movements ranged from graceful and natural to sensual and expressive, each uniquely captivating.

He felt like a voyeur, but it was the most beautiful thing he had ever seen. As the women danced, their movements and expressions filled him with awe. He watched Sarah move fluidly next to Antonio, her energy seemingly unbound and unselfconscious. Darius caught Antonio's eye, unsure if he should avert his gaze, but Antonio's reassuring smile seemed to say, "It's okay. Just appreciate it."

The music shifted through different moods, from soft and sensual to more dynamic and natural, mirroring the spectrum of feminine energy. Darius couldn't help but marvel at the authenticity and raw beauty of what he was witnessing. The women weren't performing; they were simply being. The room was alive with the unfiltered power of femininity, and Darius felt a new appreciation for every aspect of it.

He understood now, with a clarity he hadn't possessed before, that his role as a partner wasn't just about love or provision but about creating an environment where a partner could feel safe to be herself—her true, feminine self, beautiful and free like so many of the women here. It was a lesson that cut deep, forcing him to reckon with the ways he had failed in the past. But it also carried hope and the potential for growth—not just for himself, but for the kind of relationship he might one day be able to cultivate.

By the time the night ended, it was long past midnight. He had to call it a night, find some time to sleep, but he couldn't stop reflecting on what he had seen and heard. This day would stay with him forever.

Chapter 70
Dancing in the Aussie Rain

I t couldn't get any better. And yet, it always did.

They hadn't gone to bed until almost 4 AM, but three of them were still up by 9, working out, energized, and buzzing with excitement. They gathered, sitting around, exchanging their incredible experiences from the day before and eagerly anticipating what was to come.

The first exercise of the day was eye-opening. His old rules were terrible. What he'd sensed all along was absolutely true: his rules weren't set up to help him, to make him happy, or to help him feel good about himself. So he had to make new ones.

His old values had started with number one being success and number two being achievement. Now, three of his old rules didn't even make the list, including the Top 2! Love, meaning, success, adventure, intimacy, giving, and fun. His new values, in order, were now Faith and Honesty, Love and Warmth, Healthy to Health, Gratefulness and Cheerfulness, Playfulness and Fun, Passion, Learning and Growing, Contributing and Charity, Curiosity and Wisdom, and lastly, Achievement.

Tony had spoken earlier about how to be careful with physical anchors, how they can create negative situations, and the importance of aligning values with your goals. "What kind of person does it take to hit your goals?" he'd asked. "That's who you need to become. That's your destiny. Create the values that pull you toward what you want."

Darius was beyond excited to start designing these new rules and values, and he was excited to share.

Several times throughout the event, there had been a chance to participate in an exercise led by Scott Harris. It was another chance to deep dive into Tony's content, to have that feeling of accountability placed on you from the whole group that, yes, you *were* going to enact these changes. He had volunteered himself several times, but wasn't called on … But today was different.

He raised his hand and, to his surprise, Scott pointed directly at him.

"Alright, mate. You're up," Scott said, gesturing to Darius with a smile.

Darius felt the eyes of everyone in the room on him, but he was ready. "Sure," he said, standing.

Scott raised an eyebrow. "Well, go ahead, mate."

Darius began: "A person with these values, in this order, might be great in the following ways—"

He was interrupted by the blaring sound of a horn. Darius froze, confused. Scott started shaking his head with a look of mock sorrow.

"Oh mate, I hate it. It hurts my heart!" Scott exclaimed.

Darius was baffled. What had he said wrong? The answer came when Scott hurled a foam hat into the audience. It was a silly-looking creation—a smiling shit emoji. The hat landed near Darius, who picked it up.

"Rules are rules!" Scott declared, grinning mischievously.

Still unsure of what was happening, Darius placed the hat on his head. The room erupted in laughter as Scott produced an enormous water gun, a monster of a device that looked like it could soak someone from across a stadium. Without further ado, Scott took aim and fired a powerful stream of water directly at Darius's chest.

The icy spray hit him full force. For a moment, Darius stood stunned, drenched, as laughter filled the room. But as the music— something quirky and upbeat—blared through the speakers, Darius decided to roll with it. He shrugged, broke into a grin, and began to dance.

The crowd roared as Darius leaned into the spray, turning to let the water drench him from every angle. He moved with enthusiasm, bouncing in place, spinning, and even doing a little jig as water poured over him. His good humor was infectious, and the applause grew louder with every move. By the end of the song, he was completely soaked, but his spirit was intact, even elevated.

As the music faded, Darius wiped water from his face and gave the audience a theatrical bow, eliciting more cheers. He couldn't help but laugh at the absurdity of the moment.

"All right, mate," Scott called out from the stage, still grinning. "You get another chance. Go ahead."

Still dripping, Darius's mind raced as he still had no idea what he had done wrong. He wasn't about to get soaked a second time. He adjusted the foam hat on his head, gave a playful smirk, and said, "I'm just going to be completely honest. I don't understand what I did wrong. I thought what I was doing was what I was supposed to do."

The crowd chuckled, and Scott's eyes twinkled. "Well, that's mistake number one, mate. What does Tony always say? Don't cheat ahead. Focus on the exercise, do it step by step."

Darius nodded, accepting the correction. He wasn't supposed to share anyone's perspectives but his own. He was supposed to bring something new to the table, to build on what he wanted to see emerge in himself from everything he had been learning. So, soaking wet with the most unflattering hat he could ever wear on his head and the biggest smile on his face, he did just that.

"Nailed it!" Scott clapped his hands together; the room erupting into applause.

As the room started to move on, one of the Tony Robbins team members, a young woman, approached to collect the foam hat he was wearing. "Wait," Darius said, feigning mock protest. "I don't get to keep the hat?"

She laughed, shaking her head. "No, you don't get to keep the hat."

"I mean, after being soaked and humiliated, I feel like I've earned it," he teased.

"Rules are rules," she giggled as she walked away.

"Hang on, hang on, everybody!"

The room quieted as Scott again pointed at Darius, who was still dripping wet after the exercise, "I want to say this in front of everyone. You, my friend, are a stud." The crowd chuckled and murmured in agreement as Scott continued. "I want everyone to understand what just happened. The way you handled that, the way you leaned into it and rolled with it, it was magnificent. Well done."

Applause rippled through the room, and several people nearby gave Darius congratulatory pats on the back. The old version of him might not have handled that moment with the same grace and humor, but the person he was becoming felt proud to have embraced it.

Ironically, the adrenaline rush hadn't stopped him from realizing one thing: he was freezing. After five minutes of sitting in damp clothes, he dug into his backpack and found a spare T-shirt. He quickly made his way to the bathroom to change.

As he emerged in his dry shirt, feeling significantly warmer, he was met with a surprise. Three women had gathered near the bathroom entrance, smiling at him. One by one, they introduced themselves, complimenting him on how he'd handled the entire situation. Some even subtly asked if they could exchange numbers.

"Holy cow," Darius thought, "Apparently, I made quite the impression."

Chapter 71
Darius Reimagined

A s he sat back down in his seat, they were told to write a letter to their "old self." Darius took a moment to center himself, said a little prayer, and dove in. He decided to write it as a letter to himself from God.

"I love you, Darius. I want you to understand that I created you perfectly. Before you were born, I wrote about you in the Book of Life, the Book of the Lamb. I had plans for you, and I longed for you before I breathed life into you in your mother's womb. But then you entered a broken world, and things didn't go exactly as planned. You got lost, and that's okay. I was patient. I never left you.

Now you are awake. You are stepping into a place where you will eventually be fully awake, and you're beginning to understand your purpose. In the past year, you came to me, and I gave you eyes to see and ears to hear because you truly asked for it and sought me out.

I love you, Darius, and I made you perfect in my love. Everything special about you, your talents, your heart, your generosity, I gave you all of it. Life didn't always go as you expected, but that's part of your journey. You lost your way for a while, but now, by continuing to seek me, I will heal you.

You are becoming more aware, Darius. I gave you a mind for learning, a brain for understanding and connecting, and now you have a platform to share your charitable heart and touch others with the love I've placed inside you. You're ready to step into the person I always meant for you to be.

You're headed in the right direction now. You are a faithful, compassionate, courageous, and loyal man of God. I will open doors for you. I will lead you on a path of purpose and greatness so that you can influence others, give back, and bless those around you while giving me the glory.

I want you to grow and prosper, not just in business and charity but personally too. I want you to have influence as a connector, bringing charity, love, and blessings to my people. Through this process, you will become who I always meant for you to be.

Darius, you have all that you need. Be faithful, be strong, and trust in me. As you know, I keep all my promises, and you can rely on mine."

Darius felt a wave of peace wash over him as he finished reading what he wrote. With each exercise, he was starting to see the incredible potential that lay within him—and he was more than ready to step into the future that was unfolding before him.

As the next day stretched into the late hours, and with each new exercise, insight, and revelation, his head spun. While UPW was amazing, DWD was special and a level above.

It was almost 1:00 AM. By now, they had been working on their power virtues, mission statements, and away from values, and reflecting on the most important lessons they had learned. For the last hour, Darius had been with a group of three women, collaborating on some key components of their transformation. He was buzzing with excitement, feeling a renewed sense of purpose.

Some of the mantras and new rules he had written for himself were powerful, and he couldn't wait to implement them. He felt a deep conviction that implementing what he had learned at DWD and UPW, would help him continue to reprogram his mind and body. Meditation, breathing exercises, cold plunges—these practices were starting to feel like second nature. He wondered: Where would he be in six months?

He looked down at his "power virtues" list. He was genuinely excited about them. As part of the exercise, they shared their virtues with one another, and if the group wasn't convinced, you couldn't move forward. His list was as follows:

- I am faith and love.

- I am compassion, courage, and curiosity.

- I am gratefulness and playfulness.

He had written these down, worked through them, and felt more aligned with them than ever. The mission statement was even more powerful:

I, Darius, see, feel, hear, and know that the purpose of my life is to live at a high level of consciousness and use the gifts that God has given me to bless others and give unconditional love.

Along with his mantras from UPW:

"I am outstandingly worthy and blessed, and my future success is guaranteed and ordained by my Creator. Everyone who meets me and knows me loves me and wants to spend more time with me because of my high level of consciousness and incredible positive energy."

With his new set of rules, it felt like playing with house money in Vegas. Darius was determined to focus his efforts in ways that would ensure regular victories rather than beating himself up. The entire experience had been nothing short of amazing, and he couldn't help but feel a deep sense of gratitude. It had opened his eyes to something deeper than he ever thought possible. He had been living in a cave before, not fully aware of the world around him. How had he not learned about all this sooner?

Looking back over the last seven months, Darius felt an undeniable sense that everything had happened for a reason. Each step had led him here, to this moment, and it had been by design. It had all happened exactly the way it needed to happen—no sooner, no later.

As he reflected on the goals he had written, something remarkable had happened. He had met a publisher, a woman named Marjah, at UPW. She was hard to describe—formidable didn't seem quite right. She was tall, radiant, and her energy was captivating. Her smile lit up the room, and when you met her, you couldn't help but feel an undeniable spark.

Now after the events of the final day, Darius had set a goal to write a book. He wasn't sure how it would all come together, but he had a deep sense that there were multiple books inside him, waiting to be written. Over the past year, he had started presenting at conferences on talent management strategies. His sessions had been well received, and he had been asked to speak more. The idea of writing a book on the subject had been simmering in his mind, but doubts crept in. Was it driven by ego? Who would actually buy the book?

As he pondered the idea of writing, Darius realized that the concepts he discussed at these conferences were not only well received but often overlooked—despite their critical impact on the success of companies. He felt he was starting to develop a niche, focusing on why businesses succeeded or failed.

Startups faced harsh odds: most failed within a decade, with the medical field proving even more unforgiving. For Darius, the root cause was clear—poor leadership. Misaligned priorities, costly bad hires, and high turnover plagued companies, with top performers leaving due to lack of connection or growth opportunities.

The solution? Hire for culture. Darius knew companies succeeded when they aligned values, prioritized emotional intelligence, and fostered engagement. The result: better alignment, fewer wasted resources, and sustained profitability. But so few people actually understood this, so what if he could write something to help people not only understand it but implement it?

This realization hit Darius hard. As he looked at his goals for both business and charity, the idea of writing a book began to feel less like a fear and more like a calling. He knew there was a story to be told about leadership, talent, and the power of data in the modern business world. His message had the potential to resonate with leaders everywhere.

Determined, he sought out Marjah. He gently placed his hand on her shoulder and said, "Hey, I think I need to write this book."

She smiled warmly. "Let's connect after this to see if it makes sense," she said, giving him a hug. "I'm excited to be part of this journey."

What an incredible night, Darius thought, as the clock edged past 2:00 AM. The experience at DWD had been more than he could have ever imagined. His head was spinning, but this time it felt like it was spinning in the right direction. Since May, his world had been in chaos, but through all the pain and challenges, there was a new awareness. A new opportunity. He couldn't help but feel—no matter how tough things got—that the future would be brighter than he ever could have dreamed. And for that, he was deeply grateful.

***

Darius finished his work, cleaned up, and headed downstairs to the ballroom, where the after-event party was getting underway. He had moved from the rental house to the Marriott property to make it easier. The crowd was a mix of tuxedos, suits, and amazing dresses, and as he walked in, he decided to grab a glass of wine. He had not had any alcohol the entire event but decided he might have a glass or two in celebration of the amazing week.

Tamara came up in an incredible dress and gave him a hug. She looked stunning. His housemate James was there as well. They took pictures together and then moved around to socialize. He saw Amanda on the stage. The company hosting the after-party was sharing opportunities to invest in international properties and she was helping out. Darius made a mental note to make sure he said goodbye before leaving.

He made his way over to his new friend, Marcos, from Brazil. He was amazing! He had no limbs, was in a mobile wheelchair, and had gotten laws changed to drive a car across Brazil. They talked shop, Marcos introduced him to his son, and then he exclaimed, "Man, you have to come down to Brazil!"

"I'd love to," Darius smiled. "It's a country that is on my list to visit for sure."

Two others came over to talk to Marcos. Darius and Marcos took a quick picture together, and Marcos moved over to talk to the newcomers.

After dinner, great conversations with friends, and meeting some new friends, Darius was ready to call it a night as he had an early morning flight. He made his way into the main hallway and turned the corner. Next to his friend Chris was a taller man with brown hair. After a high-five with Chris, the other man introduced himself as Adam.

"Great to meet you. Have you been to DWD before?" Adam asked.

"No, this is my first. UPW was my first event in November. I really had no clue about the Tony Robbins' world," Darius confessed.

"I got involved a year ago," Adam said. "Isn't it amazing?"

"Phenomenal!" Darius said. "Like nothing I have ever experienced. What do you do?"

Adam's smile was big and contagious. "Brother, I have been on a journey! I now help companies set up charitable foundations."

Darius's eyebrows went up. "Really?"

Adam smiled. "Yeah."

Darius shared some of the charities that his company had been supporting, and that he had wanted to set up a charitable foundation for some time.

"What led you down this path?" Adam asked.

Darius smiled. "Well, I have always believed in God, but a long-time friend gave me a book called *You Can't Outgive God,* and it started me down this path. When I started the company, I told God I would give every time the company made money. I have a heart for charity and want to help grow it."

"That's awesome!" Adam exclaimed. "God showed me the truth this past year. I was saved and gave my life to Jesus."

"Wow! Praise God!" Darius smiled as they embraced with slaps on the back.

The conversation continued with the two men learning more about one another. Adam shared more about his journey and his mission, and in turn, Darius shared his personal and business situation.

Adam seemed surprised by the challenges and the divorce. "I am surprised. I don't see it."

"What do you mean?" Darius asked.

"You don't give off the energy of somebody going through those types of struggles," Adam replied.

"Well, I have been working on myself a lot, so I'll take that as a compliment," Darius said with a nod and a smile.

They exchanged contact information and promised to connect in the New Year, with Adam even promising to send a Platinum folder with several Dispenza meditations.

Darius headed to his room, not forgetting to say goodbye to Amanda, and packed for the early morning flight home. He shook his head with a smile, thinking of the many impactful contacts he had met in Florida and suspected some would end up being lifelong friends.

Chapter 72
The Book Whisperer

In his younger years, Darius had entertained the thought of being an author. At some point, though, he dismissed it as a fantasy. It struck him now as remarkable that this long-dismissed idea was reemerging, almost tangible. Meeting Marjah in the Tony Robbins circle had been, in a word, phenomenal. As Darius reflected on the past year of his life, he considered "stranger than fiction" an apt description.

Over a year ago, someone at a conference had told him he should be the one presenting at such events. His immediate reaction had been to dismiss the idea as absurd. Yet, after reflecting on the conversation and praying about it, he'd realized they might be right. Seven and a half months later, he gave his first presentation on talent management strategies in 2023. It was a culmination of more than eight years of experience and talent management on top of his corporate career, focused on why companies succeeded or failed and how to improve processes for greater efficiency.

The presentation went well. Since then, Darius had spoken at six more events, each emphasizing the significant costs of mishires and the high rates of annual voluntary turnover in companies—25% on average. The numbers were staggering: recruitment costs, HR oversight, time spent on interviews, onboarding, and training—all wasted when someone left prematurely.

From his data, the top reasons for voluntary turnover were clear: poor chemistry with immediate leaders, feeling unappreciated, doing work they didn't expect to be doing for a prolonged period of time, and believing the only way to advance was to leave. Companies often failed to align candidates' personal motivations with the company mission. Leadership often overlooked the importance of emotional intelligence and cultural fit during the hiring process.

Leadership IQ, another company in the field, had compelling data revealing that 89% of mis-hires weren't due to a lack of technical skills but rather to deficiencies in emotional intelligence, coachability, temperament, or poor motivation. Darius marveled at these figures. When candidates didn't mesh with a company's mission or were poorly matched to their roles, it spelled disaster—for morale, for productivity, and for financial outcomes.

His own company had achieved impressive results historically for their partners. Then, over the past few years, they had designed a process that was unique, efficient, and wowed everyone he shared it with, but the economy was a hindrance, and many weren't spending money currently. Yet, despite their success and unique process, with a challenging economy, Darius felt like they were the "best-kept secret" in the industry.

Scaling his company had been another defining decision. For Darius, growth wasn't just about profit—it was about increasing his impact, particularly in supporting charitable causes. He dreamed of founding his own charitable organization. Over time, he'd also started webinars and a podcast, further solidifying his role as an industry leader. In talking to Marjah while they were at DWD, she seemed to think his story might be worth telling. Darius wasn't so sure, but that's what they were meeting to discuss.

She said he had skills and knowledge that needed to be shared; a story that could help other people find his level of success—even if, right now, he didn't feel all that successful. So once Marjah had come into his life, he'd resolved to at least explore the idea further.

As they joined the video call, Marjah's face lit up, and her warmth was contagious.

"Hi, Darius!"

"Hi, Marjah!"

They exchanged small talk and caught up for a few moments before delving into the reason for their meeting—the book, her team, and the significance of embarking on this journey.

"Okay," she said, leaning forward. "Here's what I want you to do, dearest. Explain to me, what have you been presenting? Why is it important? What do you have to share?"

Darius took a deep breath and began. "Well, the history of the company is a big part of it. From the beginning, I've always been outcomes- and analytics-driven. I didn't really know much about the big picture in the first three or four years, I was just trying to survive. Trying to stay in business."

She nodded understandingly, and he continued.

"But over time, we've seen incredible results. Over nine years, we've achieved a 94% offer acceptance rate, 53% of candidates have been promoted within 24 months, and our retention rates are a third longer than the industry average."

He paused, reflecting. "In my third year, I was at a conference, and I met someone incredibly successful. They'd built over a million dollars in revenue every year for ten years straight. I shared our metrics, and he looked at me and said, 'You should be shouting that from the rooftops! That's remarkable!' At that moment, I realized just how unique our results were."

"That's incredible, Darius. And what did you take from that moment?"

"Honestly," Darius said, "It became clear to me that I needed to articulate our value proposition better. I've always worked hard, and integrity has been my foundation, but I wanted to create more consistent profits and bring greater value. I decided I wanted to scale the business, not just for myself but to make a greater impact on the industry and on charity, which is close to my heart."

He went on to describe the evolution of the company: the creation of webinars, launching a podcast, and implementing innovative strategies to enhance the candidate experience. "It's been about transforming recruitment, helping companies hire better, more efficiently, and creating positive experiences for candidates. I wanted to address inefficiencies, reduce wasted resources, and help companies find and keep the right talent."

Marjah listened intently, then asked, "That's all fantastic, but tell me, why does all of this truly matter to you?"

Darius hesitated.

"Close your eyes, Darius," she instructed. "Open your heart. Forget the analytics, speak from the heart. Why does this matter?"

He closed his eyes, took a deep breath, and, after a moment, began to speak. His words flowed with conviction. "I never thought I'd be doing this, not in a million years. But I love it. My corporate career showed me how much inefficiency and waste there was ... resources, time, even people's potential, all wasted. No one ever talked about mission or vision. That bothered me deeply."

He paused. "Running this business has given me a purpose. I want to help companies be more efficient and successful. I have always wanted to create a more positive candidate experience for the benefit of the companies. When companies hire the right people for culture, employee engagement goes up, waste goes down, their employees are happier, their products are better, and their families are better off. Everyone can thrive. If I can help with that, I can make a bigger impact on the world ... and on charity. That's what drives me."

Darius opened his eyes. Marjah was smiling warmly. "Wow, Darius," she said. "That was amazing. I felt that. Did you feel it?"

He nodded, his voice soft. "Yes. Every word."

"You have an incredible story, one that needs to be told," she said. "And this book, it's worth writing now, not later. Yes, you're facing challenges, but that makes your story even more compelling."

Darius hesitated. "But wouldn't it be better if I waited? Right now, the company's struggling. My personal life is a mess. We're not making money. Is anyone going to care about a book from someone in this position?"

Marjah shook her head. "Your story is about resilience, Darius. People need to hear that. And this book could help your company recover and thrive. It's not just about writing a book; it's about making an impact."

They discussed the details briefly, and Darius agreed to review her proposal.

As they ended the call, Marjah said, "I believe in you, Darius. Your story matters."

After the call, Darius sat back, staring at the company's mission statement printed on his mouse pad. A smile slowly spread across his face. Marjah's perspective and confidence were exciting. He just wasn't sure if this was the right time with all the challenges. He needed to pray about it, but he was pleasantly surprised and intrigued.

Chapter 73
A Growing Chasm

The situation with Darius's mother had continued to be complicated, to say the least. Ever since he set the boundary with her in the summer, their contact had been minimal, if any. He had invited her over to celebrate Christmas with his children, but she had gotten sick and couldn't come. He did make the trip to bring her some food and wish her a Happy Holiday, but their conversation was limited and he didn't stay long.

There was something unsettling about being in her house. It wasn't just the physical space—it was everything around him. His perception had shifted. So much of his life had been focused on the five senses, the physical world, and his mind, but now, his understanding of spirituality, energy, and realms beyond the material was deepening.

Darius had been reading Hawkins' and Joe Dispenza's work, which spoke about how matter interacts with matter and how there's so much more beyond the physical world than meets the eye. It was as if God had been handing him small crumbs of insight, leading him down a path of awakening. He was beginning to see that, if he was faithful and did the work, God would continue to reveal more, expanding his understanding piece by piece. It was remarkable how much his perception had changed just in the last year.

Tony Robbins had spoken about moving from the mind to the heart, and Darius had found himself reflecting on that more and more. It made sense now, in a way it never had before. He was more attuned to where his awareness and consciousness sat, but what fascinated him was the energy he was putting out—and how it interacted with the energy of others. He noticed the differences everywhere.

At home, the air in the basement, like the entire house, felt heavy, suffocating, almost like a tomb. But when he went to his office, it felt like the opposite—light, free, and peaceful. Strangely, his mother's house felt the same as his basement. It was a familiar, uncomfortable energy that he could sense the moment he entered, and this energy lingered whenever he visited.

When he saw his mother, he gave her a hug and a kiss. She greeted him from her chair, watching TV and snacking on grapes. She spoke to him, about the same topics—his sister, her brother, or the show she was watching. Darius listened respectfully, but inside, he couldn't help but reflect on how bizarre her behavior seemed now, given everything he was learning.

Her tendency to monologue was something he had always found interesting. She spoke about God and aspects of faith, but there was a disconnect. It had often felt like she was speaking at him rather than to him. It was almost as if she was putting herself on a soapbox, offering advice and direction while delivering her judgment.

As he went deeper into David Hawkins' work, studying levels of consciousness and emotional trauma, he understood more about his mother's behavior. He was gaining understanding while he considered the results of his emotional trauma therapy sessions, the deeper truths in the Bible, the demonic, and levels of consciousness. It gave him empathy for her, as he realized how difficult her own childhood must have been and how much fear, guilt, and shame had shaped her.

From a Biblical standpoint, Darius was also seeing things differently as he continued his commitment to read all the books in a year. The more he read, the more he saw how much religion had been twisted by human hands, manipulated for power and control. Hawkins showed how man took higher-level works and then diluted them for selfish reasons via force. The Bible stated in multiple places that Satan was the ruler of this world, the demonic were everywhere, and the Earth was God's footstool. His discovery of the poisonous chemicals in food since the 70's, the growth of big pharma, added to the mess of Hollywood and their politicians, was eye opening. Satan did seem to be the ruler of this world based on the data. Darius was starting to wonder, was he in the churches as much as he seemed to be in everything else?

His relationship with the Bible, with religion, and with God was evolving. He was finding truth in places he had never expected and was learning that the majority of people, including his mother, seemed to pick and choose the parts they liked, dismissing or ignoring what didn't fit with their beliefs versus what the Word said.

He had once shared something he had read about the apostle Paul, and his mother remarked that she didn't care for Paul. She didn't like him. Darius found the perspective odd. Who on earth would criticize an apostle of Christ? Was it an incredible lack of awareness, an incredible amount of pride, or both?

At that point, there was little left to discuss. He felt no support from her and a growing sense of alienation. His mother seemed more interested in the bond she had with his wife than him. She had said numerous unkind things to his face, and to his children, and he didn't trust her. During the summer, his wife had shared information in her second "hate email" that she could only have gotten from his mother, which was also totally out of context.

One day, after a visit, he had gotten up to leave and gave his mother a hug and a kiss on her forehead and told her that he loved her. She replied, "I love you, and you're welcome here anytime." But after leaving, as he was driving back to the house, he got a text from his mother:

OK, the door is unlocked. Darius has left. Do you want to do tomorrow since there is no light?

That was weird.

The next day, he received another text from his mother as she must have realized she'd texted the wrong person:

Jessica is coming over to fix my Christmas present. I did not think you would want to be here together.

You're welcome here anytime, Darius. So very sorry for all the sad things going on. God loves us all. Mom.

"What in the world?" Darius thought, shaking his head. "Didn't think we'd want to be there together? It was like his mother had zero awareness. It was as if she wasn't even really his mother," Darius thought.

He got another text a few minutes later:

We all love God and he loves us. We'll get through this. Love, Mom.

Darius didn't respond. He didn't even know *how* to respond. He prayed for his mother every day. He'd worked through the emotional trauma therapy to release any negative emotions toward her, prayed for her daily, had cut soul ties, and was working hard to hold no grudges against her. He forgave her and didn't feel any anger toward her. He didn't feel like he had any unforgiveness toward her but her actions made it hard to be sure.

The next day, he got another text from her:

Are you going to Ben's game this Friday and Saturday?

As Darius was headed to Canada for the Tony Robbins Wealth Mastery event, he responded:

I will not be there.

Thank you! It is stressful when we don't sit together. I did not know if you would want to sit together with Jessica's parents. I could sit with you if you were going.

Darius thought about that again, thinking of how absurd the whole thing was. The whole thing was incredibly awkward. His mother chose to align with his soon-to-be-ex-wife rather than with her son.

The older two kids, who had suspected an affair since the summer, didn't want anything to do with Jessica. Darius had encouraged them to support her, love her, and give her grace. They didn't know about the affair for sure at that point, but after the truth of the relationship came out in the fall, there was really nothing else for Darius to do in that area. He didn't comment on any of it to his children. When they complained about it, his response was:

"God is all about Grace. Jesus died on the cross for all of our sins. You will have to decide what relationship you will have, but I wouldn't want you to not have a relationship due to me."

At this point, even if he could make it to the game, there was no way Darius was going to be sitting with his mother, his wife, and her girlfriend at his son's basketball game. Darius couldn't quite decide whether that was the right or wrong thing to do. There was a part of him that wanted to be able to sit around them, to be at such a high level of consciousness that it really just didn't matter, but ... he wasn't at that level now.

Darius finally responded:

There are too many unkind things being done, including Jessica going after full custody of our son. Since she has been in a relationship with Ash, I will not be sitting by them at any games. I'm at a conference this weekend.

Why do you think they're in a relationship? I think they are just friends.

Why does divorce have to be so ugly? What conference are you going to?

It was a barrage of questions, with only the last one directing any kind of interest toward him. He couldn't believe how unsupportive she was. He sat there looking at the phone and shook his head. How could she not see what was right in front of her?

Then he got another text:

I love you, Darius, because I carried you and raised you the best we could. You are our son. I love Jessica because you loved her. She is the mother of my grandchildren and has always been good to me. I read my Bible and try to follow it. Try to leave judging to God.

Once again, Darius just shook his head. He thought about it and just decided not to respond. He needed to pray about it. He definitely didn't want to be reactionary as he continued to work on changing.

But the next day, as Darius headed to the conference, he got another text from her that she'd been wrong about the date of the game. He thought about the situation more and decided that he needed to respond.

I'd prefer you not respond to this. What you've said doesn't come across as supportive or kind. When I told you that Jessica and Ash were in a relationship, I wasn't speculating or guessing, I was stating a fact. She's been having an affair, and they've been together for some time. It's been confirmed in multiple ways, and she's even admitted it to our children that she is with her. So when you said, "you don't think," it felt disrespectful and unsupportive, even if you don't realize that.

What's even harder to take is how she's tied up my company assets, assets that I worked so hard to build, assets that the company created, which could help the business during this difficult time. You told me you didn't understand what that meant, and then you went on about how she and I used to love each other, how sad it is, and how glad you are that you and Dad worked through your issues in the past. That wasn't helpful. It wasn't nice. Because despite everything, I still do love her. I wasn't unfaithful, and I didn't give up on our marriage. Divorce isn't the problem. The problem is when people are unkind during divorce.

You can have whatever relationship with her you want, and I've never told you not to. But most of your communication with me lately seems to be more about your feelings than about supporting me. I get that you might not understand what I'm going through, but Jessica has been unkind and, at times, downright hateful toward me during this whole process. I'm doing my best to take the high road and show her grace, even when it's hard.

The lawyer she hired has a reputation, and from where I'm standing, it seems like she's trying to hurt me financially. She's been dishonest and manipulative about many things: going for full custody of our 15-year-old son for more child support money, expecting the house, trying to control everything. It was surprising. But I'll let my lawyer handle it. I'm continuing to work on myself, letting go, and giving it all to God. I don't want to fight any more than I absolutely have to. I just want to move on with my life and let God lead me through this.

Enjoy your weekend.

Her response:

Darius, I always want what's best for you. I mean no disrespect. Just because we do not see things the same way does not mean I disrespect you. That surprises me about their relationship. I can give you money if that will help.

The response Darius got was not surprising to him. His mother had no ability to validate, apologize, to hear. Darius had nothing nice to say or think and didn't respond. I don't want your money, he thought. He would continue to honor her as his mother but he had no interest in being around her.

Dealing with the guilt of the realizations of the past had been extremely difficult for him over the last year. It's why David Hawkins' work had been so beneficial for him. Understanding that letting go of shame, guilt, and judgment was essential. "You did the best you could with what you had." Who ever trained you to deal with these things?

He hadn't been taught or learned how to navigate his feelings, and therefore, unfortunately, he hadn't done a good job of teaching his children either. So many things he wished he'd understood, especially when it came to supporting his daughter during her challenges. He thought about his youngest son and how the dysfunction in his relationship with his wife had impacted him. Neither of them had taught him how to communicate well, and Darius, certainly, hadn't been a good role model for managing emotions in a healthy fashion. He knew his wife's catering to Ben was a disservice to him but, in this new light, he was also realizing how unhealthy certain aspects of Ben and Jessica's relationship were.

He'd done the best he could, was working to continue releasing guilt while working to grow. He'd admitted his mistakes countless times, swallowing a lot of his pride. He smiled, grateful for the opportunity to change. Darius wanted to keep growing while giving grace and working not to judge. He refused to behave like a victim.

Chapter 74
More Emotional Mysteries

Darius stepped into the building, climbed the stairs, turned the corner, and saw Larissa's door, closed tight. The cold February air nipped at his skin, but he was excited to see her. He hadn't had an appointment with her since last year, but now, it felt like it was time. This was his ninth session. So much had changed since that first meeting. He thought of Larissa as family, someone he would do anything for. He would never forget how she had opened his eyes to evil and new truths and how deeply her help had impacted him and his family.

Over the past few weeks, a persistent pain had settled in his right arm, a dull ache that defied explanation, and he couldn't sleep on his right side. It hurt near his kidney. It made no sense, but it seemed like the perfect reason to schedule another appointment. The door creaked open, and a woman stepped out, nodding to him as she passed.

"Hey there, stranger," Larissa said, a smile spreading across her face. He walked in, and they embraced. "It's good to see you."

"It's good to see you too," Darius replied as he settled onto her couch.

"How are things going?" she asked.

Darius let out a small, resigned laugh. "Well, it's still in a holding pattern. No progress on the divorce."

"At all?" she asked, concern flickering in her eyes.

"No, it's just back and forth on the assets. It's not a great division of the pie," he said, forcing a smile.

"What do you mean?" she asked, tilting her head.

"Well, the initial pass was 65% her, 35% me, based on the spreadsheet. So, we're still going back and forth, and nothing is moving fast. And on top of that, the tax money is looming over everything," he said.

"Oh my gosh, Darius," Larissa said softly.

"Yeah, I don't get it. I can't understand why she won't let me pay off the taxes. It's like she thinks she gets to take advantage of any plus on the spreadsheet, but if it's a negative, it's all on me. I've tried explaining that the government will come after both of us, but there's no reasoning with her," he said, shaking his head.

"I'm sorry," Larissa said. "How's your business holding up?"

"Not well. I'm about to lose my last employee, and I'm still not making any money. I never imagined we still wouldn't be making money at this point. I don't get it, but I keep working, holding on to faith that things will turn around," Darius said, a note of exhaustion in his voice.

"How are the kids?" she asked.

Darius sighed, rubbing his temples. "Well, since the affair came out and she's in this relationship ... the two older kids won't have anything to do with her. They're angry about the whole situation and the deceit. My youngest, though ... I'm not sure what's going on."

"What do you mean?" Larissa asked, her brow furrowing.

"I mean, since we got back from Christmas, he won't talk to me. I've asked him what's wrong, if he's mad at me, but he says that nothing's wrong. He says he's not mad, but he won't tell me anything. It's just strange," Darius said. "She controls everything regarding his schedule. I mean, he's got people with him at all times. He's either going someplace or has people at the house. I hoped I'd be able to cook for him, guide him down the same path of self-healing I've walked, and help him get off the medications he's on for ADHD. I thought we'd do the same things we did in North Carolina: workouts, breathing exercises, Scripture. I can't even imagine how much those meditations would have helped him. But now ... Now he won't even look at me."

Larissa's expression softened as she listened. "I'm so sorry, Darius."

"What about Jessica?" she asked.

Darius looked at the ceiling. "Honestly, I thought that being around her, interacting in the house, she'd see how much I've changed, all the work I've done. We'd start having positive interactions. She's still making herself scarce, ever since the relationship came out last year. I assume she's at her girlfriend's place, but I really don't know. There's no communication. David Hawkins talks about the three unhealthy ways people deal with problems, and one of them is projection. People project their own issues onto others. Jessica's done a lot of that. Being down in that basement is like being in a tomb. I'm in my own house, but I get no respect and have no authority. She doesn't tell me anything while projecting her own behaviors on me."

Larissa nodded, her expression troubled. "That's not good. I don't know how you're managing. That sounds awful."

Darius let out a heavy sigh. "It is. Being down there, hearing every sound ... It's like living in a constant state of tension. I'm not saying they're doing it on purpose, but it's just so disrespectful. It's bizarre. Every day, it feels like I'm living in the Twilight Zone. Plus, I can feel the spiritual oppression."

"I'm sorry," Larissa said, her voice soft but firm. "Just keep praying and pushing forward. This won't last forever."

"I know," Darius said, though the words felt hollow.

"What about you, though? How have you been?"

He leaned back. "Well, on one hand, I'm doing really well. I started doing Dr. Joe's meditations in December, and I feel like I've gained so much from those meditations—what I call 'active' meditations," Darius said, his eyes lighting up. "I now call what I was doing at first passive meditation. When I started, it was just sitting still, clearing my mind, praying that God would speak to me in any way He wanted, whether it was through dreams, visions, music, or just thoughts. Just working to be still."

Larissa nodded. "That makes sense."

"But with active meditation, you take a more intentional approach. You engage in a thought process that rewires your brain, gets into the subconscious and helps you reprogram unhealthy behaviors, thought patterns, that sort of thing while also manifesting positives," Darius said.

Larissa's eyes grew wide with interest. "That's absolutely fascinating."

Darius smiled. "This self-healing journey ... You got me started with Dr. Whitman, the lip, getting off the medications, healing my eyes from needing reading glasses. Then these meditations in November, just following his YouTube channel. And then, at DWD, I met Adam, this incredible guy who helps companies start charitable foundations, who gave me more Dr. Joe meditations. He's even going to help me with mine."

He took a deep breath before continuing. "I don't know how to explain it, but even with everything falling apart, and all these unkind things being done ... I am not thinking about it! I am happy most of the time. The meditations along with *Letting Go* have been game changers."

Larissa shook her head, a slight smile playing on her lips. "I don't know, Darius. I can't keep up with you. It's one book after another, one thing after another. I'm always excited to hear what you're doing and how God is moving in your life, but you're ... Well, you're progressive. Let's put it that way."

They both laughed.

Darius ran a hand through his hair, his smile fading. "The point is, on the surface, everything's a mess. The business, all the money it's created, none of it is available to me because it's tied up as marital assets. The divorce needs to finalize, or I have to start making money. Something has to change, or bankruptcy is my only option."

"I'm sorry," she said again.

"I know," Darius said, a bitter chuckle escaping him. "But here's the thing. Even with all of this ... I'm not focused on it. The meditations have helped so much. That's why I'm doubling down. I just ordered *Becoming Supernatural,* and I'm planning to go to a conference in June."

"Wow, that's amazing," Larissa said, her face lighting up with genuine admiration. Then she looked at the time, realizing how long they'd been catching up. "Alright, we'd better get moving. What do you want to focus on today? Why are you here?"

Darius looked down, a flicker of unease crossing his features. "I don't know what's going on with my right arm. It's been hurting for weeks, from my wrist up to my elbow. It feels like there's pressure all over it. And then there's pain on the right side, near my kidney. I can't sleep on that side, but I don't really know what it could be."

"Okay," Larissa said, her brow furrowing as she considered it. "Let's start with prayer."

She prayed for Darius and the session, asking for guidance and clarity. Then, with a deep breath, she said, "Let's focus on emotional release first to see if that is what's causing the arm issue and side pain. That right side ... It could be related to your adrenals, so that could be something Dr. Whitman can maybe help you with. It might also be something emotional, but we will see.

She started muscle testing and then stopped, saying, "I am pulling up a lot of challenging emotions from the age of 8."

Darius's jaw clenched, and he nodded. "That was when I was molested the second time."

"I know," Larissa said softly. "I want to do heart walls around it and focus on releasing emotions 24 hours before it happened and 24 hours after. We can focus on taking out the shame, guilt, and trauma around that time." Larissa paused, but then continued, "The energy from the person and the demonic influencing them who harmed you leaves a mark. The demonic influences involved plant seeds that can linger."

"Alright," Darius said, settling back.

After she finished the muscle testing process, she asked Darius to move to the chair to start the process of releasing the emotions. She tapped the top of his head and began, moving the magnet up and down his spine, guiding him through deep breaths and reciting the familiar incantations.

I release these energies to God, and I don't have to hang on to them any longer.

1. *Failure, helplessness, hopelessness, lack of control, low self-esteem*
2. *Anger, bitter, guilt, hatred, resentment*
3. *Shame*
4. *Disgust*
5. *Humiliation, lust (absorbed)*
6. *Love unreturned*
7. *Fear, bad memory, shame, tainted, penance*

8. *Sexual aggression*
9. *Dissociate*
10. Insecure

When she finished, Darius stood and returned to the couch, exhaustion weighing on him. Larissa continued to frown; her eyes focused intently on him.

"What's going on?" he asked, curiosity in his voice.

Larissa's face softened into a smile. "How's your arm feeling now?"

Darius shifted, flexing his fingers. "Not much different. It still hurts."

"That's what's confusing," she said. "There's something spiritual going on here."

"Spiritual?" he asked.

"Yes. I don't know if it's a curse or ... witchcraft, perhaps."

Darius looked at her, a mix of confusion and anger in his eyes. "Witchcraft?"

"I don't know, Darius," she said, her eyes narrowing with concern. "Honestly, it's above my pay grade. We're going to have to contact Karl."

"Karl?" Darius echoed. "Who's Karl?"

A small smile crossed Larissa's face. "Karl is a friend and a bit of a mentor to me. How should I put this? His calling is to serve God and engage in spiritual warfare at the highest level. When I come across something I can't fully grasp or have never encountered before, I reach out to him."

Darius's eyes widened slightly. "Okay. So, you'll call him?"

"Yes," she said. "I'll make sure he connects with you."

Darius let out a breath. "Witchcraft and curses," he mumbled. "This is going to be interesting. I don't get it, though. I pray over my house every day, and I've staked it out."

Larissa's eyes softened as she met his gaze. "There's so much more to learn and understand about the spiritual realm, Darius. The demonic presence in the house—"

"You can't control what your wife is willingly bringing into the house." Larissa's voice dropped, the weight of her words settling in the air.

Darius frowned, trying to process her words. "Okay, I get that. But I don't see how that changes anything. I can't do anything about her choices, but the rest of the house should be fine, right?"

Larissa hesitated before responding, her eyes still locked on his. "The thing is, the demonic presence isn't there for her. It's there for you, Darius."

"For me?" He looked at her with a serious gaze.

"Yes," she said quietly. "I can't fully explain it, and maybe Karl can shed some light on what's happening with your arm, but whatever this is, it wants to destroy you."

Darius stared at her, the gravity of her words sinking in. "Destroy me?" He questioned, the words lingering. "I don't understand."

She exhaled slowly. "You're going to be okay, and Karl should be able to help. Hopefully, Dr. Whitman will have answers for what's going on with your adrenals, too. When you came in today, your stress level was at a ten. After this, it's at a one. That's progress. So, let's see what Karl says."

After they said goodbye, Darius shook his head as he started up his car. Witchcraft, sorcery, and divination were all in the Bible, just like the demonic, though not as prominently. He was just starting to learn about it.

Twilight Zone, he thought. What's next?

Life was definitely not boring.

Chapter 75
Listen to Your Body

D r. Whitman pulled up his most recent results. It had been over a month or two since his last visit, and so much had happened between then and now. Darius had gone to Nashville and met with Steve Hemphill and attended two Tony Robbins events. He had gone deeper into his meditations and felt a transformation physically, mentally, emotionally, and spiritually. And as Dr. Whitman started going through his file, he could see evidence of his work right there on the screen.

SUBJECTIVE :

Chief Complaint : hip pain
Status : remained unchanged
Discomfort/Pain Intensity / Severity : 1
Timing / Frequency : Intermittent
Problem side : Bilateral

Chief Complaint : low back pain
Status : improved
Discomfort/Pain Intensity / Severity : 2
Timing / Frequency : Intermittent
Problem side : Bilateral

Notes: The patient updated the changes in their chief complaint(s) as noted above. Patient is here for their nutritional re-examination. They will also be adjusted. Doing better. Right forearm still some sore. Left shoulder pain at times, from working out. Lower back is a lot better.

Pre-existing conditions :
High Blood pressure , High cholesterol , Joint/back pain

OBJECTIVE FINDINGS :
A pre-manipulation P.A.R.T. assessment was performed in the area(s) of chief complaint. Further biomechanical evaluation revealed the presence of additional misaligned segments that are contributing postural imbalance and affecting the chief complaint. The findings are listed in the above P.A.R.T. exam. It was necessary to manipulate the subluxated segments as they are complicating factors. • The patient has had pain for more than eight days: according to the Mercy Guidelines, recovery may take 1.5 times longer. • This case is classified as chronic; lasting more than 16 weeks. According to the Mercy Guidelines, patients with chronic disorders may require more treatment/care to resolve symptomatic episodes.

Patient has no pelvic pattern.
Patient has anatomical short leg.
Fixated right hip.

Nutrition: Rescanned by Dr. Whitman
Color: B/G
PEP - Heart, CV19, Lung
PPP - Prostate
Immune: parasite 4
Metals: Arsenic, lead, iron, mercury, cadmium
Chemicals: Pesticides, plastics, hydrocarbons

"You've reached a significant point now, Darius," he said, his eyes steady. "Your inflammatory index is down to one. And do you know what that means?"

Darius shrugged and smiled. He had been in the program for almost 5 months. First, they had fixed his cortisol levels, leading to good sleep, and next, his leaky gut. It had been a remarkable journey as they had next aligned his pelvic area and legs, removing pain from his left hip that had existed for over 30 years. He had made great progress, but some new issues were strangely flaring up.

"It means the primary stressor affecting you now isn't physical. It's emotional," Dr. Whitman continued, his voice calm but firm. "Stress, emotional stress, has become the biggest pump of inflammation in your body. Unfortunately, the problem with your side and your shoulder isn't physical but emotional."

"Emotional!?" Darius complained with disgust.

"It's not unusual," Dr. Whitman added, "For patients to hit a point in their treatment where they plateau. They'll say, 'I'm better, but why do I keep falling back? Why does this keep coming up?' Nine times out of ten, it's tied to an emotional or spiritual component. Something unresolved, something buried deep, triggering their inflammatory response. I'd say 95, maybe 96% of these responses are subconscious. Old programs imprinted in our systems that we don't even realize are running. Until they surface."

"I've learned this the hard way myself, Darius," Dr. Whitman said, his tone softening. "For the longest time, I'd never had trouble sleeping. But then I hit a patch of mild stress and anxiety. Suddenly, I couldn't sleep. So, I had to take a step back and ask myself what was going on. And you know what it was?"

"What?"

"I couldn't accept that I was sick. That fear, fear of not being in control, crept in, and it fed the anxiety. It became this endless loop. Fear translated into anxiety. Anxiety robbed my rest. And it all spiraled from there."

Darius leaned forward, contemplative. "And that fear was pulling energy away from your body, energy it could've been using to heal."

Dr. Whitman nodded. "Exactly. You've nailed it. Fear, anger, resentment, they're thieves. They rob the body of resources, energy, and focus. Once you see it for what it is, you can start breaking the cycle. But first, you've got to see it."

Darius exhaled sharply, the truth of the statement hitting its mark. "Yeah," he admitted, running a hand over his face. "I mean, it makes sense. The divorce, business issues ... all of that, it's been a lot to handle." He slowly shook his head, thinking, Sorry, son, you aren't injured, you're just an emotional basket case. Darius leaned back in the chair and thought about the work he had done with

Larissa, with well over 150 emotions taken out of his body since last summer as well as the demonic chord.

Dr. Whitman nodded, his expression unyielding. "It's a lot, no doubt. But still, you've got to address it anyway. There's no sidestepping this one."

Darius nodded back. "Yeah, for sure."

Dr. Whitman didn't let the silence linger for long. "Usually, the way we approach something like this is with a structured program. Once a week for six weeks, during that time, we run tests, refine the protocols, and assess your progress. Then after six weeks, we do a full rescan and we look at what's improved, what hasn't. For you, for instance, it took two full cycles to get that leaky gut repaired. Remember that?"

Darius nodded.

"We will get you on a new regimen and then rescan as needed until we get it fixed."And just like then, once we've got the baseline results, we adapt. Every other week for twelve weeks after that, with regular rescans." Dr. Whitman tapped the side of his desk lightly, as though marking the rhythm of the plan. "It's all about peeling back the layers, one at a time."

"The layers?" Darius echoed, frowning slightly.

Dr. Whitman smiled. "Each improvement in your inflammatory index lets the body shift its focus, to cool down one chapter, and move on to the next. And what we find, what we always find, is that the body knows what's most important to address for survival. The stressor that shows up next? That's what we deal with. No skipping ahead. No rushing. Just step by step, layer by layer."

Scrolling through Darius's files, Dr. Whitman pulled up his other files.

"Back in August," he started, "Under nutrition, it listed: color BG, P, EP," Whitman continued, scanning the document. "No PPP at the time. It said small intestine: six; foods: eight; immune: three;

metals: seven; chemicals: two. Now remember," he added, looking up briefly, "The higher the number, the bigger the problem. As we work, those numbers come down, but only when the body is ready to start the repair and healing process."

Darius nodded.

"The range is usually one to ten," Dr. Whitman went on. "That's where we start, where the body's inflammatory response is at its highest. Over time, with the right protocols, those numbers drop, and the body shifts into repair and healing mode. That's always the goal in the first six weeks."

"So you got me into repair and healing after those first six weeks when I came back to you in October?" Darius asked.

"Exactly," Whitman replied, flipping to another section of the file. "October 17th. That's when your system first shifted. From there, I ran another full assessment. It showed progress, with some areas clearing up, and others still needing attention. Let me see ... Here it is: small intestines were at a nine, immune system at an eight, metals still high, particularly arsenic, lead, mercury, and aluminum."

Darius frowned. "I remember aluminum being a problem," he said. "It was strange, though, things were improving, then suddenly the metals spiked again. You explained it had something to do with the body releasing stored toxins during healing."

Dr. Whitman nodded. "That's right. It's what we call a healing release. When the body finally reaches a point of efficiency, it starts clearing out the stealth burdens, metals, toxins, even dormant infections. The immune system identifies them, releases them into the system for elimination, and you see a temporary spike in those markers. It's a good thing, even if it looks worse on paper. It means the body is doing its job."

"Stealth," Darius repeated.

"We use that term a lot," Dr. Whitman said. "It's becoming more common in the medical field too. Stealth organisms, bacteria, viruses, and even metals are things that hide in the body. Take shingles, for instance. That's a stealth virus. The immune system suppresses it, but it never really goes away. It hunkers down, and when the system weakens, it flares up again."

Darius nodded.

"It's the same with toxins and metals," Dr. Whitman explained. "They linger in the tissues, hiding from detection until the body is strong enough to expel them. That's what happened in your case. Once your immune system improved, it started flushing out those hidden burdens. That's why you saw those spikes before the numbers came back down."

"That makes sense," Darius muttered, pondering over his most recent file. There were a lot of things *"resolved,"* but, like Dr. Whitman said, they had discovered new things, new layers that needed to be addressed.

He must have slumped slightly in his chair, or perhaps his expression turned, as when he sat back in his chair, Dr. Whitman was grinning.

"Darius, you have to remember, this is a process. It will take time. Let me tell you, son, you are doing great!" He said, patting him on the shoulder.

"I know."

Dr. Whitman nodded. "It wasn't something I fully understood years ago. I had cases where people weren't responding, and I couldn't figure out why. When I went back and re-checked, I found those stealth elements showing up. I hadn't cleared them completely. That's when I realized I needed better methods. For example, now, we use the lymphatic system to help move those toxins out. Certain supplements are key for targeting those stubborn areas and supporting the lymphatic process."

"It's not going to be like this forever," he reassured, his voice steady., though there was still a hint of uncertainty. "This divorce will pass and your body is going to have healed all these past issues. You've got to clean out all the stuff that's caused your body to be out of balance. And once it's all cleaned up, then you can start living again."

Darius nodded.

"Even since October, you've made huge improvements. Every area of your mind and body is in healing."

Darius ran a hand through his hair, exhaling slowly. "I can feel it," he admitted. "I know I'm not where I need to be, but I feel like I'm getting there."

"Just can't fall into those old habits," Dr. Whitman repeated. "The body's resilient, but it also remembers. Once you've healed it, you've got to maintain it, but look at your pelvic efficiency! It was in alignment for the first time in November, and your results show it's still in place. You're past the point now where we're dealing with pelvic inefficiency. When we checked your test results, you've corrected all of that."

Darius grumbled. "I understand I am dealing with a lot of stress. But I am eating well, meditating, in Scripture, I am not on drugs or drunk in a bar, I don't know what else to do to keep going, to keep improving."

Dr. Whitman leaned back in his chair, his fingers drumming lightly on the surface. "You will get through this. Most people don't realize just how deeply emotions and chemical imbalances affect the body. It's not just physical stress, it's emotional stress, too. You'll get arm pain, for instance, and 9 times out of 10, I'll go back and recheck you and find that it's tied to stress. It's just how it shows up. I wish I could explain why it shows up differently in people, but I can't. Some people experience chronic digestive issues under stress. Others, like you, feel it in the muscles, fatigue, tension, pain. It's a cycle that doesn't break easily."

Darius shifted in his seat, feeling the weight of the truth in those words.

"Just remember," Dr. Whitman added, leaning forward a little, "As you continue to heal, listen to what your body tells you. You can't ignore the signals, not if you want to stay ahead of the game. It's a constant process. But you're doing well. Don't lose sight of that."

"Thank you, my friend," Darius said, getting up from his seat.

Dr. Whitman rose also, a thought clearly marked on the expression on his face. He moved around his desk, and as he led Darius to the door, he asked, "How's your son?"

Darius stopped. "What? Ben?"

"I remember us talking about him before. I was just curious how he was doing."

Darius shook his head, stepping a little further back into the room. "Honestly, I don't really know. He doesn't speak to me much anymore. After talking to you in the Fall, I copied twenty pages out of the book and shared it with him and my wife, hoping I could bring him. If I could bring him here to start the process himself, I think it would be incredible. It's done so much for me; it could do so much more for him. My wife and son ignored it, unfortunately."

"You know," Dr. Whitman began, "It's been over 20 years now. I was a partner in a nursing home for a while, and I had this employee, an LPN. She worked hard, took pride in her job, but her life wasn't easy. Her sister was a drug addict, and that led to a lot of trouble. The sister's child, her nephew, had his own set of problems, problems that piled up and seemed impossible to manage."

"What happened to him?" Darius asked.

"He was a handful," Dr. Whitman admitted. "I remember hearing that at school, he was stabbing other children with pencils. It was ... it was bad. But she didn't give up. She insisted on bringing him to me. I don't know if it was hope or desperation, but she had heard something about me, and she thought maybe, just maybe, I could help. So she brought him in. Long story short, we worked through some things, and, well, I get a Christmas card from him and his family every year, without fail, all because—"

"Because you changed his life," Darius interjected, almost reverently.

Dr. Whitman shook his head, a slight smile touching his lips. "No, he changed his life."

Darius blinked. "So, let me put it another way. God gave him a wonderful opportunity through you. And through the work you do, God gave him awareness, a pathway to change everything."

Dr. Whitman's expression softened even further, as though the memory of that young boy, and so many others like him, were both bittersweet and empowering. "I have a bucket full of stories like that. I've been blessed, truly blessed. And when I hear about cases like your son's, I see the potential he could have, if he didn't have all these issues weighing him down."

Darius felt a lump rise in his throat. In Dr. Whitman's words, he found hope—the potential for change, for transformation, that felt just out of reach but not impossible.

"I have complete confidence that you could help him," Darius said, his voice steady, though his heart swelled with emotion. "I know you could help him turn his life around, take everything that's upside down, and make it incredible."

Dr. Whitman gave him a long, thoughtful look. There was no promise in his gaze, but there was understanding. "Perhaps one day that door will open for him. But it's not for me to decide. I'm just here to offer the path."

As they parted, Darius contemplated all the doors that had opened in his own life, and the doors he still hoped to open for his son. Maybe, just maybe, his son could benefit from this path one day.

Chapter 76
God has a Rowdy

D arius' thoughts churned his mind into a storm of reflection and realization. Sometimes, it was dizzying, this unraveling of everything that had been his life over the past year after his wife told him their marriage was over. Just last spring, when this whirlwind had begun, his wife had so casually dropped the bombshell: their marriage was over. No lengthy explanation, no attempt at counseling—just a few curt sentences, a door shut, a holiday over.

Now, understanding her involvement with this woman even before the separation, certain behaviors began to click into place. Her actions, her treatment of him—it all made a twisted kind of sense. He even looked at the summer "hate mail" differently now. It was all more about her than him; she had to make him as big of a monster as possible to justify her dramatic new lesbian lifestyle. Yet, despite the clarity, there had been countless moments when he'd questioned his own sanity. The strange, supernatural occurrences, the oppressive weight of the demonic—it was enough to make anyone doubt themselves.

Through it all, though, he found himself grateful for the newfound wisdom, insights, and higher awareness, even in considering the pain, to arrive here. Ever since his eyes were opened and his ears attuned to the divine, he had pursued God relentlessly, seeking knowledge, understanding, and truth.

He was close to finishing the entire Bible in a year, well ahead of August, which had seemed daunting when he had made the commitment—a feat he'd once thought impossible. Additionally, over seventy books devoured, each a breadcrumb on the path God seemed to be laying out for him. Darius felt that the more faithful he was, the more God revealed. Connections clicked into place, revelations about Scripture that made little sense to Darius and had once seemed impenetrable.

But the journey wasn't without its weight. Moving back into the house had been a test of endurance, not the redemption story he'd envisioned. Even knowing his wife's infidelity and her embrace of a lifestyle he hadn't foreseen, he had held onto hope for their family.

Remarkably, he'd forgiven her. Forgiveness was something he didn't believe the old Darius would have had the capacity for in this situation. The old him would have chewed on the betrayal, gnawed on it like a dog with a bone, unable to let it go. But now, with God's grace, thanks to the tools and people that had entered his life, he could release it. The Scripture, teachings of David Hawkins, and the meditations had been a lifeline, a cleansing, healing anchor in this storm.

The blessings felt endless. Spiritual, emotional, and even physical healing. Medications had been left behind. Presence, once an elusive state, had become his norm. He could mainly exist in the moment, unburdened by the past, unworried by the future. The discipline of halting negative thoughts, identifying emotions, and letting go so that he didn't waste the energy.

To Darius, Larissa would forever be an instrumental catalyst in his journey. Originally, he had thought of it as chasing Alice down the rabbit hole, but he was starting to think of it as coming out of the rabbit hole into the expanse of a much greater truth. Every step of his journey—learning about energy, consciousness, muscle testing—was validating the truths of other spiritual realms. He had started by using these tools to examine himself, but curiosity had led him to test others: his wife, his children, books, and different situations. Each time, the techniques proved eerily accurate, offering insights he couldn't have anticipated as he continued to calibrate, validate, and learn.

David Hawkins' teachings had opened his eyes to a deeper understanding of truth and energy. Testing objects, ideas, and intentions through muscle responses revealed so much. Whether it was organic foods or toxic substances, lies or truths, the results were mostly immediate and undeniable. It was a new way of perceiving the world, and he couldn't help but feel that every step, every revelation, every trial, was drawing him closer to something greater.

***

After his appointment with Larissa, Darius met with Rowdy two days later. The encounter was extraordinary, like stepping into a story too wild to script. Rowdy's story itself was incredible, but the circumstances of their meeting felt divinely orchestrated. It began when Darius met Adam at the DWD conference in Florida. They had quickly bonded over their shared journey to faith in Jesus, faith in God, their passion for charity, journeys with Jesus, and their mutual fascination with Dr. Joe Dispenza's work. Adam had shared Rowdy's contact information and set up the video call, saying he thought they should connect.

When the call began, Darius was sitting alone on a couch in his quiet office, the absence of employees amplifying the stillness. As soon as the conversation started, Darius felt something almost tangible—a warmth, a presence, an unmistakable goodness radiating from Rowdy. The Spirit was evident without words.

Rowdy shared his life story, one that had been both miraculous and deeply challenging. He was direct, sharing that from a young age, he could see the demons or spirits that others couldn't, which made him believe for a time that he was crazy. He became a nurse, seeking to help people, and along the way, began hearing the voice of God clearly. The Holy Spirit spoke to him, guiding him, shaping his path.

"Have you always been able to see them? Demons?" Darius asked, amazed.

"Yes," Rowdy responded, nodding.

"I have interacted with them several times now and can feel their presence if they are near, but I don't see them," Darius shared.

Darius began to share his own journey: how the challenges in his marriage had led him to seek God and how God had started opening his eyes. He spoke about his fight to reclaim his health, get off medications, and understanding how the world's systems—food, chemicals, pharmaceuticals—were corrupted by greed, creating illness while profiting from the suffering. Darius believed Satan's influence could be seen clearly in these industries, deceiving and exploiting humanity.

Rowdy nodded, his smile encouraging. He then shared his moment of awakening: standing in a hospital, pulling medication from a machine, when God spoke to him directly. "Why are you poisoning my people?" God had asked. Rowdy was stunned. He was helping as a nurse, wasn't he? But God insisted, "You know what these do in the long run." Rowdy responded, "What do I do?" "Trust me," God said. From that moment, guided by faith, Rowdy began a new journey by quitting his job and working to set up a website teaching others about energy healing and how to trust God for restoration.

The conversation flowed naturally into topics of meditation, energy, and healing. Darius spoke of how practices like meditation had transformed his life, and Rowdy explained how the parasympathetic and sympathetic nervous systems influenced health and stress. They found a shared language in their experiences, both marveling at how these seemingly disparate ideas—science and faith—fit together under God's design.

Before they ended the call, Rowdy made an offer: access to his website, a platform for healing and spiritual growth. He knew Darius was struggling financially but encouraged him to explore it now, and once his business recovered, he could contribute monetarily.

The conversation shifted to deeper matters. Darius shared the details of his divorce and the details of the spiritual battle it had brought into his life. He talked about his prayers—how he'd been praying fervently for his wife, for her heart to soften, for their marriage to be restored until November. Rowdy listened carefully, his expression thoughtful.

"That's beautiful," Rowdy finally said, "But it's not how you should be praying."

Darius blinked. "What do you mean? Last year, I prayed for her and our marriage every day. I asked God to put the blood of Jesus on the covenant of our marriage, to open her eyes and ears, to remove any deception. I prayed if our marriage was restored that it might be a testament to His people of two broken people that leaned into God."

Rowdy nodded but repeated, "It's not how you should be praying for your marriage. You need to pray in the Spirit."

Darius tilted his head, confused. "I don't understand. It's over. She's a lesbian. We are getting divorced. What do you mean?"

Rowdy smiled. "Pray in the Spirit, pray in tongues. Do you know what that is?"

Darius hesitated. "Yeah, I know about it. I just finished reading Acts. I've studied everything about Peter, how the Holy Spirit came down like tongues of fire, how they spoke languages they didn't know, and people from all these countries understood them, how they healed and cast out demons. Is that what you mean?"

"Exactly," Rowdy said. "That's the power you need to pray with. That's how you should pray over this situation, Darius. It's not just words or praying in the mind. It's aligning with the Spirit."

Darius sat back, his mind churning. He really didn't know what to think, but he knew with what he had been reading in the Bible that there was something he was missing about the Holy Spirit. Maybe this was it? The idea unsettled him, yet it resonated with something deep within. Maybe this was the missing piece—the key to unlocking the next chapter of his faith and his fight.

He stared at Rowdy for a moment, then shook his head slowly. "I don't know how to do that," he said.

"Well," Rowdy said with a smile, "Don't you think you ought to figure it out?"

"Okay. How do I do that?"

"I'll send you some sermons and information," Rowdy replied. "Ever heard of Kevin Zedai?"

Darius shook his head.

"Well, he's someone I've been following for a while. Amazing story. He died on the operating table at thirty, went to Heaven, met Jesus, and then was sent back by God. Now, he has this incredible ministry. Travels the world, flies fighter jets, teaches about the truth of the Holy Spirit, spiritual warfare, and the gifts of the Spirit. Like your friend, Steve Hemphill, he understands and shares the truth about the demonic."

"The truth of the demonic last year was eye-opening and overwhelming," Darius admitted. "I've been trying to understand the gifts of the Spirit. I've been learning about that connection.

Higher levels of consciousness, spiritual realms, it's starting to make sense. But I don't fully grasp the Holy Spirit, how to access the gifts, or pray in the Spirit."

"You will," Rowdy assured him. "Everything starts in the spiritual realm before it manifests in the physical."

"I never understood that," Darius said. "Last summer, my buddy Sully, who runs the Life Center in South Bend, was explaining that the spiritual world is way ahead of the physical. I never understood that, but through the past year and the work in the Word, I think I'm getting there."

"Yes, you're already on the path, and it's going to be incredible." Rowdy paused, then said, "Hang on. God wants to tell me something."

Darius watched him as Rowdy closed his eyes, silent for a minute before speaking again.

"You're going to learn how to pray in the Spirit, and it's going to be a game-changer," Rowdy said. "God just shared something with me ... You've got a wild ride ahead of you, my friend."

"A wild ride?" Darius asked, shifting in his seat. "It's already been pretty wild."

Rowdy smiled. "Yes, but you've sought the Lord through it all, and now things are going to accelerate. It's up to you how much and how fast, depending on how you continue to seek Him. God won't give you more than you can handle, but the pace of your transformation will match your pursuit of Him."

"Since last May, when He gave me eyes to see and ears to hear, I've never looked back," Darius explained. "I can't stop moving forward. I have to know the truth, have to keep growing, have to become who He meant me to be, who He wrote about in the Book of Life before I was even born. Now, I finally understand how someone could wander in the desert for forty years, but I'm so grateful for His kindness, His grace, His patience. He never gave up on me."

Rowdy's smile softened. "Your story is incredible, Darius. What God's doing in your life is going to bless so many others. Let's stay in touch and keep supporting each other."

"Absolutely," Darius agreed.

They shared a brief prayer before ending the call.

Sitting on the big couch in the empty office building, Darius leaned back, shook his head, and murmured, "Lord, Lord, Lord. You are so amazing." His head was spinning. As he reflected on how far he'd come, he couldn't help but wonder what lay ahead.

Chapter 77
Karl & Curses

“ How are you doing, Darius? It's nice to meet you,” Karl said in a thick Kentucky accent.

Darius smiled. “Nice to meet you too.”

They exchanged pleasantries over the phone, Karl joking about his Kentucky roots, explaining he'd lived in various places before settling in Indiana.

“Did Larissa tell you how we met?” Karl asked.

Darius paused. “Well, she said you started working together after she met you through a couple she helped. Something about a church in Indiana, where the couple had a demon problem that you helped them with.”

“Yep,” Karl nodded. “That's about right.”

“She mentioned you deal with spiritual or demonic problems that are beyond her expertise,” Darius added.

“That's right,” Karl confirmed.

"And ... " Darius hesitated, "She said whatever's going on with my right arm might be related to witchcraft or ... something similar, and that we needed to bring you in."

"Yup."

Darius sat back, staring out the window, trying to process where this conversation was headed. In the space, Karl recounted the details of how he and Larissa met. He told the story of a couple struggling with severe marital issues and, even on the verge of divorce, until Karl got involved, explained they had demonic influence afflicting the house, and he helped them confront it and remove it. Afterward, the couple reconciled. It was like something from Hollywood.

Darius couldn't help but think, Well, this guy would have been useful a year ago.

"So, your calling is to deal with evil spirits?" he asked.

"For over 30 years," Karl replied. "The Lord has been using me to help people recognize and rid themselves of spiritual afflictions, to understand who God is, the truth of the enemy, and to seek deliverance."

There was a moment of quiet between them. Darius was struggling to find words—he was struggling to process his thoughts.

"So what's going on?" Karl finally asked, creating that space for Darius to tell his story.

He did, recounting the details of how the situation started in Mexico and then remembering the story about the little girl Larissa had shared while sitting on the lawn mower. Darius shared another story of his demonic experiences while in DC the previous 4th of July, while adding he had wondered more than once if he was losing his mind. Eventually, Darius got to the end, explaining about the pain in his arm, about the "curse," and about Larissa's recommendation that the two of them speak.

Karl nodded. "You're not losing your mind, brother. By chance, do you know who Ashtoreth is?" he asked.

Darius thought for a moment. "I didn't before August. Then, after reading the book *Radical*, I committed to reading the Bible in a year. The demonic is everywhere, and that name, along with Bhaal, is mentioned consistently."

"Well, that's the head of the critters that your wife has opened the door to. The main demon is there for you."

"For me?"

"Oh, yes," Karl said. "It's a powerful one and a nasty one. It loves to destroy: families, lives … everything it can touch. And it seems you've had multiple curses placed on you."

"Multiple curses?" Darius asked, dumbfounded.

"Yes," Karl confirmed. "Your business, your health, even your manhood. All of it has been targeted."

Darius blinked. Some of it made sense, but there were other parts that didn't—at least not currently. His health? With everything he was doing, the health part didn't make sense. He was certainly improving his health, so perhaps he was staving off the curse through everything he was doing with his meditations, exercises, and diet. His business made more sense. He had always made money … But now he was facing every problem imaginable, and after a horrible 2023, hadn't made money in almost six months. But his "manhood"?

He refocused. "I have a clinical background, so don't worry about embarrassing me. So, when you say manhood, do you mean like erectile dysfunction?"

"Yup," Karl said plainly.

Darius frowned. "I mean, it's not like it's getting much use anymore, but it still works fine."

Karl laughed. "Well, they're trying to destroy that, too."

Darius shook his head. "I don't get it. How does this even happen? What should I do? Who's behind it?"

"Brother, I think you already know who," Karl said gently.

Darius's mind drifted to his wife's girlfriend. Could that even be possible?

"Think about it," Karl said, interrupting his thoughts, "What has your wife opened herself up to, who has she opened herself up to? There is so much going on there, and that has allowed the darkness in. You've said it yourself: the basement feels like a tomb, this is part of the reason why it's becoming your tomb."

"So ... What do we do now?" Darius asked.

Karl's expression turned. "We're going to pray. We're going to break the curse on your arm, and that has been set against you."

They began to pray, Karl leading with a heartfelt invocation. He thanked God for the redemptive blood of his son, Yeshua, Jesus Christ. His blessings, for being the one true God, and for the power of Jesus Christ. Then, to Darius's surprise, Karl began praying in tongues. He was speaking, praying in the Spirit, and Darius could feel the power in those words.

Karl's voice grew firm. "In the name of Jesus, I break any curses of witchcraft, sorcery, or spells that have been put on my brother. In the name of Jesus, I am thankful that no weapon of the enemy will prosper against my brother. I pray for healing and the removal of all afflictions through the Holy Spirit. I pray for healing and truth to cover my brother and cover him in the Holy Spirit."

As Karl prayed, Darius's arm began to tingle. It felt strange, like the rush of adrenaline, the kind you would experience from riding a rollercoaster. It started in his arm but soon was all over his body.

"Hallelujah. Hallelujah. We praise you, Father. Hallelujah," Karl sang, then added, "Thank Him, Darius."

"Thank you, Father. Praise Jesus."

"Hallelujah," Karl said. "How's your arm?

Darius flexed his fingers, testing it. "It doesn't hurt anymore," he said, astonished.

"Praise God!" Karl exclaimed. "How do *you* feel?"

"I don't know ... tingly, I guess," Darius admitted.

Karl let out a chuckle. "Ain't God great? That's the Holy Spirit, brother."

Darius sat there in the office, shaking his head, smiling. He didn't fully understand it, but he knew Karl was right.

"I am available usually between 10 AM and 2 PM most days. Let's catch up again next week and see how you're holdin' up, sound good?"

"Okay, yeah, I'd appreciate that," Darius said.

They said their goodbyes, and he ended the call.

Darius sat for a moment. "What in the world?" he thought. Was it even possible for things to get any stranger? Then again, maybe "stranger" wasn't the right word. Perhaps he should think of it as one of the most unique weeks of his life. How could it not be, with everything that had happened?

Darius was starting to understand the complexity of Satan's kingdom and minions. He had a feeling he was going to start getting a crash course on the details of what witchcraft and sorcery in the Bible really meant.

He leaned back, reflecting on the whirlwind of events. At times, it felt like he might be losing his mind. How often had he muttered to himself, "This is crazy?" But as he immersed himself in Dr. Joe Dispenza's books and explored the miraculous ideas it introduced, he realized his perspective—and his vocabulary—needed to shift.

"God's not crazy," he thought, the hint of a smile tugging at his lips. "God's amazing."

Chapter 78
Not That Book

D arius sank into the loveseat in his office, feeling a little out of sorts. February was here and with it, his birthday. He would be 52, and this might just be the strangest birthday in memory.

The month had started with Wealth Mastery and Tony. He hadn't planned on attending, but after DWD, it felt non-negotiable, and the people around him were just as convincing. "This is one of the most important things, you can't miss it," they insisted. Was there anything he could miss?

When he arrived, he immediately doubted being there. It was like a replay of his journey to Africa, where his first thought was, What the hell am I doing? I don't belong here. They had just shown a slide of the financial prowess in the room, and he was in the bottom 1%! But then, when Tony came out and addressed the crowd, it was as if he was speaking directly to Darius: "It doesn't matter where you're at right now. You got yourself here. 99% of the world isn't here … What you're going to get out of this will be remarkable."

That helped Darius reset, and he was glad it did. The program was a whirlwind of strategies for investments and wealth-building—things that gave him a new perspective, even in his uncertainty. It was an incredible week of learning what was possible. He wanted to be around these types of innovators, positive thinkers, and creators. The week made him contemplate more on Dr. Joe Dispenza's work and its impact since December.

As his life continued to appear as if it were moving to the edge of a disastrous cliff, he mostly wasn't thinking or focussing on the negatives. He was happy the majority of the time, sleeping well, learning higher-level emotions, and actually liked himself for the first time in his life. He realized that all of these things were working together in a phenomenal fashion—he had stopped asking himself if he was going mad; it was all too real to be a result of madness.

At that point, Darius had ordered three of Dr. Joe Dispenza's books, diving headfirst into his work. He was already halfway through *Becoming Supernatural*, and it was blowing his mind. The concepts of self-healing, creating incredible manifestations, and shaping one's destiny—all backed by science—resonated deeply with him. Just like David Hawkins' teachings and other insights he'd been absorbing, this material made absolute sense.

Inspired, Darius had committed to meditating for an hour and a half each day moving forward. He was particularly excited to begin the "Tuning into New Potentials" meditation, seeing it as a way to approach his financial situation from a transformed state of mind and learn manifestation. He felt a surge of anticipation, curious and eager to see how things might unfold. It was a beautiful thing—this journey into a realm where you focus on creating the future you want from a place of Power, Gratitude, and Faith as you created your memories in advance!

At the same time, Darius couldn't deny how the supernatural was becoming, well, more supernatural. His recent appointment with Larissa, the bizarre curse on his arm—witchcraft, of all things—then there was meeting Rowdy and Karl, which had been another wild twist in an already extraordinary chapter of his life. It was utterly surreal.

He couldn't help but laugh to himself. What's next? he wondered.

He half-joked that any day now, he'd discover that aliens were not only real but living in his office—and that he'd be hosting dinner parties with them. The thought made him shake his head in disbelief. "My goodness gracious," Darius muttered, amused by the absurdity of it all. Life was full of surprises, and he was learning to lean into the mystery.

As remarkable as everything had already been, things seemed to be accelerating. He found himself diving deeper into various meditations, loving the clarity and sense of purpose they brought each day. He felt like his life was heading in a transformative direction.

Lately, his thoughts had been occupied with a meeting he'd had with Marjah about writing a book. Initially, the mere idea felt overwhelming. The pressure, the effort, and the vulnerability it would require seemed like too much to handle, especially given all the emotional weight he was already carrying.

Sitting on the loveseat in his office, Darius decided to meditate on it. When he finished, something extraordinary happened. God spoke to him.

It wasn't an audible voice, but it was undeniable—imprinted so clearly in his mind it felt like a conversation. It reminded Darius of the first time he felt the Holy Spirit's presence while in Africa. The message was direct: *You're going to write a book.*

Darius, still in the afterglow of the meditation, responded inwardly. Yeah, I know. Marjah wants me to write a business book. I wasn't sure if I could handle it, but okay, I'll do it.

But the voice came again. *"No, not that book."*

Darius frowned. What do you mean?

The reply was startling: *"You're going to write a book about your story."*

Confused, Darius asked, My story?

"Yes," God said. *"You're going to write about what's happened to you this past year. You'll tell the truth about evil and the demonic. You'll share your journey, your failures, your struggles, and the unworthiness you've felt. You will explain that because you were not truly seeking Me, were not in covenant with me, living selfishly and fooled by the enemy, that you were lost and unworthy, and coming from a place of lack because you didn't understand where your value comes from. You'll explain how you were once blind but now see, how coming to me gave you clarity. You'll expose the lies and the tactics of the Evil One, and how he works to destroy my people through the occult. You'll describe your self-healing journey, your path to freedom from medications, and how because you are seeking me and the Word, I am teaching you the truth about the enemy, spiritual realms, prophecy, and most of all, my absolute love for my people."*

Darius sat in stunned silence. His immediate reaction was resistance. I don't want to do that! he thought, not fully realizing he was telling God no.

But God continued: *"This is what I want from you. You will admit your failings, trust me, and you will give me all the glory. And this book will bless many people."*

Still, Darius couldn't shake the thought that it was crazy.

When the moment passed, he was left wondering how he could ever take on such a task. Who would believe this? People who were once his family and his supposed friends already think I'm nuts, he thought.

For the next week, the idea lingered in his mind. How could he reveal this to anyone? He thought about how, after meeting Steve and learning the truth of the demonic, he had shared it. It had helped a lot of people, but those closest to him thought he was unhinged. But if I did this, they'd think I was insane!

Finally, he devised a plan: he would call Marjah and explain everything.

"Hey, Marjah, great to see you. So, I did this meditation, and God visited me. The business book is on hold, and I have been told to write a book about my Jōb-like year, about all my personal issues and failings and lack of awareness. About how God gave me eyes to see and ears, truth and about how Satan really is the ruler of this world. That, by coming to God, He took me through a journey of healing and awareness to share with others. Sound like a plan?!"

Then surely, she'd tell him it was a terrible idea, he should just focus on the business book, and that would be the end of it.

But when the call finally happened, Marjah's reaction was the opposite of what he expected.

She didn't laugh.

She didn't call him crazy.

Instead, with a smile on her face, she said, "That's incredible, Darius. You absolutely need to put the business book on hold and write this one. This is what you're meant to do."

Her response left him surprised and a little dazed. But then she went on to share her own story of divine inspiration, telling him how, years ago, she had received what she believed was a blessing from God—a sudden download of information that had led her to write a book. At first, she'd doubted herself, shoving the manuscript into a closet for two years. But when she finally acted on it, everything in her life changed for the better.

"Trust me," she said. "You need to do this."

Darius sat there, still unsure. How could I share all this? he wondered. Who would believe it? He didn't know if he had the courage, and it would be four months of avoiding his publisher before another angel visitation and the Holy Spirit would give him the courage to change his mind.

Chapter 79
Logarithmic vs Arithmetic

D arius had just finished his meditation in the office, feeling the strange quiet of a space that once held employees. It was a shift he hadn't fully adjusted to yet.

Often, he would meditate or read next to the biocharger in his office, stacking positives, as Tony Robbins would say, or—as he would have said in the past—killing two birds with one stone. But since January, he had moved away from the Tony Robbins morning active meditations, and fully immersed himself in Dr. Joe Dispenza's work, loving the meditations. He felt he was evolving and transforming in ways he hadn't imagined. Adding these meditations and kickboxing to his previous routine was the next level for him.

Darius was also diving deeper into David Hawkins' work, finding it to be invaluable. He felt like the more he understood it, the more applicable it became. Hawkins' *Power versus Force* had opened new doors in his mind, particularly as he continued to trial and error muscle testing for truth versus falsehood. The process was giving new meaning to the information Tony and Dr. Joe shared that 50% of our memories are myths to validate what we want to believe.

He was drawn to how Hawkins explained muscle testing, a technique that Larissa and Dr. Whitman had opened the door to his curiosity that now couldn't be closed. Darius wanted to understand it fully, knowing that in certain situations, it could become a useful tool—another key to unlock a deeper understanding of the truth of his own life. Since God was Absolute Truth and His Word was the Spirit and Sword of Truth, Darius found it remarkable that God would allow Hawkins to identify a technique relevant to energy, or the Quantum field, according to Dr. Joe, that a person could identify whether anything from the past was true or false. The whole idea felt like a new world.

One concept in the book that stood out to him was the idea of a "deterministic linear sequence." Hawkins had described it like a series of billiard balls striking each other sequentially—A causes B causes C. That was how Darius's mind had always worked. But Hawkins' research suggested that causality operated in a completely different way, where what we see is merely the surface-level result of something deeper at play. The sequence that humans observe might not be the true cause—it's a perception built on limited understanding. Hawkins' diagrams and explanations suggested that what we see is just the visible portion of a much larger and hidden reality operating behind the veil. Everything Darius had experienced since last May was proving this to be true, relevant to energy, spiritual realms, and the Bible, and was validating his experience.

As Darius absorbed these ideas, he couldn't help but think about the implications for human understanding and society's evolution. What was visible and observable in the world might be entirely different from the true causes at play. What would the world be like if we could all open ourselves to higher awareness and the truth? What would it look like if we could lift that veil for every person? Was his perspective too altruistic that he was blind to how terrifying it might be? The thought was as incredible as it was terrifying—so much could change for the better, as it already had for him.

It was remarkable to Darius, and it only became more remarkable when he read about Hawkins' personal journey.

Hawkins had once been an atheist, much like Lee Strobel before him. While Hawkins didn't set out to prove Jesus wasn't resurrected like Strobel, he still found himself on a spiritual journey that led him to faith. Hawkins' viewpoint was especially interesting because he believed that the ego—the small, vain "I" that claims ownership of thoughts and creativity—was an obstacle. He suggested that true creativity, true genius, didn't come from this ego but from a higher source, traditionally understood as something divine.

Darius immediately felt himself smiling and circled it in the book, writing "God" next to the passage.

The more he read, the more he found connections to his own spiritual path and awakening.

The map of consciousness was another revelation for Darius. Hawkins charted the levels of energy associated with different states of consciousness, starting with the lowest levels—shame, guilt, apathy, and so on—up to the highest levels of enlightenment. What stood out to him was that anger, which Darius viewed as mostly negative, could be a turning point. Darius felt a new awareness and truth because Hawkins explained that while anger wasn't a place to stay, it could be a catalyst to break free from stagnation, and one could move from negative levels and ultimately to the positive level of courage. It could fuel action, pushing someone to move and grow. Anger wasn't a place to stay, but it could be a catalyst to break free from stagnation. It was a state of being that could be turned from a negative to a positive, and when it was, it led you to courage. Then, above courage, you could move to neutrality, willingness, acceptance, reason, love, joy, peace—and, for the rare few, enlightenment.

The scale was staggering. Hawkins had shown that most of the world lived at the lower levels of consciousness, below 200 on the scale, where emotions like fear, desire, anger, and guilt were common. It explained the pain and suffering that seemed so prevalent in the world.

Darius reflected on his own life, on how much he had defaulted to anger, fear, and pride. The idea of guilt and shame, especially from his family background, hit him deeply. It made sense that so much of the world lived in those lower emotional states. But what if it were possible to rise above those lower levels? What would life look like at higher levels of consciousness? This excited Darius.

He didn't completely understand, but with each new revelation, he knew he was onto something monumental. It was as if God kept giving him another breadcrumb, another piece, with each step of faithfulness in seeking Him. As he continued to dive into Dr. Joe Dispenza's work, he began to understand how emotions are not only internal but can be felt by others, affecting what we attract into our lives. The more he studied, the more connections he saw between the scientific principles of consciousness and spiritual truths, especially those in the Bible. It was like a deeper understanding of life was unfolding before him, and he sensed he was just scratching the surface.

He thought about his relationship with Jessica and how he had to give himself more grace. Over time, he had become better at forgiving himself, but it was still a struggle. Yes, he had too often defaulted to anger and had sometimes shown negative masculine traits, but a relationship involved two people, and she had many inappropriate behaviors as well.

Thank God for Larissa. Thank God for God, Darius thought, his heart swelling with gratitude. He smiled, realizing how far he had come. It was remarkable how these concepts were shifting his perspective on the world, on history, on the future. And as he let go of resistance and continued Dr. Joe's meditation, he was starting to feel these higher level emotions in his heart. His ultimate goal was to reach 540, with 500 being the lowest baseline—he wanted to live in that state of pure love, continuously.

It was incredible how the map of consciousness shed new light on historical events and figures. He was fascinated by the idea that psychological stress was essentially the result of resisting or trying to escape a condition. To let go was to move toward freedom, a higher state of consciousness, and the emotions that came with it.

One of Hawkins' examples that stood out to Darius was how the map of consciousness could offer a radically different perspective on the progress of history. The distinction between force and power was particularly eye-opening. Darius couldn't help but think about how this related to what he was learning in the Bible. Hawkins had shared the example of the British Empire and its colonial rule over India. The empire, which represented force, calibrated at 175 on the scale of consciousness—a level associated with self-interest, exploitation, and control.

In contrast, Mohandas Gandhi stood as a figure of immense power. Hawkins described Gandhi as an avatar of enlightenment, with a consciousness level of 760, among the highest attainable by humans. Only figures like Jesus and documents like the Gospels calibrated at the ultimate level of 1000, which represented pure divinity.

What amazed Darius was how Gandhi, operating at such a high level of power, was able to overcome the British Empire—the most formidable force on Earth at the time. Gandhi's strategy of nonviolence wasn't just a moral or ethical stance; it was an expression of true power, rooted in a far greater truth and alignment than the empire's use of force. Hawkins emphasized that whenever force meets power, force is eventually defeated. This was an extraordinary realization for Darius. It was power—not violence, coercion, or domination—that ultimately shaped lasting change.

Rising to higher levels of consciousness wasn't just about self-improvement; it was about tapping into a greater power that aligned with truth, compassion, and love. Force could only get someone so far, whether in personal relationships, work, or even historical movements. But power, rooted in authenticity and higher consciousness, had the ability to transform not only one's life but the world itself.

It was a distinction that so many people either misunderstood or simply ignored. "The pen is mightier than the sword," resonated with Darius, and this was the proof.

But that wasn't all. Darius still grappled with the mathematical explanation of the scale of consciousness. Hawkins had explained that the levels were not arithmetic but logarithmic. The difference between 150 and 300 on the scale was not linear but exponential. A small increase in consciousness could have a massive impact on a person's power. This idea blew Darius away, making him realize that even a small shift could dramatically affect his life and the lives of others.

Any level below 200 on the scale was destructive, not just to the individual, but to society as a whole. This was why emotions like shame, fear, and anger could be so harmful. But above 200, consciousness was constructive—at the critical level of 200, the shift from falsehood (force) to truth (power) took place.

However, something Darius thought about often was his own healing. He realized that he couldn't heal others unless he had first healed himself. According to Dr. Joe's book, the healed could become the healer. That was something he knew he would strive for, even if he wasn't sure how to fully integrate it yet.

It was something that also tied into the work he was doing to learn and understand muscle testing. The more he did it, the more the calibrations showed that he was getting better at utilizing the testing methods. The more he understood about truth, falsehood, and muscle testing, the clearer it became how essential it was to approach everything with an open heart and calibrate to ward off bias. The concept of self-healing was revolutionary. Darius had started to understand that healing wasn't just about physical health, but about emotional, mental, and spiritual wellness as well.

Sitting alone in his office, Darius felt an incredible sense of excitement about the future. He was no longer focusing on the negative aspects of his life. He was taking responsibility for his emotions, reconditioning his body to a new mind, and actively creating higher-level positive emotions. It was working.

He laughed to himself. "Where will I be a year or two from now?"

Then, with a smile on his face, he raised his energy, felt his heart open, and loudly declared, "I am outstandingly worthy and blessed, and my future success is guaranteed and ordained by my Creator."

Chapter 80
God Only Knows

G azing out the window, Darius watched as the last days of Spring rolled in. His eyes fell on the glass of wine he had poured, the second one of the evening. Alone in his office, a familiar sense of solitude washed over him. It was a position he had often found himself in, whether surrounded by company or drinking in isolation. He didn't feel anger, sadness, or depression; he felt a quiet sense of acceptance, a realization that he was no longer that old, dark version of himself. It would have been nice to feel strong all the time, but he knew it wasn't realistic.

The situation weighed on him, a strange paradox he couldn't shake. He was growing, healing, and gaining deep insights into life, seeing things he never could have imagined before. God had been showing him things repeatedly over the past year. As hard as it had been, he was no longer wondering if he was losing his mind like he did last year. He was becoming more comfortable with the changes, and as he continued to learn, he had lost count of how many books he had read outside of the Bible—more than sixty since last summer. His comprehension and ability to read had improved dramatically, and his mind felt clearer than ever before.

And God kept directing him to new books, as if saying, "Read this, then this," and the urgency seemed to be accelerating. He'd read the Bible, finding passages that clearly connected to what he was learning, linking the demonic to the real world in a way that stunned him.

The weight of it all, the magnitude of these truths, felt almost unbearable at times.

Darius had just returned from a conference in California, one he had attended numerous times before. His company was supposed to sponsor the event, and he was scheduled to present, but circumstances had changed dramatically. The business was now down to just him, teetering on the edge of bankruptcy, with no revenue in nearly seven months. He could no longer afford to pay the remainder of the sponsorship fee.

This conference had always been a highlight for him. He admired its founder, Parker—an intelligent, kind, and pioneering leader in the field. When Parker and Darius connected to discuss the situation, Darius was honest about his circumstances. He explained the struggles with his business, the impending divorce, and his inability to fulfill the sponsorship commitment.

"First of all," Parker began, "You're an amazing guy, and you've been a huge supporter of this conference. I have no doubt you're going to come through this stronger than ever. Many of us have been through tough times like this. I have a friend who just went through something similar, and his life is even better now. I promise you, one day you'll look back and be grateful this happened."

Darius smiled at the screen. "Parker, I can't tell you how much I appreciate that. You're absolutely right. Life feels like a mess right now; it seems like everything is being taken away. But at the same time, I've learned so much about myself. I've had to confront things that needed to change, my own issues, my own misperceptions. And through it all, I've been blessed."

He took a breath and continued. "I was on medication before, I'm not anymore. I've done a lot of emotional healing through therapy. I've started meditating. And even though everything around me is chaotic, I'm the happiest and most peaceful I've ever been."

Parker nodded, a warm smile spreading across his face. "That's amazing, Darius. Look, here's what we're going to do: you don't need to pay the rest of the sponsorship. I won't refund what you've already paid; it's too late for that, but I want you to come to the conference anyway. Just get yourself here."

Darius was surprised. "Parker, I wouldn't even ask for that. I just wanted to let you know why I couldn't attend or pay the rest of the fee."

"No, no," Parker insisted. "You've been a big part of this community, and people know it. You need to be there. And for the international meeting in the fall, I'll comp your ticket, just get yourself there. How does that sound?"

Darius was overwhelmed with gratitude. "Okay, I'll figure out how to get there," he promised. "Honestly, I just need two or three placements, and I can turn things around quickly."

"You can make that happen at the conference," Parker said with confidence.

And Parker was right. The conference had been just what he needed. Darius connected with old friends who shared his faith, opening the door for potential future collaborations. It was a much-needed boost of confidence during this difficult time, a reminder that even amidst hardship, opportunities were still possible.

God was amazing.

On the final day, he attended a church service where the Christian band King and Country was playing. Darius loved the band's music and was overjoyed and amazed he happened to be in the area to attend. After they played, they previewed their movie that was coming out called Unsung Hero. It was based on their true story: the struggles of moving from Australia to America, family dynamics, and God's promise.

The experience was surreal, but even more so was what happened next.

As Darius arrived at the airport and made his way toward his gate, he noticed the band sitting there. For a moment, he stopped in his tracks, amazed. Wow, he thought. What are the chances?

He approached them with a smile. "This is incredible," he said. "We were just at the same church two-and-a-half, maybe three hours ago. You guys were remarkable."

The group laughed warmly, and the two brothers, Luke and Joel, in the band stood up, extending their hands. After exchanging introductions, they asked what had brought him to the church. Darius explained he'd been attending a conference, and a local friend he had met at a Tony Robbins conference invited him to attend.

One of the brothers smiled. "It was such an incredible experience to make the movie. To tell you the truth, it really changed the way I saw my father. Playing him gave me a new perspective, and I've come to appreciate him in ways I hadn't before. God's grace is truly amazing."

"Yes, it is," Darius agreed.

The other brother leaned in. "Do you have a family?" he asked.

Darius smiled, but it was tinged with sadness. "I do," he said. "I have three children. I was, well, I am married, but I'm going through a divorce. My wife had an affair with a woman and has chosen a different path. It's been a really challenging time, both for my family and financially."

Their expressions softened with compassion. "Oh my, I'm so sorry to hear that," one of them said. "Can we pray for you?"

Darius nodded, grateful. "Absolutely. That would mean so much to me. I just want to say, though, that God has been doing amazing things even through this. I've leaned into Him more than ever, and He's been healing me in ways I couldn't have imagined. Moments like this, meeting you all, it's clear He's at work."

The brothers placed their arms around him, and together, they bowed their heads in the middle of the bustling airport. They prayed for God's grace to surround Darius, for clarity in His direction, for healing in Darius's heart, and for the strength to extend grace to others. They also prayed for his family—that God's love would rain down on them and that what lay ahead would be even more beautiful than what had come before.

It was a heartfelt and moving prayer. When they finished, Darius thanked them sincerely. They hugged, and he walked toward his gate, shaking his head in amazement.

Remarkable, he thought, thinking of all of the new people in his life. Steve, Jeff, Roe, Dr. Whitman, Larissa, and recently meeting Adam, Karl, and Rowdy … So many new relationships formed with amazing people. Each one proved that even as so much had been taken from him, God was putting remarkable people in his path and healing him in every way. "I mean," he thought, "what were the chances of meeting the band?!" God was amazing.

But there was still pain, deep pain, when he thought of his youngest son. Darius's children were all so different, each unique in their own right. They had all faced their own challenges, but despite everything, his older son, along with his daughter, had been supportive as they navigated the difficulties of the past year. But with his youngest, it was different.

The away football game in November had been amazing, and he had bonded with his son similar to their time on the horse ranch in July. Then, he had taken the boys on the scuba diving trip over the holidays, and that hadn't gone as well as he'd hoped.

He hadn't understood some of it, and other parts were just mistakes on his part with Ben dealing with his emotions and anger—mistakes he wished he could take back. He has asked them to be in Scripture each morning, spend 30-45 minutes learning to meditate, and to read a chapter of *The Masculine in Relationship* a day because he wanted to help them learn some of the valuable lessons he was learning. He didn't think it was that much to ask for taking them to Thailand. He still didn't understand because at no point had Ben made any effort to communicate with him though apparently he had been complaining back home to his mother and Sheehan's girlfriend. On the surface, it seemed ridiculous to Darius. Ben wouldn't speak to him and harbored an anger or resentment Darius couldn't understand.

Now, Ben was on vacation with his wife and her partner, and Darius had no idea what was happening. His texts went unanswered. He tried to push the pain aside, but it was always there, a heavy ache in his chest. He knew he had to avoid dwelling on it, as Tony Robbins and Joe Dispenza said: ***where focus goes, energy flows.*** Most of the time, he did a good job of that, but he was human and still imperfect despite the growth. Darius thought about the challenges they faced together and how difficult it was to keep moving forward.

As he finished his second glass of wine, debating whether to have a third, he sighed, and corked the bottle. The future was uncertain, but one thing was certain: he would never return to the man he once was. He refused.

Chapter 81
Will an Angel Report You?

I t was a Tuesday afternoon, and Indiana was beginning to thaw. Darius sat in his small office, staring blankly at the ceiling. After an hour of meditation, he felt calmer. Business calls awaited him, but his mind lingered on other matters.

The divorce was a wound he'd accepted, though it still stung. Professionally, the blows kept coming. His company, once thriving, was now a hollow shell. His most trusted employee, Angela—his right-hand, his chief of staff—had left in February, urging him to fire her as the situation deteriorated. Before that, Jake, instrumental in managing social media and analytics, had exited in January. The team, once confident in their technology and abilities, had dwindled, defeated by circumstances they couldn't comprehend.

Darius had started his business in 2015, right in the middle of the last recession. The first six and a half months were brutal—no revenue, mounting stress, and an ever-shrinking runway. He had reached a point where things were so tight that a few more months without income might have sunk him. Nine years later, the landscape was different. This time, his business had to weather another economic downturn, but now, he knew it. And yet, knowing didn't seem to make it any easier.

This recession wasn't just an external challenge; it arrived at the worst possible time for him personally. After three consecutive years of significant growth, the downturn caught him off guard. He'd over-leveraged the business, pouring too much money into the wrong areas in his drive for expansion. The timing couldn't have been worse. The divorce compounded everything, adding another layer of devastation to an already precarious situation.

Still, as fall arrived, he had clung to hope. He believed in his core team of three or four people and the solid foundation they had built together. Their track record, paired with the systems and strategies they'd refined over time, made him confident they could push through the recession. He envisioned their survival and eventual explosion of growth on the other side of this challenge.

And explode they did—just not in the way he'd imagined.

They didn't surge forward; they collapsed inward. Now, it was just him. Alone.

The reality of it was still hard to comprehend. The team he'd cultivated and the business he'd poured so much into over the years had unraveled.

The irony of his current situation wasn't lost on him. Back when his family was together—before everything unraveled with his wife—he had done whatever it took to make things work. Long hours, late nights, endless effort—it didn't faze him. For years, he worked tirelessly, sometimes staying at the office until 6:30 or 7:00 at night, never thinking twice about it. He had seen it as his responsibility to protect his family, to provide, and to secure the life they had built together.

But now? Now, he was locking up a 3,800-square-foot building that used to hum with energy, that used to be alive with employees and momentum. It was just him, alone in one small office, trying to make it work. He paused for a moment, taking in the stillness of the space around him. He sighed. He'd be going home, but he wouldn't be going *home*.

When he arrived, there was no one there; the house was empty. He prepared himself dinner, descended into the basement, and watched a sermon by Kevin Zadai. During the sermon, one part in particular struck a chord with him:

"Look, you don't need to know your destiny or what you should be doing right now. If you're unsure, just do these three things: be in the Scripture, pray, and go help someone—feed the homeless or do something for a child. The angels will report you."

Much of his past philanthropic work had centered on children, which made Zadai's advice feel personal. Darius reflected on the previous year. He had given more each year, culminating in $166k alone the year before his wife said it was over. But since the turmoil began, his contributions had dwindled. He'd still given what he could—to Steve Hemphill, the Life Center, the new clinic in Africa, and the school in the Dominican Republic that he continued to sponsor—but it was a fraction of what he had done in better times.

Darius ran a hand through his hair, leaned forward, and began to pray: "God, you know my heart. You know my repentance. You know my love for my family. You know how much I've prayed for this situation to be different. Even though I haven't received anything I asked for, even though none of my prayers seem to have been answered, I will still praise you. I will praise you on the mountaintop and in the valley, in the fire and in the darkness. And as my enemies surround me."

"Lord, I know that none of this is your fault, and I trust you. I won't stop seeking you. I'll give what I can, even though I don't have much right now. If you'll guide me, tell me who to give to, I will give. I know you don't tell us precisely what to give, but you love a cheerful giver. You know my heart for giving—you planted it in me. Help me to fulfill that calling."

He sat back on the bed, exhausted yet strangely peaceful. The house was eerily quiet as Darius lay in bed.

To calm his mind, he did a few breathing exercises. Wim Hof ended his exercise by saying, "All the love, all the power", and with that, a calm settled over Darius, and he let the relaxation carry him to sleep.

Chapter 82
An Unlocked Door

The next morning began as usual at 5:00 AM. Meditation, breathing, Scripture, and cold plunges had become his anchors. Joe Dispenza's "Reconditioning the Body to a New Mind" meditation was a favorite. At first, imagining higher-level emotions like abundance and divinity had felt foreign, but persistence brought clarity. Meditation fueled his optimism, allowing him to visualize a future where he could rebuild.

Arriving at the office, he went through his routine—reading, biocharging, and meditating. He had bought the biocharger as part of his employee health plan and now he was the only one in the office to use it. By mid-morning, he was deep into business development calls. Suddenly, a noise disrupted his concentration. Startled, he looked up to see a man standing outside his door, visible through the glass pane.

He was a stranger—a shorter Black man in maybe his fifties, seemed out of place and frazzled, clutching a piece of paper. Darius approached cautiously.

"Can I help you?" he asked.

The man glanced at the paper, then at Darius. "What's the address here?" he stammered.

"This is 4231 Jeremiah Drive," Darius replied. "What are you looking for?"

"I'm supposed to be at 4640 Drake Drive," the man muttered, his agitation growing.

Darius frowned. "That's not here, but I can help you find it. Come to the front conference room."

The man nodded, and Darius led him through the office. In the conference room, he pulled out his phone. "What's your name?" he asked.

"Michael," the man replied.

"Nice to meet you, Michael. I'm Darius," Darius said, shaking his hand before entering the address into his maps app. "Good news, it's only two miles from here."

Michael's eyes widened. "Two miles?"

"Yeah," Darius confirmed. "It's not far, just toward the interstate. Won't take long at all."

"Two miles?" Michael repeated.

"Yeah."

Darius sensed the man's frustration turning into confusion. Two miles wasn't that far ... by car. Then he looked out the window and saw it, only his car sat in the parking lot.

"How'd you get here?" Darius asked.

Michael looked down, hesitant. "I took the bus from downtown and then walked from the closest stop to here," he admitted.

Darius paused. "Okay, well, what do you need to get to this address for?"

"A job interview," Michael said quickly. "I *need* this job."

Darius nodded. "When do you need to be there?"

Michael shifted nervously. "Soon."

"Alright," Darius said. "I'll take you."

Michael blinked, startled. "You'd really do that?"

"Of course," Darius said. "No problem."

There was something about Michael, something Darius couldn't quite put his finger on. But he felt it. This man wasn't bad; he was trying to turn things around.

"So, why?" Darius asked. "What's making you come out here?"

Michael looked down, then met his eyes. "I've been homeless for months," he began, his voice laced with desperation. "It's been a really tough situation. I finally got into a place, but they told me if I don't get a job, they'll kick me back out. I have to get a job, or I'm back on the street."

"Michael?" Darius asked, "Do you have faith? Do you believe in God?

Michael paused, then nodded. "Yes, I do."

Darius felt a nudge in his spirit. "I feel like God's telling me to pray for you. Can I pray for you?"

"Yes," Michael said, almost a whisper.

Darius stepped forward and extended his hands. Michael took them hesitantly. Darius bowed his head, and prayed aloud:

"God, Father, Creator of all, we come before You in faith. I pray that You bless Michael. Thank You for bringing him into my path today and for giving me the opportunity to help him. Lord, fill him with the Holy Spirit, heart, mind, and soul. Bless his interview, Father. Help him secure this job so he can keep a roof over his head and continue on a path to many blessings. We trust in Your will and Your timing. I pray this in the name of the Father, the Son, and the Holy Spirit. Amen."

When Darius finished, Michael looked up, tears brimming in his eyes. "Thank you," he murmured.

"Come on," Darius said, clapping him lightly on the shoulder. "Let's get you to your interview."

They stepped outside, and Darius unlocked the car. As Michael climbed in, he hesitated. He remembered the prayer he had made the night before, asking God to show him who he could help. The realization struck him like lightning—Michael was the answer to that prayer.

In his office sat $1,000 in cash from some recently sold furniture. An idea formed in his mind. Turning back, he used an excuse. "I need to set the alarm. Hold on." Then he asked abruptly, "Are you hungry?

"I am always hungry."

Darius rushed back inside. Excitement surged through him. At his desk, he pulled $100 from the cash and slipped it into his pocket. Then he moved to the pantry. It was stocked with snacks leftover from better days when the office had been full of employees. Darius grabbed trail mix, jerky, and chips—whatever he could find—and returned to the car.

He handed the food to Michael, whose eyes widened in surprise. "Oh my gosh," Michael exclaimed. "Thank you so much!

"You're welcome," Darius said with a smile as they set off.

Curious, Darius asked, "So, how did you end up in this situation, if you don't mind me asking?"

Michael hesitated, then began to speak. "I made a lot of bad decisions," he admitted. "I had a place, a car, a life. But I messed up ... drinking, living with someone I shouldn't have. That ended badly. I lost my car, got into drugs ... It spiraled from there."

Darius placed a hand on his shoulder. "It's okay, Michael. We've all made mistakes. You're here now, trying to fix things. That's what matters."

Michael nodded but continued, "I was homeless for three months, living in the park. I finally got into a shelter, but it was horrible. People stole from me, broke into my locker, took everything I had."

"I'm so sorry," Darius said, shaking his head.

Michael sighed. "Now I've got this chance, but if I don't get this job, I'm back on the street."

"You'll get this job," Darius said firmly. "You're on a new path now. Stay positive."

Michael grew quiet, staring out the window.

Darius glanced over at him. It was like he could see the weight he was carrying sink him further into the seat. "Michael, can I tell you something?"

"Yeah," Michael said, his voice barely audible.

"You believe in God, right?"

"Yes, but I have made so many mistakes."

"I understand, but it's okay." He paused. "You understand that evil is real, too?"

Michael nodded.

"Okay," Darius said. "Then listen to me. God made you, Michael, in His image. He made you perfect. Scripture tells us that He wrote about you in the Book of Life before you were born. You were created special. Yes, we live in a fallen world, and bad things happen. But you are worthy.

"Whatever mistakes you've made, whatever guilt or shame you feel, none of that comes from God. He's already forgiven you. If you believe in Christ as your Savior, you are redeemed. The fruits of the Spirit are love, joy, peace, patience, kindness, goodness, generosity, faithfulness, gentleness, and self-control ... That's what comes from God! You're trying to do the right things, and God sees that."

Darius placed a firm hand on Michael's shoulder. "You need to forgive yourself, Michael. Keep moving forward. God's got you."

***

Darius pulled into a parking lot and glanced at the building in front of him. "Is this it?" he asked.

Michael looked down at the paper in his hand. "Yeah, I think it is."

"Alright," Darius said. "Go in and make sure it's the right place. I don't want to drop you off until we're sure."

Michael nodded, got out of the car, and disappeared inside.

As Darius sat waiting, his thoughts raced. This is unbelievable, he thought. I prayed for God to send me someone to help ... Now this? His mind wandered back to the morning. He was certain he'd locked the office door, just as he'd done every day for the past month. But as certain as he was, he must have forgotten. If the door had been locked, Michael would never have walked in, and none of this would be happening.

He shook his head, marveling at the sequence of events.

Michael returned a few minutes later, opening the door. "This is it," he confirmed. "Thank you so much."

"Hang on," Darius said. "Get back in for a second."

Michael hesitated, then climbed back into the car and closed the door.

"I want to pray for you before you go in," Darius said.

Michael nodded. "Okay."

Darius extended his hand, and Michael took it. Bowing his head, Darius prayed, "God, Father, I lift Michael up to You. Be with him in this interview. Give him courage and confidence. Help him to connect with the interviewer and to answer in the way he needs to get this job. Lord, You know what he needs, and we trust that You will provide. In Jesus's name, Amen."

Michael squeezed Darius's hand. "Thank you," he said, a genuine smile breaking through the tension on his face.

Darius reached into his pocket and pulled out the cash he'd taken earlier. He handed it to Michael.

Michael's eyes widened as he stared at the money. "What? Why are you doing this?"

Darius met his gaze. "Michael, none of this happened by accident."

Michael's face twisted in confusion.

"You see, last night, I prayed. My life's been tough lately. My business is falling apart, my marriage is ending, and I've been struggling. But last night, I prayed and asked God to guide me. I told Him I'd help whoever He sent my way. And then you walked into my office." Darius sighed. "Michael, I lock that office door every day. Every single day. But for some reason, I didn't today. If I had, you never would've gotten inside. We wouldn't have met. None of this is by chance. So, take the money. I hope it blesses you."

Michael's eyes filled with tears. "I don't even know what to say."

"You don't have to say anything."

"I'm a worker," Michael said, his voice cracking. "If anyone needs help, yard work, projects around the house, I can do it. I'm not afraid of hard work."

"I'll give you my number," Darius said, smiling. "After your interview, text me. Let me know how it goes."

"I will. Thank you."

They shook hands, and Michael got out of the car.

***

As Darius drove back to his office, his thoughts swirled. What just happened? He parked, headed inside, and tried to focus on work. But later that evening, as he drove home, a thought struck him out of nowhere as if it was spoken into his head, just like when he was told to pray for Michael: *What about the homeless people?*

He frowned, confused. What homeless people?

The thought persisted; this time, more specific thoughts entered his mind: *What are you going to do about the homeless people?*

Darius's heart raced as he recalled Michael's words about living in the park, and that there were others living there.

He thought about Kevin Zedai telling stories of feeding the homeless. On his wife's birthday, the Holy Spirit told him to give a homeless lady his last hamburger and the little money he had in his pocket to her. He was reluctant because that money was to buy his wife's birthday present and they didn't have much money then. But he was obedient, the homeless lady smiled at him, and said, "It's okay, Kevin, please keep the money." Kevin was astonished as he hadn't told her his name. "God loves your obedience," she said, and then she, an angel, disappeared right before his eyes.

Taking a deep breath, Darius pulled into his driveway. He couldn't shake the idea. Okay, hamburgers it is, he thought, grabbing his phone and texted Michael:

Where were you homeless? What park?

About an hour later, Michael replied:

The military park downtown. Not far from the Scottish Rite.

How many homeless people are usually there?

It depends. Sometimes 40, 50, 60. Sometimes more, but usually around 30 to 40.

Darius stared at the message, overwhelmed. "What am I supposed to do about this?" he thought. But as crazy as it sounded, he knew he needed to act.

Sunday. I'm going to take food down there. If you want, meet me, and show me where people stay.

Are you serious?

Yes.

Chapter 83
A Rainbow in the Storm

S unday mornings always had a rhythm for Darius: wake up, meditate, Scripture, take a cold plunge, work out, and head to church. After his meeting with Michael, the plan had been set, and he would hit the store to buy hamburgers and head downtown to feed the homeless around 5 PM. He'd bought burgers, buns to go with them, a bottle of ketchup and mustard, and two cases of bottled water.

Michael met him and showed him where most people hung out. It was remarkable. He offered each person a hamburger and water, asking if he could pray for them. He'd ask for their name, hold their hand, or place a hand on their shoulder while praying. Sometimes, they hugged him. A few declined his prayers or didn't give their names. That was fine with him—he silently prayed for them anyway. The whole experience really touched him, and he resolved to return the following weekend.

***

The next Sunday, after church, his phone buzzed.

Hey, are you still going?

Yes. I bought a little more this time, and I'll start cooking around four. You're welcome to come by.

Sure!

Gina's text made him smile. She and her husband were friends from church, and they had known each other for years. Last Sunday, they had told him how sorry they were about the divorce and invited him for dinner that week. At the dinner, he talked about meeting Michael and subsequently going to the park to feed the homeless; her husband seemed disinterested, but Gina expressed interest in helping if Darius ever went to the park again.

By 4:00, his kitchen was in chaos. A griddle on the stove could only handle three burgers at a time, and grease splattered everywhere. He was juggling flipping patties, assembling burgers, and stowing them in a box when there was a knock at the door.

"Come on in!" he called, hardly looking up.

Gina came through the garage door and lingered near the kitchen's half-wall—even in the chaos of his kitchen, Darius could sense her nervousness.

"How many homeless people will there be?" she asked.

"I don't know," Darius replied, flipping another burger. "There were about 28 or 30 last time."

"How can I help?"

"Grab the buns. I'll slap the burgers on, and you can assemble them."

As Darius grabbed the cooler from the porch, they worked together to prepare the rest of the burgers. Gina's movements were slightly hesitant at first, and after a while, she asked, "Aren't you nervous?"

"Nervous?"

"About me being here ... Just us."

He stopped and gave her a perplexed look. "Why would I be nervous? We're making hamburgers for the homeless."

"What if someone comes by and sees us?"

"Who cares if anybody sees us?" Darius asked, adding a half-laugh on the end in an attempt to lighten the mood.

Gina gave her best attempt at a smile. "Well ... I mean ... I don't want anybody starting rumors ... "

"We're making burgers for the homeless," Darius repeated, annoyed. Quickly, he sighed and apologized. "Gina, we've known each other for years. We go to the same church. If you're uncomfortable, you can wait somewhere else or meet me downtown after I'm done. But I'm not worried about rumors. My wife's divorcing me, she's a lesbian, and frankly, I don't care what people think. It's a bit late for me to worry about rumors. This isn't a date; it's a service project."

Gina sighed, visibly frustrated. "I get it," she muttered, focusing back on the assembly line.

By the time they finished, his son and an unfamiliar friend walked in. They barely acknowledged Darius before disappearing down the hallway. He shook his head. "That's just how it is," he said to Gina, who looked at him questioningly.

As they loaded the car, she broke the silence and asked more about his situation.

"It's not good," he admitted as they drove downtown. "My business isn't doing well. My wife's been staying at her girlfriend's place, and my son barely talks to me anymore. I tried to ask him what he wanted, but he wouldn't say much. I would have fought for him in court, but he would only say he wanted to live with her. It hurt, but I am not having him testify in court against his Dad."

"Why do you think that is?" Gina asked.

"Last year, things were great between us, the best they had ever been. Then, at the start of this year, everything changed. He found out about his Mom's relationship, and ... I don't know. After she talked to him, he stopped speaking to me. Now, he avoids me whenever he can."

"That sounds hard."

"It is. Jessica wanted full custody; I wanted 50/50 custody. Last fall, he told me the opposite, that he'd never want to live with her full-time, but when I asked him about it recently, he said he wanted to live with her. I just don't understand."

"Maybe he's confused or angry about everything happening at once."

"Maybe," Darius said. "But I've tried to talk to him. He just won't let me in."

They arrived downtown, and Darius parked the car. From the trunk, Darius grabbed the case of water, and Gina carried the box of hamburgers, complete with ketchup and mustard. They began walking through the park, handing out food, offering prayers, and connecting with people. It was awesome to have her there, lending her support and sharing comforting touches.

As they made their way around the park, there was so much encouragement, and among it, Darius felt a spiritual presence as well. He would introduce them, ask their name, then hold their hand or place a hand on their shoulder as he prayed.

"Lloyd, it's good to meet you ... "

" ... God, I pray, we pray to you, our Creator, the infinite power of the universe, and through the redemptive blood of your son Jesus. I pray for Nancy ... "

" ... Father, I ask that you bring the Holy Spirit to Nathan, that he may see and hear clearly, and that you fill his heart with hope and optimism. Help him know how much you love him ... "

" ... You knew him before he was born; you formed him in his mother's womb, and he is made in your image. Even in difficult times, please, remind David of his worth. I pray that you bless him and that he sees your work in his life over the next few months, so he may glorify and praise you ... "

" ... In your name, I pray."

Almost every time, they were met with gratitude—a smile, a thank you, or an enthusiastic "Praise God." On one occasion, when Darius and Gina prayed for three men, the men were so moved that they turned around and prayed for Darius and Gina in return. It was amazing.

By the end of their rounds, only about eight burgers were left. Unsure of what to do with them, one person suggested they go to the bus station. Darius agreed, and they gathered up the remaining water bottles and burgers and started back toward the car. Just then, Darius paused and said, "Oh my gosh, would you look at that."

"What?" Gina asked, glancing in the direction he was pointing, and gasped. Above one of the government buildings was a brilliant rainbow.

"It must have been storming all around us, but the rain never touched us once. It's been a storm all over Indianapolis, but we've stayed dry."

Gina's eyes grew bigger. "You're right. And look, right after we finished feeding the last person, there's a rainbow. Look at this, Darius. It's God's blessing."

Darius nodded. "We have to get a photo of this."

Setting the leftovers aside for a moment, they snapped a picture, and as they did, Gina let out a laugh that made Darius chuckle, too.

"This is incredible," she said.

They drove to the bus station, parking where they could. Darius stepped out and began looking for people to share them with. Two men stood off to the side.

"Hey, would you like a burger?" he asked.

Their faces lit up.

"Really?" One said, surprised.

"Absolutely," Darius replied, heading back to the car. He leaned into the back seat, grabbed two burgers, and motioned for Gina to bring a couple of waters.

"Do you want ketchup or mustard?" Darius asked.

"Yes, please," they replied.

Darius added the condiments as Gina handed them the waters.

"Thank you so much," they said, their eyes wide with appreciation.

Darius asked, "What are your names?"

One man responded, "I'm Mike, and this is Will."

"Can I pray for you?" Darius asked. They nodded, surprised. Darius's prayer was simple, asking for blessings and an open door for their future. When he finished, he noticed a tear running down one of their cheeks.

"Thank you," Will whispered, his voice thick with emotion. "Thank you so much."

Darius smiled and said, "You're welcome." They sat down to eat, and Darius kept looking around for others to share with.

Darius continued scanning the area, finding a young Hispanic man next. Though the man spoke little English, they managed to communicate through gestures and the few Spanish words Darius knew. He handed the man a burger and a water, seeing the gratitude in his eyes.

With only two burgers left, Darius turned back toward the car but paused when he saw Mike and Will again. "Hey," he called out, "Do you guys want one more hamburger? We've still got two left!"

"Really?" Will asked, his voice lifting in disbelief. "Can we?"

"Of course," Darius said, bringing the burgers over.

As he handed them out, Will hesitated. "Can I ask you something?"

"Of course," Darius replied.

"Will you pray for me? A specific prayer?" Will's voice broke, and tears streamed down his face.

"Absolutely," Darius said gently. "What can I pray for you?"

Will took a deep breath, struggling to find the words. "My friend here is going back to St. Louis on the bus. I've been homeless for a few months now. I'm trying to work. I want to work, but I can't get a job."

Darius frowned. "What's keeping you from getting a job?"

Will shook his head, clearly frustrated. "I don't know. I don't understand. I've never been arrested. I don't have a record. I've just been through a really hard time, and I lost everything. But I'm willing. I just ... Please, will you pray that God will give me a job? Help me get back on my feet?"

Darius felt his heart tighten. "Yes," he said softly, pulling Will into a firm embrace. He prayed that God would not only give Will a job but one that would bring stability and abundance. That Will would soon have a home, a roof over his head, and a fresh start.

When he finished, Will's tears kept falling. "I'm sorry. This is so embarrassing," he said.

Darius looked at him gently. "Don't be sorry, Will. I've cried so many tears this past year, you can't even imagine. Don't be ashamed of your tears. The Bible says God hears every prayer and catches every tear. One day, He will wipe them all away. I believe incredible things are coming for you."

"Thank you," Will said, his voice breaking.

They embraced, and Darius stood up, looking at Gina as she approached the car. All the burgers and water had been distributed, and the two of them got in and drove away from downtown.

They rode in silence for a while, the car filled with a quiet sense of fulfillment. Finally, Gina broke the stillness. "There really aren't words to describe that, are there?"

"No," Darius agreed, eyes focused on the road ahead.

Gina sighed. "We have so much to be thankful for. It's just remarkable."

Darius nodded. "Most of my life, even when I was going to church, I believed in God, loved Him, or at least I thought I did. But I spent 99.9% of my life focused on myself. I'd go to church, sit through sermons daydreaming about lunch, or whether we'd skip out to watch the game. Giving my creator so little of my attention, my time. I was always stuck in my own lack and unworthiness, never truly present."

Gina looked at him curiously. "Yeah, I think I understand. But, what do you mean, 'never truly present?'"

Darius glanced over. "Have you ever heard of Joe Dispenza?"

"No," Gina said.

"Well, he's got this incredible story. He's a chiropractor who was hit by a Bronco during a triathlon. It destroyed his back. Doctors told him he'd need major surgery, but he refused. Over six months, he self-healed through meditation."

"That's not possible," Gina said, shaking her head.

Darius laughed. "It makes you rethink what you believe is possible, doesn't it?"

"Yeah," she laughed, "I'd love to know more if you've got more to share."

"I'll text it to you," Darius promised.

They continued driving, the silence between them now filled with wonder. "I can't thank you enough for letting me come tonight," Gina said.

"I want to do this more often," Darius said. "There are times I wonder if I've lost my mind, but God keeps speaking to me. This is what I'm supposed to do, so I'll be back, and you're always welcome to come with me."

"Thank you," Gina said, her voice quiet with gratitude.

When they got back, they exchanged a quick, heartfelt hug.

"You better not let anyone see you hug me!" Darius joked.

Gina frowned and punched his arm.

"That was special," she said, her eyes shining.

"Yes, it really was," Darius said. smiling as he watched her drive off.

Chapter 84
Where Focus Goes, Energy Flows

T he absurdity of it all. A bankruptcy lawyer, a divorce attorney, and an ongoing lawsuit. Each encounter was more surreal than the last.

He had met Bill, a bankruptcy lawyer, after a straightforward internet search. The first lawyer he called didn't handle business bankruptcies and referred him to Bill, who was pleasant enough over the phone. "Tell me about the situation," Bill had asked, and Darius gave him a condensed overview: a failing business, frozen assets, looming federal taxes, and a pending divorce.

Bill grunted periodically as Darius spoke, his nonverbal reactions oddly comforting. After a moment, Bill said, "In my opinion, as a professional, it's really not that bad."

It's not really that bad?

Bill elaborated, "You're not in default on anything. You're still paying on your buildings, right? You've got some cash reserves. Yeah, the credit card debt and the loan are a problem, but you've got options. One good month, and you're back in the black."

The unexpected optimism caught Darius off guard.

"Take a deep breath," Bill advised. "You're handling this better than most. Call me if things get worse, but I think you'll pull through."

The conversation ended on a hopeful note, leaving Darius with a faint but tangible sense of reassurance.

Meanwhile, his divorce attorney, Janice, was the epitome of competence; to say she was good at what she did was an understatement. She was in his corner, and as the proceedings dragged on, she grew more empathetic of his situation, particularly the developing situation with his son.

The first offer from his wife's attorney was lopsided—65% in her favor. "This is nuts," he muttered. But Janice was unfazed. "This is just their opening move. We'll negotiate it back to something reasonable," she told him. Darius trusted her, even as he grappled with the absurdity of selling assets he'd owned before the marriage, before he even knew her, like a plot of land in Tennessee. "It's part of the estate now," she explained. "We'll argue for a credit in your favor, but this is just something you're going to have to deal with and accept."

Darius tried to push the thought aside, but it clung stubbornly, a shadow lurking at the edges of his mind. The divorce had been complicated enough without the lingering frustration over the way things had been handled. His ex had waited to file, timing it strategically, and had sold off certain assets beforehand so they wouldn't appear on the official records. It all seemed absurd to him—the way the system only accounted for assets starting from the date of filing, while making him give her money from an asset he owned before knowing her.

Divorce and lawyers suck, he thought, rubbing a hand over his face. What was the point in dwelling on it? It didn't matter anymore. Not really. In the past ten years, how much had God provided? The answer was clear: more than he could have ever imagined. It was remarkable, truly. Everything that had been built came from God. And now, even as it slipped through his fingers, Darius couldn't help but feel a strange sense of peace.

Coming to the end of their meeting, they sent an offer back—one that would likely not be accepted and that they'd have to amend, but it was a start.

And then, in the middle of the divorce came the first lawsuit from a former employee—one of the strangest episodes in an already tumultuous year. The employee had resigned right before getting fired under tense circumstances and filed a claim for unpaid commissions. To Darius, it seemed absurd.

Darius leaned back on the couch in his office, phone pressed to his ear. His lawyer, Sully, was speaking, his tone confident as always. Sully wasn't just any lawyer; he'd graduated from Harvard Law and now ran a charity that Darius had supported for a decade. Thankfully, Sully was helping pro bono—Darius didn't have a lot of extra money for more legal fees, and Darius had supported the center substantially over the years.

This whole situation still baffled him. Running a business had always been hard, but he'd learned some very difficult lessons the hard way. Darius was great at creating, making money, and influencing, but he'd done a poor job of hiring and holding people accountable, and the lack of an HR person or HR support was a problem. While he had good intentions, he had been too generous in certain situations and wasn't always documenting and discussing challenges with employees clearly.

This situation pained Darius even more because he cared about the individual and it was his longest-tenured employee. When Jude had started, he was driving one hour each way for his job. Darius gave him an opportunity in a new industry and significant autonomy close to home. Jude had a child with difficulties similar to one of Darius's children, and Darius had been very supportive.

But while Darius was trying to be generous, he had really shot himself in the foot. Darius had taken he and his wife on a company trip to Europe, and even though Jude didn't qualify based on his billings, Darius hoped it would be great motivation. The next year, Jude had missed his goal by over $50k and then became indignant about missing the next company trip, claiming it should have been gifted for other contributions. Jude had not been hitting metrics and had also missed a lot of time in the second quarter. Along with the fact that Darius had just brought on new employees, it made no sense to give him the trip.

Then things had spiraled from there—disrespect, telling Darius he had no idea what the fuck he was doing, unmet expectations, and finally, a resignation that came just before Darius had planned to let him go. In hindsight, Jude wasn't wrong in accusing Darius of not knowing what he was doing—if only he had understood two years ago what he knew now.

Jude filed a complaint in civil court, demanding unpaid commissions from money that wouldn't materialize for months. It seemed crazy to Darius as no company he'd ever worked for paid commissions after someone left, voluntary or not. Though Jude hadn't contacted Darius to discuss his complaint or communicate after his last day, in hindsight, Darius regretted not just paying the money.

Sully, though, was confident. "There's no way we lose in court," he'd said more than once.

But Darius couldn't ignore the persistent tug at his conscience. On three separate occasions, he'd felt God urging him to settle out of court. The first time, he brushed it off. The second came that week while reading his morning Scripture, Matthew 5:24-25: *"leave your gift there before the altar and first go be reconciled to your brother, and then come and present your gift. Settle the case quickly with your accuser while you are with him on the way, lest your accuser hand you over to the judge, and the judge to the officer, and you be thrown into prison."*

Then, after a meditation session, Darius picked up his cell phone to find a missed call—from Jude, the very employee suing him.

"What in the world?" Darius muttered, staring at the screen. No message. Nothing. He hesitated, but the nudge from God seemed clear: *Call him back.*

The conversation started tense. Jude accused Darius of cheating him out of money, claiming the company had profited unfairly from his work. Also, Darius wasn't consistent with commissions or bonuses to recruiters versus operations personnel.

Darius took a deep breath. "Look, I'm not going to argue with you. I am getting divorced, and everything in my life feels like it's being taken away. Business isn't good. No disrespect, but this doesn't matter to me. If I had to do it over, I'd pay the money just to avoid all of this."

Jude softened. "I didn't think that was an option."

"Well, you never reached out, did you?" Darius replied. "What do you want? I am willing to settle and not go to court."

From there, they started negotiating.

At one point, Jude started to bring up a negative perspective of the past. Darius respectfully interrupted, "Look, Jude, I did a lot for you, and things that I didn't have to do that come to a lot more money than you believe you are owed. Obviously, we don't agree on the situation. I am not going to debate it with you. If you want to settle, then let's agree and settle. Otherwise, you can take your chances in court with Sully."

The phone was quiet for a minute, and then Jude concurred.

Half the disputed commission in cash, plus assets like office furniture and a few personal items. Jude agreed. When he came to pick everything up, he even brought a Bourbon County Stout to split—a gesture of reconciliation.

They sat together for half an hour, talking about life. It was the first time they'd spoken in over a year. They both agreed that they wished things had turned out differently.

Darius shrugged. "Water under the bridge. I've got no hard feelings. I wish you the best."

They shook hands, hugged, and Jude left.

Later, Darius called Sully. "It's over."

"What do you mean? We're going to court next week!"

Darius explained.

"You're kidding," Sully said, stunned. "Man, I was looking forward to crushing him in court. He needed to be humbled!"

"Maybe," Darius replied and then shared how he felt God told him through Scripture, meditation, and then the missed phone call. "But I think this was more about God continuing to humble me. I had to obey, even if it didn't make sense. And maybe God will use it to bring Jude to him in the future? And now ... I feel peace."

Sully sighed, "You're probably right, but man, does that arrogant punk need humility!"

They laughed together.

"God's certainly pruning you, Darius," Sully laughed, "And amazing things will come from it. Just keep leaning in."

Darius smiled faintly, hanging up. Alone in his office, he looked up at the ceiling and whispered, "Thank you, Lord."

***

Monday marked the beginning of what Darius would later call Manifestation Week. After returning from Whistler, he had thrown himself entirely into the teachings of Dr. Joe Dispenza. Back in December, Adam had introduced him to some of Dispenza's meditations during DWD. Since then, Darius had been meditating daily for 30 to 45 minutes. By February, the results were undeniable. He felt lighter, and the weight of negativity—the financial pressures, the chaos of his business, the betrayal of his wife flaunting her girlfriend, even his son's coldness—wasn't as painful. He wasn't focused on it and felt mostly happy and optimistic.

The bizarre circumstances of his life weren't triggering him. It was astonishing, really. Events that would have crushed him before were now opportunities for growth. He wasn't drowning his sorrows in alcohol, nor numbing himself with distractions. He was happy. He was meditating, centered, and remarkably detached from the chaos.

Through the practice of letting go, Darius was rewiring his mind. Bad habits and old defense mechanisms were dissolving, and he was learning to harness higher emotions in real time. Instead of reacting to situations, he could pause, assess, and choose not to engage if it didn't serve him. If he made a mistake, he could quickly acknowledge it and identify the mistake he had made to help him choose differently the next time. For the first time in his life, Darius had found peace—an ironic revelation, given the madness that surrounded him.

By February, his commitment had deepened. He extended his meditation sessions to an hour and a half each day and devoured three more of Dispenza's books, starting with *Becoming Supernatural*. Having read it once, he returned to it after finishing *You Are the Placebo*. Each morning, he would sit by the biocharger, read a chapter, and start his day with a smile. Everything he was learning about healing, manifestation, and the interplay of science and spirituality seemed to align seamlessly with Hawkin's work on consciousness, what Tony Robbins taught, and, to Darius, was backed by Scripture. Hawkin's teachings on energy and muscle testing relevant to truth, as well as the information Dr. Joe shared on waves, energy, and the quantum, lined up remarkably with what the Bible taught about spiritual realms.

The teachings reinforced truths he had begun to embrace. Suffering was optional—it was a choice, as Tony Robbins often said. There were no victims, only volunteers. Negative emotions, Darius believed, were clearly the currency of the demonic realm, feeding off lower frequencies to manipulate, control, and create chaos. Conversely, higher emotions like gratitude and joy were scientifically proven to create biochemical conditions for thriving. What you focused on expanded as one activated specific genes to create specific chemicals leading to those emotions.

Armed with this understanding, Darius threw himself into meditations designed to recondition his body to a new mind. He practiced opening his heart and pulling up positive emotions, even in the face of adversity. While he was vastly improving his ability to bring in and shift his emotions, manifestation was still a frontier that both intrigued and challenged him. The Scripture pointing to manifesting via faith, emotion, and intention seemed correct as well.

One of Dispenza's meditations, "Tuning Into New Potentials," became his focus. The exercise involved writing down goals—first in symbolic shorthand, and then in detailed intentions fueled by elevated emotions. The science behind this, as detailed in Dispenza's books, fascinated him. Darius recalled an experiment involving DNA strands stored in jars within refrigerated cabinets. Groups meditated on unwinding the tightly bundled strands. Intentions alone had no effect, nor did meditating with elevated emotions without a clear goal. However, when intention and elevated emotions were combined, the DNA strands unwound.

With this in mind, Darius crafted his own list of intentions. At the top, he wrote the letter *F*, flanked by squiggly lines, symbolizing financial freedom. Beneath it, he outlined his desires:

- *In the next 90 days, I will generate $250,000.*
- *I will bring on 2 new clients.*
- *One old client will return and want to work with me again.*
- *Something extraordinary will happen.*
- *The divorce will be finalized.*
- *The $164,000 owed in federal taxes will be paid off.*
- *The $250,000 owed by the business will also be paid off.*
- *I will close on a new property to live in within six months.*

As he looked at the list, Darius considered the emotions he would feel if these manifestations came to pass: limitless, grateful, bountiful. He added another line: *"I will give $20,000 to charity."*

Sitting back, Darius read over the list, nodded, and thought, Yes, this is exactly what I want to create.

For weeks now, he had been faithfully meditating every single day. Each session began with bringing his mind into coherence during the first 10 to 15 minutes. Then, as the meditation shifted to the specifics of his intentions, he would focus on each item from his list, imagining those desires already fulfilled. He infused these thoughts with powerful emotions: gratitude, abundance, excitement, and a sense of being limitless.

"Live it," Dr. Joe Dispenza would say during the meditation, prompting Darius to vividly picture the outcomes he desired. He imagined himself receiving job offers, speaking on larger stages, presenting confidently, and walking through the new house he envisioned as his next home. The final part of each session was steeped in gratitude. Dr. Joe emphasized, "Gratitude is the greatest act of receivership. Get up like your prayers have already been answered."

Darius had been following this process for about 10 weeks, and then it started happening. Manifestation Week.

It began on a Thursday. Out of nowhere, a top-12 global medical device company, one he hadn't worked with in four years, reached out with four engineering roles. Darius was stunned. This company, while impressive on paper, had been notoriously difficult in the past to work with—slow processes and endless red tape. Before his Jōb-like year started, he would have declined to work with them, but now he couldn't afford to be choosy. He accepted and started on the roles, grateful to have something to work on again.

The following Monday, something even more remarkable occurred. Nancy, a favorite client from a few years ago, reached out. She had helped set up the contract and was the first person Darius had worked with at one of his largest Medtech accounts, where he had filled many roles. When Nancy moved to a new Pharma company, she brought him along, and he successfully filled 11 roles at the company. But after the pandemic, positions had slowed, and they'd lost contact, which was a mistake on Darius's part. That Monday morning, after finishing his meditation and sitting down for business development, he saw her email.

She had a confidential, critical position reporting to the CFO and needed someone she trusted to fill it. Darius couldn't believe it. They scheduled a video call, during which Nancy explained the details. Toward the end of the conversation, she asked how he was doing. Darius hesitated, then decided to be honest, sharing the challenges he'd been facing: the divorce, the struggles with the business, the financial strain. Nancy was empathetic and shocked.

"Oh my gosh, Darius, I'm so sorry," she said, then half-jokingly added, "I'd like to punch her in the face." Darius laughed, her kindness a balm to his weary soul. She was surprised—his social media posts had painted a picture of success.

"Well, why didn't you call me?" Nancy asked. "I would have given you business."

Darius reminded her of a video message he'd sent over Christmas that had gone unanswered. She explained she'd assumed he wasn't taking on work without upfront payment anymore.

"That's not true," he clarified. "I am still willing to do exclusive contingency roles with people I trust."

"Hang on," she said, turning away from the screen. Moments later, she returned and announced, "I just sent you four more jobs."

"What?" Darius's eyes widened.

"I'll send you the notes about the managers," she added. "I'll do anything I can to help you get through this."

After the call, Darius sat in stunned gratitude. If he filled just three of those roles, it would bring in over $100,000 in revenue. He glanced at his phone, his mind swirling with disbelief.

Three days later, another message came through. Ruth, a candidate Darius had placed three years ago, reached out about a product management marketing role. She'd been a joy to work with, and the placement had been a win-win for everyone involved. Though he hadn't worked with her company in over 18 months, Ruth assured him the role was already approved, and she was hopeful Darius could take it on.

Darius agreed immediately, feeling as if he were riding a wave of alignment. By the end of the week, he had secured multiple opportunities across three different clients. Sitting at his laptop, he calculated the potential revenue: $251,000—an exact match to the financial freedom goal he had been meditating on.

He leaned back in his chair, overwhelmed by the sheer precision of it all. Looking upward, he whispered, "God, You are amazing."

Joy surged through his body as he reflected on the transformation of his life. The divorce might still be in progress, and challenges remained, but everything was changing. He thought about the quantum realm, as Dr. Joe described it, and the parallels to spiritual realms. Darius had been working hard his entire life moving matter against matter—or in force, depending on the appropriate teacher's perspective. He believed God was opening his eyes to how energy, faith, and true blessings were meant to work. He believed that God was leading him down a path that would keep leading to greater enlightenment if he kept moving forward.

Darius realized he was learning to create his life with focused intention, gratitude, and purpose. What could that mean for the rest of his life? It wasn't about him—it was about blessing others and living out his higher calling.

"Where focus goes, energy flows," he murmured, laughing at the simplicity of the statement while now understanding the power of the concept. His future was bright, and for the first time in his life, he was starting to wonder or possibly realize if he was in covenant with God, honoring his statutes and direction, seeking Him first and His Will, with this new understanding and tools, maybe he really could be limitless.

Chapter 85
Three's a Crowd

arius positioned himself in the Brew Pub, choosing a quieter spot in the bar area where there weren't as many people. He knew most of the staff and liked them—they were always kind to him. One of his children had worked there for a while, so his relationship with the staff wasn't just transactional. They knew him on a more personal level. Many were aware of his struggles over the past year and, to his surprise, had been empathetic, even overly considerate. He appreciated their kindness, though he sometimes felt it was more than he deserved.

His lifestyle had changed dramatically. There was a time when he could eat out wherever and whenever he wanted without giving it a second thought. Money hadn't been an issue. But now, things were different. There was the divorce, the business finally had jobs but was not making money, and then there was his diet.

For the first few months of his holistic health journey, he ate exclusively organic, which meant cooking at home most of the time. Restaurants rarely catered to that standard—most sauces, side dishes, and even vegetables contained additives or chemicals.

Occasionally, he'd grab a burger from Five Guys or stop at Chipotle, but otherwise, he cooked. Even after completing the intense cleansing process, Darius was committed to maintaining his health. Dr. Whitman had advised him to stick to a mostly organic diet, at least 70–80% of the time, to sustain this new homeostasis.

The results were worth it. Darius felt better, slept better, and his body worked more efficiently. Remarkably, he even managed to sleep well despite the ongoing stress in his life—a small victory in an otherwise overwhelming time.

But tonight, he decided to treat himself. Screw it, he thought. He was exhausted from the unrelenting pressure brought by his situation. The divorce proceedings with his wife had spiraled into chaos, and living in the basement tomb of their shared house felt suffocating.

He hadn't expected it to be well-received when he moved back in, but he'd felt he had no choice. His financial situation, compounded by the struggling business and tax issues, made renting an apartment impossible. Staying with friends wasn't an option anymore, either. Spiritually, he believed this was the path he was meant to take, though the reality was far from what he had hoped for.

Initially, it had been tolerable. For the first few weeks, there was an uneasy calm. Conversations were brief and neutral. She was polite, exchanged pleasantries, then disappeared. But once her relationship with her girlfriend became public knowledge, everything changed. She began spending her evenings away, often not returning until late. While she had just filed for divorce in August, her behavior showed she had mentally checked out long ago. Darius didn't mind her absence—it was easier that way—but the atmosphere in the house grew darker and colder. The basement, where he was staying, felt oppressive, like the depths of a dungeon.

He had hoped moving back in might help him reconnect with his son. They'd had a promising time together in North Carolina, meditating, reading Scripture, and talking about healthy living. Darius had shared research on how diet could affect conditions like ADHD, believing wholeheartedly that his son could benefit from making similar changes. He'd even presented pages of highlighted studies, hoping to spark interest. But nothing came of it. Change was hard, and his son seemed unwilling—or perhaps unable—to consider it. His wife had ignored the information Darius shared.

The distance between them grew. His son became more withdrawn, always out with friends or busy. His wife continued scheduling their son's time without consulting him. When his son was home, it often felt chaotic, with kids coming and going at all hours. Darius had been woken up multiple times in the middle of the night by the commotion. Admittedly, he hadn't handled it well at first. One night, the noise upstairs became unbearable. He awoke and snapped. Marching upstairs, he found his son in bed and two friends wrestling in the middle of the room at 1:30 AM.

"If you want to act like this, you're welcome to go home," he'd said sternly. The boys stared at him as if he were a ghost. His son shot him a dirty look. Darius retreated to the basement, immediately regretting it. He hated that he'd lost his temper, but the frustration was mounting.

Another incident occurred with the boys at 3:30 in the morning. Darius approached them and, although he spoke more calmly than before, expressed similar sentiments. He mentioned that even if his son didn't respect him, he still had to wake up at 5:00 AM and would appreciate it if they considered the time. One of the boys had responded, "Yes, Sir," while the others remained silent.

Darius returned to the basement, feeling as if everything was falling apart. While he had beaten himself up a lot over the summer as his awareness grew, he was done beating himself up since the Tony Robbins events. He had put in an immense amount of effort to grow, endured great humiliation while eating large amounts of crow, and made significant sacrifices. Now, here he was, living in the house he paid for, a house he had been funding alone until February, when he finally ran out of money.

He was fed up with being taken advantage of, especially considering the attitude his soon-to-be ex-wife had. It felt as though he was just expected to foot the bill while she lived her life. The sense of entitlement, the extreme lack of any respect, and the dismissive attitude as she brought her girlfriend around their son and into their home with the divorce pending were becoming intolerable.

After the relationship had been openly acknowledged and his wife had confessed to their children, the situation in their home shifted dramatically. For a while, she was rarely there and had avoided bringing her partner into the house like she had previously, as she thought no one knew the truth. But by February, moving into March, things took a surprising and unsettling turn. Darius found the situation not only disrespectful but dark and cruel.

The first instance that left him reeling occurred when he came home from work one evening. He walked into the house to find his wife and her partner outside, firing up the grill for dinner. Stopping in the kitchen, Darius's immediate thought was, *You have to be fucking kidding me.* While he had consciously reduced his use of profanity since last summer, this caught him by surprise. He had now read 55 of the books in the Bible, and the consistent direction on what came out of your mouth was clear. But at that moment, it was too much. It was blatantly disrespectful and in his face.

He glanced at them outside, then at the microwave and stove, and thought, What in the world? He couldn't fathom what it would be like if he were bringing another woman into the house six months after filing for divorce, as if it were perfectly acceptable. The thought made him furious, but he pushed it down. What was he going to do? He got food out of the fridge and made a meal.

At one point, his wife came into the house. Since the revelation of her relationship, they hadn't spoken. They would pass each other in the house, avoiding any interaction—it had become routine. There was no need for him to bring it up; she had nothing to say to him, and he wasn't going to guilt or shame her. She clearly had no reservations about the situation and wasn't hiding it. There were a few moments when he thought about confronting her, but in those instances, he reflected on all the progress he'd made with the Marriage Reset Program, his spiritual journey, and personal growth. What good would it serve? He realized it would only fuel his ego and come from a place of judgment or victimhood, and he was not a victim.

So, in the rare moments when he wanted to say something, he chose not to. He sat with his feelings to start letting them go, prepared dinner, ate, and then left the house. He went to the park, lay on a blanket, meditated for an hour, and let the emotions pass.

The second incident came when his wife's partner brought a young boy over, and they were back in the backyard. It irked Darius, and he thought about how selfish his wife and her girlfriend were relevant to their children.

The third situation, however, which happened just the week before, was baffling. It was a Friday night, and Darius had planned to make chicken and asparagus. He entered the house through the garage and was met with an unexpected scene: his wife sitting cross-legged on the kitchen counter, a position he'd never seen her in before. To her right was one of her close friends, whom he had considered a close friend, too. His son was standing near the kitchen table, and at the sink, leaning casually against the sink, was his wife's girlfriend—wearing a boa constrictor or possibly a python around her neck. Darius paused mid-step as they continued their conversation as if he wasn't even there.

Darius didn't know what to do. He stood frozen in place, thoughts swirling aimlessly. Eventually, he walked into the kitchen, trying to collect himself. I'm not going to let them intimidate or bother me, he thought firmly. Deciding to make dinner, he turned on the stove. No gas. That made no sense. Then he realized nobody was paying the bills anymore since he had stopped.

His mind felt hazy, overwhelmed by the tension in the house. He placed the small bag of groceries he'd intended to cook with into the fridge, shut it, and turned away. Without a word, he walked out of the house, got into his car, and drove off. *You cannot make this shit up,* he thought. *What in the world is going on?*

Then, there was that look their friend, Beth, had given him earlier. That expression—like he was the one in the wrong, like he'd been caught stealing—stung deeply. He wondered how they could think this was okay. The sheer absurdity of it baffled him. What if the roles were reversed? Him inviting friends to hang out with a new girlfriend while still living in the same house during a divorce? Who would think that was acceptable?

Yet somehow, he was the bad guy. He had also given Beth and her husband a lot of financial assistance in the past. Would she enjoy him showing up at her house with her husband and his girlfriend while acting like she was trespassing? It seemed insane to him!

When he had told his wife there was no more money to cover bills or utilities, she exploded, demanding he move out if he wasn't going to pay.

Maybe you should get your girlfriend to pay, or maybe you should move into her apartment? he thought. She was shameless. He decided no response was the best. If she didn't like it, she could move out.

He had always been the majority breadwinner, and that was fine. Since the separation had started, he had continued paying the majority of their expenses, but that was over. Friends had told him he was crazy, but back then, he had hoped they'd work through things. Now? She was chasing company assets while he was barely staying afloat. He still had some money in the business account, but he wasn't generating income. Paying for everything while being disrespected so flagrantly? Enough was enough. He was trying to understand his own attitude. He wasn't a meek person, but in thinking about some of his business mistakes, he sensed a pattern and something he needed to uncover and learn from.

***

Darius went to the park to reset. He'd managed to shift his mindset in just 10 minutes. As he arrived, a thought struck him: *What are you going to do? Have a pity party? Drink yourself into oblivion?* The idea made him laugh. Nobody deserves that satisfaction. He was in control of his emotions, nobody else.

He laid out his blanket and meditated to Dr. Joe's "Reconditioning the Body to a New Mind," grounding himself. After an hour of stillness, he felt clarity return, and shortly after that, he decided to make for Brewlink.

The bartender brought him a beer without him even asking. "How's it going, man?" he asked, offering an ear if Darius wanted or needed it.

"About as well as you can imagine," Darius laughed before chatting and learning about Jack's recent happenings in return. Darius ordered food and settled in to watch basketball on the TV across the bar.

His phone buzzed and he looked down to see a text from Karl.

If you want to understand the specific demons that attacked your home, you need to get this book.

There was a picture of a book called, Return of the Gods by Jonathan Cahn.

Darius texted back. Ok. Never heard of Cahn. Who is he?

A Messianic Jew who does a lot of work on prophecy. Several best selling books. He's good.

Ok, sounds good, brother. I'll get it.

Wee wee, brother, Karl texted back.

Darius laughed and shook his head. He immediately went to Amazon and ordered the book.

Darius had made a joke about Karl's Kentucky accent along with his spelling. During a conversation, Karl had mis appropriated a particular word and Darius was confused. Karl laughed, explained, and said "you know what I mean!"

After the clarification, Darius said well, "you Frenchmen from Kentucky are difficult to understand!" They both laughed heartily and not long after Karl would sometimes end a call with oui, oui but if he texted it would be wee wee.

Darius smiled again thinking about it and their growing friendship. After the 3rd interaction, Darius realized that not only was Karl unlike anyone he had ever met, but that they were going to know each other for a long time. He had never met anyone previously that God spoke to directly and now he had met two, Karl and Rowdy, that God was sharing information with specifically meant for him. The conversations Darius had with Karl and the information he shared from God always blew Darius away and there was no way Karl could know the specifics he was sharing, unless It was coming from a greater power. It was.... Wild, Darius thoughts.

Jonathan Cahn, huh, Darius thought. Well, no doubt this was going to be interesting.

As he sipped his drink, it was hard for Darius to fully comprehend how much his life had changed. In just over a month and a half, it would be a year since he had met with the emotional trauma therapist. Less than four weeks after that, his wife had told him it was over.

More than a year and a half earlier, he had felt like he was on top of the world. An incredible trip to Africa, a thriving business, and big plans ahead. But now, he reflected on everything that had unraveled. He thought about *Prayers Satan Hates* and what happened when the light of truth came on. If a person's light started getting too big, evil tried to snuff it out. When he read that, it hit him hard.

He didn't see himself as special or righteous—far from it. But he couldn't help but draw parallels between his life and Jōb's story. The way God spoke to Satan in the book, saying, **"Have you considered my servant Jōb? Indeed, there is no one like him on the earth—a blameless man and upright and God-fearing and turning away from evil"**, made Darius pause.

During a recent Kevin Zedai sermon, Kevin had suggested some people look at challenges incorrectly. *Did you ever consider maybe God was bragging about you?* That hadn't made sense to Darius at first because, with his new awareness of certain past behaviors, he couldn't imagine God bragging about him. But he was definitely a different person, and he was starting to wonder what God had planned for him all this time.

He thought, If Jōb were here, we'd have one heck of a conversation. Darius shook his head. The dysfunction was overwhelming—he was back in the Twilight Zone.

He had been cutting alcohol out of his life, only drinking wine or beer occasionally. But sometimes, the stress and pain still made it hard to resist old habits.

As he sipped his second beer, he thought to himself, And you know what? I'm okay with that. I've come a long way. He took a deep breath and reminded himself of the progress he'd made—physical, emotional, and spiritual healing.

"God, I just need some financial healing now," he chuckled.

Darius realized he was in a new phase, even if everything crumbled around him. He had learned so much over the past nine years. He had managed to make back his retirement money and generate millions in revenue. And if he lost everything, he could start over—smarter and wiser, without repeating the same mistakes.

He finished the beer and nodded to the bartender for the check.

It was time to head back to the tomb.

Chapter 86
Supernatural Love With Obedience

Darius couldn't put down *Becoming Supernatural*. The ideas Dr. Joe Dispenza presented were blowing his mind, especially the connections between emotions, energy, and health. The way Dispenza explained the detrimental effects of living under the influence of stress hormones struck a deep chord with him. It wasn't just about the external factors like chemicals, pesticides, or medications, although Darius knew those played a role, it was also about his own inability to properly manage his emotions.

He thought about it for a moment. Inability. Was that the right word to describe it? He'd never been taught how to process emotions healthily, and that "inability" had built up like a boiler gaining too much steam. Dr. Whitman had told him something similar the previous summer, pointing out that his body had never been in a state where it could properly heal. Instead, it had been in constant survival mode, overwhelmed by stress, toxic overload, and poor lifestyle habits.

What fascinated Darius most, though, was the science behind shared energy and emotions. Dispenza's insights into how people with the same emotions and energy naturally bonded—just like atoms—were remarkable. It made Darius think about the connections between his thoughts, his environment, and the people he interacted with. The more he learned, the clearer it became that everything was interconnected: thoughts, emotions, health, and relationships.

This wasn't just about his physical body—it was about understanding how his entire way of being was shaping his life. The deeper he dove into Dispenza's teachings, the more hope he felt that he could continue to fundamentally transform himself in all areas— physically, emotionally, and most importantly, spiritually.

Darius was captivated by the insights he was learning.

One section explained the transition from beta to alpha, theta, delta, and gamma brain waves and how they related to meditation so one could best enter the subconscious mind to reprogram it. By doing this correctly, a person would then waste less time and energy on lower level emotions or past traumas. Where focus goes, energy flows, he thought, smiling at how Tony Robbins' voice seemed to echo in his mind.

Understanding these concepts, especially how to harness the "sweet spot" of the generous present moment, was transformative. In this state, as Dr. Joe Dispenza described, you weren't tethered to the familiar past or its predictable future. Instead, in the uncertainty of the present moment, you unlocked the greatest potential for creation. By meditating consistently, overcoming the habitual thoughts and emotions tied to past experiences, the meditator could break the cycle that kept his future the same.

It was the concept of "nerves that fire together wire together," and by shifting his focus away from past traumas or unkindness and staying in the present, he could reclaim energy previously lost to those memories. That reclaimed energy became a powerful tool for creation. He could consciously craft a positive energy field, attracting what he wanted and repelling negativity.

It felt as if, for the first time, he was truly present—not mired in the past or bogged down by current challenges. That clarity allowed him to escape the pain of unkindness or chaos in his surroundings. He realized now how rare it was in his past life for him to actually *be* in the moment.

He thought about past trips and milestones: climbing a mountain, completing a vacation, only to immediately plan what was next. It was always about significance and certainty. He laughed, remembering how he used to obsessively plan vacations, kids' activities, or even outcomes in business months or years in advance. He saw now how those behaviors were rooted in his need for control and stability. But now, his drivers were growth and contribution. The certainty, which once dictated his every move, would no longer hold him captive.

Sitting in his office, he reflected on the uncertainty surrounding him. A year ago, it would have driven him mad. Now, he felt calm, energized, and present.

As he was continuing to learn to muscle test, he realized how his level of consciousness had grown. It was wild. Testing himself from various angles and using different methods, Darius found the results consistent—all the data points were coming together, creating a cohesive understanding.

Reflecting on his journey, Darius thought about the people in his life who he felt had wronged him or been unkind: his wife, his mother, the employee setting up a business dishonestly, and employees suing him. As the Scripture continued to show nothing done in the dark or dishonestly stays hidden. But it surprised him that he had no anger toward any of them. He had prayed for all of them consistently and only wanted to take accountability for his flaws, to not judge, and to grow.

Just like Dr Joe had suggested: living in the present moment was the key. He wasn't ruminating on the past or worrying about the future. It was a liberating way to live. Tony Robbins' advice echoed in his mind: *"The fewer rules you have, the happier you'll be."*

He thought back to when he had started the Marriage Reset Program, recognizing how much he had changed. While the journey had no end date, as he continued to do the work, he wasn't seeking love and validation now. Being present meant learning not to respond, control, or dictate, but to understand, validate, and connect—to respond versus react. Perhaps this was a key aspect of showing love in its purest form—simply showing up fully for others with no agenda or preconceived notions.

Darius saw so many parallels to Scripture. He thought he was beginning to understand the role of the Holy Spirit and how that could lead to access to the gifts of the Spirit: knowledge, wisdom, healing, miracles, discernment of spirits, speaking in tongues, interpretation of tongues, faith, and prophecy. So much of what people perceived of religion or God was wrong. People oftentimes took Scripture out of context, and it was obvious Satan had used Scripture incorrectly to tempt Jesus and Jesus had rebuked Satan by correcting him with Scripture. Even more remarkable, he realized it was the Holy Spirit that had been communicating with him!

Darius thought of love. Paul shared that if you had the Holy Spirit and all the gifts but didn't have love, then the law and the prophets didn't matter. Part of true love was obedience. Darius had lost count how many times God stated you must honor the covenant, uphold His statues and if you did he would bless you. Additionally, He shared clearly why: because if you didn't you wouldn't be able to handle the enemy. It was for your own good.

In Luke 6:46, Jesus said, *"And why do you call me 'Lord, Lord,' and do not do what I tell you?"* Darius believed he was starting to understand why fear of the Lord was the beginning of wisdom. So much of religion came across as judgemental, but the Scripture taught humans were not to judge or take up vengeance. One of his favorite new verses was 2 Timothy 2:22-26:

"But flee from youthful desires, and pursue righteousness, faith, love, and peace, in company with those who call upon the Lord from a pure heart. But avoid foolish and uninformed controversies, because you know that they produce quarrels. And the slave of the Lord must not quarrel, but be kind toward everyone, skillful in teaching, tolerant, correcting those who are opposed with gentleness, seeing whether perhaps God may grant them repentance to a knowledge of the truth, and they will come to their senses again and escape from the trap of the devil, being held captive by him to do his will."

Most churches didn't seem to believe in the gifts, Darius thought. He was 52, had grown up in the church, and had no real understanding of prophecy, of the Holy Spirit, of the gifts, and no understanding of the demonic forget about witchcraft or curses. It seemed obvious to Darius that sin opened doors to the demonic and then the lower level emotions that allowed them to manipulate, influence, and open doors that weren't good.

What was clear to him was how much God loved his creation and how much the enemy hated God's creation. While God brought his followers the fruits of the Spirit, peace, and prosperity, Satan brought chaos, death, infighting, human sacrifices, and destruction.

Darius thought witchcraft, curses, and sorcery were ... fables or myths of a superstitious past. Now he was confused, but realizing that didn't seem to be the case at all. He had so much more to learn and understand.

Darius wanted to get to Unconditional Love on the scale of consciousness. He didn't know if he would be able to, but he knew he would not stop trying to grow and reach it. For the first time in his life, he thought he might understand the truth behind Agape Love. For humans, it started with being obedient to God's direction, sharing the truth of God's love, power, and prosperity for his creation while sounding the alarm regarding the enemy.

For the first time in his life, Darius wanted to share the gospel. It was sharing a message of truth, hope, and prosperity while sounding the alarm but with no judgment or pride. In Isaiah, God stated He will be in heaven with the humble and contrite of heart. It had been a challenging year of humility and destruction of pride, Darius thought, and unfortunately, it had been needed.

Chapter 87
Dad—Wake Up!

While Darius was not focused on it for the most part, in regards to the divorce, time dragged on, and he hated spending money on lawyers. Looking at the spreadsheet, he would think, *What the hell?*, then quickly catching himself, and whisper, "Oh, sorry, God."

His lawyer became a broken record: "We'll get there. We're moving toward a fair settlement. We'll get to the 50/50."

Darius despised lawyers. One of his favorite jokes was, "What do you call 500 lawyers at the bottom of the ocean? A good start." He thought they were the pariah of the world and had even considered handling the divorce without one. He had offered to have her share what she wanted directly, and then, once they agreed, her lawyer could draw it up. Her response was that she had talked to her lawyer, and he couldn't represent them both. "No kidding," Darius thought. "That's not what I offered."

The last meeting had been a flurry of negotiation, horse-trading, and posturing. They were now less than two weeks from mediation, an event that would cost thousands at best and if they went to court—$30,000, $40,000, maybe even $50,000 in total. Who knew? Going to court wasn't what he wanted, especially with the $160,000 tax debt hanging over their heads. He'd tried to sell assets last fall to cover it, but once again, she had refused.

After that meeting, he just wanted to escape and do something fun. He loved live music, and even better if it took place outdoors. So that Friday, he decided to visit one of his favorite German bars, the Rathskeller, downtown for dinner and live music. The weather was perfect, and the beer garden was buzzing with life. His middle son, Sheehan, and his girlfriend joined him, and they spent the evening eating, listening to the band, and enjoying a few drinks.

They moved on to a nearby bar with arcade games. Laughter and the clinking of glasses filled the air while they played different video games. As they were about to leave, his son said, "Hey, there's a party over at a bar near the house. My girlfriend's family's there, dancing and having a good time. Want to go?"

Darius hesitated, then nodded. They drove 25 minutes to Mooresville, and when they arrived, a group of 10 to 15 of his son's girlfriend's family were gathered, drinking and dancing. He accepted another drink, then another as the fun continued. The stress of the divorce, the hope of avoiding mediation or court were gone for the evening. He remembered leaning in to talk to Kim, one of the family friends, his hand resting on her back. She was kind, pretty, and fun. It had been 11 months since this whole situation had started; the divorce wasn't final yet, but he had to admit, even though dating wasn't on his mind, it was nice to talk to somebody and nice to be flirted with.

He had a blast dancing, but then, trying to steady himself, he realized he'd had one too many. It was time to leave.

As Darius pulled into his driveway later that night, he knew he'd had too much. He stumbled into bed and fell into a restless sleep.

***

"Dad, wake up! Dad, wake up!" His son's voice jolted him awake.

Darius blinked, confused.

His head throbbed, and he struggled to piece together what was happening.

The only thing he could think was, *Where am I?*

"Dad!"

His son shook him awake, and suddenly, he knew exactly where he was: the basement.

"Dad, Dad, Dad, come on, we have to get everything together."

"What's going on?" Darius muttered, the hangover making it hard to focus.

"We're moving everything out today," Sheehan said. "The guys are coming soon."

Darius's heart dropped. What did I do?

He sat up, head pounding, the weight of the morning pressing in. His mind raced as he processed the situation. The divorce had forced him into a corner. He assumed certain things would be his since she was getting the house—his massage chair, the lawnmower, and his art he'd bought in different countries. But reality had blurred those lines.

After getting ready, he stumbled and climbed the steps out of the basement and found Sheehan and his girlfriend, Rachel, standing in the kitchen. She gave him a hug, "My folks will be here soon with the truck."

Darius, still foggy, nodded.

"So what are we starting with?" Sheehan asked.

Rachel took the lead. "Well, let's drain the hot tub first. That'll be the easiest."

The process of draining the hot tub was not as simple as it first appeared, but Rachel's app guided them on how to disconnect the hot tub. Darius rubbed his forehead, the tension building. He felt the alcohol from last night creeping into his thoughts, twisting everything into a storm of uncertainty.

What did I do? he thought.

"Dad, what are we taking?" His son's voice snapped him back.

"I'll take the hot tub, the massage chair, my desk, and a few paintings. Everything else stays," Darius said, the fatigue laced in his voice. It seemed reasonable, especially since she was keeping the house and was getting all the appliances and the $100k pool that was put in the prior year with it while he had to find a place.

The process continued. He took down art from the walls—pieces that reminded him of places he'd been, memories that felt distant. After getting those down, he headed back to the back bedroom. There were a few things he wanted to pick up. He reached the locked door of their old bedroom, and it was locked. What? She installed a new lock. No way to retrieve the painting and the encyclopedia from his grandfather now.

As he came back, the sound of voices and moving equipment filled the air. His phone vibrated on the kitchen table. It was a text from Jessica, a message that sent a shiver down his spine:

You all need to stop. What you're doing is not right. You can't take anything out of the house.

Darius sighed, frustration and exhaustion coiling together in his chest. When he moved into the office last fall, she'd told him that he could take anything he wanted. The irony. He tapped out a reply:

You told me last fall that I could take anything out of the house that I wanted, so I'm just taking the things that are mine.

That's ridiculous. This needs to go through the lawyers.

Go back and look at the text history. You texted me that I could take whatever I wanted. You're getting the house; you're getting everything in it. I'm just taking some of the things that are mine, that I paid for.

He put the phone down, rubbed his temples, and watched as people moved in and out, carrying the last items to the trucks. The hot tub was nearly drained, and two of his son's friends lifted the massage chair onto the back of the van.

Suddenly, in the haze or in a moment of clarity, Darius thought back to when he had moved back into the house. Concerned that Jessica might lock him out or otherwise prevent him from accessing the property, he had unlocked all the windows as a precaution. Smiling at the memory, he walked over to the window of what had once been the master bathroom and bedroom he used. Testing it, he lifted the window. Still unlocked.

With a grin, he crawled through the opening, landing quietly inside. He walked over to the closet that had once been his and began pulling out the remaining clothes left there. After unlocking the bedroom door, he carried the clothes downstairs to the basement.

Then, he turned his attention to Jessica's closet. In the top right corner, exactly where he remembered it, sat the old encyclopedia his father had given him—a fragile relic passed down through generations. Its pages were crumbling, its binding barely holding together, but it was part of his family's legacy. For reasons he couldn't fully explain, it mattered to him. Carefully, he removed it and carried it to the basement.

Returning upstairs, he approached the large portrait of African elephants that hung on the wall. The painting, purchased in Tanzania during a memorable trip, made him smile. Taking it down, he walked outside, placed it in one of the trucks, and secured it before grabbing another painting from Africa and two he had purchased while in Greece.

As the team worked on loading the hot tub onto another truck, it became clear that the balance was off. Darius jumped in with some of the crew to help counterweight it, ensuring it was safely loaded.

As everybody started to disperse, Darius walked back into the house. His phone started to ring, and he washed his hands before picking it up. It was a business call, a call with a candidate about certain opportunities that they could both benefit from. Heading out into the garage, he intended to continue the call on his way to the office, but then her car pulled up in the driveway.

Jessica got out and started yelling at him, demanding he stop. Darius, mid-call with a business candidate, could only nod, a forced smile on his face as he tried to mute the conversation. Jessica stormed past him, her voice echoing. Going to his car, he sat to finish the call, trying his best to act like nothing had happened. His nervous system was on fire, but he tried to temper it for as long as he was on call.

After the call ended, he ran a hand over his face and steadied his breathing. He knew he couldn't engage, couldn't react, but he decided to go back into the house. Darius stood in the kitchen, the air thick, as Jessica stormed in, her voice sharp and cutting.

"That's it! You need to stop taking things out of the house!" she yelled.

He turned to her, calm on the surface but feeling every nerve in his body alight. "Okay."

"This is insane!" She continued. Her frustration twisted her face as she jabbed the air between them.

"You told me last fall that I could take anything out of the house that I wanted," Darius replied, keeping his voice steady. "I assumed that meant things I paid for, things that are mine. I didn't think it would be a big deal."

"That's ridiculous, and you know it!" she snapped. "This is all tied up with the courts and the lawyers. You can't just take whatever you want."

Darius said nothing, standing firm.

"When is your lawyer going to respond to mine?" she demanded, her tone dripping with accusation.

Her fury seemed to fill the room, her words tearing at his composure. He thought of Wim Hof as he used his embodiment exercises to tighten his diaphragm, his breath steadying as he rooted himself against the storm.

"I'm not sure what you mean," he said finally, his voice calm but measured.

Jessica rubbed her hands over her face, pacing furiously. "I'm sick of this! I'm sick of waiting on your lawyer. You haven't provided all the forms or done what you need to do!"

"That's not true," Darius said, shaking his head. "I've spent hours putting together over a hundred pages of documents, everything you asked for going back five years."

"No, no, no!" she interrupted, throwing her hands in the air. "Your lawyer told my lawyer that there are discrepancies, that she hasn't received everything, that they had to get back with you because there were issues with the numbers."

"That's not true," he repeated, his voice unwavering.

Jessica was relentless, pacing and gesturing emphatically. "I keep asking myself which one of you is full of shit," she spat.

The insult made Darius want to laugh, as he thought, *Maybe it's you?* but he didn't respond.

His initial instinct was to retort, to lash out, but he swallowed the anger and let it pass. "That doesn't make sense to me," he said instead. "Your lawyer has everything, my business records, personal information. I don't know what else to tell you. I don't know what else you need from me."

Her eyes narrowed into daggers. "You're the most manipulative person I've ever met," she hissed. "I can't trust you."

He blinked, taken aback but refusing to show it. The words stung, but he kept his composure. *I am actually one of the people you could trust the most*, he thought.

"You have been trying to sabotage this house. The pool. Unplugging things." she accused.

Darius looked at her, perplexed. "That isn't true."

"Things are being unplugged around here. You are messing with the pool," she snapped.

"No, I am not. I would never do that. There is no truth to that," he responded.

What in the Hell is she talking about? She's nuts, he thought, *I have to get out of here before she plants a dead body in the basement.*

She shifted the conversation to their son, hurling accusations he barely registered. His mind raced, countering her claims silently. He wanted to defend himself but bit his tongue, knowing it would only escalate the argument and do him no good.

"When are you going to be out of here?" she finally demanded.

"Well," he said, carefully choosing his words, "Based on the communication between our lawyers, it seemed like we were close to finalizing things. That's why I've started moving stuff out."

"When are you going to be out of here?" she repeated, not caring for his explanation.

He drew a long breath. "Well, your lawyer wanted me out of here in a week, but I've nowhere to go, so to give me time, my lawyer asked for a month so I could get things in order."

She sneered. "A month? I want you out of here now! It's been a year!"

His thoughts flared. *Are you crazy? It appears the affair started a year ago, but you only filed six months ago.* But his thoughts stayed in his head, and instead, he said calmly, "This is what you wanted, lawyers ... This is what you chose. You were the one who made this as difficult as you could by bringing your affair into the house."

"Affair?" she snapped. "I didn't get with her until after I filed for divorce!"

"That's not true," Darius countered, his voice controlled. "I know for a fact you were with her before you filed and during the summer."

"That's not true!"

He shook his head. "I already told you that her wife came to the office to talk to me about the lawyer's fees, and in that conversation, she had said the two of you had been together since February."

"That's a lie! I'll swear on a Bible!" she yelled.

Darius stared at her, amazed. *You want to swear on a Bible?* he thought, thinking of her actions. Adultery, licentiousness, sexual immorality, selfish ambition ... *Thinking of Galatians,* he thought, *Maybe throw in enmity and outburst of anger for today, as well! Can we trust your hand on a Bible!? Yeah, I don't think so.*

Jessica ranted further, pacing and throwing up her hands. "I'm sick of this. I want you out of here. It's ridiculous. I can't even have people over without you coming in and trying to make dinner."

Because bringing your girlfriend over in the middle of a divorce is perfectly normal! His nerves were on fire, but he bit the anger down. *She isn't worth the effort,* he thought sadly.

"Don't take anything else out of the house!" she shouted before storming down the hallway.

Darius stood in the kitchen. He looked around, the noise still raging. His nerves were raw, his body tense. He took a deep breath, centering himself.

Well, you complained to your Brother in Arms this last year that you didn't get any chance to get up to bat! Congratulations, son, you got up to bat! he thought, shaking his head at the comic relief going on in his brain, he took another slow, deep breath. It was time to get out of there and start the process of letting go.

Chapter 88
A New World of Possibilities

D arius was electric with enthusiasm. The joy he felt blew him away. These meditations were just amazing. It wasn't just the practice itself; it was how everything was interconnecting. He marveled at the revelations about energy centers and chakras, concepts he hadn't even been aware of until recently. While he had understood the body in terms of cardiopulmonary, neurology, and certain physiology, he was continuing to uncover an entirely new layer of knowledge rooted in energy and consciousness.

Dr. Whitman had introduced him to this realm, gifting him recordings that explained the energy centers in the body. At first, he didn't understand the meditation called "Blessing the Energy Centers" but he was starting to get it. It wasn't until Darius started learning "the breath," as Dr. Joe called it, and began practicing the "Blessing of the Energy Centers" meditation for a few months that everything suddenly clicked. He learned to use the breath Dr. Joe taught to move energy from the lower centers—where emotions like fear, guilt, and anger resided—into his heart and brain. The result?

He was happier, more energetic, and it also amazingly reduced any aches he once had.

The science behind it amazed him. Stories of people healing themselves from chronic diseases like ALS, Parkinson's, MS, and stage 4 cancers that weren't supposed to be curable through meditation had initially seemed hard to believe. After thinking about Hawkins' work and his own journey of self-healing, the science made sense to him. The meditations aligned with quantum physics, frequency, and coherence. Energy trapped in lower centers could be liberated and redirected toward healing and creativity, and strengthening the energy field around a person. The energy in that field additionally attracted or repelled similar positive or negative energy. Darius thought of the section in the book *Letting Go* where Hawkins talked about certain people having the ability to see the actual aura of other's energy fields.

The implications were astonishing. Only a fraction of "reality" was perceivable to human senses. The actual light spectrum and the array of colors that humans could see made up less than 1% of all frequencies of light that exist was astounding. This meant that the physical world and what we could see was nothing compared to what we couldn't see?! Talk about a check in the column of the quantum and spiritual realms! Time really wasn't linear!

He was awestruck by the science: waveforms carried information, and intention combined with emotion was the key to unlocking it while meditating. Studies showing DNA strands uncoiling in response to meditative focus underscored the power of this practice. But it wasn't enough to have intention without emotion or emotion without intention—both had to work in harmony. That balance could lead to manifestation, healing, and transformation.

Darius couldn't stop thinking about how this knowledge applied to him, his family, and his son. He remembered seeing his son's scans last summer showing brain waves out of coherence—some regions too fast, others too slow. The color-coded images were identical to what Dr. Joe's research demonstrated. Brain coherence between the heart and brain was critical for emotional and physical balance and healing.

He thought of how much he missed his son, how much he wanted to help him. He was under so much pressure, and Darius wasn't even sure he was aware of just how much pressure was weighing down on him from all these different directions. It was causing the anger, the agitation, the anxiety, and meditation could help redirect and lift all of that from his shoulders. Darius knew it could help!

Yet, after four months of estrangement, Ben still wouldn't speak to him. He wasn't sure exactly how long this was going to last, but for the first time, Darius thought he might be starting to understand. He reflected on the story of Abraham and Isaac, which had never made any sense to him. In fact, in the past, he thought it was cruel. Why would a loving God do such a thing? But in the heartache of this situation, Darius finally understood, realizing he had to trust God, relinquish control, and continue moving forward in faith. God created Ben just like he created Isaac, and he could take them or give them back.

Darius believed that by continuing to focus on growing personally in unconditional love and judgment-free living would ultimately win in this situation. The Scripture stated that through faith, lack of judgment, and continuing to pray and show unconditional love, at some point, love would have to win out. That was his hope and prayer. That at some point, surely, he would be able to help his son.

Darius started to think of the meditation called "Reconditioning the Body to a New Mind" and laughed, thinking of Dr. Joe's voice.

What would limitless feel like? What would nobility feel like?

These were the lights that awaited him at the end of all of this. They were no longer concepts or abstract ideals, they were states of being he was beginning to embody. For the first time, he felt he was stepping into the best version of himself, one that could radiate love, wisdom, and strength to those around him.

Darius sat in quiet reflection, tracing the arc of his journey over the past several months. He couldn't help but marvel at the contrast. For so long, his emotional landscape had been dominated by guilt, shame, anger, and fear. Those emotions were as familiar to him as his own name—ingrained, automatic. But higher-level emotions? Gratitude, love, joy, divine presence? They had been like foreign languages, beautiful yet incomprehensible.

He remembered the first time he tried this meditation. It had felt ... empty. What does it even mean to feel divine? To be the healer? To give life to life? he had wondered, frustrated by the lack of any tangible sensation. How would I know? It was as though he had no reference point in his heart or mind.

Now, five months into his practice, things were shifting. Slowly but surely, he was starting to grasp what those elevated emotions felt like—not just intellectually but viscerally, in his heart. The meditations, the repetition, and the commitment were paying off. Half of those once-foreign emotions were now becoming familiar, and he was beginning to understand the profound connection between the heart and the mind.

Heart-mind coherence, he thought, letting the phrase settle in.

The progress he'd made in his daily life was perhaps the most remarkable. When negativity arose—whether from external events or old, internal programming—he found himself responding in entirely new ways. Rather than reacting, he could pause, take a higher perspective, and simply say, "No, I'm not going there, or I don't choose that emotion." More than that, he had discovered the power to actively replace negativity with elevated emotions. Gratitude, joy, love—he could bring those into his heart intentionally and feel an almost immediate lift.

But what really captured his imagination were the stories of possibility. The healings, the manifestations—people transforming their lives, finding love, building businesses, and experiencing profound changes. Darius watched these examples unfold in videos, read about them in books, and felt a growing sense of excitement. What was possible for him?

Just having that higher consciousness, the improved skills, the improved health was amazing, but being able to understand polarity, be in a positive masculine state, be present with people, and actually listen to them, validating them ... Think about all the conflict that you would avoid in life and how much more of a blessing you would be to people.

The thought made him smile as he sat quietly in the office, a space that once bustled with staff but was now empty, save for him. Soon, even the building would be gone, sold off.

He reflected on what this loss meant: not losing everything, but rather losing everything that didn't matter. The material things. He hated framing it that way, not wanting to diminish the relationships slipping away, his soon-to-be ex-wife, the estranged relationship with his son, friendships he had cared about. Those losses hurt deeply. But the physical realm? The material things just weren't important.

What I'm gaining, he thought, is so much more than I'm losing.

He could feel it deeply: the spiritual, emotional, and physical healing. The financial recovery would come eventually, but that didn't matter anymore. *How am I going to bless others?* That was the question that filled his heart now.

Even with the pain surrounding his son, Darius held onto hope. His prayers were rooted in the verse from Malachi 4:6: ***"God will turn the hearts of the father's back to their sons and the hearts of the sons back to their father's. "*** He recited it often, clinging to the belief that unconditional love, proven both spiritually and scientifically, would win out in the end.

He was eager for the next step: the upcoming June conference in Mexico. The agenda excited him, especially the concept of coherence healings. These meditations, where groups of people came together to focus their energy on healing the sick, were yielding miraculous results. Darius didn't fully understand how it worked but was excited to learn. The best part of it? He realized he didn't need to understand everything anymore. He trusted what was happening—completely. He trusted God, the process, and the divine plan for his life. Everything that had happened was happening *for* him, not *to* him. He'd learned that foundational lesson when he first joined the Marriage Reset Program. At the time, it felt like empty words. Now, he knew it was the absolute truth.

He thought about the bigger picture—the way all of this tied into prophecy and purpose. My life is written in the 'Book of Life,' the 'Book of the Lamb,' he thought. That realization connected his personal journey to a universal one, grounding his newfound purpose in something eternal. And as remarkable as prophecy was, was that a direct prophecy on each person's life? He believed strongly it absolutely was and perhaps might be why evil had come after him in the way it had.

Darius no longer sought love or validation. He was continuing to find it from within and working to give love unconditionally. He didn't need certainty about what was coming, and he didn't need significance in the way he once had. It wasn't about him anymore. It was about growing, contributing, and aligning with God's plan.

He smiled as he thought about what lay ahead. What does God have planned? he wondered. Whatever it was, he trusted it would be extraordinary.

Chapter 89
The Calm in the Chaos

I t was a week after Darius had taken his belongings from the house, anticipating a potential divorce agreement. He was still deeply conflicted, torn between the emotions and thoughts that raged inside him. On one hand, he considered his actions in light of his faith. What would Jesus have done? He was pretty sure Jesus wouldn't have done what he had done. If they ask for your shirt, give them your coat too—or something to that effect.

But the truth was, Darius was tired of feeling like he was always the one who had to swallow his pride. He'd taken the high road time and again, and while he didn't regret most of his choices, there was one incident that left him feeling regret.

He'd come home to find her and her girlfriend sitting on the couch with his son, playing cards and watching a game. A wave of frustration washed over him. He turned and walked out, his emotions boiling over. Without a second thought, he stormed to her car, yanked the keys out of the ignition, and flung them out into the yard, muttering a few expletives under his breath before getting into his car and driving off.

After a mile, a moment of clarity hit him, and he considered what he'd done. With a sigh, he turned around, pulled back into the driveway, and after five minutes of searching with his phone's flashlight, he found her keys and put them back where they belonged before leaving for the office. He wasn't proud of it. While he was in good physical condition and enjoyed kickboxing, he wasn't a brawler. However, if his ex-wife had brought a man into the house in the middle of the divorce instead of a woman, it would have gotten ugly. After telling one of his female friends about his actions, she laughed and said, "That's amazing cause I would have jumped the bitch!" He tried to give himself some slack for that as he laughed at the memory.

But the financial strain had become relentless. Despite how hard he tried to let it go, it weighed on him, especially given the circumstances. It was painful, this sense of being undervalued, of feeling as if his years of dedication, the sacrifices he had made, had been erased. Loving someone, building a family, carrying the financial load for two decades, and now being made to feel as if he were worthless, it was … hard to swallow. And the added sting of her bringing her girlfriend into their home, in front of their son—it was cruel.

Her lack of honesty to their son and lack of humility was confounding to Darius. His hard work had bought all those "things" and paid for their trips. It was difficult to swallow the notion that even his own belongings were now disputed. He wanted to blame it on the hurt, on the anger of his youngest son not speaking to him, but deep down, he knew that reaction was juvenile. The silence from his son stretched on for months, with no acknowledgment, no effort to speak, until he took some of the items out of the house. Then suddenly, the silence was broken, and there was a nasty text accusing him of being a thief. Ben even spread the story on social media, saying he was stealing from him and his mother. How could he think that? How could he believe such things?

Ben had apparently reached out to Sheehan for his perspective. He defended Darius, telling his brother that their father had paid for almost everything in their lives—homes, trips, the vast majority of the possessions in the house. Sheehan shared that his Mom had paid for the pool installation and some other items but hadn't made much money until the last two years and that Dad had always been the breadwinner. Who do you think paid for you to go to Alaska, Honduras, and Belize? But his youngest was still adamant in his stance, sharing what his mother had said: that she had paid for half of everything.

As Sheehan got irritated, he went further, asking how he would feel if the roles were reversed. What if Mom had made most of the money? Then Dad had an affair, and not long after filing, was bringing his lover into the house and banging them while Mom was down in the basement?! On top of that, Dad was going for full custody of you so he could get child support? Oh, and Mom has to sell the buildings her business paid for to give Dad half, Dad gets to keep the house, and he wants most of what is in the house, including the stuff Mom uses and paid for. Would that seem fair to him?

Ben got angry and hung up

It was a pretty tense situation from that standpoint, as the whole family was fractured.

Later that week, as he met with his lawyer to discuss his choice to take his possessions and how to handle what was coming next, he had the chance to connect with Jeff Burkowski on the drive to her office. They caught each other up on the happenings in their lives, with Jeff able to give a more positive reflection than Darius. He was starting his own program to help men, similar to the Marriage Reset Program.

Darius was excited to talk to Jeff and catch up, but decided not to share the recent decision to move his stuff out. He figured he already knew what Jeff would say.

Darius took the elevator up and entered the legal offices.

"How are you doing?" His lawyer asked, offering a wry smile as she stepped out of her office.

He got up from the chair, feeling like a kid who'd just been called into the principal's office. There was silence between them until he sat at one side of her desk and she sat in her chair at the other.

"So, apparently you've been stealing things out of your house," she said.

"Yeah, I guess that might not have been the best decision," Darius admitted.

"It got them excited, to say the least."

"But, I mean, in my defense," Darius said, "She did tell me when she originally forced me out of the house that I could take whatever I wanted."

His lawyer laughed, shaking her head. "Did she now?" she asked.

"Yeah, I actually have it in a text. But, well, a lot has happened since then," he replied, smiling sheepishly.

"Oh boy, has it," she said. She laughed as she explained that his wife's lawyer had told her that this "little stunt" would come at a cost. She smiled. "Apparently, she is quite unhappy. She really wants that hottub, the lawnmower, and even the massage chair!"

Darius shrugged his shoulders. "You know what? After everything I've been through, I don't care. She can be mad."

The lawyer chuckled.

"It's unreasonable," Darius said, sighing. "But are we at 60/40 now?"

"More like 58/42," she said.

"I just don't get it. I don't understand how she can be so entitled and unreasonable," Darius said, shaking his head.

His lawyer sympathized, "Darius, it's strange. I've never seen anything like it. I've even said to her lawyer, 'Look, you need to talk some sense into your client.' She's getting this house, a beautiful one with all these renovations, at a significant discount. No matter how much she claims it's worth, it's still a great deal, but she thinks she's getting a raw deal."

"A raw deal?" Darius repeated.

"She believes you're hiding a pile of money."

"A pile of money?" Darius asked. "I've never hidden anything from her. She knew about my stocks, my crypto, my retirement portfolio, and my retirement strategy for properties. I wasn't buying those buildings through my company so I could sell them at a discount and give her half after she had an affair and divorced me." He smiled and pointed both his hands like pistols in the air.

"At least you have a sense of humor about it," she said, with a small laugh. "But here's the thing, Darius, she doesn't understand the reality of our financial situation. Your company made over $2 million the year before. She believes there's a hidden fortune, but it's clear she's not very good with numbers."

"Well, I don't have any Swiss bank accounts," Darius said. "It's ridiculous. I told her about the tax burden multiple times. The government doesn't care about who's responsible for it. They'll just start taking money out of our accounts. I've seen it happen to friends."

"Yeah, I know," she said. "Let's go over what you took from the house."

Darius gave her a half-smile. "Okay. I took the lawnmower, my massage chair, my desk, the paintings I bought, and the hot tub. I also took some of my clothes."

"That's it?"

"Yes. And everything I took, I paid for 100%."

She nodded. "Well, she's particularly upset about the hot tub. And the lawnmower, too."

Darius raised an eyebrow. "The lawnmower? She has never mowed a day in the twenty years I have known her."

"Well, maybe she and her girlfriend like to ride around on it," His lawyer deadpanned.

Darius laughed out loud, picturing it. His lawyer smiled at getting the desired effect.

"Well, she actually wants both of them," his lawyer added.

Darius was stunned. "Wait … She gets to keep the house, and I am not taking any appliances. The pool cost over $100,000, and she gets it for free, but I can't keep the lawnmower and hot tub that I paid for?"

"I'm afraid so," she said. "The law considers the pool and appliances part of the house."

"That's just crazy," Darius said, shaking his head. "So, she gets to keep the house, and on top of that, she's getting all the renovations for free. Not to mention my credit is taking a hit, and now I'll have to try to find a place to live at a bad time for rates. It's just … insane."

His lawyer sighed. "Look, I'll go back to her lawyer and see if we can come to a reasonable agreement. But you're probably going to have to give up something."

"I'm open to that, but I'm not moving on the hot tub," Darius said.

"I'll try, but don't get your hopes up because it sounds like she and the girlfriend like getting in it after driving around on the lawn mower," she said, standing up. "Think about it, and I'll be right back with some paperwork. But, whatever you do, don't bring up Tony Robbins! It's a trigger. Her lawyer must have brought his name up a 100 times."

She winked and walked out smiling.

As she left, Darius swiveled in his chair and gazed out the window toward downtown Indianapolis. The city skyline shimmered in the distance, and he let his thoughts drift to everything that had brought him to this moment. The challenges he faced, the unexpected twists, and the weight of the conversations he'd had recently—it all settled on him. Yet, as he took it all in, he realized how much he had been blessed.

He repeated the thought to himself. Yes, I'm blessed. None of this was easy, he knew that. The uncertainty, the negotiations, the possibility of court—it wasn't fun. But maybe they wouldn't have to go to court after all. Perhaps there was a chance for resolution, for moving forward with some kind of peace.

He glanced at his calendar, noting his upcoming meeting with the real estate agent. Darius couldn't help but marvel at the timing. Two of his commercial buildings, which he had been told might take six months to a year to sell, now seemed on the verge of being sold in less than 60 days—and with cash offers, no less. If that happened, it would be nothing short of remarkable. He took a deep breath, sitting back in the stillness of the office, feeling the weight of gratitude.

So much had happened. So much had changed. It was almost unbelievable to reflect on the whirlwind of the past year and a half. Who would even believe it all? And yet, as he thought about it, Darius smiled. He wouldn't change a thing, he realized, and for the first time, he truly meant it.

His meditation practice had taken root in his life in ways he hadn't expected, and the manifestations he was witnessing were extraordinary. Everything about him had changed—his spiritual growth, emotional healing, and even his physical health were evidence of that. Darius smiled quietly to himself. "Now, I could certainly use some financial healing," he murmured with a grin. But even so, he felt immense gratitude.

This incredibly difficult situation had brought him to a place of deep contentment. He was happier than he had ever been, more relaxed than he had felt in years, and healthier than he had been in a long time. And as he stared out at the city, the possibilities ahead felt boundless. He was certain his future would be remarkable because he now knew how to create it.

Based on Scripture, God could have stopped any of the past year. Satan was a narcissist and a blind fool to think he could beat the Creator. Evil had come after him, and everything was being taken away, but they should have left him alone, Darius thought. Now that he had been awakened to the truth, he would not stop. He would be relentless in pursuing whatever God had planned for him.

"Then God returned Jōb's fortune

when he prayed to him on behalf of his friends.

Thus God increased all that Jōb had twice as much as before."

– Job 42:10

Epilogue
The Holy Spirit Speaks

Darius was taking it one day at a time, which was something he had never done well in the past. But now, he was all about living in the generous present moment. Moving forward while trusting God with faith. This ability to stay present, free from the burdens of guilt and shame tied to the past or fears about the future, was something he deeply appreciated. It was the result of all the work he had done over the past year.

He had returned to Indiana after an extended period of travel. He'd spent a month in Mexico following six weeks in North Carolina with his close friend Burke from the Marriage Reset Program. After that, a quick trip to DC over the 4th of July marked his second straight Independence Day in the capital to stay with some close Tony Robbins Platinum friends—a new tradition, perhaps, as he'd never done so before. Then, after returning to North Carolina briefly, Darius was given the clear spiritual message: God was directing him back to Indiana.

Over time, Darius had come to realize that the Holy Spirit had been guiding him all along. In the past, he simply didn't have a high enough level of consciousness to realize it was the Holy Spirit. Now, he was learning to move by faith, and while it wasn't always easy, he at least wasn't running anymore from direction like he had with writing the book.

Darius had just arrived from the shared office space from which he was working, to the mostly barren apartment where he was now living. He decided to go for a ride on his triathlon bike. It was just past 7 PM, and the sun wouldn't set until 9, giving him plenty of time to enjoy the beautiful evening. After grabbing his gear and heading to the garage, he began his ride, his thoughts quickly turning to prayer and reflection.

So much had changed over the past 14 months. Last May, his wife had announced that their 17-year marriage and 20-year relationship were over. The shock, of course, was devastating. Looking back now, however, he realized there were signs he had missed, his awareness at the time clouded by distractions and limited self-reflection.

He reflected on that time in Mexico, where he had prayed for three nights straight, pleading with God for guidance. Those prayers opened his eyes and ears in ways he never imagined, helping him confront his flaws and view his life with a clarity that had eluded him until then. It was the moment that led him to everything that had come after: all of the amazing people and experiences that brought him closer to God and to his true self. In hindsight, he couldn't deny that his journey of growth had been divinely orchestrated.

Even in the resources he was finding, it was God and the Holy Spirit directing him. Sometimes, he would be nudged to read a book halfway through, only to stop and start another—seemingly random, but always purposeful. A few times, the new book would provide insights that refuted ideas in the previous one, aligning with God's truth.

While in North Carolina, he was engrossed in Annie Jacobsen's *Operation Paperclip*, which detailed the United States' controversial recruitment of Nazi scientists after World War II. The book's chilling accounts of atrocities were difficult to read. Halfway through, the Holy Spirit urged him to put it down and pick up *The Hunt for Zero Point* by Nick Cook. Despite his initial reluctance, Darius obeyed.

Through it all, he realized that God was not only revealing the truths about His creations but also exposing the deceptive playbook of the enemy. He saw how evil distorted and corrupted everything good, yet God's divine wisdom and timing remained unshakable. These realizations left him in awe.

As he continued to ride, pray, and reflect, Darius pondered the prophecies in the Bible and their intricate fulfillment. He marveled at how God's plan extended not just to nations but to individuals like himself. Written in the Lamb's Book of Life, each person's story was part of a divine personal prophecy. Darius was still piecing it all together, but he felt grateful for how far he had already come on this journey of faith and discovery.

During meditation in North Carolina, he had gone deeper than ever before. Deep in meditation, hands resting on his knees, earbuds in place, his Spirit had left his physical self and hovered far above the house. Ever since doing it last December, he had been able to do it regularly. Then it happened—a light of incomprehensible brilliance enveloped him, accompanied by a presence so powerful it bordered on overwhelming. The word terrifying didn't quite fit, but the sheer magnitude of the angel's power was staggering.

When he tried to focus on the angel, he couldn't seem to see anything past a profile and the blinding light. His body hadn't moved, yet his consciousness quivered in awe.

"You're an angel," he thought, though no words escaped his lips. His mind formed the question, and the response came:

"Yes."

Darius was utterly awestruck, unable to form another coherent thought. The angel didn't speak further, but its presence conveyed infinite wisdom and power, and while it seemed forever, it only lasted a minute. As the meditation ended, Darius returned to his body. Tears streamed down his face as he opened his eyes, overwhelmed by the experience, realizing Jet, Burke's dog, was actually on top of him, trembling. He had apparently jumped on him and was barking.

Suddenly, Burke had come into the room from his work office. "What the heck is going on?! What's Jet hollerin' about?" he exclaimed. Then he saw the old dog on Darius's lap. "What's he doin' up there?" His friend said with a confused expression.

Darius was calming Jet with his hands across his head and gently helped him down, then got up and walked past Burke to the kitchen. Burke followed.

"Darius?"

Darius looked at him. "You don't want to know."

Burke looked at him perplexed. "Brother, how much crazier could it be? Just hit me with it." he persisted.

Darius sighed. "You just had an angel in your house."

"Oh my ... " Burke rubbed his hands on his head. "Oh my ... I need to think about that," he said and walked back toward his office.

"What in the world?" Darius whispered, the memory and warmth vivid as he pedalled down the street. A chuckle escaped his lips. "What in the world?"

***

The day was fading into dusk when Darius approached an intersection. To his right, emerging from the tree line, he saw a young man with a backpack walking; he was limping slightly. Something about the figure struck him as odd. Darius continued peddling, listening to Lee Strobel's *The Case for Miracles*.

Suddenly, The Holy Spirit said:

Go see what he needs.

Darius heard it clearly but kept pedaling as if it would go away. After another minute of riding, the voice came again, firmer this time:

I told you to go see what the young man needs.

"What in the—" Darius muttered, shaking his head. He reached another intersection near a water tower, still wrestling with the urging. The voice cut through his resistance:

Are you going to listen or not?

Darius stopped abruptly, got off the bike, and slowly turned around, realizing he had ignored the Holy Spirit. Exhaling sharply, he turned his bike around, muttering, "He's going to think I'm crazy."

It took about ten minutes to circle back to where he'd seen the young man. As Darius approached, the boy looked startled, stepping back cautiously. Darius stopped and planted his foot on the ground.

"Hey, you got a second?"

The young man, a sturdy figure with a guarded expression, nodded warily. "What can I do for you?" the boy asked.

"Well, it's more about what I can do for you," Darius replied. "This might sound crazy, but God told me to come back and see if you need help."

The boy's eyebrows rose, but then he softened. "That's not crazy to me. I believe in God."

Darius smiled. "Well, praise God. So, what can I do for you?"

"I don't really need anything," the boy replied.

"What's your name?" Darius asked.

"Sampson."

"Well, Sampson, what are you doing out here? It's late, and you look like you're limping."

"I just wanted to go for a walk," Sampson admitted with a shrug. "And I hurt my ankle a while back."

Darius tilted his head. "Come on now. You aren't out for a stroll this late with a limp and backpack. Where are you going?"

Sampson hesitated, then confessed, "I've been homeless for a little while."

"Well, what can I do for you?" Darius asked.

"I don't really ask for help," Sampson said, avoiding eye contact.

"Son," Darius replied, "Do you think God told me to come back just so your pride could get in the way?"

Sampson looked down, then back up, finally admitting, "I'm hungry."

"When did you eat last?"

"Three days ago. I had a honey bun."

Darius shook his head, his heart aching. "Okay, the Holy Spirit is telling me to pray for you. Is that Okay?" He asked. Sampson nodded, and Darius placed his hands on the young man's shoulders, praying for blessings, guidance, and provision. Then, after the prayer, Darius, with a smile, said, "I live just up the road. I'll ride back, grab my car, and come get you to get something to eat."

Sampson agreed and waited outside an optometry building, and true to his word, Darius returned, picked up Sampson, and took him to Arby's.

They took it to Darius's apartment, and over dinner, Sampson opened up, sharing a life filled with hardship. His family life had been challenging—fractured and chaotic. Growing up in foster care, he had met his father for the first time this year.

When they finally met, the reunion had been brief and tumultuous. After spending five tense days together, things escalated into another argument, and Sampson had left disappointed.

The challenges didn't stop there. Sampson recounted a period when he had been homeless in Houston, sharing those dire circumstances with one of his younger brothers. Just that week, he had come from Houston to Indiana, and he was now sleeping outdoors near a pond by a warehouse, battling the elements and the loneliness of his circumstances.

Even with the challenges of his upbringing, he had excelled at sports as an outlet and became one of the top running backs in the State of Indiana coming out of high school.

Once at Indiana University, Sampson said, he had fallen in with the wrong crowd. Though the school and his coaches had gone to great lengths to support him, he got involved with drugs, eventually transferring and then quitting football and ultimately becoming homeless.

After eating, Darius washed his clothes and let him take a shower. Then, Darius offered Sampson a place to stay, suggesting his couch as a temporary refuge, but Sampson declined.

Over the next two weeks, Darius and Sampson developed a bond. Sampson visited Darius's apartment multiple times to shower, eat, and talk. One rainy evening on his fifth visit, after a meal, Sampson hesitated before asking, "Do you think I could sleep on the couch? I don't want to go back out in the rain."

"Of course," Darius replied, pulling out a sleeping bag and pillow for him.

The next morning, while Darius worked out in the building's gym, the Holy Spirit spoke again:

You are going to take in this young man. You cannot love and mentor your own son right now, but you can love and mentor him, which is why I sent him to you.

The words hit Darius like a wave, and he sank to his knees, tears streaming as he whispered, "Okay, Lord." Fearing it meant the challenges with his estranged younger son would not be over with anytime soon.

Returning home, he told Sampson, "God has told me to take you in. He sent you to me so I could mentor you."

Sampson blinked, stunned.

"But," Darius continued, "There are conditions. If you stay here, there will be no drugs, no girls, no visitors. You'll have to get up at 5:00 AM to learn meditation, learn Scripture, and practice breathing exercises. You'll have to get a job and pick up after yourself. If any of those rules don't work for you, then you can't stay here." The tears were still rolling down his face, and he took a moment to wipe them. "Think about it. Pray about it. And let me know what you want to do."

Sampson stood there, speechless.

The next day, Sampson told him he wanted to live there.

***

Darius had left that morning to go work out as Sampson headed to his job at Red Robin. He had been living with him for over two months and had gotten the job 3 weeks after moving in. After the workout, Darius entered the apartment, and suddenly, the Holy Spirit hit him.

Words entered his mind like a rushing stream, accompanied by a melody he could almost feel. It was wild—he had only just learned his first piano chords the day before and had only been learning the piano for four months. He quickly grabbed his phone, his fingers moving frantically as he typed the lyrics that were being gifted to him:

I see you, I hear you, I know you, I love you. I saw you, I heard you, I knew you, I loved you.

Hallelujah Elohim, Hallelujah Yeshua, Hallelujah Rauch, Hallelujah, Hallelujah.

And then came the chorus:

The beginning and the end, Where The Word, the Son, and the World began, The Creator of all, because I am the Great I Am.

I am, I am, I am. I am, I am, I am.

The words continued to flow, almost effortlessly:

How do I see you? How do I hear you? How do I know you? How do I love you? I wrote about you. I made plans for you. I longed for you and blew you into life in your mother's womb.

Because I made You. I am, I am, I am.

Hallelujah Elohim, Hallelujah Yeshua, Hallelujah Ruach Hallelujah, Hallelujah

The melody came alive in his mind, soaring higher as he continued:

I am the beginning and the end, Where The Word, the Son, and the World began. The Creator of all, because I am the Great I Am.

He paused, staring at the lyrics on his phone. It was stunning and surreal. God just gave him a song! And then it hit him—the title of the song was "I Am."

His thoughts flashed back to a day in Thousand Oaks, California. He had been there for a conference and had gone to a local bar to eat, work, and watch a bit of football. After his meal, he walked the mile back to his hotel, praying in the Spirit as he often did these days since God gifted him praying in tongues that summer.

As he walked, a tune suddenly filled his mind. Without warning, he began singing out loud in the Spirit, which he had never done before. Then suddenly, he had started belting out:

I am, I am, I am, I am.

The melody grew louder in his head, and the words spilled out, catching him off guard. At the time, he thought it was beautiful and catchy but nothing more. It was maybe weird, but the mystical moments of his life were beginning to feel almost routine.

Darius had always loved music, had always dreamed of singing and playing the piano. Unfortunately, he had no voice. Years ago, at the age of 25, he had taken piano lessons for a year, but the experience had been a disaster. Memorizing the notes felt impossible, and after months of struggling, his elderly instructor had kindly suggested he save his money and pursue something else. At the time, Darius accepted the idea that he simply wasn't musically inclined.

But something wild was happening.

In the past year, as he embraced embodiment breathing exercises, his voice was changing when he sang. People at church began to compliment his singing. At first, it was laughable to him— he had always cringed at the sound of his own voice, even in the shower. Yet now, he sounded ... good?

The signs then pointed him to the piano. He initially ignored them, just as he had once ignored the prompting of the Holy Spirit to write his book. After the angel had appeared to him in Mexico at the Dr. Joe conference, he was overwhelmed, to say the least. At the end of the event, he had decided to stay at his condo nearby since there were no renters currently. After a meditation, the Holy Spirit told him to stop running and start writing the book, including the structure God wanted him to follow. Darius was stunned ...

demons, angels, gifts, and the Holy Spirit ... He grudgingly emailed Marjah the next morning to let her know he would do it after avoiding the publisher for four months.

So when the nudges about learning the piano persisted, Darius knew better than to ignore them. He signed up for a master class at the Ridley Academy. After just three hours of instruction, he felt certain: he was meant to play the piano for God.

He didn't even own a piano during his first month of lessons. He got one the month after Sampson moved in, and they set it up together. He dove into the lessons with enthusiasm, loving every moment of his new daily practice. And now, standing in his apartment with the lyrics fresh in his mind, he finally understood the significance of the melody that had come to him during that walk in California.

With a huge smile on his face, Darius sat down on the piano bench. Opening the lid, he placed his fingers on the keys, ready to bring to life the song that God had shared with him.

Parting Prayer

Never in a million years, in any of the galaxies, in the different spiritual realities and realms, is this the book that I imagined I would write or if my vision to write a book would even happen!

When it was first told to me by the Holy Spirit that this was what I was to do, I ran from it. I would like to think I wasn't as disobedient as Jōb and with a better attitude, but after four months of avoidance, I was called very directly again to write it while also being given the breakdown of how I would write it. I was given a message so clear that I could not ignore it, and at that point, I surrendered and moved forward, even though, deep down, I still really did not want to.

But here's the thing that I hope and pray for.

I don't have any hallucinations that everybody will love it or that every aspect of it will resonate with each person who reads it. There are so many different areas of this book, so many topics and connections, that my hope is there will be aspects of Darius—his frustration, his confusion, his brokenness, his lack of awareness, his failures, his heart, his longing for success and to be accepted or loved—that will resonate differently with each person that reads it.

I hope that his journey of self-discovery, self-realization, and faith is one that you, whoever you might be, can understand, and I hope that by reading this story, you will find something that blesses you and your life. Whether it be understanding that there is a better, healthier way to live, that you could possibly be medication free, or that you don't have to feel worthless, or that you can take control of your anxieties, or that the practices, meditations, or books that Darius reads, could be of some use to you. Even if, in some way, it helps you reconnect or connect with God and His absolute truth, then my effort will have been worth it.

If the story of the Modern-Day Jōb can make even one difference in your life, then it will have been worth every second and effort it took to author this book.

Below is the Parting Prayer. As I neared the completion of the book, the Holy Spirit directed me to put it here, at the end of this part of the story, so that every reader would understand that the purpose of this book is to give them hope. To understand that there's nothing wrong with them. And to understand that whatever challenge they're going through, they can make it through.

God has a plan and a destiny for you, and He really did make you special. Nothing bad that has ever happened in your life came from God. He's not the one to blame. However, He does have the answers, and healing is just around the corner. So I hope that you can take this prayer and customize it to whatever you're dealing with right now, and know that not only can you overcome it, but you can thrive and become the best version of yourself.

God bless you.

***

I pray to you as my creator, the infinite power in the universe, through the redemptive blood of your Son, Jesus, being led and guided by the Holy Spirit.

God and Father, I know your promise. You wrote about me in the Book of Life, the Book of the Lamb, before I was born. You blew me into life, into my mother's womb. You have longed for me and all the days of my life were already counted beforehand.

In Jeremiah, as you state, "You only have plans to help me, never to harm me. If I seek you, I will find you."

Lord, I come to you for direction and for comfort.

Help me, Father, and give me direction, comfort, and healing in

---

I pray that you will lead and guide me. Your Will be done, not mine. Your timing, not mine.

Help me, Father, to see clearly your almighty power. As you show over and over again that if I come to You that I can overcome all.

You are the God that opens up doors nobody else can open. You are the God that closes doors nobody else can. You are the God of right now. Your prophecy is amazing. Your timing is perfection.

Lead me and guide me, Father, in the ways that I need to be led and guided right now.

Father, I pray this in your name.

In the name of the Father, and the Son, and the Holy Spirit.

Amen.

Parting Scripture

Our Creator made us and longs for a relationship with us, but we get to choose. In 1 Kings 18:21 Elijah states

"How long will you go limping over two opinions? If the Lord is God, follow Him but if Bhaal is god follow him." So, whom will you serve?" The following scripture is powerful.

Look at the world and all its distractions. We were created to worship and serve our Creator and we will worship something so we must choose wisely; the father of Lies is crafty. Until we understand this truth, we will never feel complete. There is a long list of people with everything the material world has to offer that still felt empty and the more they tried to fill the void with the flesh, the more it destroyed and consumed them.

The first decision to follow God is to be baptized but that is just the beginning as it is a journey and not a destination until you leave this realm. The second step is to seek Him, be in covenant with Him and be baptized in the Holy Spirit. Once that happens, watch out! The Lord may seek new covenants with you! Praise God! After my baptism in the Holy Spirit, I wanted a new, personal convent with the Lord and I sought out scripture to meditate on and memorize. I am going to share a few scripture that have been very important to me and the 12 for my personal covenant with the Lord over my life. I pray He gives you eyes to see and ears to hear, that you seek Him, and that His peace be on you. In the name of Jesus. Amen Amen

- Deuteronomy 4:29-31
- Matthew 16:19
- Proverbs 18:21
- 2 Timothy 2:22-26
- Galatians 3:13-14
- Psalm 139
- Psalm 91
- 2 Kings 17:29–33
- Romans 12:20
- Matthew 28:18
- Isaiah 12:2
- Mark 16:15

My First Personal Covenant with the Lord- 12 Scripture

Malachi 4:6 " I will bring back the hearts of the fathers to the sons, and the hearts of the sons to their fathers, so that I will not come and strike the land with a ban."

Proverbs 16:3 commit your work to the Lord, and your plans will be established

Malachi 3:10-12 bring the whole tithe into the storehouse so that there will be food in my house and test me please in this says God of Hosts, if I will not open for you the window of heaven, and pour forth for you an overflowing blessing. I will rebuke the devour for you; it will not destroy the fruit of your soil. Your vine in the field will not be unfruitful.

2 Chronicles 1:11-12 then God said to Solomon because this was with your heart, and you did not ask for wealth, possessions, honor, and the lies of your enemies and also did not ask for long life, but have asked for wisdom and knowledge, wisdom and knowledge is given to you. And I will also give you wealth, possession, and honor the like of which was not had by King's before you.

Proverbs 9:10 the fear of the Lord is the beginning of wisdom, and the knowledge of the Holy is understanding

Luke 8:17 for there is nothing hidden that will not become visible, and nothing secret that will not be known and come to light

Psalm 16 : 11 you will make known to me. The path of life in your presence is fullness of joy at your right hands our pleasures forever.

Jeremiah 30:17 for I will present healing to you, and I will heal you of your wounds declares God

Luke 6:38 Give, and it will be given to you. a good measure-pressed down, shaken overflowing- they will pour it into your lap. For with the measure by which you measure out, it will be measured out to you in return

Joshua 1:5 no one will stand before you all the days of your life. Just as I was with Moses, so I will be with you. I will not fail you and I will not forsake you.

2 Timothy 1:7 For God has not given us a spirit of fear, but of power and love and a sound mind

Deuteronomy 28:11-13 the Lord will generously, increase the fruit of your womb, the offspring of your livestock, and the produce of your soil, upon the land, which the Lord swore to your ancestors he would give you. The Lord will open up for you his rich storehouse, the heavens to give your land rain in due season and to bless all the works of your hands. You will lend to many nations, but borrow from none. The Lord will make you the head not the tail, the top not the bottom.

Next Steps

When I set out to write this book, I set out to write a story that would reveal truths that most people are not aware of. I wanted it to be a starting point for your own journey of self-discovery and understanding that leads to greater awareness because, with greater awareness, we get to choose the life we live.

As this part of the story comes to an end, I hope that I have been able to not only entertain but also give you some different resources and revelations to aid you on your journey, and I would like to invite you to visit my charity: **Blessing All God's Children**.

www.blessingallgodschildren.com

Through this charity, we hope to bring a light to as many people as possible, embodying the spirit of truth to create awareness and provide support spiritually, emotionally, financially, and even embracing an environment that leads to physical healing. We hope to create a higher level of awareness and understanding in others and hope that whether you're an individual or part of a business, you can join us on this incredible journey.

Or if you want to reach out and find out more about what I do, then I would encourage you to follow me on LinkedIn: www. linkedin.com/in/darwin-shurig. I'd love to hear from you, and hear how Darius's story has inspired something in your life!

Recommendations

Throughout this book, you will have noticed that Darius was encouraged and inspired to read as much as possible on his journey. Many of these books were pivotal to helping him see the truth in himself and his situation; they helped guide him and kickstart his transformation into becoming a better man.

I was inspired to include many of these books alongside the Bible as, in my own life, these authors and their works have inspired me a great deal. Some have opened my eyes to the truth, some have deepened my understanding of myself and my faith, and some have simply been incredible conduits for knowledge and understanding. So, in honor of these authors, I have included a reference list to all of the authors mentioned, and highly encourage you, my dear reader, to read them for yourself.

- **Christianity, Faith, and Spirituality**

In Search of the Real Heaven, Steve Hemphill.

Prayers Satan Hates, Steve Hemphill.

Radical, David Platt.

The Bait of Satan, John Bevere.

The Case for Christ, Lee Strobel.

What Are the Stakes?, Steve Hemphill.

You Can't Out Give God, Dr. Marilyn Hickey.

- **Marriage, Relationships, and Personal Development**

Better Man, Better Marriage, Jeff Borkoski.

I Hate You, Don't Leave Me, Jerold J. Kreisman and Hal Straus.

The Art of Embodiment, G.S. Youngblood.

The Five Love Languages, Gary Chapman.

The Love Dare, Alex Kendrick and Stephen Kendrick.

The Masculine Relationship, G.S. Youngblood.

The Way of the Superior Man, David Deida.

The Wife Magnet, Jeff Borkoski.

Walking on Eggshells, Paul T. Mason and Randi Kreger.

- **Consciousness, Enlightenment, and Inner Growth**

A Course in Miracles, Helen Schucman.

Becoming Supernatural, Dr. Joe Dispenza.

Letting Go, David R. Hawkins.

Power vs. Force, David R. Hawkins.

The Art of Enlightenment, Osho.

The Untethered Soul, Michael Singer.

You Are the Placebo, Dr. Joe Dispenza.

- **Visionary Thinking and Global Impact**

Good to Great, Jim C. Collins.

Leadership Styles, Mark Murphy

Operation Paperclip, Annie Jacobsen.

The 15 Commitments of Conscious Leadership, Jim
Dethmer, Diana Chapman, and Kaley Klemp.

The Healing of America, T.R. Reid.

The Hunt for Zero Point, Nick Cook.

The Language of God, Francis S. Collins.

About the Author

Darwin Shurig understands that people are the greatest asset at any company and the key qualities that growth companies need to grow market share while enhancing their positive culture and team environment. He has a clinical background as a respiratory therapist of over 30 years, including 12+ years of sales, business development, marketing, and negotiations experience within medical device, diagnostics, distribution, ventilation, and sleep therapy, 8 years of sales leadership, 3 years of operations and extensive experience in negotiations and contract management before entering the entrepreneurial world of talent management.

He founded Shurig Solutions, Inc. in 2015 and helped build a company that has produced over $6 million in revenue generation. He has created the SSI Educational Webinar Series, the SSI Executive Conversations Podcast, Candidate Prep Best Practices, and the Top Talent Accelerant™ process. Darwin was highlighted in the Creative Classics book, *The American Entrepreneur*, published in 2020, was listed as an MRI Top 10 Managing Partner for 2021, and SSI was ranked a top 15 office in 2022. He presents on Talent Management Strategies and moderates panel discussions for organizations including LSI Emerging Medtech, LSX Global Medtech Forum, Qualio, Greenlight Guru, the Florida Medical Device Consortium, and Brainlinx.

Darwin founded **Blessing All God's Children** in October 2024, and has a heart for charity. SSI supports five independent charities, and he has volunteered on the board of the MRI Charitable Foundation for 3 years. His goal is to help promote other charity activities, support unique projects for charities that bring value and resources to the less advantaged, and create a charitable explosion through more frequent and sustained giving with complete transparency.

DID YOU LOVE THIS BOOK?

*****

I'd be honored if you'd share your thoughts
by leaving an honest review on Amazon!

www.ingramcontent.com/pod-product-compliance
Lightning Source LLC
Chambersburg PA
CBHW021207130626
46554CB00004B/1124